FEUDALISM IN HISTORY

Feudalism in History

Edited by Rushton Coulborn

WITH CONTRIBUTIONS BY

JOSEPH R. STRAYER
WILLIAM F. EDGERTON
EDWIN O. REISCHAUER
DANIEL THORNER
DERK BODDE
ERNST H. KANTOROWICZ
BURR C. BRUNDAGE
MARC SZEFTEL
RUSHTON COULBORN

FOREWORD BY A. L. KROEBER

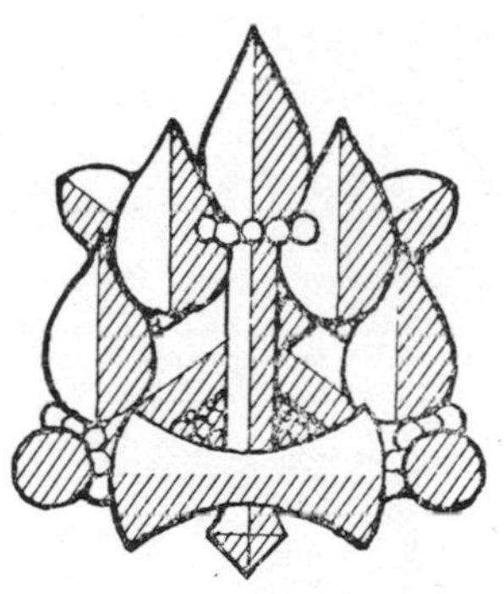

ARCHON BOOKS
HAMDEN, CONNECTICUT
1965

Reprinted 1965 with permission
in an unaltered and unabridged edition

Library of Congress Catalog Card Number: 65-24506
Printed in the United States of America

The Conference on Feudalism at Princeton University, October 31-November 1, 1950

THIS BOOK is the outcome of interest by the Rockefeller Foundation and sponsorship by the American Council of Learned Societies. The aim of the book is to test the extent of repetition in history. The Council set up a Committee on Uniformities in History, and it was the Committee which chose feudalism as an example of a more or less repetitive or uniform phenomenon in history. The Council brought together a Conference on Feudalism at Princeton University on October 31 and November 1, 1950. Twenty-three scholars were present, including Arnold Toynbee who attended by special arrangement. The eight papers constituting Part Two of the book were drafted for the Conference and subsequently revised for inclusion in the book.

COMMITTEE ON UNIFORMITIES IN HISTORY
AMERICAN COUNCIL OF LEARNED SOCIETIES

Crane Brinton, Harvard University
Rushton Coulborn, Atlanta University, Secretary
E. H. Harbison, Princeton University
Alfred L. Kroeber, University of California, Chairman
Charles E. Odegaard, Executive Director, American Council of Learned Societies (now, University of Michigan)
For the Rockefeller Foundation: John Marshall, Associate Director, Division of the Humanities

Participants in the Conference on Feudalism
Princeton University, October 31-November 1, 1950

HOWARD BECKER, *University of Wisconsin*
DERK BODDE, *University of Pennsylvania*
CRANE BRINTON, *Harvard University*
BURR C. BRUNDAGE, *Cedar Crest College*
GEORGE G. CAMERON, *University of Michigan*
RUSHTON COULBORN, *Atlanta University*
W. REX CRAWFORD, *University of Pennsylvania*
H. G. CREEL, *University of Chicago*
KARL DEUTSCH, *Massachusetts Institute of Technology*
WILLIAM F. EDGERTON, *University of Chicago*
JAMES K. FEIBLEMAN, *Tulane University*
E. H. HARBISON, *Princeton University*
ERNST H. KANTOROWICZ, *University of California (now, Institute for Advanced Study)*
ALFRED L. KROEBER, *University of California*
A. N. KURAT, *University of Ankara, Turkey*
JOHN MARSHALL, *Rockefeller Foundation*
CHARLES E. ODEGAARD, *American Council of Learned Societies (now, University of Michigan)*
ROBERT REDFIELD, *University of Chicago*
EDWIN O. REISCHAUER, *Harvard University*
JOSEPH R. STRAYER, *Princeton University*
MARC SZEFTEL, *Cornell University*
DANIEL THORNER, *University of Pennsylvania*
ARNOLD J. TOYNBEE, *University of London and Royal Institute of International Affairs*

FOREWORD

WHAT started out to be a meeting of minds in 1950 has eventuated into something double-barreled: a symposium and a comparative treatise.

The 1950 Conference on Feudalism, of which this study is the outcome, was preceded by two rather informal conferences on the Interpretation of History, which Robert Oppenheimer and Walter Stewart arranged at the Institute for Advanced Study in April 1948 and May 1949. These two earlier gatherings were designed to bring together Arnold Toynbee, then in the United States, with some of us who were interested in his views. Toynbee also attended the 1950 conference, and, besides him, Rushton Coulborn, E. H. Harbison, and I were present at all three conferences. Oppenheimer and Stewart attended both the two earlier gatherings; and at the second the philosophers Erich Kahler and Paul Schrecker and the art historians Erwin Panofsky and Curt Sachs balanced in numbers the historians de métier present.

John Marshall of the Rockefeller Foundation also attended at that time, and it was he who suggested a third conference under the sponsorship of the American Council of Learned Societies. The Council accepted the suggestion, and Charles E. Odegaard, then its Executive Director, proceeded to form the Committee on Uniformities in History. The Committee performed its function, eight papers on feudalism in different times and places were written, and the Conference on Feudalism met and deliberated for two days.

The eight papers were prepared in advance, were mimeographed, and then sent to members of the conference. After consideration there, the papers were revised by their authors in the light of the discussions. They are now printed as Part Two of the present book.

These eight essays have a dual character. They present the latest, up-to-date opinions of as many specialist scholars in their fields on the question of how feudalistic or quasi-feudalistic or non-feudalistic the institutions of a given people were in a certain period. Secondly, the eight essays represent a first stage in correlation—through the application by each author, to his own subject, of ideas developed during the conference by specialists in other subjects. Thus the feudal institutions of Japan were re-reviewed in the light of those of Europe, and reciprocally; and both were examined in comparison with the feudal or near-feudal institutions of Mesopotamia or China or Byzantium.

Some of the scholars who did not prepare papers were nevertheless experts in one or another field or area to which feudalistic institutions have been attributed, and were therefore specifically concerned in the exchange of views. Others had wider interests of a generically comparative character, or were concerned chiefly to form abstract conceptions. From a third to a half of the members of the conference were Sinologists, Orientalists, sociologists, anthropologists, philosophers; the remainder, historians.

In Part Three, Coulborn presents a detailed "Comparative Study of Feudalism." This follows a complex procedure, and then, in the concluding chapter considers the relation of the chief cases of feudalism to the stage of civilization in which they arise. Coulborn sees feudalism as a socio-political aid in the revival of civilization when this, following the death of creativity in intellectual endeavor, begins to dry rot, crumble off, and shrivel: its political and economic fabric disintegrates. A new religion may then develop or be introduced and lay the foundation for a later regrowth of the civilization. Feudalism may or may not develop; if it does develop, it is as a rude but healthy reconstructive device from the low point of disintegration and decline and as an instrument of the spread of the reconstructing civilization.

Not, says Coulborn, that the repetitions of feudalism—and similar phenomena—in history are close; but there are enough of them to make their total denial unreasonable. The uniformities in human history are not easy to extricate and justify—that is why he needs ten chapters to do the job for feudalism and a number of other uniformities with which it is intimately related. The variables impinging on man are many and human history is big and endlessly complex. But, Coulborn maintains, the uniformities are there and they can be defined.

I agree with Coulborn. And I would add that in the main the uniformities will turn out to be cultural; as indeed feudalism or any other institution is culture. So far as the uniformities lie in events, these will be "gradual events" in the histories of cultures and their forms, rather than immediate acts of individual men or specific groups of men.

And why not? For from one angle, culture *is* the regularities of human behavior. In the close-up, as in consideration of this or that particular national or tribal custom, the fact is obvious. When we range through the vast spaces and times of history, their filling is so interminably varied that we can expect only a minute fraction of the total content to find even reasonably close repetition elsewhere, especially on first inspection. It takes analysis to establish more, gradually; and it is to intensive comparative analysis that Coulborn has subjected the several feudalisms.

A. L. Kroeber

University of California
March 1954

PREFACE

FOR nearly twenty years I have devoted all the time I had for study to comparative history. This required in the first place reading much history which I previously did not know, the history of China and India, of Russia and Islam, and some prehistory necessary to an understanding of early periods of history. In the second place it required expeditions into other subjects, chiefly anthropology and philosophy. I am very conscious of my good fortune in having been able to pursue these studies, and of the large debt I owe to those who have, in many different ways, helped me to do so.

From Alfred Kroeber I have had for ten years the friendship and steady encouragement of a leading scholar, of the generation senior to my own, in the broad field of study where we both work. It has, therefore, been a peculiar pleasure for me to take part in the writing of this book and in the preceding conference in which he was the prime mover. To Joseph Strayer I am indebted for active and most valuable aid and counsel in the editing and writing. Both of them have read my part of the text, and other contributors have been kind enough to read and criticize particular chapters.

The staff and readers of the Princeton University Press have made valuable suggestions about arrangement and content of the whole book, and it has been a privilege to work with them.

I am very grateful to the Social Science Research Council for fellowships which enabled me to give all my time to study for two years, from 1943 to 1945, to Princeton University for my tenure of the Shreve Fellowship in 1946, and to the American Philosophical Society for a grant from the Penrose Fund also in 1946. Much of the material I have drawn upon in the book was accumulated in those years. The Rockefeller Foundation and the American Council of Learned Societies have sustained the entire enterprise of which the book is a result. I have relied constantly upon their interest in carrying out my part in it, and would express my thanks to John Marshall, Charles Odegaard, and Mortimer Graves for their special contributions to its realization. My thanks are also due to the Department of History, Princeton University, for a grant from the Dayton-Stockton Fund in aid of publication.

I am indebted to the following publishers for permission to quote material from their publications. Cambridge University Press: *History of English Law* by F. Pollock & F. W. Maitland and *The Heroic Age* by H. M. Chadwick; Ginn & Company: *Folkways* by W. G. Sumner.

To Atlanta University I owe many things. The most important is the opportunity to teach history comparatively to small numbers of graduate students. This exercise has served to sharpen many of the ideas propounded in the book, and has proved beyond all doubt the breadth and depth of understanding of history which proceed from studying it comparatively. Further, my duties at Atlanta University have always been light, and I sincerely hope that my colleagues will be satisfied with the use I have made of the leisure I have had, as that use is exemplified in the book. The administration of the university has invariably been sympathetic to my aims and has promoted them wherever possible. The one disadvantage I have suffered has been the great distance from Atlanta of the large libraries whose resources are essential to my work. A series of grants from the Carnegie Foundation through its Atlanta University Center and a second grant from the Penrose Fund by the American Philosophical Society have met most of the special expenses of travel.

Lastly I must thank my wife, Helen McIntosh Coulborn, for what amounts to collaboration with me in the production of the book. As a scholar in a field allied to my own, she has always offered valuable criticism of everything I produce before anyone else sees it. As an expert in styling and arranging of manuscripts, she has saved both me, my collaborators, and the publisher much. In addition, she has typed the entire manuscript and prepared the index.

RUSHTON COULBORN

Atlanta University
February 1954

CONTENTS

PART THREE: A COMPARATIVE STUDY OF FEUDALISM

RUSHTON COULBORN

PART ONE

INTRODUCTORY ESSAY

I · THE IDEA OF FEUDALISM

BY JOSEPH R. STRAYER AND RUSHTON COULBORN

The idea of feudalism is an abstraction derived from some of the facts of early European history, but it is not itself one of those facts. No contemporary of William the Conqueror or Godfrey of Bouillon ever used the term; it was invented by scholars, chiefly scholars of the eighteenth century. These scholars, looking at certain peculiar institutions which had survived to their own day, looking back to the period when these institutions had originated and flourished, coined the word feudalism to sum up a long series of loosely related facts. From its very beginning the idea of feudalism was a high-level abstraction; it described a general category of institutions rather than one specific government. Historians have found feudalism in ninth-century France, twelfth-century England, fourteenth-century Germany; they have written of feudal survivals or revivals on the Continent at the end of the Old Regime.

It is necessary to recall these elementary facts of historiography in order to justify the present book. Some scholars have insisted that feudalism is a technical term which can be used only for Western European institutions of the Middle Ages; they reject *a priori* the attempt to find feudalism in other regions or at other times. But if we consider the origins and the use of the word, we must doubt that it has such a limited meaning. Like "aristocracy," or "dictatorship," it describes a general method of political organization rather than one unique constitution. And there is no reason why this method might not have been developed by several peoples widely scattered in space and time.

This book is an attempt to test the hypothesis that the methods of feudalism may have been applied, in whole or in part, outside Western Europe: in Russia, in Byzantium, in Iran, in ancient Mesopotamia, in Egypt from the Sixth Dynasty to the Twelfth and from the Twentieth to the Twenty-sixth, in Muslim India, in China under the Chou and after the end of the Han Dynasty, in Japan during the Shogunate. The inquiry can hardly begin without a provisional description of feudalism, but it is likely that this description will be modified during the course of the investigation. No single description of feudalism has ever fitted exactly with all the facts of Western European history which it tried to cover; it will obviously be much more difficult to find a formula which will describe common elements in nine different feudal or partially feudal societies. On the other hand, in trying to discover the elements common to these societies, it may be possible to resolve some of the differences which still remain among scholars as to what the essential characteristics of feudalism are.

The larger aim of the book, however, is not to produce a new definition of feudalism, but to see if the study of feudalism will throw light on the question of uniformities in history. That question, in its simplest terms, is this: historians, for many generations, have insisted that every historical event, every historical personage, is unique and will never be duplicated or repeated. At the same time, in their writing, and in the thinking which lies behind the writing, they use words and concepts of general rather than specific meaning; they assume that every new situation has something in common with certain other situations which have preceded it. The Romans, the Chinese, the Incas had "empires"; Athens, Florence, and Manchester had citizens of the "middle class." Why is it permissible to use terms of such general meaning? Are there events which are so similar that they must produce like results? Are the possible solutions to human problems so limited in number that events which are really not very similar will produce results which are almost identical? Or is it all a mirage, caused by the poverty of our vocabulary—are we like those early American colonists who named their raw settlements after European cities in order to gain a comforting sense of familiarity?

Feudalism is a good specimen to use in investigating this problem of uniformities. Difficult as it is to define, it is still more precise, more limited in range of meaning, than concepts such as monarchy or empire. It is also less common. It recurs—if it does recur—somewhat rarely in history; the nine societies studied in this book do not include all possible examples of feudalism, but they include the majority. At the same time, these societies are well distributed in time and space—if feudalism is a recurring condition, a uniformity, then the uniformity overrides differences of race and civilization.

Now for a provisional description: Feudalism is primarily a method of government, not an economic or a social system, though it obviously modifies and is modified by the social and economic environment. It is a method of government in which the essential relation is not that between ruler and subject, nor state and citizen, but between lord and vassal. This means that the performance of political functions depends on personal agreements between a limited number of individuals, and that political authority is treated as a private possession. Since personal contacts are so important in feudal government, it tends to be most effective at the local level where such contacts are easy and frequent. Since political power is personal rather than institutional, there is relatively little separation of functions; the military leader is usually an administrator and the administrator is usually a judge. Military functions are prominent in most feudal societies, especially in their beginnings. The existence of private armies in the service of great men is a sign that the growth of feudal institutions is becoming possible, and some semi-feudal societies, such as post-Ramesside Egypt, never go much beyond this stage. The agreements between leaders and followers usually emphasize military service and some followers never have any duties except those of an expert soldier. Even when actual military service is no longer important, a strong military tradition often remains in the mores of the society—witness Western chivalry, Japanese *bushido*, and the less well known code of Chou China.[1]

The men who discharge political functions in a feudal society are not necessarily aristocrats when they first begin to gain power, but—unless the experience is an abortive one—they soon are recognized as an aristocracy. There are usually marked distinctions within the aristocracy; even in the simplest feudal society there are leaders and followers, and in a highly developed feudal society, such as that of Western Europe, many more gradations may be found. In theory, and occasionally in practice, the feudal aristocracy can be an aristocracy of ability; actually, in all feudal societies there has been a strong, almost irresistible tendency towards heredity of function. Even in Egypt between the Sixth and Twelfth dynasties, where the feudal character of the society is more than doubtful, the position of the nomarch (chief officer of local government) becomes hereditary. It is also possible for an already existing aristocracy to become feudalized—that is, for a group which already has wealth and political privilege to use its wealth and power to reorganize government in a feudal pattern. As a matter of fact, few of the societies studied in this book do not show attempts on the part of aristocracies to do something of the kind.

A connection between feudalism and landed property is implied by the very word which is used to describe the institution, for the *feudum*,

[1] H. G. Creel, *The Birth of China* (New York, 1937), pp. 278-280.

or fief, was usually (not always) a piece of land. But we should remember once more that the word comes long after the fact and that the emphasis which it puts on the fief may be misleading. Most students of European feudal institutions agree that vassalage—the relationship between lord and man—is the essential element in feudalism,[2] although there has always been a minority which places more emphasis on the fief.[3] Without attempting to settle the question here, we might point out that the fact that one man holds land of another does not inevitably create a feudal relationship, and that the powers of a feudal lord are not a mere extension of the powers of a landlord. On the other hand, it is certainly true that the lord-retainer relationship may be of great importance in a society which is not at all feudal—for example, among the early Germans. The introduction of the fief gives stability to agreements which are otherwise fluctuating and impermanent and makes it possible to build a more solid institutional structure on the basic relationship of lord and man. Thus it seems likely that in a fully feudal society there will be an almost equal development of both vassalage and the fief, whereas in a proto-feudal or partly feudal society the growth of the one or the other will be stunted. For example, in the early Carolingian Empire many vassals had no benefices (fiefs) while in pre-Muscovite Russia dependent persons could change lords at will and thus could hardly be considered vassals.

Even more difficult is the problem of discovering specifically feudal characteristics in relations between lord and peasant. Most ruling classes have been supported by the labor of peasant cultivators and have assumed the right to command, judge, and tax their inferiors. In Western Europe this power of a local lord over his villagers far antedates anything which can be called feudalism. But when feudalism does come to Western Europe it gradually regularizes and gives legal status to powers which were before somewhat arbitrary and extra-legal. There is much fluctuation at first, but by the twelfth century customary law has determined the rights of the lord and the duties of the peasant within fairly narrow limits. There are other cases in which the powers of local lords over their villagers antedate feudalism, Chou China, for example. Muscovite Russia is a special case: before the rise of Moscow, peasants, as well as small gentlemen, were notably free from their lords' jurisdiction, but the Muscovite regime granted to the lords very large powers indeed over their villagers. These powers were so large

[2] F. Lot, M. Bloch, F. L. Ganshof, C. Stephenson.
[3] Fustel de Coulanges, F. Seebohm, G. B. Adams.

that they seem to have constituted much of the substance of feudal rights—if they were feudal. In this connection we should note that when the scholars of the Société Jean Bodin investigated serfdom[4] they decided that it was most oppressive and the powers of lords most secure when a strong central government controlled lords and peasants alike. It is a fair conclusion that feudal lords have usually, perhaps always, been supported by the labor of their peasants and that they have had the right to command and judge the peasants, but that the occurrence of those rights does not prove the existence of feudalism.

No static definition can be entirely satisfactory, for feudalism, like any other political system, constantly develops. To the static definition, therefore, may be added one in dynamic terms. In those terms, feudalism can be described as a series of responses to a certain kind of challenge. A challenge which affected a good many societies was that of the decay or weakening of a highly organized political system—an empire or a relatively large kingdom. The spasms of disintegration of such a system can sometimes produce by way of response a series of moves toward reconstruction which lead in a feudal direction. In such cases feudalism usually has some tinge of legal sophistication, some relics of or tendencies toward centralization. The memory of the past throws a shadow over the feudal period; often the wraith of the old monarchy survives, as, for example, the Holy Roman Empire or the imperial court of Japan. If the society is only partially feudalized, as in Muscovy or Parthia, the old monarchy may be much more than a relic.

But we do not know that all feudal and partly feudal societies originate from that challenge. The best opinion about Chou China is that no empire or large kingdom preceded the rise of feudal relations there, and there may be other cases, real or apparent, of the rise of feudalism directly out of a simpler society than an empire. Yet the Chou monarchy did become a wraith of itself as feudalism developed, and there did remain a memory of what it had been in its early days when it was not yet feudal. The anomaly, if it is an anomaly, is the more difficult because it is only partial; it is one of the major problems arising in the comparative study of feudalism, and a part of the concluding essay in this book is devoted to elucidating it. Meanwhile, in seeking conditions favorable to the rise of feudalism, we might consider these: where government is unable to protect its subjects against either internal oppressors or external marauders; where military power

[4] *Le Servage* (Brussels, 1937).

has fallen into the hands of a relatively small part of the population; and where a former large economic unity has broken down, or where a large political unit has been built up in the absence of economic unity.

The societies which have shown strong feudal tendencies are usually ones in which agriculture predominates, in which economic interests are local and the burdens of supporting a far-flung political organization are not compensated by economic benefits. Highly organized commerce tends to inhibit feudalization. The great commercial center of medieval Byzantium, as we shall see, radiated an influence over Kievan Russia, Byzantine Asia Minor, and Iran; the effects were different in those three different regions, but were alike in obstructing the feudal tendencies which existed in all of them.

The existence of a class of local magnates, exercising considerable *de facto* political authority, is common in countries in which agriculture predominates. If the central government cannot retain the obedience of these men, their *de facto* power easily becomes power *de jure* and is inherited by their descendants. The granting of immunities from ordinary acts of jurisdiction is often an important stage in this process. It is possible for the process to prevail against the influence of commerce tending to bolster the unifying power of the central government.

The impact of barbarian invasions naturally emphasizes the weaknesses of a decaying monarchy and strengthens the class of magnates by throwing on them the burden of local defense. Yet it cannot be maintained that every feudal period begins with a barbarian invasion (witness Japan) or that the barbarians always have the same influence. There is, for example, the case of China between the Han and the T'ang; in that period the barbarians from the steppe overran much of North China, but conditions pointing in a feudal direction developed in the south, where those barbarians did not penetrate. The honorable character of the personal vassalage relation is often attributed to barbarian influence and is thought to be a modification of the relation between leader and followers in a barbarian war-band. This has been well demonstrated for Western Europe, and it will be interesting to see whether it is true also elsewhere.

Feudalism can hardly exist without a monopoly or near-monopoly of military power in the lord-vassal group. This monopoly is most easily established when a new technique of fighting is introduced, especially if this technique involves expensive military equipment. The mounted knight of Western Europe is the classic example of this phenomenon—he needed special training from the age of twelve, a horse specially bred for fighting, and expensive armor. The Japanese armored knight-archer, the cataphracts of Byzantium and Iran, the chariot-fighters of the ancient Near East and of China all belong more or less to this class. But the monopoly can also be obtained through purely political means—if the mass of the population is never called for military service, then military power becomes the monopoly of a small group. In either case the professional fighting man becomes the backbone of the feudal class.

When power is distributed on a local basis and put into the hands of professional fighting men, a good deal of rebellion and internecine war can occur. And these things have occurred often enough to cause some to say that anarchy is a normal feature of feudalism. But this is very doubtful doctrine. Even in the most disorderly regions some effective local governments survived under feudalism, and in more fortunate regions feudalism provided a solid basis for organizing powerful, relatively centralized states. Carl Stephenson has shown how feudalism aided the development of political institutions in Northwestern Europe[5] and the example of Japan under the Tokugawa Shogunate shows that the European experience is not unique. In fact, it can be argued that fully developed feudalism is one of the ways in which sizable political structures can be built out of elementary local ones, and that the large incidence of internecine troubles is the price paid for this kind of progress. There is indeed a dramatic irony in the fact that the better feudalism works the more rapidly it generates a political structure which is no longer completely feudal. By contrast, half-feudal societies, where surviving imperial institutions and new feudal relationships neutralize each other, are among those that remain weak for centuries. Frederick Barbarossa saw this clearly when, in the twelfth century, he tried to strengthen the Holy Roman Empire by including all the great men in the network of feudal relationships. He was not entirely successful, but his basic idea was sound; the strongest states of his day had been built out of feudal materials in a relatively short length of time. Toyotomi Hideyoshi, who built up the Tokugawa Shogunate, worked on a similar principle, having learned in the service of the great feudal magnate, Oda Nobunaga, both the use and the abuse of the feudal relationship.

[5] "The Origin and Significance of Feudalism," *American Historical Review*, XLVI (1941), 811-812.

Hideyoshi lifted Japan out of an age of internecine feudal struggles, but, four centuries earlier, Yoritomo Minamoto had saved the empire from collapse by direct application of the lord-vassal relationship among landed men who had eluded the authority of the central government—a policy analogous to Barbarossa's and more successful. Yoritomo's success produced a polity which lasted for more than a century, but then collapsed. We need an explanation of the collapse which overtakes part-imperial, part-feudal polities. We need an explanation equally of the access of strength, more or less rapid and on quite a permanent basis, which some feudal and feudalistic polities have gained. Besides the Tokugawa Shogunate, there are William the Conqueror's England, Iran when the Sassanids took over, and a number of other states in which such changes happened.

Finally, there is the broader and deeper question of whether feudalism ordinarily appears in an age of failure of the high culture as a whole. The question is too large for consideration here, but perhaps it may be hazarded that some feudal periods have been periods of recovery from general failure of the culture. There is another large fact, that some feudal periods have been conspicuous also as "ages of faith." This is true of the era in China between Han and T'ang and of the European Middle Ages; yet there are differences between medieval Western Christendom and China as it underwent the penetration of Buddhism. We lack information about religion and religious institutions for some of the feudal and quasi-feudal periods with which we are concerned; nevertheless, in lower Mesopotamia Marduk displaced Anu, Enlil, and Enki either during or just before a feudal period, and something obscure, but perhaps important, happened to the Mazdaean church in Iran in Arsacid times and earlier;[6] in Egypt from the accession of the Fifth Dynasty something was happening in the cult whereby the prospects for some, and perhaps all, classes of a felicitous future in eternity were improved.[7]

Such matters as these will be considered again in Part Three of this book after the evidence collected in Parts Two and Three has been studied. Meanwhile, certain matters of common knowledge have been called in here to illustrate similarities between the various periods studied, and we think that the similarities shown are already sufficient to provide the beginning of an answer to the main question before

[6] N. C. Debevoise, *A Political History of Parthia* (Chicago, 1938), pp. xxxix, 149.

[7] John A. Wilson in *Journal of Near Eastern Studies*, III (1944), 215-218.

us—the question of uniformities in history. Enough repetition of larger political and social conditions has been found to warrant the tentative extension of the idea of feudalism from the history of Western Europe to the history of other societies; feudalism may, therefore, be considered provisionally as a uniformity. It remains, of course, to substantiate this with more detailed evidence and, in so doing, to sharpen our definition of the criteria which make feudalism a uniformity. Among the matters of common knowledge called in were some which illustrated, not similarities, but dissimilarities. When both similarities and dissimilarities have been examined as rigorously as possible we may be closer to knowing what feudalism is, when it occurs, and what phenomena resemble it or lead to it but are not feudalism itself. And the description and circumscription which can be made for feudalism may suggest what order or degree of uniformity is likely to be found for other phenomena which seem to be repetitive in history.

PART TWO

SPECIAL STUDIES

II · FEUDALISM IN WESTERN EUROPE

BY JOSEPH R. STRAYER

FEUDALISM, in Western European history, is a word which has been given many meanings,[1] but most of them can be brought into two general categories. One group of scholars uses the word to describe the technical arrangements by which vassals became dependents of lords, and landed property (with attached economic benefits) became organized as dependent tenures or fiefs. The other group of scholars uses feudalism as a general word which sums up the dominant forms of political and social organization during certain centuries of the Middle Ages.

There are difficulties with both usages. In the first category there is no agreement on the relationships which are to be considered typically feudal. Is it the act of becoming a vassal, or the act of granting a fief, or a combination of the two which makes feudalism? Retainers, clients, armed dependents of a great man—all these we have in both Germanic and Roman society from the fourth century on, but does that entitle us to speak of Late Roman or primitive German feudalism? Under Charlemagne there are vassals, and these vassals receive dependent tenures. Yet the king still keeps close control over all men and all lands, and the relationships of dependency are not necessarily hereditary. If this is feudalism, then we need another word to describe conditions in the eleventh century. In the seventeenth century, in both France

[1] Pollock and Maitland, *History of English Law*, 2nd edn. (Cambridge, 1923), I, 66-67: "... *feudalism* is an unfortunate word. In the first place it draws our attention to but one element in a complex state of society and that element is not the most distinctive: it draws our attention only to the prevalence of dependent and derivative land tenure. This however may well exist in an age which can not be called feudal in any tolerable sense. What is characteristic of 'the feudal period' is not the relationship between letter and hirer, or lender and borrower of land, but the relationship between lord and vassal, or rather it is the union of these two relationships. Were we free to invent new terms, we might find *feudo-vassalism* more serviceable than *feudalism*. But the difficulty is not one which could be solved by any merely verbal devices. The impossible task that has been set before the word *feudalism* is that of making a single idea represent a very large piece of the world's history, represent the France, Italy, Germany, England, of every century from the eighth or ninth to the fourteenth or fifteenth. Shall we say that French feudalism reached its zenith under Louis d'Outre-Mer or under Saint Louis, that William of Normandy introduced feudalism into England or saved England from feudalism, that Bracton is the greatest of English feudists or that he never misses an opportunity of showing a strong anti-feudal bias? It would be possible to maintain all or any of these opinions, so vague is our use of the term in question."

and England all the technical forms of feudalism survive—most nobles are vassals and much of their land is held as fiefs. Yet it is only the form which has survived; the ideas which control the relationship of king and noble no longer conform to the feudal pattern. In short, the difficulty in concentrating on the technical aspects of feudalism is that it sets no chronological limits and provides no standards by which feudalism can be clearly distinguished from preceding and succeeding types of organization.

In the second category this difficulty is overcome by assuming at the outset that there is a "feudal age," a "feudal period" with definite chronological limits. The limits may vary, but there is general agreement on the core of the period—all authorities would admit that feudalism reached its height in the eleventh and twelfth centuries. But while this approach clears up the chronological confusion, it introduces a functional confusion by applying the feudal label to all social phenomena between the tenth and the thirteenth centuries. For example, the class structure of the late Middle Ages was very different from that of the early Middle Ages—are they both feudal? Lords used a different technique in exploiting their lands in 1200 from that in vogue in 1000—which technique should be accepted as typical of feudalism? We meet the sort of difficulties here that a modern historian would find if he assumed that the factory system were an integral part of democracy.

To obtain a usable concept of feudalism we must eliminate extraneous factors and aspects which are common to many types of society. Feudalism is not synonymous with aristocracy—there have been many aristocracies which were not feudal and there was no very clear concept of aristocracy in the early days of feudalism. Feudalism is not a necessary concomitant of the great estate worked by dependent or servile labor—such estates have existed in many other societies. Feudalism is not merely the relationship between lord and man, nor the system of dependent land tenures, for either can exist in a non-feudal society. The combination of personal and tenurial dependence brings us close to feudalism, but something is still lacking. It is only when rights of government (not mere political influence) are attached to lordship and fiefs that we can speak of fully developed feudalism in Western Europe. It is the possession of rights of government by feudal lords and the performance of most functions of government through feudal lords which clearly distinguishes feudalism from other types of organization.

This means that Western European feudalism is essentially political—it is a form of government. It is a form of government in which political authority is monopolized by a small group of military leaders, but is rather evenly distributed among members of the group. As a result, no leader rules a very wide territory, nor does he have complete authority even within a limited territory—he must share power with his equals and grant power to his subordinates. A fiction of unity—a theory of subordination or cooperation among feudal lords—exists, but government is actually effective only at the local level of the county or the lordship. It is the lords who maintain order, if they can, who hold courts and determine what is the law. The king, at best, can merely keep peace among the lords and usually is unable even to do this.

The men who possess political power also possess important sources of wealth—land and buildings, markets and mills, forests and rivers—and this wealth is naturally useful in maintaining or increasing their political authority. Yet wealth alone does not give political power—loyal vassals and courageous retainers are more important. Any sensible feudal lord will surrender much of his land in order to increase the number of his vassals, and the most powerful lords, such as the Duke of Normandy, actually possess relatively few estates. It is also true that political and economic rights do not always correspond. A lord may have rights of government where he has no land and may hold land where some other lord has superior political authority. No one finds this inconsistent, because the distinction which we have been making between political and economic rights has almost no meaning for the early Middle Ages. Public authority has become a private possession. Everyone expects the possessor of a court to make a profit out of it, and everyone knows that the eldest son of the court-holder will inherit this profitable right, whatever his qualifications for the work. On the other hand, any important accumulation of private property almost inevitably becomes burdened with public duties. The possessor of a great estate must defend it, police it, maintain roads and bridges and hold a court for his tenants. Thus lordship has both economic and political aspects; it is less than sovereignty, but more than private property.

Effective feudal government is local, and at the local level public authority has become a private possession. Yet in feudalism the concepts of central government and of public authority are never entirely lost. Kingship survives, with real prestige though attenuated power, and the Church never forgets the Roman traditions of strong monarchy and public law. The revival of Roman law in the twelfth century strengthens these traditions and by the thirteenth century most lawyers insist that all governmental authority is delegated by the king and that the king has a right to review all acts of feudal lords.

Feudal lordship occupies an intermediate place between tribal leadership and aristocratic government. It differs from tribal leadership in being more formalized and less spontaneous. The feudal lord is not necessarily one of the group whom he rules; he may be a complete stranger who has acquired the lordship by inheritance or grant. It differs from aristocracy in being more individualistic and less centralized. The feudal lord is not merely one of a group of men who influence the government; he *is* the government in his own area. When feudalism is at its height, the barons never combine to rule jointly a wide territory but instead seek a maximum degree of independence from each other. One of the signs of the decay of feudalism in the West is the emergence of the idea of government by a *group* of aristocrats.

As the last paragraphs suggest, we must distinguish between an earlier and a later stage of Western feudalism. In the early stage feudalism was the dominant fact in politics, but there was almost no theoretical explanation or justification of the fact. In the later stage feudalism was competing with and slowly losing ground to other types of political organization, and many able writers tried to explain how and why it functioned. The great law-books of the thirteenth century—the Norman *Summa de Legibus*, Bracton, Beaumanoir—fit the facts of feudalism into a logical and well-organized system of law and government. Naturally most writers of secondary works have relied on these treatises and as a result the modern concept of feudalism is largely that of feudalism in the late twelfth and thirteenth centuries—a feudalism which was much better organized, much more precise, and much less important than that of the earlier period.

The first period of feudalism is best exemplified by the institutions of northern France about 1100. In northern France the one basic institution was the small feudal state dominated by the local lord. He might bear any title (the ruler of Normandy was called at various times duke, count, or marquis) and he was usually, though not always, the vassal of a king. But whatever his title, whatever his nominal dependence on a superior, he was in fact the final authority in his region. No one could appeal from his decisions to a higher authority; no one could remain completely indifferent to his commands. His position was based on his military strength. He had a group of trained fighting men in his service; he held fortified strategic positions throughout his lands; h possessed sufficient economic resources to pay for both the army and the fortifications. There might be lesser lords within his sphere of influence who had accepted his leadership in order to gain protection or because his military power left them no choice but submission. Some of his retainers—not necessarily all—would have fiefs for which they rendered service, in which they had limited rights of government. Relations between the lord and these subordinates were still undefined. The exact amount of service to be rendered by the vassal, the rights of government which he could exercise, the degree to which these rights could be inherited by his descendants depended far more on the power and prestige of the lord than on any theory of law. It was up to the lord to defend his territory and his rights; if he failed he would either lose his lands to a stronger neighboring lord or to his more powerful subordinates. There could be great fluctuations in power and in amount of territory controlled, not merely from one generation to another, but even from one decade to another. The only thing which was relatively stable was the method of government. The customs of a region remained the same, even if the lordship changed hands, and every lord had to govern through and with his vassals. They formed his army; they made up the court in which all important acts of government were performed; they performed most of the functions of local government in their fiefs.

The second stage of feudalism—the stage described by the great lawyers of the thirteenth century—bears a closer resemblance to the neat, pyramidal structure of the textbooks. The bonds of vassalage have been tightened at the upper and relaxed at the lower level; the ruler of a province now owes more obedience to his superior and receives less service from his inferiors. Early feudalism might be described as a series of overlapping spheres of influence, each centered around the castles of some strong local lord. Later feudalism is more like a series of holding corporations; the local lord still performs important functions but he can be directed and controlled by higher authority. Appeals from the local lord to his superior are encouraged; petty vassals are protected against excessive demands for service or attempts to seize their fiefs; the central government in some cases deals directly with rear-vassals instead of passing orders down a long chain of command. Royal law-courts play a great role in this reorganization. The institution of the assizes at the end of the twelfth century in England protected the rear-vassal and brought him into direct contact with the king. The development of appeals to the king's court at Paris gave the same results in thirteenth-century France. In this much more highly organized feudalism rights and duties are spelled out in great detail. The amount of service owed is carefully stated, rules of inheritance are determined, the rights of government which can be exercised by each lord are defined and regulated. Force is still important, but only the king and the greatest lords possess sufficient force to gain by its use; the ordinary lord has to accept judicial solutions to his controversies.

There is obviously a great difference between these two stages of feudalism, and yet the transition from one to the other was made so smoothly, in many places, that it was almost imperceptible. It is true that in the later stage rulers were aided by concepts which were not derived from early feudalism, such as the revived Roman law and the Church's ideas of Christian monarchy. Yet, giving due weight to these outside influences, there must still have been some principle of order and growth in early feudalism which made possible the rapid development of relatively advanced systems of political organization in the twelfth and thirteenth centuries. Early feudal society, turbulent as it was, was never pure anarchy. There was always some government, even if rudimentary and local; there were always some centers of refuge and defense. Early feudal government, primitive as it was, was still more sophisticated and complicated than tribal government. There was a higher degree of specialization—the fighting men and the men with rights of government were clearly marked off from the rest of the group. There was a little more artificiality in political organization. Feudal government was not (necessarily) part of the immemorial structure of the community; it could be imposed from the outside; it could be consciously altered by the lord and his vassals. Early feudalism was rough and crude, but it was neither stagnant nor sterile. Flexible and adaptable, it produced new institutions rapidly, perhaps more rapidly than more sophisticated systems of government.

To understand the real vitality of feudalism we shall have to consider briefly the circumstances in which it first appeared in Europe. The Roman Empire had collapsed in the West, largely because none of its subjects cared enough for it to make any great effort to defend it. The Germanic rulers who succeeded the Emperors were not hostile to Roman civilization. They preserved as much of it as they were able; they kept together as large political units as they could. They were not entirely successful in these efforts, but they did preserve real power for the central government and they did thwart the growth of independent local lordship. The greatest of the Germanic rulers, Charlemagne, even united a large part of Western Europe in a new Empire. This was a *tour de force* which has impressed men for over a thousand years; he made his bricks not only without straw but very nearly without clay. The Latin and Germanic peoples he united had no common political tradition, no common cultural tradition and very few economic ties. Their interests were predominantly local, as they had been for centuries; only the clergy remembered with longing the peace and good order of Rome. With the moral support of the Church and the physical support of the army of his own people, the Franks, Charlemagne held his Empire together, but it was always a shaky structure. The Church profited by its existence to extend the parish system and to improve the education of the higher clergy. These developments helped to soften some of the cultural differences among Western European peoples, and to lay the foundations for a common European civilization, but the forces of localism were still stronger than those which worked for unity. Local government was in the hands of counts, men of wealth and high social position who held their authority from the king but who were not always fully obedient to him. The counts, in turn, were not always able to dominate the great landowners of their districts. Vassalage was becoming common and something very like fiefs held of the king or of lords appeared about the middle of the eighth century. Charlemagne tried to reinforce the doubtful loyalty of his subjects by making the great men his vassals, but this expedient had only temporary success. The ties between the magnates and their retainers were far closer than those between Charlemagne and the magnates, for the retainers lived with their lords while the lords visited the imperial court only occasionally. As a result the magnates had great power in their own provinces, subject only to the intermittent intervention of the king. This was not yet feudalism: there was still public authority, and the great men held political power by delegation from the king and not in their own right. But it was very close to feudalism; a strong push was all that was needed to cross the line.

The push came in the fifty years which followed Charlemagne's death. His heirs were less competent than he and quarreled among themselves. The magnates took advantage of these quarrels to gain independence; they began to consider their offices private possessions, to be inherited by their sons. Meanwhile invasions from outside threatened the security of all inhabitants of the Empire. The Saracens raided the south coast of France, the west coast of Italy, and even established a permanent fort at Garde-Frainet which interfered seriously with overland travel between France and Italy. The Magyars occupied Hungary, and from this base sent great cavalry expeditions through southern Germany, eastern France and northern Italy. Worst of all were the Northmen. For over a century their shallow-draft ships pushed up all the rivers of northern Europe and sent out raiding parties which plundered the countryside. The central government was almost helpless; it could not station troops everywhere on the vast periphery of the Empire and it could seldom assemble and move an army quickly enough to catch the fast-moving raiders. Defense had to become a local responsibility; only the local lord and his castle could provide any security for most subjects of the Empire.

It was in these conditions that feudal governments began to appear in northern France—a region which had suffered heavily from both civil war and viking raids. We could hardly expect these early feudal governments to be well organized and efficient—they were improvised to meet a desperate situation and they bore all the signs of hasty construction. But they did have two great advantages which made them capable of further development. In the first place, feudalism forced men who had privileges to assume responsibility. In the late Roman Empire, the Frankish kingdom, and the Carolingian monarchy wealthy landlords had assisted the central government as little as possible while using their position and influence to gain special advantages for themselves. Now they had to carry the whole load; if they shirked they lost everything. In the second place, feudalism simplified the structure of government to a point where it corresponded to existing social and economic conditions. For centuries rulers had been striving to preserve something of the Roman political system, at the very least to maintain their authority over relatively large areas through a hierarchy of appointed officials. These efforts had met little response from the great majority of people; large-scale government had given them few benefits and had forced them to carry heavy burdens. Always there had been a dangerous discrepancy between the wide interests of the rulers and the narrow, local interests of the ruled. Feudalism relieved this strain; it worked at a level which was comprehensible to the ordinary man and it made only minimum demands on him. It is probably true that early feudal governments did less than they should, but this was better than doing more than was wanted. When the abler feudal lords began to improve their governments they had the support of their people who realized that new institutions were needed. The active demand for more and better government in the twelfth century offers a sharp contrast to the apathy with which the people of Western Europe watched the disintegration of the Roman and the Carolingian Empires.

Feudalism, in short, made a fairly clean sweep of obsolete institutions and replaced them with a rudimentary government which could be used as a basis for a fresh start. Early feudal government was informal and flexible. Contrary to common opinion, it was at first little bound by tradition. It is true that it followed local custom, but there were few written records, and oral tradition was neither very accurate nor very stable. Custom changed rapidly when circumstances changed; innovations were quickly accepted if they seemed to promise greater security. Important decisions were made by the lord and his vassals, meeting in informal councils which followed no strict rules of procedure. It was easy for an energetic lord to make experiments in government; for example, there was constant tinkering with the procedure of feudal courts in the eleventh and twelfth centuries in order to find better methods of proof. Temporary committees could be set up to do specific jobs; if they did their work well they might become permanent and form the nucleus of a department of government. It is true that many useful ideas came from the clergy, rather than from lay vassals, but if feudal governments had not been adaptable they could not have profited from the learning and skill of the clergy.

Feudalism produced its best results only in regions where it became the dominant form of government. France, for example, developed her first adequate governments in the feudal principalities of the north, Flanders, Normandy, Anjou and the king's own lordship of the Ile de France. The first great increase in the power of the French king came from enforcing his rights as feudal superior against his vassals. Many institutions of the French monarchy of the thirteenth century had already been tested in the feudal states of the late twelfth century; others grew out of the king's feudal court. By allowing newly annexed provinces to keep the laws and institutions developed in the feudal period, the king of France was able to unite the country with a minimum of ill-will. France later paid a high price for this provincial particularism, but the existence of local governments which could operate with little supervision immensely simplified the first stages of unification.

England in many ways was more like a single French province than the congeries of provinces which made up the kingdom of France. In fact, the first kings after the Conquest sometimes spoke of the kingdom as their "honor" or fief, just as a feudal lord might speak of his holding.

As this example shows, England was thoroughly feudalized after the Conquest. While Anglo-Saxon law remained officially in force it became archaic and inapplicable; the law which grew into the common law of England was the law applied in the king's feudal court. The chief departments of the English government likewise grew out of this court. And when the combination of able kings and efficient institutions made the monarchy too strong, it was checked by the barons in the name of the feudal principles expressed in Magna Carta. Thus feudalism helped England to strike a happy balance between government which was too weak and government which was too strong.

The story was quite different in countries in which older political institutions prevented feudalism from reaching full development. Feudalism grew only slowly in Germany; it never included all fighting men or all lands. The German kings did not use feudalism as the chief support of their government; instead they relied on institutions inherited from the Carolingian period. This meant that the ruler acted as if local lords were still his officials and as if local courts were still under his control. In case of opposition, he turned to bishops and abbots for financial and military aid, instead of calling on his vassals. There was just enough vitality in this system to enable the king to interfere sporadically in political decisions all over Germany, and to prevent the growth of strong, feudal principalities. But while the German kings of the eleventh and twelfth centuries showed remarkable skill in using the old precedents, they failed to develop new institutions and ideas. Royal government became weaker, and Germany more disunited in every succeeding century. The most important provincial rulers, the dukes, were also unable to create effective governments. The kings were jealous of their power, and succeeding in destroying, or weakening all the great duchies. The kings, however, were unable to profit from their success, because of their own lack of adequate institutions. Power eventually passed to rulers of the smaller principalities, not always by feudal arrangements, and only after the monarchy had been further weakened by a long conflict with the papacy. Thus the German kings of the later Middle Ages were unable to imitate the king of France who had united his country through the use of his position as feudal superior. Germany remained disunited, and, on the whole, badly governed, throughout the rest of the Middle Ages and the early modern period.

Italy also suffered from competition among different types of government. The German emperor was traditionally king of (north) Italy

He could not govern this region effectively but he did intervene often enough to prevent the growth of large, native principalities. The Italian towns had never become depopulated, like those of the North, and the great economic revival of the late eleventh century made them wealthy and powerful. They were too strong to be fully controlled by any outside ruler, whether king or feudal lord, and too weak (at least in the early Middle Ages) to annex the rural districts outside their walls. The situation was further complicated by the existence of the papacy at Rome. The popes were usually on bad terms with the German emperors and wanted to rule directly a large part of central Italy. In defending themselves and their policies they encouraged the towns' claims to independence and opposed all efforts to unite the peninsula. Thus, while there was feudalism in Italy, it never had a clear field and was unable to develop as it did in France or England. Italy became more and more disunited; by the end of the Middle Ages the city-state, ruled by a "tyrant," was the dominant form of government in the peninsula. There was no justification for this type of government in medieval political theory, and this may be one reason why the Italians turned with such eagerness to the writings of the classical period. In any case, the Italian political system was a failure, and Italy was controlled by foreign states from the middle of the sixteenth to the middle of the nineteenth century.

There are certainly other factors, besides feudalism, which enabled France and England to set the pattern for political organization in Europe, and other weaknesses, besides the absence of fully developed feudalism, which condemned Germany and Italy to political sterility. At the same time, the basic institutions of France and England in the thirteenth century, which grew out of feudal customs, proved adaptable to changed conditions, while the basic institutions of Italy and Germany, which were largely non-feudal, had less vitality. Western feudalism was far from being an efficient form of government, but its very imperfections encouraged the experiments which kept it from being a stagnant form of government. It was far from being a just form of government, but the emphasis on personal relationships made it a source of persistent loyalties. And it was the flexibility of their institutions and the loyalty of their subjects which enabled the kings of the West to create the first modern states.

III JAPANESE FEUDALISM

BY EDWIN O. REISCHAUER

I. Introduction

THE idea of feudalism may be an abstraction derived from some of the facts of early European history, but it is an abstraction which applies with equal validity to many of the facts of Japanese history between the ninth and nineteenth century. Scholars primarily concerned with Japanese feudalism rather than with that of Europe might possibly have made some alterations in detail in the description of feudalism in the Introductory Essay or in similar definitions and descriptions of feudalism in Occidental writings, but they could not have altered the major outline.

Parallels between isolated facts may be purely accidental, but the close resemblance between the general patterns of political, economic, and social phenomena in feudal Europe and Japan indicates that feudalism is not merely a chance array of facts in early European history but is a fundamental, even though not necessarily frequent, form of human organization. Here is clearly a great uniformity of history, and the striking parallels in the whole process of development from prefeudal times through the long feudal experiences in Europe and Japan to the postfeudal systems of both areas would suggest that much is still to be learned about the historical process in the West from a comparative study of these similar experiences.

II. Isolation and the Time Scale

There appears to be one fundamental difference between the feudal experience of Japan and that of Europe: the Japanese experience took place in a land which until the nineteenth century was more isolate from all other parts of the civilized world than was any other culturall advanced area of comparable size. European feudalism seems to hav evolved at a somewhat more rapid pace than Japanese feudalism, per haps because of the great pressures and influences between a numbe of areas, each of which in size and population was roughly equal t the whole of Japan, and also because of far greater pressures fron peoples outside the fold of European feudalism.

In Japan, relative isolation seems to have permitted a slower rate c evolution and the persistence for a much longer time of distinctly pr feudal institutions. Elements of Japanese feudalism appeared as early as the ninth or tenth century, but these did not begin to take shape in a definite feudal system until the twelfth century, and not until two or three centuries later did Japan develop institutions which closely paralleled those of European feudalism at its height. On the other hand, during these long centuries of feudal growth, prefeudal institutions continued to exist side by side with the new, and some managed to survive the whole millennium of Japanese feudalism to be given new life and modern form in the nineteenth century. One of these was the concept of a centralized state as the natural and proper political organization for all Japan. Another was the imperial line, which survived the extraordinary vicissitudes of the feudal period as the unquestioned source in theory of all political power. Associated with the imperial family was a court aristocracy which continued a precarious existence on the margins of feudal society. Another important survival of prefeudal times was the whole nomenclature of office of the old imperial government, for the old court ranks and the names of extinct imperial offices were made an integral though anachronistic part of the feudal system.

Isolation may also be the basic factor which allowed Japanese feudalism to continue into a highly advanced or, one might better say, badly degenerated phase, which finds no very clear parallel in the West. In other words, if isolation permitted the continuation of more prefeudal elements during feudal times in Japan than in Europe, it also may have permitted the continuation of a basically feudal organization into a period which in point of view of technological and economic advances might best be compared with the early modern period of Europe.

The connection between isolation and the slowness of the course of Japanese feudal evolution can be illustrated in reverse by the two periods when Japan was least isolated from outside influences. During the second half of the sixteenth century, when representatives of the Western world suddenly broke in upon the isolated Japanese, feudal institutions of all sorts changed more rapidly and drastically than ever before, and there were signs that feudalism itself might be swept away within a short time. The artificially imposed isolation of the next two centuries halted this trend, but, when the Western world again descended upon Japan in the middle of the nineteenth century, feudalism collapsed almost at once and disappeared entirely within two or three decades.

The basic ingredients of Japanese feudalism offer a striking parallel to those of Europe. In Japan, as in Europe, we find a people who had a persistent tradition of tribal or clan organization, with strong emphasis on hereditary leadership and personal bonds of loyalty, falling heir to an advanced and centralized state system. But the process of union of these two factors in Japan differed sharply from that of Europe. A leading clan had established its dominance over the other clans by at least the sixth century A.D. and had then in the course of the seventh and eighth centuries embarked on an ambitious effort to imitate the Chinese political system by transforming the loose federation of clans in Japan into a centrally controlled state, based economically on a complex system of direct taxation of the peasantry. The degree of success achieved by the Japanese, particularly in the central districts, is more surprising than the eventual collapse of the effort during the ninth to twelfth centuries.

It is a question whether this collapse entailed a lowering of cultural and economic levels in Japan. Obviously such a decline occurred to some extent in the capital district, deprived as it was of much of its former political and economic control over the provinces. In the latter, however, there seems to have been rather a rise of economic and cultural levels. Certainly by the thirteenth century the Japanese as a whole were economically and culturally far ahead of where they had been at the height of imperial rule in the eighth century, and even more notable advances were to be made during the next three centuries of growing political anarchy. Thus, in Japan, where the centralized political system borrowed from China had never been more than a thin veneer and had been more a theory than a reality in large parts of the land, the rise of feudalism did not entail general economic and cultural decline. Instead, feudal institutions seem to have fostered economic and cultural growth and eventually produced a political integration far more powerful than that of the old imperial government.

III. The Manor and the Military Clique

Japanese feudalism took shape from two separate institutions which as they gradually merged produced a fully feudal Japan. One was the *shō* (or manor) with its *shiki* (or "tenures"), a land-holding pattern which evolved as a clear subversion of the land and tax system borrowed from China. The other, which was the warrior clique, seems at least in part to have been a survival from the ancient social organization of the Japanese. As might be expected in a period of declining central authority, both institutions served to give the individual participant the protections which the central government no longer could furnish, but the one was primarily economic, affording protection from ruinous taxation, and the other military, providing simple police protection.

The *shō* began to appear as early as the eighth century when newly cultivated lands, because of oversight or special permission, remained off the tax registers. They grew through further land reclamation, through slow but steady depredations on the public domain by those with sufficient political power to be able to escape the tax collectors, and through commendation by tax-paying men who by this act won the tax-free status of powerful patrons. The great Buddhist monasteries, by the receipt of benefices and by means of their influence over the government, played a primary role in the creation of many of the *shō*. By the tenth century the great bulk of the agricultural land of Japan was divided among *shō* which enjoyed complete or partial tax exemption on the various pieces of land of which they consisted.

One prime difference between the *shō* and the European manor was that its fields were usually scattered and in no way corresponded to village units. Asakawa has ascribed the difference to the fact that rice, which is traditionally cultivated in small irregular patches, was the foundation of Japanese agriculture, and there was little or no common grazing land which would be utilized and therefore owned by village units. The *shō* also varied greatly in size. At the end of the twelfth century the famous Shimazu *shō* in southern Kyushu seems to have contained over 23,000 acres of cultivated land in three provinces, but many other *shō* were probably no more than large farms supporting a handful of families.

By the twelfth century we find a complex pattern of relationships of men to land within a *shō*. These relationships were similar to the "tenures" of Western feudalism but quite different in one respect. Tenures implied conditions and obligations. The Japanese *shiki* (a word which originally meant "office" or "function") were primarily rights to income. The *shiki* were of various different levels. First of all there was the *shiki* of the *ryōke*, which Asakawa variously translates as "seignior" and "domanial lord." The *ryōke* was almost always an absentee owner, normally a powerful family of court nobles or else some great Buddhist monastery or possibly an important Shintō shrine. The *ryōke* was also known as the *honke*, but in cases where the original domanial lord had felt it necessary to commend the *shō* to some still more powerful person or institution (the *honke*) for added protection, the *ryōke* and *honke* were different, and each had his separate *shiki* or income from the *shō*. Living on the *shō* itself would be an agent of the domanial lord or some original proprietor of the *shō* or often enough both, each with his appropriate *shiki*. Then there was the actual cultivator with his cultivator's *shiki*. The cultivator was not necessarily a peasant himself but more likely a manager of hired workers who did the actual farming for him, presumably for wages.

Shiki as rights to income were commonly divisible and alienable. Of course, there were great variations in the terms of tenure, some having been entirely free and subject to no interference by supposedly higher authorities, and others, such as those of agents, having been under the strict control of the domanial lord; and there were always efforts by each group to modify its terms of tenure to its own benefit. In the twelfth century, however, *shiki* were for the most part freely divided and disposed of at will.

Primogeniture was not the custom in this age, and in each generation there was a tendency for a division of *shiki* among all the male heirs. Even women were sometimes included in inheritances, for they could hold *shiki* as well as their men-folk. The result was an extreme confusion of *shiki* rights, with *shiki* of different types on a number of pieces of land held by a single individual, so that he might be the superior of another person with regard to one piece of land and his subordinate in another. Social relations obviously were not dependent entirely on *shiki*. In general the domanial lords were of a higher status than the local *shiki* holders, and the workers who had no *shiki* were still lower, but there were no general class lines between agents, proprietors, and cultivators, social differences varying with each specific case.

The second institution which lies behind Japanese feudalism is the military clique, which in turn had its roots in the aristocratic, hereditary organization of the old Japanese clans. In the twelfth century, as probably in prehistoric times, the warrior was an aristocrat. No doubt one basic reason for this, as in Europe, was the cost of the equipment of warfare. The fighting unit was the individual knight, elaborately armored and mounted on a horse. Although he was supported by grooms and other attendants, he fought as an individual, relying on his horse for mobile bow and arrow attacks upon his adversary and using his sword for close fighting.

In the attempt to transplant Chinese institutions to Japan, the government failed to create a huge army of foot soldiers on the Chinese model. Peasants conscripted for the army were used as little more than labor gangs, while Japan's real fighting forces continued to consist of relatively small groups of aristocratic provincials. We know little of the development of these groups, but in the twelfth century they were largely identical with the local *shiki* holders of the *shō*. In part descended from local clan aristocrats and in part the descendants of members of the court aristocracy and of offshoots of the imperial family who had gone to the provinces as local officials and agents for domanial lords, this local aristocracy occupied the now largely nominal positions in the old provincial administration of the central government and at the same time were in actual control of the *shō*, which they defended by their military prowess and from which they derived their support through *shiki*.

While the *shō* still provided an adequate basis for economic organization, geographic decentralization and chaotic divisions in ownership and control kept it from being the natural unit of local military organization. It was rather the family and, beyond the family, the larger groupings engendered by long relationship and mutual dependence between members of different families which were the centers around which the provincial warriors organized for purposes of mutual defense. From such groupings, strongly reminiscent of the ancient clan, grew the feudal cliques of the eleventh and twelfth centuries, notably the two great cliques of the Taira and Minamoto. These two fought a series of wars with each other, which ended finally in 1185 in the destruction of the core of the Taira clique and the complete victory of the Minamoto. The leader of the latter, who now was the military master of all Japan, adopted the ancient title of *shōgun*, or generalissimo, and established the headquarters of his military government (*bakufu*) at Kamakura near the center of Minamoto strength in eastern Japan.

IV. Two Feudal Stages: Kamakura and Ashikaga

The year 1185 is usually taken to mark the beginning of the feudal age in Japan, because from this time until the nineteenth century the actual control of what remained of the organs of central government was for the most part in the hands of military leaders and not in the hands of the imperial family or of the court nobility. It was also in the early years of Minamoto rule that the feudal clique was integrated with the *shō* system to form a single feudal structure. This was done by placing *jitō*, or stewards, who were personal retainers (*gokenin*) of the Minamoto *shōgun*, in control of the *shō* and of what remained of the public domain of the whole land. Often these men were the original proprietors of the estates or some other local *shiki* holders who were already Minamoto retainers or who managed to acquire that status, but in other cases they were warriors from east Japan who, as a reward for past services, were inserted as *jitō* into the already complex control structure of the *shō* in other parts of the land. The *jitō* of course had *jitō shiki* for their support. They also quite naturally embarked at once upon an uneasy competition for power and income with the other *shiki* holders of their respective *shō*. Further form was given to the new feudal structure in most of the provinces by the designation of one retainer as the *shugo*, or protector, who had overall responsibility for maintaining the peace and for organizing the local retainers in time of war.

Thus, a single military clique had expanded to take over control of the whole nation, although in theory it had merely taken over the military functions of the otherwise impotent central government. Through the *jitō* it controlled the income of the old central government and of the court nobility and also exercised direct supervision over the vast bulk of the people of the land, who lived and worked in the *shō*. Through the direct loyalty of all the retainers to the *shōgun* and through their organization for defense purposes under the *shugo*, it exercised effective military control over the whole land and possessed a defense system which succeeded in repelling the two Mongol invasions of 1274 and 1281.

In Japanese feudalism legal rights and legal fictions were never as important as in European feudalism, and therefore less is heard of them. This is not surprising in view of the relative unimportance of legal concepts in the centralized Chinese system which lay behind Japanese feudalism, as contrasted with the vital role of law in the Roman background of European feudalism. At the same time, legal realities, if not legal fictions, played an important part in the transition from imperial to feudal rule in Japan. The military cliques tended to develop their own "house" laws, based on custom and precedent. With the triumph of the Minamoto clique, its "house" laws became in fact the only enforced laws of the land. In theory all *shiki*, except those of the *jitō*, were dependent upon Imperial law, but in practice under the

Kamakura shogunate most litigants came to seek justice from the Kamakura courts, since these were the only ones with power to enforce their decisions. Imperial law gradually became a dead letter, except insofar as it was recognized by the shogunal courts, and for the remainder of the feudal period the only living law codes were those of the successive shogunal families and in time those of the other independent or autonomous lords.

The period of the Kamakura shogunate has often been considered the classic age of Japanese feudalism, but in comparison with similar periods in other feudal societies it might best be regarded as a proto-feudal prelude to complete feudalization. A remarkable degree of stability, however, was achieved at this time through the adaptation of certain feudal devices. The edifice the Minamoto built endured for well over a century, and while the extinction of the main Minamoto family led to the substitution of figurehead *shōgun* who had no true personal claim on the loyalties of the retainers of the clique, shogunal regents, or *shikken*, of the Hōjō family (curiously enough descended from the Taira) and the central boards of the shogunate held the clique together. More surprising, they administered justice to all comers, with the result that *shiki* holders outside the clique did not lose out as rapidly to the *jitō* as one would have supposed. On the other hand, the constant division of *jitō shiki* through inheritance dangerously undermined the economic basis of the retainer group, and the passage of time even more seriously weakened the bonds of personal loyalty between provincial retainers and the figurehead *shōgun* and his regent. When a sudden revolt overthrew the Kamakura shogunate in 1333, the military clique disintegrated at once and completely.

With the collapse of the Kamakura shogunate, Japan entered upon a prolonged period of almost constant warfare between rival groups of local warriors. The once nationwide clique of warriors was gone, and a new basis for political integration was needed. The Kamakura *shōgun* were succeeded by a new line of *shōgun* of the Ashikaga family, an offshoot of the Minamoto, but the Ashikaga, having no real claim on the loyalty of the greater part of the warrior class, were in no position to establish anything like a *jitō* or *shugo* system and in consequence never controlled all of Japan or, for that matter, even much of the country for very long. They ensconced themselves at the old imperial capital of Kyoto and placed deputies with various titles at certain key spots in the realm, but during most of their two centuries of supposed rule they had little control over their own deputies and still less over the other military lords who were rising to power all over Japan.

The constant warfare of the Ashikaga period naturally brought with it significant changes. Between the first half of the fourteenth century and the last half of the sixteenth, Japanese feudalism evolved with relative rapidity but, as one might expect, with many local variations and complexities. This period of Japanese feudalism is both the most confused and the least known, and generalizations therefore are difficult to make, but it is a period of particular interest, because it was during this time that Japanese feudal institutions most closely paralleled those of European feudalism at its height; it was, in fact, the period of high feudalism in Japan. Though it may not be possible to give a clear picture of the situation throughout Japan at any one moment during this period, the general developments over the whole span of these centuries are relatively clear.

The lack of central control or of any organ capable of enforcing legal decisions gave the strong ample opportunity to dispossess the weak. There began a rapid reshuffling of *shiki* rights, which led eventually to the elimination of the whole *shiki* system. The first to lose out were absentee domanial lords, who, as effete court nobles in the distant capital, had little chance to defend their rights. Great monasteries, however, often possessed the military power to protect their domanial rights in nearby *shō* and even to increase their control at the expense of lesser *shiki* holders.

Meanwhile the various local aristocrats, who had served as *shugo, jitō*, agents for domanial lords, proprietors, and cultivators, embarked on a long struggle with one another for absolute mastery of their respective lands and for their further extension. Power changed hands with startling rapidity, as obscure families rose to prominence and others of long standing fell and disappeared. Because of the traditional Japanese emphasis on hereditary legitimacy, each newly risen family claimed some impressive ancestry, but never before and never again in recorded Japanese history did might so clearly determine right.

As *shiki* rights were done away with, the *shō* itself disappeared, and in its place began to appear the consolidated feudal realm which was the undisputed possession of a single lord (*daimyō*) or possibly of a great religious institution. The process was a slow and irregular one, as certain powerful local warriors extended their authority through infeudation or conquest over their weaker neighbors. The terms of infeudation and the realities of control showed great variation, and vassals often had no compunction about deserting to other lords or asserting their independence when opportunity offered. The result was that the patterns of allegiance shifted rapidly and the boundaries of effective control between the various *daimyō* were subject to constant fluctuations. However, by the sixteenth century some reasonably stable feudal domains had appeared, in which the *daimyō's* feudatories were his obedient vassals and their tenure was dependent upon his will. Throughout the period there was a clear tendency for the number of independent lords to decrease as the domains grew in size and the remaining *daimyō* increased their effective control over their vassals.

Back of the consolidation of holdings and power lay a significant sociological change. Primogeniture had become the rule, or rather a Japanese variant of primogeniture, which permitted a father to name any of his natural sons or even an adopted son as the heir of his full position, whether as *daimyō* or hereditary vassal.

As the *shō* gradually gave way to consolidated feudal realms, the local warrior aristocrats also gradually changed their military and administrative functions. In the twelfth century they had been for the most part small-scale rent collectors and farm managers. By the sixteenth century only a small proportion of the warrior class had the status of *daimyō* or of enfeoffed or sub-enfeoffed vassals of *daimyō*, and the vast majority were becoming divorced from the land, receiving their economic support not in terms of local holdings but as specified quantities of rice produced from the lord's lands. In other words they were becoming hereditary salaried officials and officers in the service of a lord. The feudal class, including both enfeoffed vassals and landless salaried retainers, was on the way to becoming a hereditary bureaucracy entrusted with the diverse governmental functions of highly organized and in some ways economically advanced realms.

The military functions of the warrior class were also undergoing rapid changes. In the twelfth century the members of the military cliques had served as individual knights when summoned. Some time after the collapse of the Kamakura regime, the popularization of the spear as a major weapon of combat led to the appearance of relatively large bodies of foot soldiers drawn from the peasantry, and by the middle of the sixteenth century firearms had reached Japan, even further changing military tactics. As a result, the hereditary feudal warriors were no longer individual knights but constituted instead a professional military corps and an elite officer class to lead peasant levies.

v. Late Feudalism: Hideyoshi and the Tokugawa Regime

During the second half of the sixteenth century the arrival of Europeans in increasing numbers at the ports of Japan brought new pressures on Japanese feudalism. The Christian doctrine of the Occidentals, entailing as it did new loyalties to persons and institutions outside of Japan, seemed to pose a political threat, and the Japanese were by no means unaware of the way in which political domination had sometimes followed the seemingly innocent activities of European missionaries and traders in southern Asia.

Perhaps because of these challenges, profound and rapid changes took place in Japanese feudalism during these years. All of the trends of the Ashikaga period were accelerated and accentuated. The consolidation of feudal domains went on even more rapidly than before, until virtually all of Japan was divided among such domains, and a hierarchic order of vassalage among the *daimyō* began to appear. Eventually Toyotomi Hideyoshi, a common soldier of obscure origin who had achieved the status of a *daimyō*, established control over so many vassal domains that the remaining independent *daimyō* felt constrained to recognize his suzerainty. Feudal Japan had at last been reunited, and a central government had been reestablished, but on a far greater and more powerful scale than ever before in Japan. Hideyoshi at once manifested his control over the energies of the whole nation by launching an ambitious building program in his capital cities of Kyoto and Osaka and by sending a great although unsuccessful military expedition against Korea, which was aimed at the eventual subjugation of China.

While unity was being established, the dynamic forces of the new age evinced themselves in other ways as well. Under the stimulus of increased foreign trade, commercial enterprises rapidly expanded. The rise of a common soldier like Hideyoshi to become the military master of the land illustrates the growth in social mobility. Armies increased greatly in size and, with the introduction of Western firearms, even more markedly in strength. There was also a veritable rash of castle building, which dotted the landscape with imposing structures. Previously in Japan, fortifications had been commonly built where the terrain offered special defense advantages, but these fortifications usually were not permanently inhabited castles. The castles built during the second half of the sixteenth century were not exactly like those of medieval Europe, even though they may have been of European inspiration. They were rather a cross between medieval castles and the more extensive European fortresses of the sixteenth century. The walls and towers of the castle were of relatively light wood and plaster construction, but beneath these walls and towers usually stood the real defenses—masonry faced earthworks of imposing dimensions, surrounded by broad moats, which were sometimes arranged in a series of concentric circles.

The reunification of Japan in the late sixteenth century might well have led to the reestablishment of an entirely centralized form of government and the ending of feudal political institutions. Instead the Japanese were able to free themselves of the pressures from the outside world and to maintain for another 250 years the feudal structure of the late sixteenth century. Tokugawa Ieyasu, one of Hideyoshi's chief vassal *daimyō*, managed to wrest national ascendancy from the more loyal supporters of Hideyoshi's infant heir in a great battle in 1600. Dominated by the desire to avoid any change which might lead to the downfall of Tokugawa power, Ieyasu and his heirs did their best to freeze the social and political situation as it existed at the time.

To do this they found it necessary to extirpate without mercy the Christian creed, which had been successfully propagated by Portuguese and Spanish missionaries, and to eliminate most of Japan's fruitful contacts with the outside world. Japan's natural isolation had been largely overcome by the enterprise of Japanese mariners during the preceding three centuries and by the subsequent appearance of the Europeans in Japanese waters. Now isolation was reimposed by law and was strictly enforced. Without this artificial isolation, which eliminated virtually all foreign pressures, it seems quite improbable that feudal forms could have survived as late as they did in Japan.

With foreign pressures eliminated and political and social change reduced to the minimum, the Tokugawa were able to give to the Japanese the longest period of uninterrupted peace they have ever enjoyed. The two and a half centuries of Tokugawa rule constitute the final phase of Japanese feudalism—a phase characterized by a surprising elaboration of centralized controls in a feudal system, or perhaps one might say a surprising continuation of feudal forms in an otherwise early modern centralized state.

Under the Tokugawa the class structure was frozen and an artificial division into four classes—warrior-administrator,[1] peasant, artisan, and merchant—was borrowed from ancient Confucianism. During the

[1] Corresponding to the scholar-administrator class of China.

fifteenth and sixteenth centuries there had been a rapid increase in class mobility, but now the warrior class of *samurai* was made into a virtual caste, which, in theory, could be neither entered nor left. This it remained until the imperial restoration of 1868, although long before that date it had started to crumble at the edges, and the increasing concentration of the wealth of the land in the hands of merchants and petty entrepreneurs had sometimes made a mockery of the vaunted social superiority of the warriors.

The Tokugawa *shōgun* personally controlled a vast domain around his capital at Edo, the modern Tokyo, and at several strategic points throughout the land, including all of the larger cities, but the bulk of the country remained divided between the domains (*han*) of the various *daimyō*. The shogunal domain was about five times as large as that of the largest *daimyō*. Grouped around this domain and occupying most of the central portions of Japan were the *han* of the associated (*fudai*) *daimyō*, who were either members of the Tokugawa family or else descendants of lords and retainers who had recognized Tokugawa suzerainty before 1600. The most distant areas of Japan were divided among the outer (*tozama*) *daimyō*, who had not become Tokugawa vassals until after 1600. (Religious institutions had been virtually eliminated from territorial rule in the late sixteenth century.)

There were about 265 *daimyō*, all of whom were direct vassals of the *shōgun* and received investiture from him. They could have no contacts with one another without his permission, nor could they appoint heirs without his specific approval. They could not even construct any fortifications without permission, with the result that castle building came to a virtual end. All were forced to keep their immediate families as hostages at the *shōgun's* court in Edo, and they themselves divided their time between Edo and their domains, according to a rigidly fixed schedule (*sankin kōtai* system). They were subject at all times to special demands for services, which, together with the *sankin kōtai* system, constituted a severe financial drain. They also were fully responsible for the administration and defense of their domains and for the military support of Edo whenever requested. On the other hand, they were not directly taxed and, within the limits described above, enjoyed autonomy within their own realms.

In theory the *shōgun* could dispossess or move any *daimyō* at will. In practice some of the more distant and powerful *daimyō* remained secure in the domains their ancestors had held since before 1600, but some of the smaller *daimyō* and especially those more directly under the control of the *shōgun* were often moved around with their hereditary retainers and were given promotions or demotions in the size of their domains as if they were nothing more than provincial officials in a hereditary bureaucracy.

The *samurai*, who with their families constituted about five per cent of the population, were the direct retainers of the *shōgun* and of the many *daimyō*, serving their respective lords as hereditary officials, officers, and soldiers. The more important retainers themselves held small fiefs from their lords, although they normally did not reside on their fiefs but at the capital cities of their respective lords. Fief-holding retainers of the *shōgun* were known as *hatamoto*. Their fiefs were smaller than those of the smallest category of *daimyō* (10,000 *koku*[2] of rice produce), but a few retainers of great *daimyō* actually had fiefs larger than 10,000 *koku*. The vast majority of retainers, however, had no land at all and received their income as rice allotments. All retainers held their lands or rice incomes only at the pleasure of their lords.

At Edo an elaborate central government grew up, manned by officials drawn from among the direct shogunal retainers and the associated *daimyō* and their retainers. Posts in this bureaucracy were determined by a man's position in the feudal hierarchy, but able men were often made eligible for promotion in office by the assignment of larger rice stipends or larger fiefs as retainers, by promotion from the status of retainer to that of *daimyō*, and by promotion in the size of the *daimyō* domain held. Without going into the details of the organization of the central government, we should note that collective responsibility through boards and through division of power between different offices was more common than the individual responsibility of a shogunal prime minister.

Shogunal lands were administered by direct agents of the Edo government. As was the rule throughout Japan, roughly half of the produce of the land was collected as taxes for the support of the government. This tax yield from shogunal lands formed the bulk of the central government's income, far outbalancing its income from taxes on trade, the issuance of currency, and mining and commercial monopolies. Shogunal commissioners (*bugyō*) were in charge of the various cities under the direct rule of the shogunate. The bulk of the country, however, was divided for administrative purposes between the

[2] Roughly equivalent to five bushels. In the course of the Tokugawa period, most fiefs developed a somewhat higher productive capacity than the official assessment.

domains of the various *fudai* and *tozama daimyō*. The administration of each *daimyō han* tended to be a small imitation of the Edo government, staffed by the *daimyō's* retainers, and the finance of each *han*, as of the shogunate, was based primarily on land taxes. Edo, while allowing the *daimyō* substantial autonomy within their domains, kept a close watch on them not only through the *sankin kōtai* system but also through a system of secret police (*metsuke*), whose duty it was to keep their eyes on the *daimyō* and on any other groups which might prove to be subversive.

The commoners, who formed the bulk of the population, were sharply divided from the feudal aristocracy of *daimyō* and retainers and were barred from all political power. In theory they were subdivided into the three classes of peasants, artisans, and merchants, but there were no real barriers between these three functional groups, while among the peasants themselves there were sometimes rather sharp social lines drawn between land-owning families, some of which had warrior status in pre-Tokugawa times, and tenant farmers and servants.

Politically the commoners were divided between the shogunal domain and the *han* of the various *daimyō*, and they were expected to be loyal to their respective lords and to remain in their domains. While the peasants in particular were the victims of an onerous system of taxation and all commoners were subject to cruel and detailed penal codes, they were allowed a considerable degree of autonomy in conducting such of their affairs as did not bear upon the finances or security of their lords. This was particularly true of the peasants, for the whole feudal elite, instead of living on the land, was concentrated largely in Edo and the various *han* capitals. The peasant village had begun to emerge during the Ashikaga period as the unit of local agrarian organization in place of the *shō*, and in the Tokugawa period it became still more clearly the primary unit of social and economic organization in the countryside. Within the semi-autonomous villages, as within the commercial towns, there was a chance for various non-feudal tendencies to develop, with the result that by the early nineteenth century tenancy and landlordism were growing fast, while a certain amount of entrepreneurial activity had appeared in commerce and in the simpler forms of manufacturing.

VI. Religion and Ethics

Since feudalism in Europe flourished in the age in which Christianity most fully dominated the Western mind, it is natural to assume that some comparable religion may have dominated the Japanese mind in the Japanese feudal age. This assumption is only in part true. Buddhism in medieval Japan had somewhat the same role as Christianity in medieval Europe, but it was never as dominant or as exclusive an ethical and religious force in Japan as Christianity was in Europe.

Originally alien to China, as Christianity was foreign to Rome, Buddhism was introduced to Japan as an integral and important element in Chinese culture, just as Christianity was a major part of the late classic civilization of the West. Well entrenched in Japan by the ninth century, Buddhism adapted itself more easily to the growing feudalization of Japanese society than did many other elements of the Chinese system. As the central government declined in power, Buddhist monasteries increasingly became the centers of learning in Japan, and by the fourteenth and fifteenth centuries Buddhist monks dominated almost all aspects of Japanese culture. Similarly, Buddhist institutions became great landowners, taking a major part in developing the *shō* of the early feudal age. As feudal landholders Buddhist monasteries also won control over large groupings of warriors and thus became important military entities. Particularly in the old capital district around Kyoto, monasteries were among the greatest landholders and military powers of the day. Only with the restoration of unity in the late sixteenth century were the monasteries divested of much of their lands and of all of their military power.

As in Europe, the feudal period in Japan was an age of religious fervor and of faith. In prefeudal days, Buddhism, because of its magnificent rituals, glorious artistic traditions, and great prestige, had appealed for the most part to the ruling classes. By the tenth century, however, there appeared a new sort of popular religious fervor. Inspired preachers harangued the multitudes on hell-fire and damnation, and the masses began to respond. In the late twelfth and early thirteenth centuries, just when the Minamoto clique was founding the first shogunate, the mounting religious tide gave rise to a new sectarian movement. In rapid succession appeared the sects which were to become the great ones of later Japanese Buddhism. Several stressed the popular concepts of personal salvation through faith and a very real afterlife in a glorious Paradise. Others of the Zen type stressed a stoical mysticism, which found a ready response among the warrior class. Sectarianism led to militancy, and for a few centuries Japanese Buddhists showed some of the same propensities for mutual self-destruction which so often characterized the history of Christianity in Europe.

By the high feudal period of the fourteenth and fifteenth centuries, Buddhist ideas dominated almost every aspect of Japanese culture. Zen monks took a leading role at the court of the Ashikaga *shōgun* as well as in Japan's trade relations with the outside world. The literature of the age was permeated with Buddhism, and the major artistic currents of the time were under the direct influence of Zen philosophy. Meanwhile the sects which stressed concepts of personal salvation through faith had come to play a larger part in the lives of the lower classes. One of these sects achieved new popularity by clerical reforms permitting the marriage of the clergy, and by the translation of Buddhist texts from Chinese into Japanese. It also organized congregations of laymen, which in time became the nucleus for political and economic action by peasants and townsmen. In the latter part of the Ashikaga period embattled Buddhist congregations of commoners sometimes fought for their rights with fair success against the feudal classes.

Many of these tendencies within medieval Buddhism in Japan were abruptly halted by the reunification of the land. Not only were the monasteries deprived of their military and economic powers, but Buddhist ideas also lost much of their influence over the ruling classes. Art and literature soon became almost purely secular, and Buddhism rapidly lost prestige. All Japanese were registered by law as parishioners of monasteries and temples, for this was the Tokugawa census system, and temple schools remained the primary educational institutions for the lower classes, but the Tokugawa period was not a Buddhist age in the sense that the preceding six centuries had been.

Despite its great role in feudal Japan, Buddhism was not the sole source of ethical ideas at this time. It supplied certain humanitarian concepts, and the stoic philosophy of Zen lent moral strength to the warrior class, but the ethics of feudalism was expressed more in Confucian terms. Early Confucianism, stemming as it did from a semifeudal age in China, stressed the lord and vassal relationship and put special emphasis on loyalty. It was but natural for the feudal classes in Japan to look toward these aspects of Confucian philosophy, and, with the decline of Buddhist influence in the Tokugawa period, Confucianism became even more important than before. It was virtually given the status of a state philosophy and was shown marked shogunal patronage.

Out of Confucianism, Zen philosophy, and the feudal experience itself, a specific code of feudal ethics was gradually evolved. This code naturally emphasized loyalty, obedience, bravery, and stoical acceptance of what fate had to offer. Though not preoccupied, as was Western chivalry, with the treatment of women, it laid stress on an acute sense of honor, which when sullied could only be assuaged by revenge or by *seppuku* (also known as *harakiri*, suicide through disemboweling). Although this ethical code did not receive its specific name of *Bushidō* until recent decades, it was already in existence by the time of the founding of the Minamoto shogunate, and it has lasted, at least in modified form, beyond the collapse of feudalism itself.

VII. Commerce and Industry

The feudal age in Japan was a period of steady and at times rapid economic growth. From beginning to end all agricultural land, of course, remained under the control of the feudal classes, and commerce and industry, as they developed, were adapted to the prevailing feudal institutions. In the case of domestic trade and production, this was done primarily through the *za*, or guild. Arising in the thirteenth and fourteenth centuries, the guilds, in exchange for monetary offerings to their patrons and protectors, won for their members local monopoly rights and protection from the multiple assessments and extortions common in a feudal society. Their patrons and protectors commonly were religious institutions or the feudal aristocracy, and around the old imperial capital they included certain members of the old court aristocracy, whose lingering prestige, if not their actual power, made their protection worth seeking.

As the feudal unit grew, so also did the scope and size of the guild. In fact, these two forms of growth, political and economic, were probably interdependent aspects of the whole process of growth in feudal Japan. By the Tokugawa period medieval guilds had given place to merchant companies which commonly operated throughout the domain and under the protection of a single *daimyō*, but in some cases spread their activities throughout the major cities of the land.

The feudal rulers usually saw fit to exact what return they could from domestic guilds and merchant companies, but they took an even more active part in foreign trade. In the thirteenth century, when trade with China and Korea began to become important in the Japanese economy, Buddhist monasteries took the lead in financing the larger commercial ventures, but by the late fourteenth century the Ashikaga *shōgun* and the lords of western Japan were themselves financing trading expeditions to the continent. During the next two centuries the overseas commercial interests of the Japanese grew rapidly as more and more mariners from western Japan took part in this international trade and extended their activities throughout the Far East as far as the Straits of Malacca. The feudal lords of the coastal fringes of western Japan came to depend on the profits of foreign trade for a major part of their income, and the spurt in foreign commerce which resulted from the arrival of the Europeans in the sixteenth century only served to increase their dependence on commercial revenues.

From the start, the Japanese overseas traders probably included among their numbers many hereditary members of the warrior class. In any case, overseas merchant adventurers became virtually a branch of the warrior class of western Japan, and they came to be known throughout the Far East more for their martial prowess than for their purely commercial activities. In other words, the overseas commercial enterprises of late medieval Japan, like those of early modern Europe, had a strong piratical tinge. Japanese merchant-pirates became the scourge of the China coast, and in the late sixteenth century Japanese mercenaries and adventurers became renowned throughout southeast Asia.

This growth of foreign trade no doubt gave impetus to economic development within Japan, and the sixteenth century witnessed rapid economic growth, particularly in western Japan, and the rise of purely commercial towns. Under the stimulus of foreign trade, Nagasaki in western Kyushu grew from a fishing village to be one of Japan's main ports. Sakai at the eastern end of the Inland Sea had long been a thriving commercial center and in late Ashikaga times achieved a considerable degree of autonomy as an incipient "free city." In the sixteenth century Osaka, a few miles north of Sakai, became Japan's leading commercial city, and it managed to maintain its independence from control by the feudal classes until 1580, when its great Buddhist castle-monastery was finally captured by the leading feudal lord of the day.

In the seventeenth century the Tokugawa eliminated most Japanese trade with the outside world and all Japanese overseas enterprises, but economic growth continued apace, presumably because of the reunification of the country and the consequent prolonged period of peace. Despite the feudal basis of government, the economy of Japan soon became basically a money economy, as was to be seen from the issuance by the shogunate and by the individual *han* of many forms of commercial paper credits and paper money. The shogunate and all of the *han* still received most of their income as taxes in kind on rice lands, but they soon discovered that they had to convert much of this rice income into money to meet various expenses. For this purpose the *han* of western Japan established business offices in Osaka in addition to the residences and offices which all *han* maintained in the feudal capital of Edo, and before the end of the seventeenth century two great rice exchanges dealing in futures had grown up in Osaka and Edo.

The *daimyō* and their retainers, with their incomes fixed in terms of rice and their expenditures in part in money, were constantly becoming the victims of fluctuations in the price of rice. As a consequence, there was a strong tendency for *daimyō* and retainers alike to fall into debt to urban merchants and moneylenders. The *han* often sought to save themselves from financial ruin by creating commercial monopolies in cooperation with local merchant firms and sometimes by becoming directly involved in commercial activities themselves. The individual *samurai* could only attempt to save himself by taking up some side occupation, such as piecework production of simple manufactured goods. This situation led to increasing intermarriage between members of the feudal aristocracy and the despised but wealthy merchant class and the gradual blurring of class lines in other ways as well.

During the Tokugawa period much of the wealth of the land became concentrated in the hands of merchants, particularly in the great cities of Edo and Osaka, each of which was approaching the million mark in population by the nineteenth century. The merchants, thus, dominated the economy of late feudal Japan, but their domination of the culture of the period was even more marked. Although excluded entirely from political rule, they made their particular form of urban culture the typical culture of Tokugawa Japan. The literature of the day was produced under merchant patronage in the great urban centers. It was written for the middle-class reading public and often was specifically about them and their lives. Printing became common, and the publishing houses usually catered to the tastes of the non-feudal city dwellers. Similarly the theatre and the other arts were dominated by merchant tastes, and the great development at this time of wood-block prints came as a direct response to the demands of the urban middle class for art works at popular prices. Culturally, and to some extent economically, Tokugawa Japan had a postfeudal rather than a strictly feudal society.

VIII. The Feudal Legacy

One final aspect of Japanese feudalism which should be mentioned is the legacy it has left to modern Japan. It seems probable that the Japanese feudal experience, which so closely paralleled that of Europe, may have had something to do with the speed and ease with which the Japanese during the past century refashioned their society and government on European models. One cannot but compare Japanese success along these lines with the slow and painful efforts at westernization on the part of the other Asiatic peoples, who for the most part had had longer and often much closer contacts with Western civilization, but lacked the feudal background. It seems possible that Japan, in paralleling the European experience, produced at least in embryo some of the same characteristics which grew out of European feudalism and helped shape the society of the modern West. The real explanation of Japan's ability to transform itself so rapidly into a modern Western-type nation may be that this transformation was less of a change for Japan than for the other lands of Asia.

Some features of similarity between Japan in its final stages of feudalism and early modern Europe will serve to illustrate the point. First, the Japanese had an aristocratic military tradition similar to that of Europe, which made military careers attractive for able young men and service as conscripts less undesirable than it otherwise might have been for the common soldier. The Japanese were ready to go about the creation of a modern army and navy with far more interest and enthusiasm than were most of the other peoples of Asia.

Second, although the Japanese had no clear concept of chivalry, they had a strong feudal code of honor. The individual was accustomed to think in terms of duty and loyalty toward higher authorities and had a deep sense of obligation, which was in some ways not unlike the Puritan conscience. The Japanese laid emphasis on the scrupulous performance of duties and unlimited self-sacrifice for some entity or ideal beyond the individual or his family.

Third, a strong national consciousness had grown up at an early date within Japanese feudalism. Appearing as early as the thirteenth century, it was perhaps not less common or less intense among Japanese in the mid-nineteenth century than among any of the most advanced peoples of the West at that time. This national consciousness, combined with the strong sense of feudal loyalty, had produced a genuine national patriotism long before the opening of Japan in 1854. As the feudal unit grew, the loyalty of the individual grew with it, until it was an easy final step to shift loyalty from the *shōgun* or *daimyō* to the Emperor and from the feudal realm to the nation as a whole.

Fourth is the concept of law which emerged from Japanese feudalism. The Far East never had anything like the Roman concept of law, but Japanese feudalism developed among the Japanese a strong sense of legal rights, including property rights, which had to be maintained if society were not to dissolve into chaos. This may well be the reason why the Japanese were able to shift with ease to an Occidental system of law in the nineteenth century and had less difficulty than many other peoples of Asia in adopting the concept of the equality of each individual before the law.

The fifth point, which is related to the legal one, is the independent development of capitalistic enterprise within the feudal framework. While the lack of protective laws kept most risk capital in China and the rest of Asia tied to the quick turnover of trade ventures, the Japanese businessman and entrepreneur received far more legal protection from the feudal regime, despite its official contempt for him and its relegation of the businessman to the lowest social class. This permitted not only the development of the stable commercial firms of the Tokugawa period but also the appearance of entrepreneurs willing to risk their capital in petty industrial enterprises. By the early decades of the nineteenth century factory organization had commenced in the spinning and weaving industry, and factory towns were making their appearance. For the Japanese the step from such entrepreneurial capitalism within the framework of feudal society to full-fledged modern capitalism was by no means the leap in the dark which it has proved to be for much of the rest of Asia.

A sixth and final point is social organization. The family unit in Japan had come to approximate that of Europe much more closely than did the family unit of China, for instance, and the institution of primogeniture, which had grown out of feudalism, had created a class of younger sons who, as in Europe, in their search for a place in society, often formed an enterprising and very active *avant-garde* of progress. Equally significant was the appearance of social elements in some ways comparable to the middle class of the West. The well-to-do city merchants clearly are to be considered in this group, but so also are some of the *samurai* and peasants in certain parts of Japan. In the Tosa *han* on the island of Shikoku, for instance, the institution of "rustic" *samurai* (*gōshi*) had produced a "middle" class between the peasants and the warriors, and in this and other ways the traditional class divisions had broken down further than in most parts of Japan. In the Shimazu *han* of Satsuma in southern Kyushu the exceptionally high proportion of *samurai* to the total population had forced a large part of the former to work as farmers or small producers of various sorts. In these two cases, elements of the upper class had in a sense become a middle class, taking on mixed functions as producers as well as hereditary aristocrats. At the same time, in the silk producing and textile weaving areas of the Kantō in central Japan certain prosperous peasants had gathered enough capital to become small local entrepreneurs, using their agricultural profits to start all sorts of small industries. It is perhaps no mere accident that the poorer *samurai* of western Japan, and notably those from areas such as Satsuma and Tosa, and the richer peasants of the Kantō, as well as the city merchants, furnished a large proportion of the Japanese leaders in government, business, and the professions during the Meiji period (1868-1912). While the *daimyō* and their more important retainers produced very few leaders for the new Japan and the true peasant masses almost none, those elements which came closest to constituting a middle class seem to have been best able to make the transition to the economic and political system of the modern West.

No one has ever clearly stated or carefully studied the general thesis that the feudal experience in Japan produced certain characteristics which were similar to some of the major characteristics of postfeudal Europe and that these points of similarity made it easier for the Japanese to adopt the political and economic forms of the contemporary West. Although the preceding paragraphs merely suggest a few of the facets of this problem, they may serve to indicate the scope and importance of the question and may also give some hint of the still unexplored possibilities in a comparative approach to the various feudal experiences of the human race.

IV · FEUDALISM IN CHINA

BY DERK BODDE

1. Introduction

THE *Periods of Chinese Feudalism.* In recent years the terms "feudal" or "feudalistic" have become increasingly popular as designations for premodern Chinese society. The justification for such usage is economic rather than political. In traditional China, the basic medium of wealth was grain, produced on small patches of land by peasants who were either petty proprietors or tenant farmers. These peasants, who constituted seventy or eighty per cent of the total population, were economically dominated by a small interlocking oligarchy of government officials, landed gentry, and rural moneylenders; the capital of this oligarchy was commonly invested in land rather than in commercial or industrial enterprise, which for the most part was small, familial, localized, and marginal to the total economy.

This meant that the bulk of the peasants, though legally free to buy and sell land or change their occupation, were in actual fact effectively bound to the land they cultivated by a variety of economic factors. These included population pressure and concentration of land in the hands of the ruling group, with consequent high land taxes and rents; a shortage of capital with consequent high rates of interest; and the failure of industry and commerce to develop to the point where they could provide real alternatives to farming. Traditionally, indeed, most peasants, should they be forced by economic circumstances to abandon the land, had little alternative but to become either soldiers or bandits. Such a society, though obviously precapitalistic, could not properly be called a slave society, since its number of actual slaves was relatively small. How then, so runs the argument, can it be described other than through use of the word "feudal"?[1]

Such an argument, however, disregards the political aspects of feudalism, which are those stressed in the Introductory Essay of this book, and which, if we examine China, are found to be largely or totally

[1] The answer, for many scholars, is that it was neither capitalistic, slave, nor feudal, but constituted yet another distinctive form of society, referred to by K. A. Wittfogel as "oriental" society, but which Wolfram Eberhard prefers to describe as "gentry" society. For the theories of these men and of Owen Lattimore, see Sect. IV below; cf. also the remarks in the concluding paragraphs of this paper.

absent under most of its major dynasties. The common characteristic of those dynasties is that they governed a centralized empire through a salaried civilian bureaucracy which was appointive, non-aristocratic, theoretically non-hereditary, and in many cases recruited by means of the famous Chinese examination system. Between these periods of empire intervened other shorter periods of political disunity and war-lordism, which, however, are too brief and obviously transitional to merit discussion here.

From the strictly political point of view, therefore, there are only two major periods of Chinese history in which feudal or quasi-feudal phenomena are prominent. The first, commonly regarded as China's "classical" age of feudalism, is the Chou Dynasty (1122?-256 B.C.), with which, however, it is convenient for our purposes to group the preceding Shang Dynasty (1765?-1123?).[2] The second is the period of A.D. 221-589, during which China was fragmented among more than two dozen short-lived dynasties and states, to designate which it is convenient to use a modern coined term, Period of Disunity. These two ages were separated from one another by the Ch'in (255-207 B.C.) and Han (206 B.C.-A.D. 220) dynasties, under which, beginning in 221 B.C., remnants of the Chou feudal system were destroyed and replaced by a new form of bureaucratic empire. The collapse of Han rule (officially in 220, though actually in 190, when the empire disintegrated into three parts) ushered in the Period of Disunity, which in turn was brought to an end by the re-establishment of centralized empire under the Sui (590-617) and T'ang (618-906) dynasties.

In the following pages we shall first discuss the rise and fall of Chou feudalism, and, more briefly, the subsequent institutional changes of the Ch'in and Han empires; then present theories which try to explain the factors in ancient Chinese society responsible for these changes, and finally, in less detail, describe the resurgence of certain quasi-feudal phenomena during the Period of Disunity.

II. Feudalism during the Early Chou Period

The Chinese Term for Feudalism. The modern Chinese equivalent for "feudalism" is a compound term, *feng-chien chih-tu*, which literally

[2] Variant chronologies exist for events prior to 841 B.C., and many scholars believe that the shift from Shang to Chou actually occurred about a century later than the officially accepted date here given. The period prior to the Shang Dynasty is too sparsely documented to permit any fruitful discussion on our topic.

means "*feng*-establishment system." Though this term became really popular in China only in comparatively recent times, following the influx of sociological and historical concepts from the West, the word *feng*, which is its key component, has a history of almost three millennia and carries with it a rich body of associations stemming from indigenous ancient Chinese civilization. As used in literature of the Chou period, *feng* means, among other things: a mound, to raise a mound, to earth up (a plant), a boundary, to determine the boundaries of a fief, to enfeoff. Its ancient written graph represents a hand beside a plant growing from the soil, and apparently is intended to portray the act of heaping earth around a plant, or, more generally, of raising a mound. As we shall see below, a mound of earth played a central part in the Chou ritual of enfeoffment.

Shang Antecedents. The word *feng* apparently does not occur on the divination inscriptions of the Shang Dynasty so far discovered. Hu Hou-hsüan, however, on the basis of an exhaustive examination of these inscriptions made from the point of view of feudalism, has arrived at the following conclusions.[8] Certain Shang kings apparently made a practice of conferring territories upon their wives, sons, and prominent ministers, as well as upon a number of unnamed individuals who are simply referred to in the inscriptions as *hou*, or (less frequently) as *po* or *nan*. These terms, as we shall see, were later to become well-known titles of nobility in the Chou feudal hierarchy. Other territorial holders included neighboring tribal leaders who, originally independent of the state of Shang, had in the course of time apparently been reduced to positions of political dependency. These various landholders, whom Hu interprets as vassals of the Shang kings, were, he believes, in general obligated to perform one or several of the following duties: (1) defense of the Shang frontiers; (2) conducting of punitive expeditions against rebels; (3) tribute payment of tortoise shell and other valuable localized products; (4) tax payment of millet and other grains; (5) supplying of *corvée* labor for cultivation of the king's lands.

Hu's inscriptional material is too fragmentary and ambiguous to be as conclusive as he seems to assume. In its totality, however, it lends

[8] In his "Yin-tai Feng-chien Chih-tu K'ao" [Study of Feudal Institutions of the Yin—i.e., Shang—Period], contained in his *Chia-ku-hsüeh Shang-shih Lun-ts'ung* [Collected Essays on Shang History Based on the Bone Inscriptions], 1st Ser. (Chengtu, 1944), 1, Essay 1.

fair probability to the thesis that already during Shang times dependency relations may have existed, perhaps not greatly unlike those which in Chou times were to develop into a feudal structure. Further than this it would be unwise to venture at the present stage of our knowledge.[4]

Origin and Stages of Chou Feudalism. The Shang capital was located in northern Honan, somewhat north of the Yellow River, on the present Peking-Hankow Railroad. Some three hundred miles to the west, near the present city of Sian in the basin of the Wei River, the Chou people rose to political prominence on the fringes of Shang civilization. Though little is known of their early history, it is evident that they were then culturally far less sophisticated than the Shang, whose script and advanced bronze-working technique they probably acquired only at the time of, or shortly prior to, their conquest of the Shang. Other cultural differences, too, seem to have existed between the two groups.

It is still a moot point, however, with the scanty evidence presently available, whether these cultural differences are sufficiently decisive to point to clear-cut ethnic differences as well. Scholars like Creel and Lattimore think that they are not. According to these writers, both the Chou and the Shang stemmed from an essentially uniform human stock common to North China in neolithic times, and the cultures of the two groups were in good part derived from common antecedents. This means that the Chou, at the time of their conquest of the Shang, were not "barbarians" in the sense of being an intruding, definitely alien group, but only in the sense of being the provincial and culturally rather backward cousins of the Shang.[5]

Eberhard, however, strongly disagrees. "Our present knowledge," he maintains, "indicates that the Chou were originally of Turkish

[4] It is not hard to find writers who assert that the Shang possessed a feudal system, but in so doing they are merely following traditional accounts composed long after the Shang period itself, and therefore far from trustworthy. H. G. Creel, writing some eight years earlier than Hu, but basing himself on essentially the same Shang inscriptional material, strongly doubts that feudalism goes back to the Shang. As pointed out by him, the mere occurrence in the Shang texts of titles which later appear in the Chou feudal hierarchy does not prove that in Shang times these titles had the same connotations as they did during the Chou. See his *Birth of China* (New York, 1937), pp. 135-136.

[5] Creel, p. 221, and Owen Lattimore, *Inner Asian Frontiers of China* (2nd edn. New York, 1951), pp. 307-308.

stock."[6] This thesis, to which we shall revert in Section IV below, is central to Eberhard's whole theory of Chou feudalism.

When the Chou, following their gradual political consolidation in the Wei valley, finally launched their eastern expedition in the twelfth or eleventh century B.C., they not only succeeded in overthrowing the state of Shang, but also in overrunning considerable areas which had probably lain outside the Shang domain proper. Then, because of the difficulties involved in maintaining personal control over these large new territories, the Chou conquerors retired to their homeland in the west, where they thereafter exercised direct rule only over a limited area known as the "royal domain." Of their newly acquired eastern territories, a part was parcelled out to various Chou leaders and the allies who had helped them in the conquest, but much was apparently simply left in the continued possession of those indigenous clan leaders who, during the Chou advance, had either been conquered or had voluntarily tendered their submission. Even the descendants of the house of Shang, in fact, were not exterminated, but were allowed to continue ruling over a state reduced in size.

In this way there came into being a host of small states or principalities—at least one hundred are known to have existed in the eighth century B.C., when we begin to have detailed historical records—each consisting of a walled capital, surrounded by tilled lands from which it derived its sustenance. During the early Chou Dynasty, most of these were separated from one another by mountains, marshes, and other uncultivated "no man's land," peopled only by "barbarians" over whom no one exercised clear-cut jurisdiction.

The relationships of the rulers of these principalities to the Chou monarchy, as well as to their own landholding subordinates, seem in a general way to merit the term "feudal" usually applied to them. From the viewpoint of the present book, however, there is less justification for the common assumption that Chou feudalism began as a full-fledged institution immediately with the Chou conquest, and that it ended as such only with the creation of the Ch'in empire in 221 B.C.

The objection to the first half of this assumption is that feudalism, as defined in this book, means something more than the mere existence of vassalship ties between a single group of territorial nobles on the one hand and a single ruling house on the other. In order to constitute a true feudal system, it should include a network of similar ties linking

[6] Wolfram Eberhard, *History of China*, trans. E. W. Dickes (Berkeley, 1950), p. 25.

these same territorial nobles with a descending hierarchy of lesser and more localized dignitaries beneath them, until, ideally, virtually the entire population is integrated into a complex pyramid of delegated powers and responsibilities.

On the face of it there is little likelihood that such an elaborate structure could have sprung into being full-fledged at the time of the Chou conquest—unless, indeed, the Chou at that time merely perpetuated a pre-existing Shang structure, and this, as we have seen, is improbable. Much more likely would seem the hypothesis that Chou feudalism, as known to us a few centuries after the conquest, had resulted from a gradual evolutionary process, though how and when this evolution occurred is almost impossible to say with the existing evidence. One or even two centuries may have been required before a fairly crystallized and broadly inclusive system emerged. Probably, however, the steps in that direction began very soon after the conquest, since it was already then that the house of Chou began to show signs of political weakness.

That such an evolutionary process did, in fact, take place, is suggested by two bits of evidence contained in the data to be presented in later pages. One is the loose manner in which titles of nobility were used in the early days of the Chou Dynasty, as contrasted with the fixed hierarchical sequence they assumed later.[7] Another, and one much more significant, is Maspero's thesis (see note 12 below) that, in early Chou times, the relationships of state rulers to the Chou monarch were quite different in nature from those of these same state rulers to the lesser landholders within their own states. In later times, however, as Maspero then goes on to say, this difference tended to disappear owing to the fact that these lesser landholders assimilated themselves more and more into the hierarchy of the state nobles. Such a phenomenon, if it did occur—and unfortunately the evidence is not too conclusive—would seem to point to a transition from a proto-feudal to a fully feudal stage such as we have been assuming.

Because of the difficulty of tracing this transition, however, we must be content, in the remainder of this section, to draw an over-all picture of feudal institutions as they appear to us down to about the seventh or sixth century B.C. The changes that thereafter occurred, on the other hand, can be outlined with greater assurance. By that time the weakness of the Chou monarchy had become so pronounced that it is questionable whether the word "feudal" should be used at all to describe the relationships to it of the former vassal principalities. To all intents and

[7] Cf. above p. 18 where Strayer finds the same contrast in feudal Europe.—Ed

purposes these had become completely independent states, and they remained thus until one of them, the state of Ch'in, successively annexed its rivals and established a new type of empire in 221 B.C.

Within the separate states themselves, however, feudal institutions persisted until the end of the dynasty, though to varying degrees according to time and place. Beginning about the sixth century B.C., the impact of a series of social, political, and economic changes forced a gradual transformation and eventual breakdown of the old feudal order, particularly in Ch'in, where it is quite probable that feudalism had already virtually disappeared prior to the creation of the Ch'in empire.

From the point of view of the foregoing analysis, therefore, the traditional statement that Ch'in "destroyed" feudalism in 221 B.C. is only partially true. What it really did was to destroy the localized remnants of feudal institutions and replace them by a centralized bureaucratic form of empire, the roots of which, however, can be traced back earlier, particularly in Ch'in itself. In Section III we shall examine in more detail the changes that led up to this all-important step, as well as the further consolidation of empire that took place under the following Han Dynasty.

Political Structure. The Chou rulers (like their Shang predecessors) held the title of *wang* or "king."[8] Their vassals were collectively known as the *chu hou*, "all the lords" or "all the princes."[9] Individually, however, each bore one of five specific titles: those of *kung, hou* (same as the *hou* just mentioned), *po, tzu*, and *nan*. In the course of time these titles crystallized into a fixed hierarchy of descending rank, for which reason Western scholars have found it convenient to translate them as duke, marquis, earl, viscount, and baron respectively. Some writers of the end of the Chou go so far as to equate them with fixed territorial holdings of similarly descending importance for which they even indicate precise measurements, but this is obviously a late and idealized schematization. There is abundant evidence that in early Chou times the five titles followed no absolute sequence.[10]

[8] The ancient graph represents a man, standing erect with arms outstretched and feet firmly planted on the ground. He is, so to speak, holding a piece of territory against all comers. Though this title, generally speaking, was a prerogative of the Chou kings, Creel points out (*Birth of China*, pp. 343-344) that even in early times cases are known of its use outside the royal family. This practice, as we shall see, was to become well-nigh universal in the latter centuries of the dynasty.

[9] The same *hou* that had already been used as a title during the Shang Dynasty.

[10] All of them, according to Hu Hou-hsüan (pp. 32ff.), occur on the Shang

The territories with which these nobles were invested were known as *kuo*, a word which today still means a state, country, or principality. Rulership of such *kuo* was hereditary, descent being usually by primogeniture, though favoritism or intrigue produced many violations of this principle. Smaller fiefs also existed, known as *fu-yung* or "attached territories," the rulers of which had no direct access to the Chou kings, but rendered their service to the ruler of that particular neighboring *kuo* to which they happened to be attached.

Concerning the exact nature of the ties between the nobles and their Chou overlord we must draw our information from scattered statements, some of rather late date. The nobles were confirmed in the possession of their territory through a ceremony of investiture which took place in the Chou ancestral temple. There the new vassal, after receiving from the king a solemn admonition to be conscientious in his duties, prostrated himself before him and was given a jade scepter and a written tablet bearing the terms of his enfeoffment. Often these were accompanied by other valuable gifts, such as bronze vessels, clothing, weapons, chariots, and the like. During the early part of the Chou Dynasty, at least, this ceremony was apparently commonly repeated whenever the son of a deceased noble succeeded his father as holder of a fief.[11] We shall defer to a later point in this section an account of one of its most significant aspects, that associated with a divinity known as the Lord of the Soil.

In return for their land holdings, the nobles manifested allegiance by going to the Chou court for individual audiences with the king (probably not as frequently or regularly, however, as traditionally supposed), or sent envoys for this purpose. The late ritualistic texts further speak of periodic mass audiences attended by nobles from all parts of the country, but whether or not these actually occurred on the scale described is uncertain. We do know that the nobles offered tribute on occasion, consisting of valuable but easily transportable products indigenous to their territory. In time of rebellion or "barbarian" attack

inscriptions, though the functions attached to each are far from clear. As interpreted by him, *kung* originally meant "patriarch," i.e., the ancestral head of a family; the graph for *hou* pictured an arrow entering a target, and the word was apparently used as a military title; *po* meant "senior" or "elder"; *tzu* meant "son," i.e., the son or sons of the king; *nan* meant "male."

[11] For further details, drawn from contemporary bronze inscriptions as well as the usual literary sources, see Ch'i Ssu-ho, "Investiture Ceremony of the Chou Period" (article in Chinese), *Yenching Journal of Chinese Studies*, Peiping, No. 32 (June 1947), 197-226.

they were expected to provide troops to help the king. Sometimes they were called upon for special services, such as the supplying of men and materials for repairing the city wall of the royal capital. The king had the right, if not always the power, to act as judge in disputes involving two nobles, or to send troops against those who proved recalcitrant.

Within their own states, however, the nobles were for all practical purposes autonomous. They appointed their own officials, levied their own taxes, maintained their own armies, and exercised their own justice, which was based on tradition and personal opinion rather than on any clearly defined body of law.

Much of their land, nonetheless, was further subdivided in the form of domains, known as *yi*, which they distributed to their relatives, officials, and courtiers. The same was true of land within the Chou royal domain. Such *yi* were measured by the number of peasant families occupying them. The early portion of the *Book of Changes*, for example, speaks of an *yi* as having 300 families. However, the fact that in other contexts this word is also used to designate a city, seems to show that it underwent a semantic evolution similar to the Latin *villa*, from which are derived the French *ville, village*, etc.

It was possible for a single individual to hold more than one *yi*, sometimes scattered in different parts of the state to which he belonged. Often he himself lived in the state capital, leaving his domains in charge of an administrator or steward known as *tsai*. Such stewards were sometimes highly influential men, who constituted the *alter ego* of their master.

Instances are known in which a state noble took back a domain that he had given to a subordinate, or transferred it to another man. In general, however, such domains became the hereditary property of those who received them, and were administered by them without external interference. This parallels the fact that the official positions in the various feudal states tended to be held hereditarily by certain families, some of whom ended by becoming more powerful than the nobles they served.

It is commonly assumed that this intra-state subdivision of land was simply a further extension of the process whereby fiefs were allotted by the house of Chou to the state nobles. Maspero, however, believes that the two systems were originally quite distinct. In his opinion, the investiture ceremony which marked the king's granting of a fief to a noble did not take place when a noble conferred a domain on a subordinate. Therefore, such subordinates, strictly speaking, did not belong to the feudal hierarchy, and their status was that of landed proprietors, not of vassals. He points out, for example, that should an official be dispossessed of his property by his master, he then owed him nothing and was free to seek service under another lord, from whom he could obtain a new domain.[12]

Even if this distinction originally existed, however, it seems evident that in the course of time it became obliterated for all practical purposes. Maspero himself admits that there was a constant tendency for the great officials to convert themselves into actual vassal lords. Moreover, he draws attention to an institution, about which we unfortunately know little, whereby an individual could, by swearing a solemn oath, entrust himself to a patron, whom he thereafter served unto death with unswerving fidelity. This practice he compares with that of commendation. "Each great lord thus had his bands of followers who played an important role in the troubles of this epoch."[13] We have indicated above the importance this theory—unfortunately difficult to prove conclusively—may have for tracing the early evolution of Chou feudalism.

Many scholars further assume that all land, in the last analysis, was regarded as actually belonging to the Chou kings. As one piece of evidence they cite the famous early Chou poem (*Book of Odes*, no. 205) which reads:

> Everywhere under vast Heaven
> There is no land that is not the king's.
> To the borders of those lands
> There are none who are not the king's servants.

Here again, however, Maspero disagrees. What this poem expresses, in his opinion, is merely the concept of political sovereignty, not that of any definite right of property. The ancient Chinese philosophical theory, as summarized by him, was that land was not the inalienable property of any one man, but belonged to "everyone." Everyone, in other words, enjoyed the right, varying in degree according to his position in a strongly hierarchical society, to make use of a portion of it. What the sovereign did, therefore, by determining its specific allotments, was merely to regularize this right which was common to all.[14]

[12] Henri Maspero, "Le régime féodal et la propriété foncière dans la Chine antique," *Mélanges posthumes sur les religions et l'histoire de la Chine*, III. *Études historiques* (Paris, 1950), 133, 143-144.

[13] "Le régime féodal," p. 144.

[14] Maspero, "Les termes désignant la propriété foncière en Chine," *Mélanges posthumes*, III, 204-205.

The Aristocracy. A common designation in Chou literature for members of the upper class is *chün-tzu* or "rulers' sons." Originally this was a term primarily indicative of good birth, but later, under Confucian influence, it acquired a strongly moral coloration in a manner very similar to our word "gentleman." Lowest among the *chün-tzu* was the class known as *shih*, which Creel defines as meaning, among other things, "a young man" or a "stalwart," and which he compares with the word "brave" as used to denote the warriors of an American Indian tribe. Though not all *shih* were warriors, he suggests that as a class they were perhaps roughly comparable to the knights of medieval Europe.[15]

All these aristocrats, regardless of whether or not they bore titles of nobility, differed from the rest of the population in that they maintained family genealogies, performed no agricultural or artisan labor, did not engage in trade, and lived according to an elaborate but (in early times) unwritten code of ceremonial and etiquette known as *li* (variously rendered as rites, ceremonies, traditional mores, customary morality, etc.). These *li*, which took the place of any fixed code of law, were designed to cover all the major activities of life and required much time to learn. On the military side they remind us in some ways of the code of chivalry of European knighthood. Warfare, if we are to believe the historical records, was waged more for prestige than to gain loot or territory. One should be generous to the enemy, not push one's victory too far, and not resort to unfair stratagems. In 638 B.C., for example, we read in the *Tso Chuan* that the Duke of Sung suffered a serious defeat because he allowed the enemy to cross a river before launching his attack. On being criticized for his act, he said: "The superior man[16] does not inflict a second wound, and does not take prisoner anyone with gray hair. When the ancients had their armies in the field, they would not attack an enemy when he was in a defile."[17]

Warfare was endemic during most of the Chou Dynasty. The aristocrats went into battle wearing leather armor and riding in four-horse chariots, each bearing a driver, a lancer, and an archer equipped with the powerful Chinese reflex bow. A company of foot soldiers, recruited from the common people and traditionally said to number 120, accompanied each chariot; seventy-two such chariots, with their infantry

[15] *Birth of China*, pp. 278-279.
[16] *Chün-tzu* or "ruler's son," the term that has just been described.
[17] See also Marcel Granet, *Chinese Civilization* (London and New York, 1930), pp. 266-281, for a vivid account of the military code during the early Chou period.

complement, were regarded as comprising the army of a first class state.

When not engaged in warfare, the Chinese aristocrats, like their medieval European counterparts, amused themselves by feasting, hunting, and engaging in such games as archery contests. To a greater extent than in medieval Europe, however, they seem also to have been seriously interested in the administrative affairs of peace. Many were well-educated men who, at diplomatic assemblies or court gatherings, could buttress their arguments with appropriate quotations from such ancient literature as the *Book of Odes*.

One striking difference between Chou China and medieval Europe was that the former possessed neither a universal church nor a professional priesthood. There were, to be sure, certain men who specialized in religious ritual, divination, and the like, but their role was that of assistants rather than chiefs in the great religious ceremonies, in which the aristocrats acted as their own priests. A primary reason, no doubt, is that these ceremonies were in large part concerned with the cult of the ancestors. Such a cult was necessarily divisive rather than unifying, since the ancestors of each aristocratic clan were of immediate concern only to the members of that clan. Hence it was unable to develop into a universal church with an organized priesthood.

Nevertheless, this ancestral cult was probably the most vital psychological factor from which the aristocratic class derived its power and prestige. Each important clan maintained its own elaborate genealogy, through which it traced descent from ancient heroes who were locally and even nationally famous. These ancestors received regular food offerings from their descendants, by whom they were consulted on all important occasions. They were powerful spirits capable not only of aiding their own family, but also of injuring anyone outside the family who might arouse their ire. This, no doubt, is one reason why the Chou conquerors permitted the descendants of the Shang kings to continue ruling as heads of a lesser feudal state, rather than draw possible retribution on themselves by causing the sacrifices to these Shang ancestors to be interrupted.

In a society as ancestor-conscious as that of ancient China, it is obvious that relationship ties between the leading clans were of paramount importance. Political alignments, in fact, were determined more often by these ties than by abstract obligations of vassal to overlord. Or rather, it would perhaps be more correct to say that the vassal-lord relationships were to a large extent based on those of family. To quote

Ch'i Ssu-ho, "the whole empire was converted into a great family system."[18] So strong, indeed, was the stress on family that in later Confucian thinking the state itself was regarded as simply an enlargement of the family system. Even during early Chou times, in fact, we find the ruler commonly referred to as "the parent of the people."

Aside from the ancestral cult, however, other religious ceremonies were psychologically important for the political system. Symbolic of territorial sovereignty, for king and noble alike, were the sacrifices paid by both to a divinity known as Hou T'u, Lord of the Soil. Actually there were many such lords: lesser ones presiding over local villages, a greater one for each fief, and a supreme one (sacrificed to by the Chou king alone) presiding over the country as a whole. Each had its own altar, consisting of a flat open-air square mound of earth. A tree or trees were in ancient times (not later) grown on this altar, and the cult almost certainly originated as one of fertility.

We, however, are concerned only with its political aspects. When a new fief was created, the invested noble received from the king a lump of earth taken from the altar of the national Lord of the Soil, which then became the nucleus for the localized altar built by the noble in his own fief. We have examined at the beginning of this section the meaning of the word *feng* ("a mound," "to raise a mound," etc.), used to designate this ritual. A fief's Lord of the Soil was, like the noble's own ancestors, among the most powerful divinities to whom he sacrificed, and, as long as he retained his fief, these sacrifices continued. Should the fief be annexed, however, its altar of the soil was then roofed over, thereby destroying the power of its divinity, after which the new ruler built another altar of his own. Maspero, as we have seen, believes that this investment ritual did not apply to the lesser domains distributed by fief holders to their subordinates, even though each peasant community within such domains had its own localized Lord of the Soil.[19]

Finally, the Chou kings themselves were specifically confirmed in their rule of the entire country by a further religious sanction, connected

[18] Ch'i Ssu-ho, "A Comparison between Chinese and European Feudal Institutions," *Yenching Journal of Social Studies*, IV (1948), 11-12.

[19] The classical study of this cult still remains that of E. Chavannes, "Le Dieu du Sol dans la Chine antique," Appendix to his *Le T'ai Chan* (Paris, 1910). The reader should beware, however, of the remarks there made regarding the use of the five colors in conjunction with this cult, since Chinese naturalistic speculations centering around the five colors, five directions, five elements, etc., did not crystallize until the fourth or third century B.C.

with their supreme divinity, T'ien or Heaven. The ancient graph for T'ien clearly represents an anthropomorphic figure. It is, indeed, very similar to the early graph for *wang*, "king," save that it omits the latter's lower horizontal line representing the ground on which the figure stands. Already at the beginning of the Chou Dynasty, however, the word was used not only religiously to designate a supreme divine power, but also non-religiously as the term for "sky." Creel suggests that it may have originated as a collective designation for the ancestors of the Chou kings, taken as a group, and that it thereafter became the name for the realm above in which they lived, thus changing into an impersonal supernatural concept very similar to our word "heaven."[20] This theory would explain very conveniently why no one but the Chou kings bore the title of T'ien Tzu, "Son of Heaven," and why, although Heaven could be appealed to by all, sacrificing to it was a Chou royal prerogative.

Certainly there seems no doubt that T'ien was a Chou and not a Shang divinity, and that the Chou were the creators of the important political theory known as that of T'ien Ming, the "Mandate of Heaven." Creel, indeed, believes that this theory was used as political propaganda by the Chou to justify their overthrow of the Shang Dynasty. Their claim was that they had supplanted the Shang because of the latter's moral unworthiness, and that Heaven had therefore transferred its Ming or Mandate to themselves, thus giving them the divine right to rule. This theory, however, proved to be double-edged, for it involved the idea that the Mandate does not necessarily remain "eternal." That is to say, should its holders at any time prove to be incompetent, it could quite conceivably be transferred by Heaven to yet another ruling house. As later elaborated by the scholar-bureaucrats of imperial China this idea was to become an important instrument for criticizing the ruler and thus strengthening their own influence. It has been repeatedly invoked to justify the many changes of dynasty in Chinese history and is still perpetuated in the present Chinese term for revolution, *k ming*, which literally means "transferring the Mandate."

The Commoners. The economic basis for the feudal structure w have been describing was the great bulk of non-aristocratic commoner known as *min*, "the people," or as *shu jen* or *chung jen*, "the masses. Unlike the aristocracy, the *min* had no family names or genealogie no ancestral cult, and but little knowledge of the complex rules of

[20] *Birth of China*, pp. 342-344.

which governed the lives of the ruling class. Between them and the latter, however, there was a series of gradations rather than an absolute gap, for cases are recorded, though admittedly rare, in which commoners were raised to aristocratic status or aristocrats fell to the ranks of the commoners.

This non-aristocratic population belonged to various categories. Some were artisans or menials who served the ruling class. Both groups apparently included slaves, consisting either of war captives or of persons who had been enslaved for crime; these, however, do not appear to have been numerically or economically significant. There were also merchants, a few of whom seem to have succeeded in acquiring a fair amount of wealth. No fixed system of metal coinage yet existed, however, so that trade largely consisted of barter. All these groups lived in walled towns or were attached to the establishments of the landed proprietors in the countryside. Economically they did not play an important role, and there was, during the early Chou, no development of artisan guilds or of an urban bourgeoisie comparable to that of medieval Europe.

Far more vital to the total economy was the great mass of peasants. They appear to have had no formal rights to the land they cultivated, to which they were bound as serfs, and with which they could be transferred whenever its control passed from one overlord to another. There seems to have been no trace of free landholders, as in Europe. It is uncertain whether the serfdom of the peasantry derived from a formally recognized right of the overlord over the lives of those who cultivated his land, or simply from the fact that any peasant desperate enough to flee from his own overlord would have great trouble in obtaining land from another. Maspero tends toward the second view.[21] In any case, we know that the peasants were obligated in peacetime to surrender a portion of their crops to their overlord (said in late texts to be about a tenth, though probably the actual amount was considerably greater), and were subject to conscription for wall and road building, irrigation and flood-control works, and other public construction. In time of war they supplied the foot soldiers who accompanied the chariots of the nobles.

Much has been speculated but little is definitely known about the precise system of land tenure of the early Chou. The difficulty lies in the fact that what little information we have is mostly late, fragmentary, and ambiguous. Much of the discussion centers around the

[21] "Le régime féodal," p. 126.

ching-t'ien or "well-field" system, the first comparatively detailed account of which, however, dates only from Mencius (372?-279?). According to what he says, such a *ching* consisted of nine plots of land: eight "private fields" (*ssu t'ien*), each occupied by one peasant family, surrounding a ninth central plot known as the "public field" or "lord's field" (*kung t'ien*; the word *kung* may be translated either as "public" or "lord"). The produce of this central field, which was communally cultivated by the eight families, went to the overlord, whereas that of the "private fields," cultivated by each family individually, was retained for personal use. Traditionally, the term *ching-t'ien* is explained on the basis of the graphic resemblance of the character *ching*, "well," to the layout of the nine plots of land. Conceivably, however, the nine plots may have actually centered around a well used for irrigation.

That such a checker-board pattern could ever have been laid out over wide areas with the mathematical exactness described by Mencius is very improbable. On the other hand, it is the belief of most scholars at present that his account does reflect some kind of actual economic and administrative unit of early Chou times, the essence of which was that part of the land was communally cultivated by the peasants for their overlord and part privately cultivated for their own use. Ch'i Ssu-ho goes so far as to compare the public or lord's field with the "demesne" of the European manor, and the private fields with its "land in villeinage."[22]

Various Chinese scholars have proposed theories to explain this and other ancient land systems ambiguously referred to in Mencius and elsewhere. Though ingenious, they are generally not too convincing and hardly provable, and it would lead us too far afield to discuss them here.[23] One of the more probable, followed by Maspero,[24] is that in very early times, before a fixed land system had yet evolved, the peasants practiced a system of communal cultivation in which they shifted every few years from one piece of land to another, preparing the new land for agriculture by burning off its cover of bush and grass.

[22] Ch'i Ssu-ho, "The *Ching-t'ien* Theory of Mencius" (article in Chinese), *Yenching Journal of Chinese Studies*, Peiping, No. 35 (December 1948), 101-127, esp. 124-126.

[23] That of Hsü Chung-shu, however, will be touched on briefly in Sect. IV below. For a convenient summary of it and several other recent Chinese theories, see Yang Lien-sheng, "Notes on Dr. Swann's *Food and Money in Ancient China*," *Harvard Journal of Asiatic Studies*, XIII (1950), 531-543.

[24] "Le régime féodal," pp. 124-126.

This theory is supported by passages in certain early texts, as well as by modern parallels in Indo-China and elsewhere. It is weakened, however, by the fact that a word occurring on the Shang divination inscriptions, where it has been commonly interpreted as referring to this method of "fire farming," has now been conclusively shown to refer in actual fact to the burning of the fields as a preparation for hunting rather than for agriculture.[25]

III. Disintegration and Disappearance of Chou Feudalism

Decay of Chou Royal Power. The picture of Chou feudalism which we have been painting necessarily glosses over, for want of adequate information, the many regional and temporal variations that undoubtedly existed. An era of increasingly sharp change perhaps began as early as 771 B.C., when, according to the traditional account, a sudden attack by "barbarians" forced the house of Chou to abandon its capital in the west and to establish a new one some two hundred miles farther east near the present city of Loyang. There, though perpetuating its rule until 256 B.C., it succeeded in doing so only because the question of its continued existence or non-existence no longer had any practical significance. The history of the last several centuries of the Chou is that of the struggles for power between half a dozen or so of the major states—by that time completely free of any Chou overlordship—in which the Chou kings rarely figure at all.

Indicative of this political change in its early stages is the fact that the *Tso Chuan* (an extremely detailed historical chronicle of the period 722-481 B.C.), though mentioning hundreds of nobles by name, records only nine of them as having undergone the ceremony of feudal investiture. In not one of these nine cases, moreover, did the noble in question actually go himself to the Chou capital. On the contrary, the king in every instance sent his own envoy to the noble's home state to perform the ceremony.[26]

Even better known is the way in which, during this same period, the more powerful of the feudal lords endeavored to arrogate to themselves various royal functions. The first step came in 679, when one of them assumed a new title, that of *pa,* "lord protector" or "tyrant" (in the

[25] See Hu Hou-hsüan, "Yin-tai Fen-t'ien Shuo" [On the Burning of Fields during the Yin—i.e., Shang—Period], *Chia-ku-hsüeh Shang-shih Lun-ts'ung,* I, Essay 4.

[26] See Ch'i Ssu-ho, "Investiture Ceremony of the Chou Period," pp. 224-226.

Greek sense). This title was thereafter successively taken by the rulers of four other states before it finally lapsed in 591. Under the aegis of these *pa*, assemblies of the leading nobles were convoked, at which the latter solemnly, and somewhat cynically, signed treaties pledging themselves to maintain the peace and "assist the royal house [of Chou]." These efforts at peacemaking failed, perhaps in part because no one state was powerful enough to retain the title for more than one generation. Had it been otherwise it is conceivable that an institution might have developed comparable to that of the Shogunate in Japan.

Changes, ca. Sixth Century Onward. The latter centuries of the Chou were marked by widespread change and innovation which speeded the dissolution of the feudal order, though remnants persisted within the individual states down to the Ch'in unification of 221 B.C.

(1) *Technological changes*: These include the appearance of iron (first mentioned in 513), and of improved agricultural techniques (better plows and fertilizers, building of irrigation and water-control works, etc.). A growth in population was one important result, as evidenced by the increasing size of cities and armies. An impressive indication of technological advance, and of the ability to mobilize large masses of manpower on public works, was the wall-building in which the leading states engaged during the fourth and third centuries B.C. Walled fortifications, hundreds of miles long, were built not only along the northern frontiers to separate China as a whole from the steppe peoples as a whole, but also elsewhere to separate the individual Chinese states from one another.

(2) *Military changes*: With the advent of the appropriately named Warring States period (403-221), warfare lost its chivalric character and turned into large-scale conflict, waged in deadly earnest by armies of tens of thousands for the primary purpose of territorial annexation. It was backed up by political alliances, diplomatic intrigue, and such techniques as bribery and assassination. The result was that by the third century B.C. all but a handful of the larger states had been crowded from the scene. Complex siege engines and other techniques were devised for the assault on walled cities. What is more important, at the end of the fourth century the northern and western states, notably that of Ch'in (now centered at what had been the Chou capital prior to the shift of 771), learned from the neighboring steppe peoples the use of mounted archers in place of the old cumbrous war chariots.

(3) *Economic and social changes*: From the lower fringes of the aristocracy, many members of which had become impoverished through the constant wars, there now arose a new class of unattached politicians, educators, and thinkers, who often travelled from state to state, seeking a ruler who would put their ideas into practice. The golden age of Chinese philosophy owes its genesis to these men, of whom Confucius (552/551-479) was the earliest example. Other members of the aristocracy specialized as professional military warriors and "bravos" attached to the various state rulers.

Yet another phenomenon of the times was the appearance of a money economy based on metal coinage (and with it no doubt a growing merchant class). This development is commonly said to date from the late fifth century.

Most significant evidence of the disintegration of feudalism, however, was the changing relationship of peasant to land, culminating in the disappearance of serfdom. The imposition of new forms of land taxation and military levy in two states (Lu and Cheng) in the years 594, 590, 543, 538, and 483 is probably indicative of this change. Though we know virtually nothing of their precise details, it has been thought that they were attempts, on the part of the state administration, to extract taxes directly from the peasantry, instead of through their immediate overlords, the local landed proprietors.

In the state of Ch'in the changes were most sweeping. There the famous statesman, Shang Yang (died 338), is credited with abolishing the old system of land tenure in at least parts of that state, and giving to the peasants the right to "sell and buy" land. On such land he seems to have instituted a tax-in-kind paid directly to the state in place of the labor services formerly rendered by peasant serfs to their immediate overlords. Through these measures, Ch'in successfully encouraged settlers to migrate from other states.

(4) *Institutional changes*: With the institution of written law codes, mentioned in two states (Cheng and Chin) in 536, 513, and 501, we find a new concept emerging: that of an impersonal body of law, to which all men, high and low alike, should be subject, in place of the old personalized feudal relationships, based on the traditional mores or *li*. This new concept, fostered by the Legalist school of thought, reached its highest development in Ch'in, where it undoubtedly helped that state in its ultimate triumph.

Another phenomenon equally indicative of the increasing complexity of social organization was the trend toward specialization in administration. Civil and military functions, for example, which in earlier centuries had often been conducted by the same men, came to be differentiated during the Warring States period by being allocated to a civil and a military hierarchy, the former headed by a Prime Minister (*hsiang*) and the latter by a Military Commander (*chiang*). This bifurcation was to be perpetuated in imperial times.

In the more important states there was a steady curtailment of the power of local officials and landed proprietors. In Ch'in, for example, this political centralization is evidenced by the land reform described above. It also appears both there and in other states in the rise of a new administrative system based on the *hsien* (prefecture) and *chün* (commandery). These territorial units seem to have originated in land newly annexed from other states, or in the militarized zones of states bordering the steppe peoples on the north. Gradually, however, especially in Ch'in, they were established in territory lying well within the state frontiers as well. What distinguished them from the domains of the landed proprietors seems to be that they, unlike the latter, were directly controlled by the state government by means of state-appointed governing officials who, at least in principle, were non-hereditary. The *hsien* (which was smaller than the *chün*) is first mentioned as early as 688 and 687 in Ch'in, while the *chün* appears considerably later, first in the neighboring state of Wei around 400 and again in 361. Though the *chün* was to give way to the province in later times, the *hsien* survives as an administrative unit to this day.

Yet another innovation, carried out in Ch'in in the year 350, was the institution of a new aristocratic hierarchy of eighteen degrees, having purely honorary rather than territorial or hereditary significance. These degrees were acquired, not by birth, but by military exploits, or later (the first case is reported in 243) through purchase.

(5) *Concept of a universal empire*: The administrative system of the early Chou, inadequate though it had proved to be in practice, undoubtedly represented an attempt to create a political universality probably greater than any that had previously existed in China. In the last two centuries of the Chou, with the intensification of war and social upset, the dream of almost all thinkers became that of recreating a universal empire that would bring peace to the world. In literature, this dream is manifested in the highly idealized writings of the ritualists and others, purporting to give detailed pictures of early Chou and even pre-Chou institutions and customs.

Politically, the same ideal is symbolized in the history of the words *wang*, "king," and *ti*, "emperor." In 370 B.C. the new ruler of Wei usurped the title of *wang* (hitherto, with few exceptions, a royal designation); his example was speedily followed by other state rulers. This title, however, no longer sufficed to express the aspirations of the leading contenders for power. Hence a new title was looked for and found: that of *ti*, a word rich in religious and historical associations. Ti (or Shang Ti, "Supreme Ti") had been the name of the most powerful divinity of the Shang Dynasty; by the Warring States period it had also come to be attached to the names of certain legendary heroes supposed to have ruled in the predynastic golden age. Finally, during the last decades of the Chou (in the years 288, 286, and 257), several state rulers tried to adopt it as their political title. Though these efforts failed, owing to the jealousy of rival states, the founder of the Ch'in Empire took the word as part of his title in 221 B.C., and it has since remained as the permanent Chinese equivalent for emperor.

Establishment of Bureaucratic Rule under the Ch'in and Han Empires. Having conquered the last of the opposing states in 221 B.C., the king of Ch'in adopted for himself the new grandiose title of Shih-huang-ti, "First Sovereign Emperor." At the same time, so we are told by the *Shih Chi* or "Historical Records" (the official history of the period), "he caused the Ch'in [Empire] to be without a foot of land of investiture [*feng*]," and removed "the rich and powerful people of the empire, amounting to 120,000 families," to the Ch'in capital, where they could be kept under the watchful eye of the central government. Their weapons were confiscated and cast into bells and monumental human statues. Though certain noble titles were retained, they were honorary only and had no territorial significance. The empire was divided, in 221 and the years immediately following, into a total of forty-two *chün* or commanderies.[27] Each commandery was governed by a centrally appointed triumvirate of Administrator, Military Governor, and Overseer, and was subdivided into an indeterminate number of *hsien* or prefectures, governed by Prefects.

[27] Thirty-six is the number stated in the *Shih Chi* as having been established in 221, and this figure is repeated in D. Bodde, *China's First Unifier: A Study of the Ch'in Dynasty as Seen in the Life of Li Ssu (280?-208 B.C.)*, *Sinica Leidensia*, III (Leiden, 1938), pp. 135, 144, 238, which, however, on p. 246 lists four additional commanderies as having been created in 214. From scattered references we can deduce that the actual total number created during the dynasty was probably forty-two.

A major technological achievement of the Ch'in was the Great Wall of China, built by hundreds of thousands of conscript laborers, who in part utilized for this purpose the walls previously erected by several of the major states along their northern frontiers.

When the Ch'in Empire disintegrated only twelve years after its founding, many of the former nobles or their descendants returned to power in the resulting civil wars. Moreover, when the founder of the Han Dynasty (206 B.C.-A.D. 220) mounted the throne, he, though a commoner himself, created a new land-holding aristocracy in 202 B.C. This he did by dividing almost two-thirds of his new empire into "kingdoms" and "marquisates," bestowing these on his brothers, sons, and meritorious assistants, each of whom possessed full authority over the people within his boundaries.

In following decades, however, the power of the new aristocracy proved to be dangerous and so was checked in various ways, especially after the unsuccessful Revolt of the Seven Kings in 154 B.C. Thus a decree of 127 B.C. destroyed primogeniture by compelling all kingdoms to be equally divided among the sons of deceased kings. In 106 the empire, including the kingdoms, was divided into thirteen Circuits, each headed by an imperially appointed Inspector charged with keeping watch over it on behalf of the central government. Many noble families met violent ends as the result of intrigue or attempted rebellion, so that, during the first two centuries of the Han Dynasty, the average noble life-span of such families was only 2.31 generations. In fact, we know that of the marquises created by the Han founder, not a single descendant retained that title by the year 86 B.C.

Furthermore, the *chün* and *hsien* system was continued and gradually extended, so that by the end of the first century B.C. there were 83 *chün* and 1,314 *hsien*, as against only 20 kingdoms and 241 marquisates. (The holdings of the latter ranged in size from 100 to 20,000 families, with 2,600 as the average.) The nobility, to be sure, lived lives of great luxury, but the real administrative power by this time lay in the hands of the centrally appointed bureaucracy, which under Emperor Ai (6-1 B.C.) amounted to 130,285 officials, and which was paid in cash or grain, not in land (though much of its capital was invested in land).

Thus was created the vitally important official-gentry class, which in most later periods has been the effective ruling group in China, and which, though it tended to be self-perpetuating as a class, was non-titled and individually non-hereditary in the government posts it held. The orthodox ideology of this group was Confucianism. The Han also saw the beginnings of the examination system, greatly elaborated in T'ang and later dynasties as the instrument for recruiting the official bureaucracy.

This internal political consolidation was accompanied by a military expansion which pushed the imperial frontiers into modern Indo-China in the south, Manchuria and Korea in the northeast, and the westernmost reaches of Chinese Turkestan in the northwest, thus making of the Han one of the three or four largest empires in Chinese history.

Private ownership and buying and selling of land were now the rule, and resulted in such a concentration in the hands of the wealthy that the government was often urged to impose limitations on the size of landholdings. The climax was reached with the famous decree declaring the nationalization of all farm land, issued by the usurper Wang Mang in A.D. 9, which, however, had to be rescinded three years later owing to the tremendous opposition of the landed gentry.

IV. The Dynamics of Chou Feudalism

What were the forces that shaped early Chinese society along the lines we have been describing? No answer to such a complex question can, in the present state of our knowledge, be really conclusive. Nevertheless, the theories of Owen Lattimore and (more recently) Wolfram Eberhard, because of the care and detail with which they have been worked out, deserve serious consideration.

We shall begin with Lattimore's theory, as developed in his *Inner Asian Frontiers of China.*[28] Though deriving much from K. A. Wittfogel's concept of what the latter calls "oriental society," it goes considerably further by combining this with Lattimore's own concept of the nature of nomadic society. In this way it seeks to explain what has been a major theme of Chinese history: the interplay of forces between the agrarian society of China proper and the nomadic society of the steppes, mountains, and deserts fronting China's northern periphery.

The Agrarian Way of Life. Lattimore's theory begins with the thesis that Chinese civilization evolved in North China out of a relatively uniform antecedent neolithic culture, based on a mixed economy of hunting, fishing, and food-gathering, to which were later added the domestication of the dog and pig and a primitive agriculture. The trend

[28] See especially Chaps. IX-XIII, which are those most pertinent to the period we are discussing.

toward agriculture occurred first in the north rather than in the potentially richer Yangtze Valley, owing to the fact that the loess soil which covers much of the Yellow River basin was comparatively free from vegetation and could be easily worked with stone tools, whereas the Yangtze Valley was still a thick jungle land. Even in North China, however, agriculture did not develop evenly everywhere. At first it tended to be concentrated in certain valleys in the loess highlands, which, being well watered and sheltered, combined favorable conditions for crop growing with continued opportunities for hunting and fishing. Only later, probably, did agricultural communities spring up in the lower reaches of the Yellow River, for there the land, though fertile, was marshy and required drainage.

Somewhere along this line of development, however, a vital factor intruded itself: the comparative sparseness and seasonal irregularity of the rainfall in North China, which meant that agriculture could not progress beyond a certain point without the help of irrigation. We cannot as yet precisely date the beginnings of Chinese irrigation, but when it started, its need for the cooperative labor of communal groups must have powerfully reinforced the already-present tendency of agriculture to develop in a few nuclear areas rather than evenly throughout the country.

The Shang state was one of these nuclei. Another was the Chou, which, starting from the same general neolithic background, matured later than the Shang but eventually outstripped it. Still others were the little principalities—each a self-contained economic cell centered upon the walled city where it could store its precious grain—that came into political existence under the Chou.

From these nuclei the agrarian way of life spread outward wherever the terrain was favorable. The demonstrated ability of grain-production to support a larger population than any other occupation encouraged the use of manpower for increasingly ambitious water-control works. These enabled ever more land to be brought under cultivation, thus in turn making possible a yet greater population. Such works—built not merely for irrigation, but also, especially later, for flood control, drainage, and water transport—enabled the Chinese progressively to overcome environmental obstacles such as in the beginning would have been insuperable.

At the same time, the increasing concern with agriculture caused other economic activities to decline to marginal importance. Hunting, for example, once economically significant, became the sport of the aristocracy. The pig, rather than cattle or sheep, was used as the chief food animal, because, as a scavenger, it did not require extensive land for its pasturage such as could more efficiently be devoted to crop growing. In short, the production of grain—wheat or millet in the north, and, later, rice in the south—became *the* great Chinese way of life.

The amalgamation through military means of smaller states into larger states, characteristic of the Chou period, was a political reflection of the growth of key economic regions. Because, however, this growth was not uniform, but advanced more rapidly in some areas and times than in others, the balance of political power likewise fluctuated between different regions. The culmination was reached with the creation of a single universal empire in 221 B.C.

Having outlined Lattimore's theory, let us now try to formulate some conclusions. In the first place, as pointed out in the Introductory Essay of this book, one of the stimuli for the rise of a feudal system may often be "the decay or weakening of a highly organized political system—an empire or a relatively large kingdom." A few lines later, however, the essay wisely warns us that this is not necessarily true for all feudal societies, and points to China by way of illustration. This warning is well taken because, in the case of Chou feudalism, it is highly doubtful whether any such antecedent "highly organized political system" did in fact exist, irrespective of whether we think of it in terms of the Shang state, or of the hegemony established by the Chou themselves at the time of the conquest (from which, presumably, gradually evolved the later full-fledged feudal system). In the words of Maspero: "Chinese feudalism does not emerge from the decomposition of an antecedent regime more or less strongly centralized."[29]

In the second place, the reason why Chou feudalism was doomed to eventual failure, at first nationally and then locally, was that, initially and nationally, even the moderate political unity demanded by it outstripped the economic integration of the scattered units to which it was applied, whereas, later on and locally, the economic growth of these units outstripped the organizational ability of feudalism to handle them effectively. The resulting tensions brought about the changes and eventual breakdown already described, thus clearing the way, first, for the transformation of the former feudal principalities into states entirely independent of the Chou monarchy, and then, finally, for the amalgamation of these states into a new kind of bureaucratic empire. This,

[29] "Le régime féodal," p. 144. Cf. also Lattimore, p. 370, for a similar view.

however, did not happen without tremendous resistance on the part of the old order. The wall-building activities of different states during the fourth and third centuries B.C., for example, are interpreted by Lattimore as "a general phenomenon of the last phase of . . . feudal separatism in China."[30]

In the third place, the growing economic monoculturism of the Chinese, with its need for the efficient utilization of concentrated manpower, led even in early times to a bureaucratic tendency in Chou feudalism. "It was necessarily interested in public works of a kind that were not characteristic of European feudalism. . . . The labor of the whole community had to be regulated for the maintenance of public works—water rights had to be allotted and grain stored and issued for the labor gangs. Even under feudal conditions, accordingly, there was a more urgent need for clerkly functions than in Europe."[31] In the end, the ruling aristocracy of feudal China successfully transformed itself into the ruling scholar-gentry of imperial China.

Finally, the factors which we have been describing gave to Chou feudalism a homogeneity far greater than that of Europe, with its diverse origins and varied local economies. This fact was to have lasting consequences, for, as pointed out by Lattimore,[32] it is no accident that "Europe changed in a way that led to a money economy and industrialism, while China changed in a way that created a centralized imperial bureaucracy, . . . whose combination of landed interest and administrative interest kept capitalism well in check and prevented industrial development almost entirely."[33]

The Pastoral Way of Life. The other side of Lattimore's theory concerns the nomadic steppe peoples of China's northern frontiers. In his view, the pastoral economy of these peoples was in good part an outgrowth of that same general neolithic North China culture from which had arisen the grain economy of the Chinese. This happened because,

[30] p. 404. From our point of view, of course, the term feudal is not entirely accurate at this point, since feudalism had by this time disappeared from the national scene, even though its remnants persisted within the individual states.

[31] Lattimore, pp. 375-376.

[32] p. 393.

[33] This, like most generalizations, requires some qualification. The growing complexity of Han society, for example, inevitably led to an industrial and commercial development which was very considerable, judged by previous standards. Nevertheless it remains true, then and later, that this development was consistently opposed by the state bureaucracy and never reached the position where it dominated the state, as in Europe.

in the beginning, only those groups occupying certain favorable localities had followed the trend toward specialized agriculture which caused them eventually to become "Chinese." In less favorable intervening terrain other groups retained their earlier mixed economy, thus becoming the "barbarians" who in early Chou times occupied the uncultivated no man's land between the feudal states.

It is not surprising that in the Chinese historical accounts of Chinese-barbarian conflicts during the first half of the dynasty, the latter are usually pictured as aggressors. Viewed in their larger historical context, however, what these conflicts really seem to represent is a series of losing rear-guard actions on the part of the barbarians against the spreading tide of Chinese agricultural economy. Some "barbarians," engulfed by this tide, accepted the Chinese way of life and thereby themselves became "Chinese." Others who resisted, however, were driven progressively farther into the mountains and finally even out into the inhospitable steppe.

It should not be supposed that at this time these "barbarians" were as yet true nomads. We read in the records, for example, that in their clashes with the Chinese they fought on foot. But gradually, as they reached the steppe, their old mixed economy evolved into a new way of life. They "found themselves in a terrain and environment that would not tolerate either the old mixed economy as a whole or the special emphasis on agriculture that had become the mark of 'being a Chinese.' They were forced, instead, to work out for themselves a new line of specialization in the control of herded animals in the wide steppe. This emphasis on a single technique produced in due course a society even more one-sided than that of China, but sharply different from it and in the main antagonistic to it."[34]

Thus there developed in the steppe lands fronting northern China a genuine nomadism which from the time of its appearance powerfully affected Chinese history. We have already seen, for example, how at the end of the fourth century B.C. certain of the Chinese states, including Ch'in, learned from their nomad neighbors the use of mounted archers in place of the former war chariots. The building of the Great Wall during the Ch'in Dynasty is commonly regarded as an artificial attempt to demarcate the Chinese from the nomadic way of life.

[34] Lattimore, p. 381. He is careful to point out elsewhere (p. 355), however, that the pastoral nomadism of Inner Asia derived its origins not only from the steppe margins of North China, but also from the edges of the Siberian forests and of the Central Asian oases.

This attempt, however, foundered on the geographical fact that between agrarian China and the pastoral steppe there is no clear-cut physical demarcation, but only an ill-defined transitional zone, to some extent suited for either farming or herding, but ideally suited for neither. In this zone, therefore, a mixed agricultural-pastoral society developed. Politically, its members enjoyed a peculiarly strategic position, because, though conversant with both ways of life, they were definitely committed to neither and therefore were free to join either one in its struggles against the other.

From the Han Dynasty onward, as a result, Chinese and nomads have repeatedly struggled to control this intermediate zone, and from it have gone on to try to establish domination over the other's homeland. In this struggle each has enjoyed temporary but not permanent success, because each, in order to rule the other, has had to accept the other's psychology and way of life, thereby losing its own cultural and political identity. This fact is important for the discussion in Section V of feudalistic phenomena during the Period of Disunity. Before turning to this, however, let us first consider Eberhard's theory of Chinese society and compare it with that of Lattimore.

Chou Feudalism and Chinese Gentry Society. Eberhard's theory of Chou feudalism, and of its evolution into what he calls Chinese "gentry" society, is presented in the first chapter of his recently published *Conquerors and Rulers: Social Forces in Medieval China* (Leiden, 1952). There he begins by applying to China A. Rüstow's theory of "superstratification,"[35] i.e., the theory that feudalism results from the stratification produced when there is the conquest of one group by another that is ethnically and culturally different. This, in the case of China, means, for Eberhard, that "Chou society is the result of an *ethnic superstratification.* The Chou rulers came from Western China accompanied by a group of militarily organized tribes of non-Chinese affiliation. . . . They conquered and occupied East China and started an expansionist, colonial activity."[36]

Elsewhere (pp. 24-25), Eberhard emphasizes the wide general applicability of the "superstratification" concept: "We regard feudal conditions as the result of superstratification of a basically agrarian group by an essentially or at least originally pastoral group. . . . Feudalism came into existence when the originally pastoral tribes of the migration period

[35] See A. Rüstow, *Ortbestimmung der Gegenwart*, I (Zurich, 1949).
[36] p. 4 (Eberhard's emphasis).

had conquered the Roman Empire; when the originally pastoral Chou and their allies had conquered Shang-China; when nomadic Mongol and Turkish tribes had conquered India, or Persia, or Russia." However, as Eberhard is careful to add, this fact "does not mean that any conquest of nomads inevitably led to feudalism."

In Chou China, Eberhard believes, the conquest resulted in a deep dualism between the rulers and the subject population, manifesting itself in such fields as religion, literature, and law. Above all, however, it is conspicuous in property relations. The Chou conquerors, when they settled on their new fiefs in Central and East China, built city fortresses there which stood like islands in the sea of the indigenous population. Being unable to rely wholly on this population for their food supply, they were obliged to develop alternative sources of food of their own. They therefore "organized their tribesmen in semi-military cadres of eight families each. These groups left the fortress in early spring, cleared a piece of land and cultivated it for one or more seasons until the soil was exhausted, after which a new clearing was made."[37] These clearings, ideally possessing regular size and shape, and quite possibly cultivated collectively by their eight-family occupants, were the *ching-t'ien* or "well-fields" of Mencius and other late Chou writers. Their rigid organization contrasted sharply with the freer organization of the indigenous "natives," who lived in villages of their own more or less independently of the conquest group, to which they merely had to pay sporadic "tribute" as a token of submission.

In the course of time, the fortress cities of the ruling nobles lost their exclusively administrative and military character and became industrial and commercial centers as well, increasingly frequented by the surrounding "natives" who were anxious to acquire the goods produced by the city artisans. This development was accompanied and facilitated by the rise of a merchant class and a money economy. As the result of it and other complex factors, much of the land originally belonging to the "natives" was probably bought or otherwise acquired by the nobles and their city-dwelling followers. In this way new relationships of a landlord-tenant character came into existence. These, though "shaped after the model of feudal institutions," such as had hitherto prevailed, differed from them in the "absence of the moral element (loyalty), [or of] the mutuality of rights and obligations," and in the fact that they were "more or less purely economic" in character.[38]

[37] p. 7.
[38] pp. 10-11.

This development was of crucial importance, for it speeded the cultural assimilation of the ruling group with the subject population, made it possible for the former to regularize the latter's occasional tribute into a fixed tax indistinguishable from the "tithe" received by the nobles from the communally-cultivated "well-fields," and caused these "well-fields" themselves to disappear entirely as separate units. Commissioners—many of them recruited, Eberhard believes, from the merchant class—were now employed by the nobles to travel about the countryside and collect the new taxes. "The lords regarded these collectors as their 'officials' and shaped their relation towards them after the model of their household administration."[39]

These and other changes of the sort we have described in Section III led to the gradual dissolution of the old feudal relationships, and their replacement by a new network of economically-centered landlord-tenant relationships. The process culminated, as we have seen, with the creation of a new type of empire in the third and second centuries B.C., dominated by a new social group to which Eberhard gives the appropriate name of "gentry."

The two major characteristics of this gentry class that distinguish it, in Eberhard's eyes, from the "burgher" society of the West, are that (1) it was economically dependent upon landed property, not industrial capital; (2) its three major professions were those of landowner, scholar, and politician—all normally represented within a single gentry family, and often, indeed, in a single individual. The key to the great stability of this class lay in the fact that a gentry family normally possessed both a city and a country home. The former was occupied by those family members who were engaged in political careers, while in the latter lived other members who administered the family's rented-out landed property. At the same time, this rural seat provided an economic base to which the city members could retire in times of political disfavor or uncertainty. "The extreme stability of Chinese gentry society was the decisive factor which prevented the disintegration of Chinese civilization and militated against the success of foreign rule over China. But it also prevented change. It prevented the development of modern science—the instrument of change."[40]

The Theories of Eberhard and Lattimore Compared. Eberhard's description of gentry society differs little in its broad outlines from Lattimore's conception of post-Chou society. Nor does Eberhard objec

[39] p. 11. [40] p. 16.

to Lattimore's theory of the development of pastoral society along China's northern periphery, and its interaction there with Chinese agrarian society; on this point, indeed, he seems to be in essential agreement with Lattimore.[41] It is the agrarian side of the picture, however, that Eberhard in the second chapter of his book heavily attacks. In so doing he by-passes Lattimore himself and concerns himself exclusively with K. A. Wittfogel's formulation of the theory of "oriental" society. This formulation, however, has, as we have noted earlier, been of basic importance in shaping the agrarian side of Lattimore's own theory.

Reasons of space prevent us from considering in detail all of Eberhard's arguments. The more important of them, however, have to do with Wittfogel's central thesis, according to which the preoccupation of the state with water-control works, especially those for irrigation, has been the decisive factor shaping the evolution of Chinese and other examples of "oriental" society. Eberhard, by way of refutation, adduces historical evidence from which he seeks to prove that (1) irrigation was not vital to the wheat and millet culture of North China (where Chinese civilization had its start), but assumed real importance only in connection with the later rice culture of the South; (2) Chinese political interest in water-control works cannot be traced with assurance far back into the feudal period, and became conspicuous only during the imperial epoch, when, moreover, it centered more around canal-building activities (themselves but one aspect of the rising interest of the time in improved communications), than it did around irrigation projects per se; (3) when, as we sometimes read in the literature, purely irrigational projects were undertaken, their initiative usually came from the local populace and not the central government.

Despite questions of detail, Eberhard's total arguments convince this writer that Wittfogel has probably considerably over-estimated the all-embracing role of irrigation in China, at least as far as the North is concerned. Certainly the criticism, made by Eberhard on the final page of his book, seems justified that Wittfogel, by his blanket application of the word "oriental" to a wide range of civilizations—some not even found in Asia at all—has tended to obscure the actual differences among them. The safer course, suggested by Eberhard himself, is to approach each of these civilizations, including China's, as an "individual case."

Eberhard's own socio-political approach, on the other hand, does not—at least to this writer—provide a fully satisfying explanation for

[41] See Eberhard, pp. 8-9, 72.

the evolution of Chinese society from its feudal and pre-feudal stages to its later form. His theory does not, in other words, convincingly explain why, for example, Chinese society from early times displayed tendencies toward an economic monoculturalism and a political bureaucratism, such as eventually transformed it into the gentry-dominated monolithic state of imperial China. For problems such as these, the environmentally-based and economically-based functional approach of Wittfogel and Lattimore seems to provide a more dynamic and consistent rationale.

Even if we accept Eberhard's strictures on Wittfogel, it is perhaps still possible to utilize the Wittfogel-Lattimore theory in a modified form. Thus it seems reasonable to suppose, with Lattimore, that the early development of agriculture in North China tended to be concentrated in those areas that were environmentally favorable to it, and that this concentration encouraged the growth of population in the same areas, thus leading to the rise of local political entities. It seems likewise reasonable to suppose that the thinner population that occupied the less favorable intervening areas tended at first to retain the old general mixed economy, but that it then began to move toward a more exclusively pastoral way of life when it discovered this to be better suited to its environment. In this way the stage was set for that bifurcation, postulated by Lattimore, which led toward a specialized agriculture on the one hand and a specialized pastoralism on the other.

Given the seasonal unevenness and relative sparsity of rainfall in North China, moreover, it would be strange if the occupants of the agricultural areas did not at some stage try to remedy this condition by means of irrigation. This they might very well do even though their irrigation projects were of only marginal importance to the agricultural situation, were neither grandiose nor all-pervasive, and stemmed from private groups rather than from any centralized political authority. The net effect, in any case, would be the stepping up of agricultural productivity, resulting in the further growth and spread of a population now increasingly wedded to an agrarian way of life. These factors would in turn induce the local political structure to develop more and more along bureaucratic lines in its efforts to handle the enlarging population.

In this way a chain reaction would be produced which, once started could continue under its own momentum until China finally became a centralized empire. All this could plausibly happen even though the state as such waited until the imperial age to play a major role in water control activities, and even then interested itself more in canal-building than in irrigation-works per se.

We have, moreover, so far said nothing about such forms of hydraulic activity as the drainage of lowlands and flood-control, about which Eberhard himself says relatively little. Yet it is obvious that they must have become of crucial importance to the Chinese when their agrarian way of life expanded from the valleys of the loess uplands out onto the great alluvial plain of the lower Yellow River. The difficulties then encountered must have been so formidable that they could hardly have been overcome by private initiative alone, unaided by centralized political supervision.

If we turn now to Eberhard's own theory of "ethnic superstratification" as the key to Chou feudal institutions, we are confronted by certain difficulties. One is the uncertain support provided by the available data for Eberhard's supposition (see Sect. II above) that the Chou were "originally of Turkish stock," and hence ethnically distinct from the peoples they conquered. Certainly it seems strange, if this be the case, that linguistic traces of the fact have not survived, similar to those found in the case of the many alien invaders of China of later periods.

In the second place, Eberhard's attribution to ethnic superstratification of the "deep dualism" believed by him to characterize Chou society, is to some extent weakened by a factor already noted by us in Section I. This is, that when the Chou people conquered East China, they retained only a part of the new territories as fiefs for themselves and their allies, leaving other portions in the continued possession of indigenous clan leaders. This means that the new ruling aristocracy did not in all areas consist of alien conquerors.

In the third place, Eberhard, it will be remembered, finds the alleged dualism of Chou society most significantly manifested in the *ching-t'ien* or "well-field" system, regarded by him as a semi-military institution created by the Chou conquerors for their own people, in contradistinction to the looser organization of the subject population. At this point Eberhard explicitly acknowledges his indebtedness to Hsü Chung-shu's theories of early Chou land tenure.[42] These theories, however, while extremely ingenious, depend on so many scattered and sometimes dubious bits of evidence that they definitely do not bring

[42] Eberhard, p. 6. Cf. Hsü Chung-shu, "A Study on the Ching T'ien System" (article in Chinese), *Chung-kuo Wen-hua Yen-chiu Hui-k'an* [Bulletin of Chinese Studies], Vol. IV, Pt. I (Chengtu, 1944), 121-156.

conviction to this writer. What is much worse, moreover, is that this complex evidence is used by Hsü to prove, not that the *ching-t'ien* system was inaugurated by the Chou conquerors, but that it was a survival from the Shang dynasty![43] Yet Eberhard reverses this equation for his purposes without a word of explanation.

In summary, we would like to suggest that Eberhard's application of the superstratification theory to Chou China does not really seem to require the ethnic differentiation he himself postulates for it. Such at least, is the conclusion we might draw from Eberhard's own opinion quoted earlier, that the source of feudalism lies in the "superstratifica tion of a basically agrarian group by an essentially or at least originally pastoral group." Cultural patterns such as these do not necessarily have to be associated with ethnic differences.

What we ourselves suspect really resulted from the Chou conquest wa a superstratification that was primarily political rather than ethnic Though certain cultural differences no doubt accompanied this proces of political superstratification, it would seem wiser to regard most o them as functionally arising out of the very fact that the population was divided into a ruling and a ruled group, rather than as indicativ of innate ethnic or cultural differences between the two groups, ante dating the conquest.

In this modified sense we are quite ready to accept superstratification as the immediate factor responsible for the rise of feudal institutions i Chou China. At the same time, however, we believe that other longer continuing forces—probably both environmental and economic—mus also be looked for, if we are to explain the processes which finally pro duced Chinese gentry society. These forces may well have been muc more varied and less exclusively "hydraulic" than Wittfogel an Lattimore assume, but that they existed, and in the end proved decisiv seems reasonably certain.

Though we may glimpse the main contours of Chou feudalism, an theory as to its dynamics is necessarily rendered uncertain by th limitations of the available data. With the humbleness of the tru scholar, Eberhard admits as much when he concludes his book b saying: "The theory developed here is only an attempt at an interpreta tion. Our knowledge of Chinese society is still far too limited to mak any final explanation possible."

[43] Hsü, pp. 131ff., esp. p. 139. Cf. also Yang Lien-sheng in *Harvard Journal Asiatic Studies*, XIII (1950), 536, which summarizes Hsü's theory.

v. Feudalistic Phenomena during the Period of Disunity[44]

Comparison with the Chou Dynasty and with Medieval Europe. The Han Dynasty officially ended in A.D. 220 (though the empire had already disintegrated into three parts thirty years earlier). The subsequent Period of Disunity (221-589) falls into three main divisions: (1) the Three Kingdoms (221-280); (2) the Western Chin Dynasty (265-316), during which most of China was momentarily reunited following the year 280; (3) the Northern and Southern Dynasties (317-589), during which South China was ruled by five successive dynasties with capitals at Nanking, while the North was fragmented among almost a score of ephemeral states and dynasties, of which only the Northern Wei (386-535) succeeded in lasting more than a century. Finally the period was brought to an end by the reunification of North and South under the Sui Dynasty (590-617).

The Period of Disunity, as an age of prolonged political division, invites comparison with the Chou Dynasty on the one hand and with medieval Europe on the other. Such comparison shows that whereas it differs from the Chou on several vital points, its similarities with medieval Europe are striking, even though subject to important qualifications.

(1) Like the European Middle Ages but unlike the Chou, the Period of Disunity followed the collapse of a major empire, whose memory and political institutions, however, it preserved to a greater extent than did medieval Europe. The result was twofold: it meant that on the one hand the Period of Disunity differed from the Chou in its political system, but that on the other its break with the past and decline in learning were neither as sharp nor as prolonged as was the case in Europe.

(2) Like the Middle Ages but unlike the Chou (after the conquest itself), the Period of Disunity witnessed a continuing series of major barbarian invasions which destroyed native Chinese rule in North China for almost three centuries, imposing a sequence of alien dynasties ruled by Turks, Mongols, Tibetans, and Tungus. Unlike Europe, however, where barbarian invasion actually helped to overthrow the Roman

[44] The writer is keenly aware of the difficulties involved in the discussion of this period, for which the basic monographic studies are largely lacking, so that the remarks below are necessarily tentative and subject to correction.

Empire, the invasions of China during the Period of Disunity did not begin until the early fourth century, i.e., until a century after the Han Empire itself had already collapsed. Even then, in fact, the term "invasion" is something of a misnomer, for the first alien state, that of the Former Chao (304-329), was not created by the inroads of peoples from the actual steppe, but by a coalition of Hsiung-nu (Hun) tribes who had already been settled in North China for more than a century. There they had acquired military power after having been used as mercenaries by the northernmost of the Three Kingdoms. In other words, they were partially Sinified by the time they founded their state, and were the products of that undefined frontier zone between China proper and the steppe whose importance we have described in the preceding section. Some, though not all, of the subsequent alien states and dynasties of the Period of Disunity were likewise dynasties of "infiltration" rather than dynasties of conquest.[45]

(3) Like the Middle Ages but unlike the Chou, the Period of Disunity was an "age of faith." Buddhism, which had entered China during the Han Dynasty, spread during the Period of Disunity to become *the* great religion of high and low alike. Here again, however, the similarity with Europe must be qualified, for whereas Christianity there became the state religion already under the Roman Empire, Chinese Buddhism did not become really influential until the late third or early fourth century, i.e., again, as in the case of barbarian invasion, until about a century after the collapse of the Han. Even then, in fact, it had to meet the continued challenge of the rival ideologies of Confucianism and Taoism, which, though temporarily weakened, were never permanently submerged. Chinese Buddhism, furthermore, always remained a congeries of different sects and monasteries, rathe than a truly universal church united under a supreme spiritual hierarchy. Though spiritually, socially, and even economically, its impac was profound, its political power was much less than that of Christianit in Europe or even Buddhism in feudal Japan.

(4) Unlike the Chou, and also, though to a lesser extent, unlike th Middle Ages, the Period of Disunity had no central pivot of politica unity. That is to say, it had no single ruling house to provide politica continuity, such as the house of Chou had provided during the earlie period. Dynasty followed dynasty, with little regard for politica

[45] The terminology is that of K. A. Wittfogel and Feng Chia-sheng, *Histor of Chinese Society: Liao* (Philadelphia, 1949), pp. 15-16.

legitimacy, and the schism between the Chinese South and the alien North effectively inhibited any feeling of common allegiance to a single overlord.

Feudalistic Phenomena. Aside from these partial similarities with the European Middle Ages, the Period of Disunity displays other phenomena which elsewhere are the frequent, if not invariable, marks of a feudal age. There is, for example, the very fact of political disunion itself. Warfare, coupled with famine and other disasters, exacted an enormous toll, and more than once the historical records contain the grim word "cannibalism." Nevertheless the drop in population from Han times, if it actually occurred, was far less than traditionally supposed.[46]

A by-product of disorder was the southward migration of Chinese—especially those of the upper class—to escape the invasions from the North. It has been estimated that by the end of the fourth century about one million northerners had fled to the south of the Yangtze River. This movement, on a scale heretofore unprecedented in China, gave to the South a growing economic importance which caused it ultimately to outstrip the North.

Another by-product was the widespread dislocation of economic life. Trade, which despite Chinese agricultural monoculturalism had developed to sizable proportions under the Han, was choked off in many places. From the third century onward there was a shrinkage in the use of metal coinage, and between then and the fifth century there were periods when copper coins were reported as being out of circulation. The result was a reversion to barter trade in many places.

With the wane of central authority, governmental functions were often monopolized by powerful local landowning families. Despite decrees to the contrary, it became common practice for wealthy clans to enclose large amounts of public land for their own use. Helpless families and individuals frequently attached themselves as *k'o* or "guests" (retainers) to such a clan, thereby gaining support and security

[46] Census figures recorded in the dynastic histories indicate a drop from about 48 million to about 16 million between the years A.D. 140 and 280. The two sets of figures, however, are in actual fact useless for comparative purposes, because only the first seems to be a moderately complete census of the total population, whereas the second is almost surely merely an enumeration of the country's taxpayers. Cf. Hans Bielenstein, "The Census of China during the Period 2-742 A.D.," *Bulletin of the Museum of Far Eastern Antiquities*, Stockholm, No. 19 (1947), 125-163, esp. 128, 139-145, 153-155.

for themselves, as well as exemption from the levies and services imposed by whatever central government existed. Similar reasons caused other people to become Buddhist monks, or to attach themselves or their lands to powerful monasteries. Like the rich families, such monasteries enjoyed special privileges. They commonly owned large amounts of land, and not infrequently acted as trade centers or money lenders.

Individuals who became *k'o* were hereditarily owned and could be transferred as gifts to friends; the chief difference between them and slaves (who also existed) was that unlike the latter they could not be sold. This institution was on several occasions recognized by the ruling dynasty, which tried to regularize it by placing limitations on the number of *k'o* permitted to be held by protectors according to the latters' rank. On the other hand, we also read of cases in which slaves and *k'o* were freed by imperial decree and drafted as soldiers or transport workers in spite of objections from powerful families.[47]

Aside from such general phenomena reminiscent of feudal ages elsewhere, attention should be drawn to a political move on the part of the founder of the Western Chin Dynasty, Emperor Wu (265-289), which, though not "feudal" itself according to the definition of this book, might conceivably, under differing circumstances, have led to the eventual development of an institutionalized feudal system. On his accession, he enfeoffed twenty-seven or more of his relatives as *wang* or kings, giving them *kuo* or principalities converted from former commanderies and ranging in size from 5,000 to 20,000 families. Each had its own private army and staff of administrative officials, modelled on that of the central government. In addition, there was created an indeterminate number of lesser dukedoms and marquisates.

At first the new nobles apparently preferred the pleasures of life in the capital to living on their own fiefs. In 277, however, they were compelled by imperial edict to retire to the countryside. Three year later, following the unification of the empire, the central governmen

[47] The above data (save those on population, for which see preceding note are conveniently summarized in Yang Lien-sheng, "Notes on the Economic Hi tory of the Chin Dynasty," *Harvard Journal of Asiastic Studies*, IX (1946), 11 117. Cf. also the pertinent data in Wang Yi-t'ung, "Slaves and Other Compar ble Social Groups during the Northern Dynasties (386-618)," *ibid.*, XVI (1953 293-364, and in Etienne Balazs, "Le traité économique du 'Souei-Chou,' *T'oung Pao*, XLII (1953), 113-329. As clearly indicated by Wang (pp. 344-358 *k'o* or "guests" were in actual fact only one (perhaps the most conspicuous) several serf-like social groups, whose status was little better than that of slaves.

attempted a general disarmament program, which, however, failed on the one hand to apply to the new aristocracy, and on the other led to the selling of many government arms to the Hsiung-nu or Huns. The combination of these events was disastrous. The Revolt of the Eight Kings, beginning in 291, was not suppressed until 306. This left the dynasty so weakened that it fell an easy prey to the Huns and was completely expelled by them from North China ten years later. Had the Chin rulers proved more competent, it is conceivable that the Period of Disunity might have been shortened by two centuries, and that the domination of the North by the barbarians might have been avoided almost entirely.[48]

Was the Period of Disunity an Age of Feudalism? Despite the facts just cited, the answer to this question is definitely no if we accept as valid the central criterion for feudalism advanced in the Introductory Essay of this book. To quote this essay: "Feudalism is primarily a method of government . . . in which the essential relation is not that between ruler and subject, nor state and citizen, but between lord and vassal." Such a relationship did not exist during the Period of Disunity, save in sporadic instances.[49]

During this age the main struggle was no longer really one of bureaucracy against feudalism, or centralism against localism, for this had already been decided in favor of the former several centuries earlier. Rather it was that described by us in Section IV: the struggle between the Chinese agrarian way of life and the nomadic pastoral way of life. In this struggle, the Period of Disunity represented a phase of nomad ascendancy, just as the Han Dynasty before it and the Sui and T'ang dynasties after it represented phases of Chinese ascendancy.

The Chinese migrants who fled southward from the fourth century onward carried with them the typical Chinese social pattern. For those with money and influence it was, despite political uncertainty,

[48] For these events, see Teng Chih-ch'eng, *Chung-hua Erh-ch'ien-nien Shih* [Two Thousand Years of Chinese History] (Shanghai, 1934), II, 40ff.

[49] It is only fair to point out that this verdict—based as it is on rather specific political criteria—is not universally shared by all scholars. Balazs, *op. cit.*, for example, several times uses the word "féodalité" with reference to the Period of Disunity (without, however, defining what he means by the term). A good example is the sentence on p. 125 of his article which begins: "However, opposed to the feudalism of the Chinese baron emigrés in the South, there is in the North the new feudalism of the Turco-Mongol conquerors. . . ." Concerning possible differing interpretations of the nature of Chinese society during the Period of Disunity, see also the concluding paragraphs of this essay.

a boom period. Great estates were created out of land which, through the efforts of innumerable peasant tenants and "colonizers," was cleared, drained, and put under cultivation. The holders of these estates, the landed gentry, were interlinked or identical with the members of the official bureaucracy. Their common characteristic was that they all belonged to "old families"—families with lengthy pedigrees and cultured backgrounds. Like members of an exclusive club, they were careful to bar all parvenus from their ranks.

An example of how they did this is found in the system known as the "rectification of the nine categories" (*chiu-p'in chung-cheng*), used as a basis for making official appointments. Under this system, government boards in different localities periodically graded the local populace into nine ranks, ostensibly according to their moral and intellectual qualifications, but actually on the basis of family backgrounds. In the words of a Chin Dynasty critic, Liu Yi (died 285): "In the upper categories there are no 'cold gates' [socially insignificant families]; in the lower categories there are no 'hereditary families.'" It is hardly surprising that few people from the "cold gates" ever gained official rank.[50]

Yet though the men who ruled South China thus constituted a privileged oligarchy, for whom family and social connections were of paramount importance, they did not form a titled nobility nor belong to a feudal hierarchy of overlords and vassals. Though their government was weakened by corruption, incompetence, and political strife, its form followed that of the Ch'in and Han bureaucracies. It cannot, therefore, according to the definition used in this book, be said to have been a feudal government.

In the North, the Huns, Tibetans, and other invaders had their own tribal organizations, varying from group to group, but all reflecting to some degree their pastoral background. Beneath them, however, the overwhelming bulk of the population remained Chinese in culture and economy. In dealing with this Chinese population, the aliens had four main alternatives. On the one hand, if they wished to preserve their own way of life, they might drive the Chinese peasants south, convert them into slave herdsmen, exterminate them, or allow them to remain as subjugated peasants, while installing themselves over them as a ruling military caste. On the other hand, they had the

[50] Though statistical data confirming the great stability and exclusiveness of the gentry class during the Chin Dynasty have not yet been made, Eberhard has prepared comparable data covering the Northern Wei Dynasty (386-535). See note 52 below.

possibility of deliberately giving up their own nomadism and assimilating themselves as much as possible to the Chinese way of life.[51]

None of the alien dynasties that attempted any of the three former alternatives succeeded in surviving for more than a few decades. The fourth and peaceful alternative, most notably tried by the comparatively long-lived Northern Wei (386-535), yielded greater success because it enlisted the invaluable cooperation of the Chinese landed gentry. Yet in the end it too led to the same result: through the very fact of making themselves a part of Chinese society, the conquerors lost their political identity and disappeared from history. Thus it is significant that when China was reunited, the dynasty that did this, the Sui, was Chinese and not alien, though it originated in the North. In the long run the tribal organization of the nomad could not withstand its new Chinese environment.[52]

The process of Sinification of the barbarians is reflected in the land policies of North and South. Under the Han, the general policy—formulated but hardly enforced—had been to set limitations on the amount of land owned by wealthy individuals. During the Period of Disunity this policy shifted to that known as the "equalization of land" (*chün t'ien*), under which peasant families received land allotments from the government on the basis of the age, sex, and number of their members, these allotments being periodically equalized through subsequent readjustment.

This policy, which represented an effort to extend centralized control at the expense of local interests, was never, however, more than partially effective. This was not merely because of the technical difficulties involved, but more especially because the policy in general applied only to "government land"—that is, to land not privately owned; in particular, it probably extended only very rarely to the estates of the powerful landed gentry.[53] Significantly, the policy was advocated most

[51] Eberhard, *History of China*, p. 112. In the fourth chapter of his *Conquerors and Rulers*, Eberhard discusses these several alternatives in detail.

[52] In his *Das Toba-Reich Nordchinas: Eine soziologische Untersuchung* (Leiden, 1949), Eberhard has prepared statistical analyses (also touched on in *Conquerors and Rulers*, pp. 116f.), indicating that under the Northern Wei Dynasty, only 28 per cent of the known leading gentry families were of alien stock; that of the remaining indigenous gentry families, no less than 92 per cent had already belonged to the leading political class prior to the establishment of the dynasty; and that as the dynasty wore on, the importance of the alien gentry steadily diminished while that of the Chinese gentry increased.

[53] This point is emphasized by Balazs. Cf. his translation (pp. 278-281) of a Chinese document of c. 577-580, from which we gain a vivid picture of the great gap between theory and application of the land regulations at that time.

actively in the long-settled and heavily populated North, especially during and following the period of Sinification of the Northern Wei Dynasty. In the South, where a sort of "colonial" expansionism was taking place, and where the thinner population made land control less needed, little was done along this line, even on paper. In this respect, then, the alien North was less "feudal" than the Chinese South.

VI. Conclusion

In the Introductory Essay of this volume, criteria of two sorts have been advanced for the identification of feudalism: those that define it in static terms, i.e., try to tell us what feudalism itself is; and those that define it in dynamic terms, i.e., try to tell us how it operates and what are the attendant conditions under which it is likely to arise.

The static criteria include those of vassal-lord relationships (regarded as particularly important); a personalized government which is most effective on the local level and has little separation of political functions; heredity of functions; a system of landholding consisting of fiefs given in return for service; regularization of the rights of the lord over the peasant; existence of private armies; and a code of honor in which military obligations are stressed.

The dynamic criteria include those of an antecedent empire which has disintegrated; the impact of barbarian invasion; the outstripping of economic unity by political unity, leading to the waning of central authority and rise of local magnates exercising considerable *de facto* authority; monopolization of military techniques by a special group; warfare as a means of building larger political units out of lesser ones; and the existence of a universal religion which makes of the feudal period an "age of faith."

If we apply these criteria to China, a curious fact emerges: the Chou period, on the whole, meets the static criteria better than it does the dynamic criteria, whereas the Period of Disunity, on the whole, meets the dynamic criteria better (though with certain qualifications) than it does the static criteria. In other words, though the Chou Dynasty produced a genuine feudal system, it seems to have done so through forces, some of which, at least, differed considerably from those commonly associated with feudalism elsewhere. The Period of Disunity, on the other hand, though it experienced conditions theoretically favorable to feudalism, did not see the rise of a true feudal system. The superficial conclusion, if we compare this situation with other civilizations is that differing conditions may give birth to similar institutions, and similar conditions may give birth to differing institutions.

From the point of view of our particular case study, however, the second part of this generalization requires qualification. In Section IV we have already tried to suggest what may have been some of the important forces underlying ancient Chinese society. The important point to remember is that these forces not only operated during the feudal age itself, but also deeply influenced the entire later development of Chinese society. This continuing influence explains why the Period of Disunity developed the way it did, despite the appearance of certain conditions at that time which in a different society might have led to a full-blown feudal system.

In conclusion, the writer would like to draw attention once more to the definition of feudalism made in the Introductory Essay, which has been that followed in the present paper. Feudalism, as thus defined, is "primarily a method of government, not an economic or social system." Because of this political emphasis, the Introductory Essay, while recognizing the importance for feudalism of certain economic phenomena, denies that these phenomena are themselves decisive factors unless occurring in conjunction with a rather specific set of political relationships.

There are many writers, however, who would prefer to broaden the concept of feudalism by applying it to a wider range of landlord-tenant relationships, the common feature of which is that they in effect bind the peasant so closely to the particular land he cultivates as to make him little better than the serf of his landlord proprietor. Such relationships—often based more on economic than on political sanctions—do not necessarily have to occur only within the specific political framework we have been discussing. In recent years wide currency has been given to this broadened interpretation of feudalism by numerous writers who have used it to describe conditions characteristic of many Asian agrarian societies.

In the case of China, such a more generalized concept would almost surely require a modification of some of the conclusions we have been making. It is evident, for example, that the "equalization of land" program of the Northern Wei Dynasty, though no doubt intended, at least in good part, to improve the livelihood of the peasant, at the same time—to the extent that it actually operated—severely curtailed his freedom of economic choice by confining him to whatever plot of land happened to be allotted to him. As such, it could be interpreted as an instrument for the economic control of the peasantry, and hence as a "feudal" institution, even though, since this control operated from the state rather than from a personal overlord, some special term like "state feudalism" or "bureaucratic feudalism" might have to be coined for it.[54]

Such a formulation rests on an interpretation of feudalism which, while often convenient for purposes of ordinary discussion, lacks the precision of the narrower political interpretation, and has the further defect that it tends to obliterate the all-important distinction between China's bureaucratic-gentry form of society and other non-bureaucratic forms found elsewhere. On the other hand, its merit is that it centers attention upon vital economic factors such as the political approach may tend to overlook, and which, despite their importance for China, have hitherto received not nearly the systematic study they deserve.

[54] The latter term has, in fact, already been used. See, for example, Joseph Needham, "The Chinese Contribution to Science and Technology," p. 221 of *Reflections on Our Age* (London, 1948), where Needham remarks that "Chinese society has been called 'bureaucratic feudalism.'" Cf. also the comparable Chinese term, *kuan-liao chu-yi chung-yang chi-ch'üan ti feng-chien chih-tu* or "bureaucratic centralized feudalism," as used in Fan Wen-lan, chief editor, *Chung-kuo T'ung-shih Chien-pien* [A Short General History of China]. Thus in the first (1947) through third (1949) printings of this work, Chap. I of Pt. II bears the title: "Establishment of Bureaucratic Centralized Feudalism—Ch'in." In the 1950 printing, however, this is changed to read: "Establishment of a Bureaucratic Centralized National State." For the relationship of Fan Wen-lan's theory of Chinese society to those of other Chinese scholars, see Eberhard, *Conquerors and Rulers*, p. 50. For a further discussion of the views of various Chinese scholars concerning the nature of Chinese society, see Benjamin Schwartz, "A Marxist Controversy on China," *Far Eastern Quarterly*, XIII (1954), 143-153.

V · FEUDALISM IN ANCIENT MESOPOTAMIA AND IRAN

BY BURR C. BRUNDAGE

1. Introduction

THE search for feudal institutions in the history of the ancient Near East is fraught with great difficulties. Some of these are the usual difficulties of working upon ages of political fragmentation which leave scanty records, but to them must be added the chances of archaeology since the record is partly in archaeological form. Moreover, the present inquiry is for the purposes of comparing institutions in different times and places; it will be of little avail, then, unless institutions can be defined closely enough to show how far the terms which have come into use for European feudal institutions may properly be applied to those of the Near East. This special requirement is sometimes very hard to meet, but we recognize the responsibility to check the applications of those terms which have been made by others who were not especially concerned with their effect in comparative study. These circumstances—those inherent in the material and those inherent in the special aims of the study—are amply sufficient to warrant a strong note of caution at the outset. The reader will not find answers to all questions, and in particular he will not find a definitive judgment as to whether feudalism ever existed in the ancient Near East in anything approximating its full development in medieval Europe.

Localism in government, private armies, and private courts are key elements in a feudal society, as well as, in many cases, a recollection of a former political unity. Other elements are subinfeudation, homage, fief-holding, and personal immunities; these will be noted where and when they appear. We believe, with the Introductory Essay, that feudalism is essentially a political phenomenon, and that questions of church and land tenure are not by necessity relevant to the definition, however enlightening they may be in other respects. It is, however, exactly on the subject of political relationships that our texts are singularly silent; so in some cases we have been forced to rely perhaps too heavily upon the facts of land tenure. As for the attempt to visualize feudalism in the ancient Near East as a process, our meager documentation does not permit us that luxury.

II. Political Institutions before the Kassite Period

The political form of the entire pre-Kassite period in Mesopotamia was that of a culturally continuous but war-englobed society in which the autonomous city-states strove energetically to maintain their individuality—which, of course, they equated with survival. Periodic disturbances of magnitude occurred in this sprawling structure, giving rise to increasingly successful attempts to realize benefits of a larger political integration. The cities of Akkad, Ur, Mari, Babylon, and others exercised hegemony over all or parts of the Tigris-Euphrates Valley, and the kingdoms and empires they constructed have become milestones in Mesopotamian history. Did feudalism or feudal elements exist in this pre-Kassite period?

In spite of the slow crystallization towards centralized empire in this period, we believe that there was never any fundamental deviation from the polity of the city-state, and we are almost tempted to add that as a consequence there could have been no *indigenous* institution even remotely resembling feudalism in the Valley prior to the Kassites.

A congeries of city-states—such as here in south and central Mesopotamia or later in Hellas—seems an even more unlikely setting for feudal developments than does a highly centralized territorial state. Under the latter, the forms at least, and some of the substance, of fief-holding and vassalage can exist, as well as many of the social prerogatives of a feudal aristocracy. If this be true, then we must seek for traces of feudalism in the Valley in periods when the typical or indigenous political climate was altered by the introduction of new elements. These conditions can be found especially in those periods following the invasions which so liberally dot Mesopotamian and general Near Eastern history.

In the far background lie the Obeidian and proto-Sumerian strata of Mesopotamian culture. Speiser's statement, however, that "the Sumerian city-state represents a commercial theocracy in which private enterprise had an important place,"[1] is not encouraging to those who would see feudal elements in this period. And back of this period of temple-dominated life lies Jacobsen's "primitive democracy,"[2] wherein the Sumerian city was essentially republican, having formulated its constitu-

[1] *Journal of the American Oriental Society*, Supplement No. 4 (1939), p. 27

[2] T. Jacobsen, "Primitive Democracy in Ancient Mesopotamia," *Journal of Near Eastern Studies*, II (1943), 159-172.

tion into an upper and a lower assembly with plenary powers. The very beginnings of Sumerian domination in the lower Valley might possibly tell another story if we possessed sufficient remains to judge. The conjecture may be made here that Kramer's recently propounded Heroic Age of the Sumerians (following Obeid and preceding Early Dynastic I), who were themselves invaders from the eastern mountains, may have been followed by an age having feudal tendencies. In that early period Kramer would see the lower part of the Valley preempted by a rich culture, the Irano-Semitic, the irruption of a dominant military caste of barbarian Sumerians no longer subject to tribal law, an institution of personal following very much like the Germanic comitatus, and finally the hacking out of crude principalities.[3] If correct, this hypothesis might date the first appearance of elements leading in a feudal direction to a significantly early period (some time in the last quarter of the fourth millennium B.C. and the first century of the third millennium), but still subsequent to the *floruit* of a more sophisticated, semi-urbanized culture.[4] This, however, is purely speculative.

We must now deal briefly with the coming of the Amorites into the Valley around 2000 B.C., for, by use of terms borrowed from European history, it has been implied frequently that feudal elements begin to emerge in Mesopotamia by the middle period of the Amorite First Babylonian Dynasty.

If fully developed feudal conditions existed in the period of the greatest Amorite ruler, Hammurabi, we would surely expect to see hints of it in the law code promulgated by that remarkable administrator. Such is not the case. All classes of men mentioned in the Code come within its terms. Royal judges are indicated, and in cases of adultery, which perforce must apply to the noble class as well as others, we see the king exercising dominium over the lives of all his subjects. There is thus no private jurisdiction, nor are we told of any special class of immunities affecting the nobility as a whole. To clinch the overriding incidence of the Code, we note that the state in certain cases secured greater redress for damages than did private persons (law 8); and the responsibility of the state and municipal government is amply outlined, as for instance in the case of unrecovered stolen goods.

[3] *American Journal of Archaeology*, LII (1928), 156-164.

[4] Kramer's theory is based almost entirely upon analogy from the realm of literary genre, and can scarcely be tested archaeologically as yet. I find it difficult to harmonize with Jacobsen's "primitive democracy"; if Kramer's idea is correct, there is some conflict, but perhaps that is with the word "democracy."

Laws 26-41 refer to military obligations connected with the usufruct of certain lands, orchards, or flocks, a type of service known as *ilku*, and Meek in his translation has used the term "feudal" to describe these.[5] This group of laws, while it definitely refers to precarious benefice-holding, does not give us any reason to infer personal vassalage under the king with bucellarian or jurisdictional rights, and the situation politically is therefore best equated with the landholding of the Roman *limitanei milites*. It is not therefore essentially aristocratic.

Private armies are by implication denied throughout the pertinent sections of the Code. In the king's army the hiring of substitutes for military service seems to have been fairly common (laws 26, 33) which certainly does not bespeak a class which monopolized the prerogatives of war. Furthermore, we see that high military officers stand in a legally regulated position of responsibility toward the foot soldiers under them (law 34), which fact again tells strongly against the existence of private troops. The only specifically stated immunities from military service apply alone to land owned by the church (law 182).

From the Code of Hammurabi we see a class of nobles, as we would expect, but neither private armies nor private jurisdiction, and localism in government only under the shadow of a strong state. And inasmuch as the law codes of Lipit-Ishtar of Isin and Bilalama of Eshnunna, preceding the Hammurabi Code and apparented to it, similarly give us no reason to assume a developed feudalism in the Valley, we may conclude that our investigation should begin with the Kassite period, which overlaps and succeeds that of the First Dynasty of Babylon.

We cannot overlook the fact, however, that the Amorite kings of the First Babylonian Dynasty had created a group of military dependents who were at times granted certain immunities in their persons. At the same time they were professional officers in the royal army, and the estates they held did not confer on them governmental or jurisdictional prerogatives. We might remove the dilemma by assuming that some of the elements of feudalism were present in the Old Babylonian period, but were disparate and muted by the stringent and unrelaxed exercise of the central power. I can see no evidence that the *ilku* and personal immunities which obtained during the First Dynasty of Babylon influenced the development of feudalism in the Kassite period, which we must now discuss.[6]

[5] *Ancient Near Eastern Texts Relating to the Old Testament*, ed. J. B. Pritchard (Princeton, 1950), pp. 163ff.

[6] A private communication to the author from Mr. Taha Baqir, archaeologist

III. The Kassite Regime

The Kassites were a hill people who inhabited the valleys back of the first high ranges of the Zagros Mountains. The splendor and sophistication of civilization in the Valley under the kings of the dynasty of Hammurabi initiated among these outlanders the magnetic "forest-to-farm-to-forum" movement with which we are so familiar from the later history of the Roman Empire. After their first violent attempt to invade the empire by force during the reign of Samsu-iluna, son and successor of Hammurabi, had failed, they continued to exert pressure—this time, however, by the slow, osmotic process of drifting in by small groups and taking up tasks as hired farm hands, grooms, and common laborers. We would also expect to see them as mercenaries, but of this we have small evidence. This process continued for almost a century and a half before they elevated their first king, Gandash, to the throne. So began the long, inglorious, and generally very obscure passage of Lower Mesopotamian history known as the Kassite period (ca. 1595-1171 B.C.).

Unlike the Amorites, the Kassites do not appear to have assimilated with the native peoples of the Valley. This fact alone should lead us to guess that they established an aristocracy of a different order from the Babylonian upper classes.

Beginning with Gandash, commercial activity showed signs of strangulation—perhaps the result of the ineptitude of the first Kassite house. From village holdings and collective tribal lands the king now acquired by purchase or outright requisition large tracts of land to distribute among his favorites, priests, seers, and others. The charters recording these grants under the king's seal were inscribed upon stelae, termed *kudurru*, whose purpose was to invoke divine sanction for the protection of the newly acquired property. The custom probably arose at this time because the Kassite government was inadequate to the task of safeguarding private property. The royal officials, however, actually laid out the land in question. Of these transactions it has been said:

---

in the service of the Iraq government, is pertinent at this point: "Unfortunately our partial work at Aqar Quf has not shed any new light on the subject. . . . As far as I know, feudalism in the strict sense of the term (e.g., the European type of the Middle Ages) seems to be lacking in Babylonia. My general feeling, and perhaps I am mistaken, is that if something like feudalism had occurred in certain periods (e.g., the Kassite period) it would have been similar to the type of feudalism in some phases of the Arab Caliphate (*iqta*) or like Ottoman feudalism; that is, it was chiefly due to weakness or deterioration in the central government."

"Le fief créé par le roi est attribué à titre héréditaire et définitif, et non point à titre précaire comme les biens ilkou de la période précédente; le donataire reste soumis aux charges et impôts dont ce fief est grevé, à moins d'obtenir—et c'est le cas le plus fréquent—une tablette de franchises."[7]

By terms of these charters of immunity, the king would give over such rights upon the lands in question as the collections of various levies, assessments and taxes, the *corvée* upon the dikes and canals, water and pasture rights, and the right of military protection.[8] We are also informed that these benefices became hereditary, at least in some cases.[9] One benefice in particular was in litigation under the crown for the duration of three reigns.[10] In this instance we can see that the king could bestow the estate if the owner died without issue, or if there were a dispute over ownership. Yet apparently the crown was not powerful enough to secure reversion, except to grant the benefice out again.

Cities, and of course villages, were also from time to time parcelled out as benefices to deserving officials, generally without immunity from military service. Such grants may have been subject to recall by the crown.[11] It should be noted that this was in the later period when the Kassite kings were deified. Here at least was the fiction of unity in the state, and perhaps a fair amount of the substance.

We do not know what were the *personal* relationships which bound together benefice-holder and king, and we can therefore state nothing definite concerning Kassite vassalage (or other form of dependency if the word vassalage is not justified) as it was conceived apart from benefice-holding. Possibly as time went on there was a general loosening of the feudalistic elements in Kassite society—this is an assumption we make as a corollary of what seems to be the gradual strengthening of the central power. Ultimately, however, Kassite rule, ground between the upper and nether millstones of Assyria and Elam, after years of bloody struggle died out in the Valley.

[7] L. Delaporte, *La Mesopotamie: Les Civilisations Babylonienne et Assyrienne* (Paris, 1923), p. 113.

[8] A. T. Olmstead, *History of Assyria* (New York, 1923), p. 512; and Delaporte, *Mesopotamie*, pp. 114ff. where a typical *kudurru* is quoted at length.

[9] For an instance where a fief granted by Kurigalzu III was later confirmed to the descendants of the original patentee by a succeeding king, see *Cambridge Ancient History*, II, 244.

[10] L. W. King, *Babylonian Boundary-Stones and Memorial Tablets in the British Museum* (London, 1912), pp. 7-18.

[11] H. Radau, *Babylonian Expedition of the University of Pennsylvania*, Series A: *Cuneiform Texts*, XVII (1908), Part I, 49ff.

Before we leave this area, we should note that the unsettled conditions of the times under the succeeding Pashe Dynasty repeat the pattern. The great king Nebuchadnezzar I, as a reward for meritorious military service, granted to one of his captains of the charioteers a march on the dangerous Elamite frontier. The villages in this march were granted immunity from all crown taxes and levies, and the inhabitants were freed from the incidence of arrest by imperial officers and from the billeting of soldiers. In the same reign similar immunities were bestowed upon lands granted to certain priests in the name of their god.[12] This is possibly evidence that feudal vestiges survived Kassite domination in the Valley.

IV. Hatti and Mitanni

We must turn now to a consideration of those regions peripheral to Babylonian culture and briefly describe each in turn. Although, in the cases we shall review, Hatti, Mitanni, Syria-Palestine, and Assyria had all absorbed the basic Mesopotamian culture, the feudal or similar institutions we can see in them are not necessarily related generically to each other. On the contrary, it is our feeling that whatever feudal comparisons can be drawn between them and their congener, Kassite Babylonia, are in general the result of a simple uniformity which will be detailed in the summation.

At the source of the great northern and eastern invasions of the first half of the second millennium were the Indo-European movements out of an original homeland in the steppe of southern Russia. The Kassites, an Asianic people, had been somewhat influenced by the eastern segment of that group, the Indo-Iranians. They were not, however, the only people bowled out of the mountainous rim of the Fertile Crescent in advance of these widespread ethnic disturbances. Another people speaking an Asianic tongue, the Hurrians, now under the domination of a closely knit Indo-Iranian aristocracy, flooded across northern Mesopotamia and Syria. In this open area they ultimately founded the powerful state of Mitanni.

The western segment of the Indo-Europeans from Russia moved two prongs down into the warmer lands, one into the Balkans, and the other, which here concerns us, across the Bosporus or through the Caucasus into the Near East. These conquering tribes subdued the Asianic inhabitants of Anatolia, who had been under the tutelage of an attenuated Sumerian culture, and set up a group of kingdoms in central,

[12] King, *Babylonian Boundary-Stones*, pp. 29-36, 96-98.

eastern, and southern Asia Minor, chief of which was the Hittite state called Hatti, with its capital at Hattusas (modern Boghaz-koy).[13] Over the native element they ruled as a small elite class. In this respect the situation is analogous to that which obtained among the Kassites and Hurrians.

The Old Hittite Empire was formed by the expansion outward of one of the small city-states in the center of the Anatolian plateau. As its neighbors were successively brought to heel, the king generally installed his sons as princes over the new appanages. These princes were assured, by written contract, guarantees of the integrity of their territories and of the hereditary descent of their power—a type of private agreement between lord and man, the great king remaining in theory, nevertheless, the sole sovereign.[14] The dependent kings in return owed undivided homage, tribute, and quotas of armed men to their Hittite overlord. The performance of homage was an annual ceremony wherein the dependent prince was constrained to appear in the royal capital in person. In the New Empire, following a temporary collapse of the monarchy, this system of princes (not necessarily of the blood royal) was still utilized for newly conquered provinces, but within the confines of the kingdom itself gave way to the installation of royal governors recallable at will.[15] A petty king of one territory might at the same time be an appointed governor in another. It is of interest to note that this Hittite system of government, feudal or not, does not follow upon the disintegration of an antecedent centralized rule, for no great autonomous power preceded it on the plateau, unless Akkadian or Assyrian rule from the Valley be brought into the picture, which is a tenuous assumption in the light of the known facts. The system, then, is a makeshift whereupon an increasingly powerful conception of kingship is enabled to erect itself and grow.

Besides these petty kings and governors, there appears to have been an Indo-European warrior nobility centered more closely around the king, perhaps a tribal inheritance. While the dependent kings held power by written agreement, this noble caste held theirs by traditional prerogative. This can be proved by reference to the Assembly of Notables.[16] Two classes appear, the "Great Ones" and the warriors. The

[13] For excellent references see A. Goetze, *Kulturgeschichte des alten Orients* III, Part I: *Kleinasien* (Munich, 1933).

[14] L. Delaporte, *Les Hittites* (Paris, 1936), pp. 180, 196.

[15] *Les Hittites*, pp. 181ff.

[16] Delaporte (*Les Hittites*, pp. 171-172) considers the existence of this assembly

lords, or Great Ones, were certainly members of the Assembly. They had to swear fealty to the crown at periodic convocations expressly called for that purpose, and further, they were obligated to provide armed men and chariotry and follow their king in battle. In the Assembly, however, they exercised the right of sitting in judgment upon the king in the case of a crime committed against the royal blood, the king having to appear before them in person, and they were, in the early period at least, called upon to ratify the choice of the royal heir.[17] The king swore in the Assembly to uphold the privileges of the lords. At the same time, the social caste was not so rigid but that a nobleman, for certain high crimes of state, might be degraded to the social level of a peasant or worker.[18]

The warriors were men, no doubt, of Indo-European blood and speech like the king and the Great Ones, who were supported by landed grants from the king, though their fields appear to have been no larger than what could maintain a family and equip them as fighting men. Certain groups of warriors were by written charter exempt from the *corvée*.[19] The king is expressly charged to respect their prerogatives as well as those of the lords.

It is difficult to join this picture of the social structure with what we know of land tenure from the Hittite law code because the benefice-holders mentioned therein are not identified expressly by the ranks of nobility mentioned above.[20] There appear to have been three types of land-holding, exclusive of the tenure of the clergy and certain collective properties belonging to towns. The ordinary holding could be bought and sold, but at all times owed taxes or service to the crown. There was additionally the land held by the *ḫipparas* man (the warrior class?) which was permanently entailed in the family and owed service to the

---

as evidence of the *feudal* structure of the Hittite state. I do not believe that this institution alone allows the strict use of the term. He further makes the following unsupported statement: "Les Hittites indo-européens sont venus d'Europe; c'est de là qu'ils ont apporté l'idée du régime féodal: on la retrouvera plus tard dans les institutions monarchiques des poèmes homériques." This statement is echoed by G. Contenau, *La Civilisation des Hittites et des Hurrites du Mitanni* (Paris, 1948), p. 111. There is absolutely no evidence that any of the known Indo-European peoples practiced feudalism before their entry into the Near East. That feudalism can be imported like an article of commerce by an unorganized people moving into a high-level cultural area would be difficult to maintain.

[17] Delaporte, *Les Hittites*, pp. 63, 66ff., 170-172.

[18] *Les Hittites*, pp. 66, 184. [19] *Les Hittites*, p. 185.

[20] English translation to be found in *Ancient Near Eastern Texts*, pp. 188-197. The laws cited from the Hittite code are from this translation. Laws 39-42 and 46-56 are pertinent.

king (law 48). This *ḫipparas* man in his person possessed important privileges of freedom from arrest and immunity from the consequences of theft (law 49), the community in the latter case having to bear the fine. There was a third class of landed proprietor (not the *ḫipparas* man) who was specifically exempt from services to the crown. This group may have been true feudatories with immunities, though we are not told whether they were nobles, whether their privileges included private jurisdiction, or indeed whether their estates were large enough to include serfs. As a sign of the granting of such a benefice, the king bestowed upon the patentee a loaf from his table (law 47).

In its broad outlines the picture is not hard to discern. Three elements are present in the Hittite state: the tribal peerage, presumably inherited from the past, out of which the nobility grows; kingship, in some part no doubt of primitive provenience, but coming rapidly to approximate the pattern of Near Eastern kingship; and the system of dependent princes. These three elements, with some similarities to European feudalism, nevertheless did not produce a full-blown feudal society. Why they did not must remain doubtful, but three matters concerning the power and functions of the monarchy should be considered in this connection. First, the Hittite lands were pressed vigorously and continuously by wild tribes around them, notably by the Gasgas in the littoral mountains to the north. Such a threat by no means rules out the probability of feudal developments, but in this instance it led instead to a centralized military power to protect the plateau. Hatti in consequence was a warlike state comparable to Assyria, the king appearing annually at the head of a standing army pieced out with the infantry and chariotry of his dependents.[21] Secondly, we are aware of the profound importance of the crown as the religious guardian of the state and the intermediary between the people and the whims of the gods. The well-being of the state and the fertility of the fields depended upon the king. The nobles did not share this tremendous responsibility with him. Lastly, there was the great Sumero-Semitic tradition of legalism planted at an early date on the plateau, the nomistic sanctions of which militated powerfully against too great particularism in jurisdiction. The Hittite law code was the king's law, was dispensed by his officials, and apparently prevailed over a large part, if not all, of the empire.

The Mitannian picture is less well known to us, but seems much the same—a strong monarchy supported by a horse-breeding aristocracy,

[21] Delaporte, *Les Hittites*, pp. 206ff.

the *maryannu.*[22] From the Nuzu excavations it is clear that a system of land-holding obtained similar to that of the Hittite *ḫipparas*, lands held by commoners in return for either military service or the performance of the *corvée*,[23] but we are not told whether a like system was extended to the nobility. In a treaty from this period we have an explicit reference to the dangerously independent position which the Hurrian *maryannu* could assume during the breakdown of the central power in the kingdom of Mitanni.[24] This aristocracy is stated to have possessed both charioteers and foot soldiers.

Consideration of the Hurrian state of Mitanni leads us directly to Assyria, for the two were mortal enemies during the fourteenth century. Greater Assyria, as it stretched across northern Mesopotamia later in history, was duplicating in territorial terms the former Hurrian achievement of the fifteenth century. But before we turn to this later period, we must first survey the contemporary picture to the west.[25]

[22] For the *maryannu* as a social caste see R. T. O'Callaghan, *Aram Naharaim* (Rome, 1948), pp. 66-68.

[23] The typical Nuzian sales-adoption cannot be forced into a feudal picture inasmuch as such transfers of *ilku*-land pertain apparently to a village class, warriors in some cases perhaps, but not of the upper nobility. For the sales-adoption controversy see P. M. Purvis, "Commentary on Nuzi Real Property in he Light of Recent Studies," *Journal of Near Eastern Studies*, IV (1945).

[24] *Ancient Near Eastern Texts*, p. 318.

[25] Other regions within the spread of Mesopotamian culture might be brought n if enough information were available. The greater Anatolian massif throughout he history of the ancient Near East seems to have been particularly congenial o feudal tendencies, and would by itself make an interesting study in this respect. Concerning Urartu, perennial foe of Assyria in the Vannic region, Nicolas Adontz ays, "L'état d'Urartu était basé sur la même conception que celle qui dominait es Empires d'Assur et de Hati. C'était une monarchie féodale, d'òu le titre de roi des rois' des souverains de l'Urartu. . . . L'organisation de la cour royale n'est as connue, mais elle ne pouvait être autre que celle de la cour assyrienne" *Histoire d'Arménie: Les origines*, Paris, 1946, p. 215). By the *rabute* (Great Ones) of Urartu one understands "peut-être les grands seigneurs terriens dont es uns, issus des anciens dynastes déchus, auraient gardé une partie de leur ropriété patrimoniale; les autres été dotés par les rois de terre à titre de fiefs" p. 219).

In the Hellenistic period, and therefore by implication in the preceding Persian eriod, Pontus and Cappadocia preserved these tendencies. "As in Pontus, so in Cappadocia the land belonged to the king or to the holders of large estates, both acred and secular. . . . [The priests of Comana and Venasa] ranked second and ird, respectively, to the king himself. The other principal landholders were the reat nobles, who probably had their seats in some of the strongholds known to ave existed in Cappadocia. They appear to have enjoyed greater power here than Pontus, and their position seems to have been comparable to the barons of urope in the Middle Ages. When the royal house eventually became extinct,

v. Syria and Assyria

The second millennium in Syria-Palestine had opened auspiciously with a period of gradual resettlement and reurbanization following the decline of Early Bronze in that area. The revival of Egyptian activities in this whole littoral area and the now expanding contacts with Mesopotamia introduce us to a slowly quickening culture in an Egyptianizing Amorite-Canaanite milieu.

A stunning series of invasions shattered this semi-rustic world. Between 1750 and 1600 B.C., those same waves of mixed Asianic and Indo-European warriors which had produced Kassite Babylonia, Hatti, and Mitanni now surged down the coast, seizing power most firmly in northern and eastern Syria, but also descending far down into Palestine.[26] The period which they initiate in Middle Bronze II is one of much greater commercial interchange than heretofore, and it witnessed the institution of a new regime of city-states. For the sake of convenience we shall refer to those motley rulers as Hyksos.

The Hyksos brought with them much of the cultural apparatus of upper Mesopotamia and the Iranian valleys. They were not, therefore, a mere horde of untutored barbarians, but on the contrary, a horse-breeding warrior caste effectually equipped with the latest and most terrifying paraphernalia of war: chariotry, compound bow, metal arrow-heads, helmet, scale armor, and the scimitar, few of which had been seen in this area before.[27] New towns and strongholds sprang up everywhere along with many ingenious improvements in the arts of fortification, such as the rectangular city-camp and the sloping revetment. From the excavations signs of violent local strife and constantly recurring city destruction are evident.[28] All signs point to greater wealth in the Hyksos period as well as greater insecurity.

We know too little to make more than an intelligent guess as to the type of society that obtained among the conquering Hyksos. Many small well-defended cities existed in Syria, such as Aleppo, Alalakh

one of them was chosen king of the country" (David Magie, *Roman Rule in Asia Minor*, I, Princeton, 1950, 201; also 179-180).

[26] Out of this whole area they cast veritable tidal waves of Amorite and Hurro-Iranian adventurers (accompanied undoubtedly by ragtag tribal elements from the trans-Jordanian steppe) into Egypt, where they became known to history as the Hyksos.

[27] H. E. Winlock, *The Rise and Fall of the Middle Kingdom in Thebes* (New York, 1947), Chap. VIII.

[28] W. F. Albright, *The Archaeology of Palestine* (Harmondsworth, Eng., 1949), pp. 90ff.

Khashshum, Qatna, Carchemish, and others, as well as those in Palestine. The inscription of Idrimi, local prince of the crude, warlike, semi-Hurrianized state of Mukishke (capital city Alalakh) about 1500 B.C. gives a uniquely vivid picture of the insecurities, heroic raids, revolts of rebellious vassals, destructions of cities and sudden reversals of this period.[29] In this respect it resembles the confusion of a typical prefeudal or proto-feudal society. The picture, however, is one of a city-dwelling warrior group (housecarles) clustered retainer-fashion around their hereditary prince—not a landed aristocracy. The same period is covered by our recension of the Keret epic of Phoenicia, which discloses the heroic tastes of the nobility. In this epic the ruler Keret refers to his seventy peers and his eighty barons who have been invited to a great banquet.[30] Very occasionally a Hyksos ruler such as Khyan, who ruled as pharaoh from the Delta, seems to have extended a strong arm over a portion of these small Syrian and Palestinian principalities; otherwise they seem to have enjoyed autonomy.

Concerning types of land tenure in Syria-Palestine of this period we have no evidence. Of this aristocratic congeries of city-states a little later under the Egyptian Eighteenth Dynasty, Wright and Filson have written: "The social organization of Canaanite society [under the Egyptian Empire] . . . was a feudal system with a king and an aristocracy of partly foreign 'chariot warriors' at the top, while at the bottom was a lower class of serfs and slaves. An independent and energetic middle class was nonexistent."[31] Whether Hyksos society was indeed loosely feudal, as claimed, it was at least aristocratic. It looks as if we are dealing here with a heroic rather than a feudal age.

For our purposes, we organize Assyrian history into five periods, as follows: (I) The period coincident with the decline of the First Dynasty of Babylon down through the first dozen kings of the Third Babylonian Dynasty (Kassite) is almost a complete blank. It would seem that Ashur was at some times a city-state of very limited dimensions, and could scarcely have been feudal. (II) In the succeeding

[29] W. F. Albright, "Some Important Recent Discoveries: Alphabetic Origins and the Idrimi Statue," *Bulletin of the American Schools of Oriental Research*, No. 118 (1950), pp. 14ff.

[30] H. L. Ginsberg, "The Legend of King Keret," *BASOR*, Supplementary Studies, Nos. 2-3 (New Haven, 1946), p. 24. The translation "peers" and "barons" , of course, merely analogical.

[31] Wright and Filson, *The Westminster Historical Atlas to the Bible* (Philadelphia, 1945), p. 36.

period (the Amarna Age and somewhat later) strife between Assyria and her larger neighbors, Mitanni and Kassite Babylonia, was incessant. (III) From Ashur-uballit (acceded 1362) through the reign of Tiglath-Pileser I (acceded 1114), the imperial idea begins to reorient Assyrian history profoundly, though with severe reversals especially during the middle of the period. Heavy annual campaigning by the king at the head of his army now became a practice whenever the royal power was in the ascendant. Tiglath-Pileser I is now a typical Near Eastern potentate, a royal hunter, and the lord of a crudely conceived empire comprised mainly of dependent princes, provincial administration being used in the home territories alone.[32] (IV) After him darkness suddenly descends; usurpers are now the order of the day, and for about two hundred years until Adad-nirari II (acceded 911) Assyria is again weak, and again we know next to nothing about the period. (V) Beginning with Adad-nirari II Assyria moves slowly and hesitantly into her great imperial period, that of the Sargonids, which was to end only with the resounding fall of Nineveh itself in 612 B.C.

A priori we might seek for signs of feudalism in the latter part of Period I, in Period II, and possibly in the earlier part of Period III; such a chronological development would parallel developments in known feudal societies. Survivals and reflections of feudalism could on the same basis be expected later. What we actually get in the evidence is miserably meager: in the middle of the last period, just preceding the great Sargonids, many of the provincial governors and court officials became independent.[33] A radical weakening of the royal power began under Shalmaneser III whose *turtanu* (chief man and generalissimo) Daian Ashur usurped much of the crown's prestige as well as its responsibilities, somewhat in the manner of the Merovingian mayors of the palace.[34] King-makers and great nobles dominated the scene during the reigns of Shalmaneser IV and his two successors.[35] The great Tiglath-Pileser III, who brought an end to this exuberance of aristocratic disorders, was himself a usurping noble who had been endowed with broad acres and immunities by the preceding king, and even he had at first to be chary of the prerogatives of his former compeers.[36]

This period then, just preceding the most magnificent *floruit* of the Assyrian Empire and heir to a long, often-interrupted, and decidedl

[32] Olmstead, *History of Assyria*, p. 66.

[33] L. Delaporte, *Le proche-orient asiatique* (Paris, 1948), pp. 242-243.

[34] Olmstead, pp. 152-153. [35] Olmstead, pp. 167-168, 172.

[36] Olmstead, pp. 175, 203-204.

volcanic history, is one of a political type we recognize: it could be post-feudal, or it could be prefeudal, but it could also be neither. As to the first possibility, it is too long since a possible truly feudal period; as to the second, no feudal period actually succeeded; hence we conclude that the partial and temporary disintegration of the period in question has nothing to do with feudalism.

The Assyrians had been too long habituated to their piedmont homeland to be considered invaders. We must treat them for our purposes as an indigenous people, unlike the Kassites, Hittites, et al. Kingship here (well established by the time of Tiglath-Pileser I) was supreme, sacred, and amazingly durable, able to ride out appalling vicissitudes.[37] When rights of rule and jurisdiction were locally exercised by the nobles, as they were in the unsettled middle of the fifth period of Assyrian history, they were usurped rights and formed no part of the ideal Assyrian polity, whereas in parts of medieval Europe feudal localism was standard and possessed the prestige of a long history itself.[38]

Assyria, born into the most exposed portion of the Near East, was from the very beginning militaristic and imperialistic and was never on anything but a complete war footing. The Assyrian warrior aristocracy, the *mar banuti*, was few in numbers and therefore was constantly called upon to perform the various priestly, bureaucratic, and military duties necessary to the maintenance of Assyrian life. That this was essentially a court officialdom, rather than an old hereditary landed nobility, can hardly be doubted.[39] Nevertheless their rewards were in broad acres as well as bureaucratic promotion. In the former the grant was in the typical form of a royal patent, obviously derived from the Kassite *kudurru* in format and style, detailing the lands, plantations, and attached serfs in question and the immunities from taxation and corvée allowed.[40]

[37] The court correspondence of the last period of Assyrian history shows clearly the typical self-abasement of the subject before the king, and well illustrates in numerous other ways the overriding incidence of Assyrian kingship. See R. H. Pfeiffer, *State Letters of Assyria* (New Haven, 1935), pp. 113-156 especially, and passim.

[38] See Olmstead, pp. 168-169, 203-204, for the notorious case of the magnate Bel Harran-bel-usur.

[39] Some seem to have been eunuchs, which is a far cry from the country nobleman type; see Olmstead, p. 153.

[40] See C. H. W. Johns, *Assyrian Deeds and Documents Recording the Transfer of Property*, IV (London, 1923), 165-166, for the text of a typical charter from the reign of Ashurbanipal. In this late (Sargonid) period the grant seems to have been for life only, after which it reverted to the crown. The Assyrian *ilku*, or

Besides the landed aristocracy, there existed a significant group of middle class landlords or farmers, some wealthy and maintaining slaves and tenants. In addition there were free imperial cities thriving on large grants of autonomy.

VI. The Medes and Persians

The Medes and Persians must not be conceived of as raw invaders at the time of the establishment of their empire, for, during their long, sporadic journeying southward out of an Aryan heartland, their routes constantly touched the domains of Urartu, Assyria, Babylonia, and Elam, and in those three centuries of acculturation they had absorbed large doses of Valley ideas and techniques.[41] This is the period in their annals about which we have only fragmentary information, a period when most of their tribal groups had already long left behind a purely tribal-nomadic stage and were living in settlements in the Zagros, sometimes fortified. Onto this political substratum kingship was grafted somewhere in the seventh century.[42]

We have mentioned these origins—a weak and distantly remembered period of tribal pastoralism, followed by a long period of rule under village headmen (clan leaders), and finally the development of king-

---

benefice-relationship, could refer not only to fields, but to a city and its inhabitants For an Assyrian city freed by the king, but continuing to owe its *ilku*-obligation to a former prefect for building projects, see R. H. Pfeiffer, "On Babylonian-Assyrian Feudalism," *American Journal of Semitic Languages and Literatures* No. 39 (1922), p. 67.

[41] History first records the Medes and Persians in the latter half of the ninth century B.C., during the reign of Shalmaneser III (A. T. Olmstead, *History of the Persian Empire*, Chicago, 1948, p. 22), almost three centuries before Cyrus took over the Median Empire.

[42] Sargon's campaign of 714 B.C. had met only a series of local Median chieftains (Olmstead, *History of Assyria*, p. 231). Exactly a century later Cyaxares, a king at the head of a remodeled army (Olmstead, *History of the Persian Empire* pp. 31ff.), invaded the northern part of the Valley and allied himself with Nabopolassar against the Assyrians. The origins of the institution of Iranian kingship thus lie within the century 714-614 B.C. Herodotus must therefore have had this age in mind when he related the well-known story of the Medes who, previously having lived in scattered villages under their local sheiks, elected Deioces their first king with law-giving powers. Though we cannot accept this story in detail (George Cameron, *History of Early Iran*, Chicago, 1936, pp. 176-177), may well represent Iranian kingship as an essentially spontaneous Median origination, though it by no means precludes the obvious Assyrian and Babylonian parallels influencing its development. To the south of the Medes, the Persians had raised up a leader who entitled himself "great king, king of kings, king of Parsa, whereas his father had been only "king of the city Anshan" (*History of the Persian Empire*, p. 29).

ship—because it is one of the few fairly clear-cut instances of such a political succession in the Near East, and from the point of view of the dynamics of the aristocracy which arises under the early Achaemenid kings, it is a necessary part of the picture.

The salient fact of the Achaemenian polity is a centralized government expressed in terms of divinely sanctioned royal power. The aristocracy was the mainstay of this government, and the exposition of the exact balance of power between noble and crown confronts us here.

To return for a moment to the earlier period, we see that the preimperial Persians possessed a social stratification (essentially like that of their Vedic congeners) which divided the nation into priests, warriors, and cultivators. In this early tribal period the second estate were chariot warriors. When they emerge into history we see them arranged, however, in relationship to the land, the *vith*, the clan in its village grouping and surrounding domain being under the jurisdiction of its *vithpaitiš*.[43] That these offices were held by members of the warrior class is clear. Somewhere along the line the *vithpaitiš* had added to his tribal jurisdiction and prerogatives the social power that comes from the personal possession of broad acres.[44] This is apparently the situation which meets us when Cyrus, revolting from his Median overlords, brought the Persian Empire into being. Backed by immemorial tribal tradition, the prerogative of leadership in war, and the newer usages of landed position, the *vithpaitiš* so permanently established himself (as is evidenced by the "Seven"—the seven most eminent aristocratic houses) that he outlasted the Achaemenian, Seleucid, Parthian, and even the Sassanian empires.[45] From Cyrus on, these aristocrats took their places at the royal councils, in the army, the higher bureaucracy, and the satrapal system. They insisted upon certain immunities in regard to their vast lands, their persons, and the peoples attached to them,[46] and yet in general were kept in a proper subordination to the larger purposes of the royal house.

It was the great organizer Darius who preeminently seems to have harnessed this aristocracy to the royal chariot.[47] Given by Ahura-Mazda,

[43] M. Ehtécham, *L'Iran sous les Achéménides* (Fribourg, Switzerland, 1946), pp. 18-41.

[44] Ehtécham, p. 50: "L'autorité . . . des *vithpaitiš* est fondée sur l'importance de leurs propriétés terriennes, et sur le nombre considérable des individus attachés à leurs personnes." See also p. 21, n. 4.

[45] The Achaemenian *vithpaitiš* becomes the Sassanian *vaspuhran*; see below, p. 114.

[46] Ehtécham, pp. 64ff., 84, 101ff.

[47] Ehtécham, pp. 114ff.

kingship was divine; and although the nobles had to provide for their own levies in the king's service, they still had to respond to his muster by command of superior power. By utilizing the *vithpaitiš* in the administrative satrapal system, by divorcing the duties of governor from those of general, by maintaining a most searching espionage system, the Achaemenid kings effectively restrained his political power. While the empire was extant, the landed immunities of the *vithpaitiš* continued, as well as certain limited immunities in law, but we hear nothing of a system of private individual agreements between the king and his nobles for division of political power. This system sets the stage for the Parthian and Sassanian periods which follow, the two latter being inexplicable without the antecedent Achaemenian accomplishment.

In theory the king was absolute; in practice the Achaemenian state was a fairly stable symbiosis of crown and aristocracy. There is no denying that rebellious nobles often disposed of the wearer of the crown by assassination. They never, however, attacked the integrity of the crown itself. Towards the end, particularly recalcitrant satraps began to wear the monarchy down, a situation that vividly recalls the free-for-all in the third century of the Roman Empire, when aspiring generals and governors each hoped to reestablish under his own aegis the full power of the principate. But feudalism never emerged out of the disintegration of Achaemenian times.

VII. The Parthian Regime

The historic Parthians were by origin a semi-nomadic Iranian people of the Dahae tribes of the steppe country east of the Caspian. Their wanderings brought them into the Persian satrapy of Parthava some time before 250 B.C.; it was from this region that they later expanded into empire.

Rostovtzeff says, "The feudal structure of the Parthian Empire was inherited by the Arsacids from the Achaemenids and was transmitted by them to the Sassanian kings."[48] This comment must be rejected for reasons which have just appeared. The question of what was transmitted by Achaemenian Persia to later times will be considered below.[49] Here we must determine first whether the loose Parthian Empire may properly be termed feudal, and if so, what were the circumstances of its origin.

[48] *Cambridge Ancient History*, XI, 117.

[49] pp. 116-119.

Upon the death of Alexander his inchoate empire split into several succession states. One of these fragments, the Seleucid Empire, itself disintegrated into smaller pieces, particularly after the disastrous defeat of Antiochus III at Magnesia in 189 B.C. These smaller pieces, Elymais, Characene, Media, Persis, etc., had formerly been Seleucid satrapies.

When Mithradates I carried his victorious arms through the Caspian Gates westward to the creation of the greater Parthian domain, it was not therefore a coherent empire which he overran, but an already disorganized swarm of small independent states, each with its own ruling dynasty. Some of these states, such as Persis and Sacastene, were left in control of their native houses and assumed the superior status of dependent kingdoms or duchies, enjoying the rights of autonomous coinage, etc. Over some states, the Parthians installed *marzbans* (governors or generals), who seem to have been more independent than the Achaemenian satraps—in fact more like the Carolingian counts. Others, little amenable to discipline, like certain of the small Arab states or Greek cities, were perhaps jointly controlled by crown and local government. And on the frontiers a system of marches was maintained. In other words, the Parthian Empire was a patchwork that could be held together at all only by the constant exercise of force. It was, however, a recognizable state for over three and a half centuries.

In Europe, as noted above, it was the power of the Roman imperial ideal (expressed variously through the Papacy, the Carolingian Empire, and the Holy Roman Empire) which gave distinction and a theoretical integration to western feudal society. Similarly it was the long shadow of Cyrus and Darius which proved to be the cement that bonded together Parthian feudalism, if feudalism it was—with this difference, that the ideal in the case of Parthia was more nearly attainable, owing to the fact that the large urban centers continued throughout this period in undiminished vigor, as did the far-flung commerce which supported them. Ctesiphon, the royal capital, was situated within a heavy network of trade routes. Money was more abundant in the Parthian Empire than it was in medieval Europe, and to that extent anything like feudal tenure, which is based in land, must have been weakened. It should be pointed out, however, that the Parthian himself did not engage in this commerce; it was rather the Syrian, Arab, Babylonian, and Greek merchant who sustained the money economy.

Famous families such as the Suren, Karin, Gewparthran, Mihran, and Aspahbad existed. The assumption is that some of them were originally Parthian clans and had been endowed with their large estates by the Parthian king incident upon conquest. The Suren possessed vast holdings in Mesopotamia, the Karin near Nihawand, the Mihran near Rhagae in Media, and the Gewparthran in Hyrcania. It is usually assumed that it was those families which supplied the *marzbans* of those satrapies in which they held most of their lands.

This landed aristocracy must be distinguished from the indigenous aristocracy of the client kingdoms. It is hard not to make the comparison between Parthian nobility and the Frankish and Teutonic aristocracy of the ninth and tenth centuries. In the pages of history the Parthians are a singularly colorless people. Socially they may be characterized as a ruling class that lived on horseback, and who rode only to hunt or fight. Four centuries of contact with a rich Babylonian tradition, Hellenistic culture, Roman political genius, and the stimulation of trade with China produced no noticeable effect upon them. The general lawlessness of the class may be appreciated from the attempt made by a contemporary Arsacid king of Armenia to pull their fangs. Like Louis XIV he desired to maintain a close surveillance over them and to that end he ordered them off their patrimonies and into the circle of the court.[50]

We suspect that the number of this Parthian aristocracy was small. Surenas, the greatest Parthian noble under Orodes II, had in his personal retinue a thousand mailed cataphracts (heavily armored knights, equipped with spear and sword), from which one may guess with Tarn that the number of Parthian knights in all may have been only about six thousand.[51] We can be reasonably sure that a lesser order of nobility existed, perhaps like the Spanish hidalgo, represented here by the more numerous lightly-armed horse-archers.

The greater nobility possessed large landed estates which, on the Armenian analogy, were granted by the crown along with general powers of government (immunity?) and more specific public offices. That there was a tendency for estate and political authority to be equated, thus allowing for the office to take on a hereditary aspect cannot be doubted. Nevertheless a strong king was able to remove the exercise of office from one family and regrant it elsewhere.

As one would expect in a people of semi-nomadic background, the tribal flavor of the Parthian nobility is pronounced. The great aristocratic families of Parthian descent were grouped into a council of peers whose advisory and elective powers limited the sovereignty of the king

[50] A. Christensen, *L'Iran sous les Sassanides* (Copenhagen, 1944), p. 24.
[51] *Cambridge Ancient History*, IX, 601.

Like the normal feudal court, this council considered itself to be a body of the king's equals. Each family possessed its own special prerogatives, even as the family of Arsaces possessed the sole prerogative of the crown.

It is of interest that, in spite of the disruptive tendencies of the Parthian nobility, they completely respected this Arsacid prerogative. Even though they might assassinate or depose the Arsacid king, inevitably they raised another Arsacid to succeed him. Here is the hereditary instinct highly developed.

The purely Parthian tradition, coupled with the Achaemenid tradition of centralized rule, enabled a strong king to dominate the nobles. The situation therefore differs from that seen in medieval Europe. The Parthian king, like his Achaemenid predecessors, called himself King of Kings, and had his hunting parks, his gardens, his summer palaces, his eunuchs, his harem, his bodyguard, his judiciary, and his private treasury filled with the tribute from conquered territories. The powers he exercised were potentially autocratic. The Parthian state was thus a thoroughly mixed system, partly feudal perhaps, partly tribal even, and partly Oriental despotism.

VIII. The Sassanian Regime

In the year A.D. 224 Ardashir I, bearing the title King of Kings, led a successful revolt against his Parthian overlord. The result was a rejuvenated empire erected upon the ruins of the old and embracing practically the same area. Because the transfer of power was so easily accomplished, such forces as were operative in the social structure were scarcely disrupted.

The very fact of the new conquest, however, meant a new emphasis upon that tradition of centralization which had never died out under the Parthians. In fact, the Sassanian kings, sprung from the province of Pars, consciously reerected what they could of the autocratic fabric of the Achaemenian kings.

Society was more severely stratified and more complex under the Sassanians than under the Parthians. Four estates are found: the ecclesiastical hierarchy of the Magian Zoroastrian Church, the warrior class, the bureaucracy, and the masses of the people which included the bourgeoisie. The subdivisions of the second estate are instructive. In order of decending rank they were as follows:

Shahrdaran—the princes of the empire. These were the dependent princes, minor potentates of the client kingdoms (such as the Arab kings of Hira, etc.), princes of the royal house being prepared in the art of rule in various governorships, and the *marzbans*. All of these bore the royal title. Two divisions thus exist in this class, non-Sassanian or non-Iranian client kings in whose families the rule was hereditary, and the appointive Sassanian governors.

Vaspuhran—the nobles of the great landed families. Again the famous Seven Families appear, some inherited from the Parthian regime. They are the Sassanids, Karin, Suren, Aspahbadh, Spandiyadh, Mihran, and Zik(?).

Vuzurgan—the "great." The high functionaries and administrative heads of the empire.

Azadhan—the "free" or "noble" men. Minor functionaries in the provinces, a minor nobility. Here probably also belong the petty knights who served in the armies when not living on their lands.

A glance at the above list reveals that the central government disposed of paramount power. Our nobility is now only a minor part of the second estate. The central government under the King of Kings was controlled by a vizier (*hazarbadh*) and a group of state ministers each with his own divan and a corps of civil servants. The situation of the army reveals even more clearly the swelling power of the government. While the heavily armored knight—now practically indistinguishable in appearance from his medieval European counterpart—and the horse-archer were still the nucleus of the army, elephants and auxiliaries had reappeared in strength. The army was commanded by a regularly appointed official, the *eran-spahbadh*, who was both commander-in-chief and minister of war. We hear nothing of private armies of knights such as the Suren had possessed in the early Parthian period.

It is unclear what specifically were the privileges of the nobles and to what extent the crown could interfere in their estates. Immunity is nowhere mentioned. We do know that there were certain hereditary offices held in the seven great families. The crown of course belonged to the house of Sassan; to others belonged hereditary supervision of the cavalry, of taxation and the treasury, of civil affairs, and of legal arbitration, among others. That these hereditary charges were empty of real significance during most of the period may be inferred from the presence of a bureaucracy and the absolutist tenor of the government.

Though purity of blood in the families of the second estate was insured by legislation as well as by custom, there are evidences of the decline of noble houses and their final immersion in the commercial and governmental classes below them. Conversely, the king possessed the power of ennobling new houses as a reward for merit or service, though it was a prerogative seldom used. Members of the church were not recruited from the nobility, but were exclusively drawn from the ancient tribal class of the Magi, much as the Hebrew priesthood was monopolized by the tribe of Levi.

The nobility as such, the *vaspuhrs*, still retained their ancestral lands, upon which their residences presumably stood, as well as other scattered holdings in various parts of the empire. The signs are, however, that these lands were limited in extent in comparison with the crown lands. Although the members of the aristocracy supplied many of the higher administrative posts, such as that of *marzban*, these charges could not be too easily perpetuated in the family. The natural result of this decrease in real power for the *vaspuhrs* was their sublimation into a true *noblesse de cour*. The glamor, excitment, and culture of the court of the King of Kings substituted for their former power.

To bring out the implications in this courtly Sassanian period we must briefly review its salient characteristics. Imperial expansiveness, ostentation, ceremonialism, in sum the brilliant concentration of a rich cultural apparatus around the person of the King of Kings gave to the period of Kavadh and the two Khusros (A.D. 488-628) more than a superficial resemblance to the period of Louis XIV. We even note the same dull and unmitigated misery of the lower classes. The capital and its Fontainebleau outside were now the home of many of the nobility. Aristocratic sons were sent to court as pages to learn skill in literary pursuits, theology, music, astronomy, riding, hunting, etc. The noble ladies, like their sisters in the high Middle Ages in Europe, rode to the chase with the men. The nobles were subsidized in part to maintain them at court, and when serving in the army were now for the first time put on a salaried basis.[52]

[52] How sophisticated were the times may be gathered from that most interesting of all Oriental revolutions, the Mazdakite movement. This was a semi-religious upheaval among the lower classes, with, however, powerful friends at court. Its aim was to redistribute the wealth and thus destroy greed and lust at the root. It finally attracted King Kavadh himself and through him secured initially some favorable legislation. In the fury attending this social eruption, the nobles were decimated, their castles looted, their women seized, and their properties destroyed. Although church and nobility reacted violently and ultimately put down the uprising, the nobility at least were seriously weakened and thus were even more

Upon the death of Khusro II, who ruled thirty-eight years, the entire centralized fabric of the state was rent. The governors became practically independent and it is to be assumed that the *vaspuhrs* regained some of their lost power and prestige. It is of interest that some of these great families continued into the tenth century still endowed with the hereditary charge of certain administrative posts. So well established were these noble Persian houses that, as is well known, they not only retained their standing in the new world of Islam, but helped appreciably to mold that world.

In A.D. 632 the Sassanian Empire collapsed before the fanaticism of Islam.

IX. Conclusion

Turning back now to review our material, we can see that this something we have provisionally called feudalism existed in the ancient Near East in the main as a corollary of the invasions of (1) Indo-European (including Hittite), Kassite, and Hurrian groups around the beginning of the second millennium B.C., and (2) the Medo-Persian and Parthian irruptions of much later date. In the case of the Kassites the weakening of a preceding centralized government may have sowed the proper seeds of feudal development. With Hatti, inasmuch as no powerful antecedent state existed in Anatolia before the coming of the Hittites, antecedents in a weakened centralized government must be sought in the realm of institutions copied from the Valley. The case of Assyrian feudalism adduced cannot very easily be connected with invasion, but there is a good case for the memory of former unity.

Earlier invasions, such as the Amorite, failed to produce feudal institutions. How can we account for this?[53] For one thing we must attribute the difference to the fact that Hittites, Hurrians, and Hyksos were horse-breeders, whereas the earlier groups were not. The horse was then relatively unknown. Thus we can hardly avoid the idea that horse and chariot, which were instrumental in the success of the great invasions, also tended to be productive of societies of aristocratic and knightly warriors. The simple economics of an expensive, mobile, and crushing weapon of war, suddenly introduced into the midst of a peasant and commercial society, allowed groups small in numbers to effectively seize and wield power in the ancient Near East.

---

amenable to the autocratic controls of the succeeding kings, notably Khusro I and Khusro II.

[53] See below, pp. 244-245 for another suggestion as to the position occupied by the Amorites in Mesopotamian history.—Ed.

But the use of horse and chariot alone does not fully answer our question; larger and deeper social relations are also involved. In those polities in the Near East which are subsequent to successful tribal invasion, there would seem to be almost an automatic equilibrium established between military power (in the possession of the invaders) and cultural power (in the possession of the invaded), a stopgap *modus vivendi*, that is, between the coercive and the persuasive elements in the society until such time as the society has again convinced all of its members of its orderly and institutional intentions. In the case of the Kassites, Hittites, and Arsacids, we have clear-cut examples of extraneous tribal minorities seizing the rule without the requisite cultural apparatus (at first) to feel at ease with their responsibilities, the result being a poorly concealed tension, probably not quite feudalism but something like it. Oriental conceptions both of kingship and of empire mitigate this tension, and at times even totally warp it to their purposes.

The Achaemenian and Sassanian cases are different in that the peoples were far more heavily soaked in those great intangible traditions of the area they took over; the greater confidence they derived from this enabled them to immediately transmute royal into imperial rule. The Sassanian feudalistic tradition was inherited from the Parthian regime. The Sassanian case is different in another way from our other examples in that the revolution that brought them to power was a resurgence of old Persian elements, not a foreign invasion unskilled in the manipulation of cultural traditions. Consideration of these two latter cases perhaps completes the answer to the question about the Amorites raised above. The seepage of Amorite elements into the Valley was a long extended process. The culture that was met there had been from earliest antiquity powerfully affected by close and continuous Semitic infusions. A severe cultural dichotomy therefore did not operate between invaders and invaded to produce a radical redistribution of power.

In the clear-cut examples of alien conquest, those of the Kassites, Hittites, and Arsacids, the logic of the situation would operate immediately. Because of the fact that the invaders were few, stringent efforts had to be made simply to retain the captured power, and this necessitated the full utilization of every warrior and his continuous mobilization. Thus an alien aristocracy swiftly arose which floated on the surface of the indigenous people, who were correspondingly reduced. The difference can be sensed at once in the contrast made by the rule of the typical *ensi* in the early, autonomous Sumerian city-state. Here the welfare of the state centered around its continuing good relations with the divine powers, to achieve which purpose the state produced and employed its own officer, the *ensi.* The integration of means and end is thus a logical one, internally conceived and carried out. The imposition of a foreign warrior caste in the seats of rule calls for another integration, *which the new group itself imposes* without immediate reference to anything but the problem of retaining power. This integration may be monarchy or feudalism or both.

At the beginning of this section we divided the invading peoples into two groups. The second group of societies with which we dealt, Achaemenian, Parthian, and Sassanian, is a unit in that the elements follow each other in strict chronological order, unlike the first group, the societies of which, with the exception of Assyria, were all simultaneous results of a single great ethnic upheaval. Even though Persian and Parthian represent invading and horse-breeding peoples, still the horse had already long been acclimatized in the Near East by the time they appear, and so the cases are not comparable.

There is a subtle over-all difference between the earlier and the later periods which we have difficulty in analyzing. In the Near East of the Persian and Parthian rule there was greater wealth and population, and this provided a more resilient cushion, absorbing much of the invaders' energies and economically reducing the extreme burden of a particularistic nobility. The social institutions of the age into which they irrupted were older, richer, more complex, and therefore possibly more durable. This is suggested by the fact that kingship in the Persian-Parthian group is a far more potent political factor than in the Kassite-Hurrian-Hittite group, because of its extension into imperialism.

We must also advert to commerce and urban life as important factors inhibiting the development of what might have been radical feudalism in either of the periods. There is a profound generic difference between European feudalism and that of the ancient Near East. European feudalism throve in a generally rural and isolated context; over vast areas there were few towns and fewer cities. In Europe even today relics of large and small castles dot the landscape. In the ancient Near East the walled city of venerable antiquity was the seat of the aristocracy. Fortified cities were the only real protection possible in an age when large political units neighboring could launch fairly effective armies into one's territories. Under such conditions castles of the European variety would have been of no avail. So completely unjointed had European political life become that the typical feudal army was generally only a small levy of knights with some footmen bent on pillage and usually incapable of forcing the large castle. The large size of the Near Eastern kingdoms and principalities exerted its effect in placing the aristocracy in an urban context. In the case of Assyria, we see the imperial "free" city existing almost autonomously behind its charter of privileges. In the case of Parthia we see that, while the important cities of the Valley and the Iranian plateau are no longer able to command their own political destinies, they are large, vigorous, and so well oriented in their ancient patterns of religious and commercial life (expanded now by new Hellenistic influences) that their inertia proves to be a telling factor in maintaining the stability of the empire. The Parthians themselves never gave up their somewhat gypsy-like life inherited from the Chorasmian steppe, but they willingly allowed the urban life of the realm to flourish as it could. Roman, Indian, and Chinese articles of trade crossed the empire unhindered but for tolls. Canaan under the Hyksos witnessed the development of cities both in wealth and in numbers. Well-established cities like Haran dotted the plains of northern Syria and Mesopotamia under the kings of Mitanni, and even in Anatolia we hear of some of importance. This last area, however, appears to have been the least urbanized.

Kingship, empire, commerce, and the continued presence of cities and towns thus combined to reduce the intensity of feudal features in the Near East, the more so as time went on. It must be admitted finally that, while we agree with the provisional description of feudalism in the Introductory Essay as a method of government where "political power is personal rather than institutional," our Near Eastern sources give us far too little information to claim dogmatically that exactly such polities existed there. Yet at the same time the cumulative effects of such peripheral facts as we do possess lead us to believe that in varying degrees something approaching feudalism did occur in the ancient Near East. But in any case we "see through a glass darkly."

VI · THE QUESTION OF FEUDAL INSTITUTIONS IN ANCIENT EGYPT

BY WILLIAM F. EDGERTON

1. Prefatory Remarks

It seems sure that Egyptologists who have applied the term "feudal" to certain periods of Egyptian history have not had in mind any such substantive concept of feudalism as is put forward in the Introductory Essay to the present volume. Rather, they have probably thought of a "feudal" period as one in which the most important governmental powers rested in the hands of territorial or local "nobles" who owed their positions usually to inheritance, less often to royal appointment; a period in which central government either did not exist or could not fully control the local authorities. In the body of the present essay, therefore, no opinions are offered as to whether any of the institutions described are feudal; it is sought merely to show, so far as knowledge permits, what the institutions were. It may be suggested here that they were not truly feudal. The question of their character is discussed in Professor Coulborn's concluding essay.[1]

The following table is intended only to give a rough idea of the periods involved in the present essay. All dates are approximations. For the Middle Kingdom and later periods the margin of error is only a few years; for the Old Kingdom it may be as much as two centuries.

Old Kingdom, 28th-23rd Centuries B.C.
(Capital at Memphis)

Fourth Dynasty, late 28th to mid-26th century
Fifth Dynasty, mid-26th to late 25th century
Sixth Dynasty, late 25th to early 23rd century
Seventh Dynasty ("seventy kings who reigned seventy days") corresponds to no known historical reality.
Eighth Dynasty succeeded Sixth at Memphis, and merges into the

First Intermediate Period, 23rd-21st Centuries:
A Period of Disunity

Ninth and Tenth Dynasties, 2242-2060 B.C. (capital at Heracleopolis)

[1] See below, pp. 216-218, 254-269.

Eleventh Dynasty (at Thebes) began during the First Intermediate Period and ended about 1985 B.C.

Middle Kingdom, 21st-18th Centuries

Eleventh Dynasty, ending about 1985 B.C.
Twelfth Dynasty, 1985-1776 B.C.
Thirteenth Dynasty, began about 1776 and merges into the

Second Intermediate Period, Late 18th to Early 16th Century (Including the Hyksos Domination)

Seventeenth Dynasty began in the Second Intermediate Period and ended about 1580 B.C.

Empire, or New Kingdom, 1580-1085 B.C.

Eighteenth Dynasty, 1580-1350
Nineteenth Dynasty, 1350-1200
Twentieth Dynasty, 1200-1085
Twenty-first Dynasty, 1085-950
Twenty-second Dynasty, 950-730
(Twenty-third Dynasty was contemporary with the latter part of Twenty-second.)
Twenty-fourth and Twenty-fifth Dynasties, 730-663
Twenty-sixth Dynasty, 663-525

II. The Old Kingdom and the First Intermediate Period

In theory, at all times, the Egyptian king was a god, ordained by the greater gods to rule over mankind. His expressed will not merely had the force of law; it *was* the law. No other human source of legislation was acknowledged in Pharaonic Egypt.

In the Fourth Dynasty reality corresponded rather closely to this theory, or so it seems. The government was an autocratic bureaucracy headed by the king. A single official, the vizier, probably exercised supreme administrative and judicial authority under the king throughout the kingdom. Territorially the kingdom was divided into a number of administrative districts called nomes (perhaps twenty-two in Upper Egypt and twenty in Lower Egypt; complete lists are not available before the Ptolemaic period). Many nomes were derived from independent states of great antiquity. They were governed by nomarchs, royal appointees whose highest ambitions in this period were concerned with the central administration and the royal court rather than with their particular nomes. Administratively the central government was organized in a number of departments each of which doubtless functioned throughout the country; to what extent the nome administrations may have been similarly organized is not known. There is evidence tending to show that officials whose work pleased the king were freely moved from job to job. Princes of the royal house often held the highest offices; with this exception, some Egyptologists believe that birth was of little importance, though I personally am skeptical of this proposition. (The view of Junker,[2] that descendants of kings filled the majority of public offices, depends in part on the precise interpretation of an obscure title, *rḫ-nyśwt*, which may mean perhaps "descendant of a king" or perhaps merely "acquaintance of the king.")

By making and maintaining canals and dikes throughout the country, the government regulated the intake and discharge of the Nile flood. Such regulation has always been, and is today, the indispensable prerequisite for decent living conditions in Egypt. Irrigation and drainage consume a very large part of the total labor force which is or can be usefully employed in Egyptian agriculture. The task cannot be effectively performed on a purely local basis. Hence, the difference in terms of human well-being between a strongly unified kingdom and a congeries of mutually hostile localities is immensely greater in Egypt than in most parts of the world. Hence also, the government must exercise effective control over a large labor force. The compulsory labor of his subjects constituted an important part of the king's income, in the Old Kingdom as in most later periods. Another important part of his income was the right of his officials to requisition accommodations and materials of various kinds when traveling on the king's business. Perhaps the most important part of his revenue may have been derived from the royal domains: it is believed that these were partly managed directly by the king's salaried officials and partly farmed out on lease. I personally do not doubt that he also collected taxes on lands held by the temple and tomb endowments and by private individuals, but almost nothing can be stated with absolute certainty regarding land taxes in Egypt before Alexander.[3]

[2] *Giza*, VI, *Akademie der Wissenschaften in Wien, Phil-hist. Klasse, Denkschriften* (Vienna and Leipzig, 1943), 24.

[3] For a recent discussion of the problems concerning taxes or other official revenues derived from land, see Alan H. Gardiner, *The Wilbour Papyrus*, II: *Commentary* (Oxford, 1948), review by W. F. Edgerton in the *Journal of the Ame*

The supreme task of government in the Fourth Dynasty was the erection of the king's pyramid, and in general the provision of those material benefits which would insure eternal blessedness for the king and for those about him. By the king's favor, the high officials of the kingdom built their tombs close around his pyramid so that they would be closely associated with him in the hereafter as they had been on earth. Expensive tombs remote from the capital are extremely rare before the Fifth Dynasty.

Kings and officials endeavored to endow their tombs in perpetuity. Such an endowment might include lands, cattle, and "people" (serfs or slaves?).[4] It might also include income consisting of future offerings which were first to be presented but not consumed at the temple of some god or at the tomb of some exalted personage of an earlier generation. The endowment was to be administered by a "soul-servant" or a group of such; a man's soul-servants might or might not be his own descendants. Such endowments were sometimes gifts of the king, and sometimes erected by the tomb-owner out of his private property. The "god servants" (priests) who maintained the divine service in temples were supported by similar endowments.

In these two cases, therefore (soul-servants and god-servants), there was a direct connection between the tenure of lands and other property and the rendering of stated services. In neither of the two cases was the ostensible recipient of the services a living human being. Probably the recipient (the god, or the deceased tomb-owner) was the owner of the endowment in Egyptian legal theory, but it is also probable that the individual god-servant or soul-servant could effectively dispose of his individual rights and duties, at least by testament. In the Middle Kingdom and later, priestly offices were bought and sold like any other kind of property, but we do not know whether this was true in the Old Kingdom.

The reigning king paid his officials partly by stipends of food, drink, clothing, etc., and partly by donations of lands. We have no evidence to suggest that continuing ownership of land so donated depended in any way on continuing service; on the contrary, it is the current belief of Egyptologists that the holder and his heirs could keep such lands indefinitely, and I am of those who suppose that such lands could

can Oriental Society, LXX (1950), 299ff. The period directly involved here is the reign of Ramses V, about 1150 B.C.

[4] *Urkunden des ägyptischen Altertums*, I: *Urkunden des alten Reichs*, ed. Kurt Sethe, 2nd edn. (Leipzig, 1932-33), 12, 10. (Hieroglyphic texts in the Egyptian language, cited below as *Urk*. I.)

also be freely sold. The progressive impoverishment of the royal government through the cumulative effect of donations of land to officials, to temples, and to mortuary endowments, is believed to have been one of the principal causes of the collapse of the Old Kingdom. Even at the beginning of the Fourth Dynasty (the earliest period for which relevant information is available) some lands could be bought, sold, and bequeathed.[5]

The Fifth and Sixth Dynasties are characterized by progressive governmental decentralization. Nomarchs, instead of being freely shifted from one nome to another, became permanently attached to their individual nomes and made their tombs there. A new office, "governor of Upper Egypt," came between the Upper Egyptian nomarchs and the vizier: this office may have been created to keep the nomarchs from becoming independent, but the nomarchs continued to grow increasingly independent. At some times several different nomarchs were simultaneously "governors of Upper Egypt," each functioning in a limited number of nomes. Offices tended to become hereditary (a condition always desired by the officials themselves). By the end of the Sixth Dynasty the nomarch was usually[6] chief priest in the principal temple of the nome. A nomarch who inherited the highest civil (administrative and judicial) and the highest priestly offices in his nome together with important landed estates was obviously in a position to take advantage of any weakness which might appear in the central government.

A practice which surely contributed to the collapse of the Old Kingdom was the granting of "immunities" from forced labor and from other exactions which might be imposed by royal officials or by other powerful or influential persons. A number of such grants have come down to us, issued by kings of the Fifth, Sixth, and Eighth[7] Dynasties in favor of various temples and mortuary endowments. Some such grants actually forbid agents of the government to enter lands of the privileged temple.[8] By the time of Pepi II (late Sixth

[5] See E. Seidl, *Einführung in die ägyptische Rechtsgeschichte bis zum Ende des Neuen Reiches*, I, *Juristischer Teil*, Ägyptol. Forschungen herausg.—A. Scharff, Part 10 (Glückstadt, Hamburg, New York, 1939), 47ff.

[6] According to Kees, "regelmassig" (H. Kees, *Beiträge zur altägyptischen Provinzialverwaltung und der Geschichte des Feudalismus. Nachrichten von der Gesellschaft der Wissenschaften zu Göttingen*, 1932, p. 93).

[7] "Eighth Dynasty" here is Sethe's "Coptite" Dynasty; see below.

[8] e.g., *Urk*. I, 283, 8. Pirenne seems to me to exaggerate the importance of this detail, which in any case does not occur in all grants of immunity (J. Pirenne, "La Féodalité en Égypte," *Revue de l'Institut de Sociologie*, XVI, 1936, 24f.).

Dynasty) the granting of immunities had attained such proportions that the king had to authorize certain officials on certain occasions to requisition what they needed from towns, temples, etc., "without allowing any immunity."[9] The next step was to issue new grants of immunity, taking cognizance of the commissions "without allowing any immunity," and specifying that even such commissions should be void against the new immunities now granted.[10] We are dependent on our imaginations for the consequences of this double contradiction. (The situation has been misunderstood by Pirenne,[11] by Hayes,[12] and by the much more reliable Scharff.[13] Sethe has the correct interpretation.[14])

The Sixth Dynasty was followed by a period of disorganization known to Egyptologists as the First Intermediate Period. A horde of Asiatics overran at least the entire Delta and occupied it for a considerable period. Ipuwer's description[15] suggests that they may also have wrought much havoc in Upper Egypt; many of them may have established themselves there, perhaps in positions of authority. The invasion was doubtless facilitated by the greatly diminished efficacy of the royal government and the increasing disunity of the country. Whatever the causes, it is certain that public authority was not consistently maintained. The splendid tombs of the kings and grandees of the Old Kingdom were generally looted and wrecked in this period:[16] in ancient Egypt, nothing could more clearly register a state of anarchy. The new tombs and other works produced during the period are unambitious in scale and poor in execution.

The Eighth Dynasty succeeded the Sixth at Memphis with little or no interval. The Eighth Dynasty was formally recognized at least as far south as Coptos, and probably to the First Cataract: I share the view of Hayes[17] that Sethe's "Coptite" Dynasty is really the Memphite Eighth. But it is unlikely that these last Memphite rulers exercised much real power. Rival families in the chief provincial centers

[9] *Urk.* I, 131, 7. Pepi II's letter to Harkuf.

[10] e.g., *Urk.* I, 282-283.

[11] *Histoire des Institutions et du droit privé de l'ancienne Égypte*, III (Brussels, 1935), 295.

[12] "Royal Decrees," *Journal of Egyptian Archaeology*, XXXII (1946), 8.

[13] "Der historische Abschnitt der Lehre für König Merikarê," *Sitzungsberichte der Bayerischen Akademie der Wissenschaften, Phil.-hist. Abt.* (1936), Heft 8, p. 11, n. 1.

[14] *Göttingische gelehrte Anzeigen*, CLXXIV (1912), 713.

[15] Alan H. Gardiner, *The Admonitions of an Egyptian Sage* (Leipzig, 1909).

[16] J. A. Wilson, *The Burden of Egypt* (Chicago, 1951), p. 109.

[17] "Royal Decrees," pp. 19-23.

were more concerned with their own aggrandizement than with serving king or country. The nomarchs of Heracleopolis (XXth nome of Upper Egypt) took the kingly title, forming the Ninth and Tenth Dynasties. They reconquered the Delta and most if not all of Upper Egypt, but succumbed to the nomarchs of Thebes (IVth nome) who formed the Eleventh Dynasty. In the middle of the twenty-first century B.C. Mentuhotep II or III of the Eleventh Dynasty conquered Heracleopolis and reunited all Egypt. The period of union thus begun, the Middle Kingdom, lasted nearly three centuries.

During the First Intermediate Period many nomarchs became practically petty kings (not counting, of course, those of Heracleopolis and Thebes who actually assumed the full royal titles). The reunification of the kingdom under the Eleventh and Twelfth Dynasties did not proceed without conflict. Some of the great nomarchic families opposed the new Theban power, and disappeared. Others were on the winning side, and prospered. A major task of the early Twelfth Dynasty kings was the complete establishment of royal power over the traditional independence of those nomarchic families which had supported them. This task is believed to have been completed by the time of Sesostris III (second quarter of the nineteenth century B.C.).

Our knowledge of the institutions of the First Intermediate Period is scant and unsatisfactory. A nomarch might date by the years of his own tenure of power (as only kings had done before) and append the pious wish "may he live, be prosperous, and be healthy!" to his name (another royal prerogative). These superficial phenomena undoubtedly epitomize the basic realities: even though a nomarch might acknowledge the superior authority of a distant king and perhaps even pay regular tribute to the royal court, he himself was really an autocrat within his nome. The nomarch collected taxes, administered justice, suppressed robbers, protected widows and orphans, raised and commanded troops in war, and did everything which a wise, vigorous and benevolent king might be expected to do; such, at least, is the ideal which emerges from the mortuary "autobiographies" of the period.

A unique document of the reign of Sesostris I, second king of the Twelfth Dynasty (ca. 1960-1926 B.C.), reflects some details which must be survivals from the First Intermediate Period. Hepzefi, nomarch of Siut (XIIIth nome of Upper Egypt) executed a series of ten contracts by which he hoped to provide permanently for his mortuary service. The contracts have not survived, but summaries of them were inscribed in Hepzefi's tomb for the encouragement of his soul-servant. Hepzefi claims to dispose of land and/or revenue under three heads:

(1) From his paternal estate, he sells 42 arouras (28⅓ acres) of land and 27/300 (a little more than 1/13) of the annual income of the principal temple in the nome (of which he happened to be chief priest). The shares of temple income are sold to the holders of certain priestly offices, and he supports his right to sell them with the remark "for I am the son of a priest (*waab*) like each one of you." He betrays no doubt of the validity of these transfers from his patrimony.

(2) From the nomarch's estate he purports to sell to certain temple corporations,

(a) certain shares of meat and of charcoal due to the nomarch from the temple, and

(b) the first fruits of the harvest of the nomarch's estate, a customary free-will offering which future nomarchs would have been expected to pay in any case.

He clearly recognizes the possibility that future nomarchs may nevertheless claim the charcoal, and shows some uneasiness about the first fruits of the harvest, but strangely seems to feel no such uncertainty about the shares of meat. Note that he does not attempt to alienate the nomarch's land.

(3) As chief priest ("overseer of god-servants") of the temple, he sells to himself as a future inhabitant of the cemetery a certain share of meat from every bull sacrificed in the temple and a measure of beer on each occurrence of a certain festivity. These two items were paid for by 2/360 of the temple's annual income, from Hepzefi's patrimony; possibly for this reason, he seems to feel some confidence that future chief priests will keep up the payments of meat and beer.

Thus, the following legal institutions apparently existed shortly after the beginning of the Twelfth Dynasty, and may probably be regarded as survivals from the First Intermediate Period: A man could have possessions both as an individual human being and also—separately—in several different official capacities. What he owned as an individual could be sold. What he owned as nomarch probably could not be sold by any process which would legally bind future nomarchs. Shares of temple income could be bought, sold, and bequeathed, apparently without reference to duties of any kind, but perhaps only within certain recognized priestly families. Presumably other shares of temple income were attached to specific priestly offices; whether these could be sold in such manner as to bind future holders of the relevant office, is not entirely clear. From another source we know that a priestly office itself could be sold.[18]

III. The Empire and the Libyan Regime

The Middle Kingdom disintegrated in the course of the eighteenth century B.C. A new Asiatic horde, the Hyksos, conquered the country; their leaders reigned as "Kings of Upper and Lower Egypt" for probably a hundred years (seventeenth and sixteenth centuries B.C.). Theban princes led a nationalist reaction which drove out the Hyksos and reunited all Egypt in the first half of the sixteenth century (Seventeenth Dynasty and beginning of the Eighteenth). The impetus of the wars of liberation carried Egyptian armies to the Euphrates on the north and far up the Nile valley on the south. The liberating and conquering kings of the Eighteenth Dynasty rewarded their warriors with lands, slaves, gold, all of which became the unrestricted property of the recipients. But above all, the kings showered immense wealth on the gods who had vouchsafed them victory: chiefly on Amon of Karnak (Thebes), but also on Ptah of Memphis, Re of Heliopolis, and a host of less prominent deities. In my opinion, Egyptologists have usually exaggerated the extent to which these admittedly vast temple endowments weakened the royal government: the evidence seems to me to show that even the wealthiest temples remained subservient to the king's authority throughout the Eighteenth and Nineteenth Dynasties and almost to the end of the Twentieth (ca. 1580-1100 B.C.), and the forces which finally wrecked the Twentieth Dynasty were military rather than sacerdotal.[19]

Meanwhile, the warlike spirit had ebbed and the Pharaohs turned more and more to foreign mercenaries for their armies. In the late Nineteenth and early Twentieth Dynasties (ca. 1250-1150 B.C.) these came chiefly from across the Mediterranean and from Nubia. Espe-

[18] Seidl, *Einführung*, p. 46, citing P. Kahun II, 1, a document of the late Twelfth or early Thirteenth Dynasty.

[19] Kees, "Herihor und die Aufrichtung des thebanischen Gottesstaates," *Nachrichten von der Gesellschaft der Wissenschaften zu Göttingen* (1936-38), pp. 1-20; W. F. Edgerton, "The Government and the Governed in the Egyptian Empire," *Journal of Near Eastern Studies*, VI (1947), 152-160; Edgerton, "The Nauri Decree of Seti I," *JNES*, VI (1947), 219-230; Edgerton, "The Strikes in Ramses III's Twenty-ninth Year," *JNES*, X (1951), 137-145; Edgerton in *Cambridge Ancient History*, II (2nd edn.), Chap. XXIV (forthcoming). Gardiner's objections, *JEA*, XXXVII (1952), 24-33, have not altered my view of the Nauri Decree.

cially prominent are the Sherden, probably members of the same ethnic group which was later to give its name to Sardinia.[20] Sherden were prominent as landholders in the reign of Ramses V (ca. 1150 B.C.).[21] Both Sherden and the Nubians disappear from our knowledge as Egyptian mercenaries about the end of the Twentieth Dynasty (early eleventh century B.C.), their place being taken by the Libyans.

Mercenaries, foreign invasions, and civil wars made the latter part of the Twentieth Dynasty (ca. 1150-1100 B.C. and later) a time of recurrent anarchy. The royal tombs of Thebes were plundered, as those of Memphis had been at the fall of the Old Kingdom. An army officer named Herihor made himself High Priest of Amon of Karnak (the wealthiest and most powerful priestly office in Egypt), while a husband and wife of unknown origin, Smendes and Tentamon, set themselves up as rulers of Tanis in the Delta; these three worthies ignored the last King Ramses, permitting him to sit harmlessly on the throne but governing Egypt and sending emissaries to foreign lands in their own names without so much as mentioning the king. Other "great ones of Egypt" appear vaguely in the background, and may have governed this or that city with as little respect for Herihor, Smendes, and Tentamon as these three showed for Ramses. On the death of Ramses XI, first Herihor and later Smendes assumed the Pharaonic titles; later still a grandson of Herihor married a granddaughter (?) of Smendes and made some pretense of uniting the country for a time. These personages are counted to the Twenty-first Dynasty, which reigned until about 950 B.C.

Meanwhile Libyan marauders, Libyan mercenaries serving in their own units under their own chiefs, and peaceful Libyan settlers became increasingly prominent. About 950 B.C. a powerful Libyan named Sheshonk, whose family for some generations had ruled a wide territory around Heracleopolis, made himself Pharaoh and founded the Twenty-second Dynasty (950-730, capital at Bubastis in the Delta). Sheshonk's was only the strongest of many Libyan families who had established themselves in different Egyptian cities. These Libyans maintained their identity as a separate military class (something previously unknown in Egypt), continued to wear Libyan costume at least in some details (particularly, the chiefs continued to wear one or two feathers on the head, an ancient Libyan custom), but before

[20] Cf. Alan H. Gardiner, *Ancient Egyptian Onomastica*, I (Oxford, 1947), 194-99.

[21] Cf. Gardiner, *The Wilbour Papyrus:* II, *Commentary*, p. 80.

Sheshonk ascended the throne they had become thoroughly Egyptianized in religion and doubtless in many other ways. They continued to reside in organized military communities, where each soldier had his plot of ground. At Thebes, the High Priest of Amon continued to be what the soldier Herihor had made himself—the effective ruler of a principality which at times included a large part of Upper Egypt. This sacerdotal principality was regularly headed by a son or other close relative of the reigning king. Similar sacerdotal principalities existed at Heracleopolis, Memphis, Heliopolis, and probably other cities: we judge the period chiefly by Theban records, having little information elsewhere. It would seem that the sacerdotal principalities were ruled by high priests who were also generals, while the military principalities were ruled by generals who were also high priests: I am not disposed to argue that the difference was important. High priests and generals alike, though Egyptianized, continued proudly to trace their ancestry back to Libyan origins. As a rule, they recognized the supremacy of the reigning king during the early part of the Twenty-second Dynasty. Rebellions occurred from time to time, but we do not know whether these were led by disgruntled Libyans or nationalistic Egyptians. A decade or two before 800 B.C. a rival Libyan dynasty, the Twenty-third (perhaps a branch of Sheshonk's house), established itself and reigned alongside the Twenty-second under circumstances about which we know almost nothing. In the eighth century, disunion went on apace: when the Nubian Piankhi momentarily conquered Egypt about 730 B.C., he received the submission of a whole series of independent or semi-independent princes, four of whom bore the ancient title which had once meant "King of Upper Egypt"; the most influential of the lot, Tefnakhte of Sais, did not bear the kingly title.[22]

A peculiar institution especially characteristic of the Twenty-first to Twenty-third Dynasties is the political use of oracles. The concept of government by oracle was an old one going back at least to the Second Intermediate Period.[23] Thutmose III (fifteenth century B.C.)

[22] Raymond Weill has recently propounded views on the significance of multiple kingship which I cannot share ("La royauté en division multiple à diverses époques de la période pharaonique," *Journal asiatique*, CCXXXVIII, 1950, 59-80)

[23] Consider the folk tale in which the sun-god Re begets the first three kings of the Fifth Dynasty and foretells their successive reigns (A. Erman, *Die Märchen des Papyrus Westcar*, Berlin, 1890, I, 10-13. Erman in his introduction dates the papyrus to about the Second Intermediate Period ("Die Handschrift und ihr Alter," pp. 5-6) so that the practices recorded in it must go back at least to that period.

in an address to his courtiers which probably has no factual foundation, claimed that his own elevation to the throne resulted from an oracle of Amon of Karnak: the claim, even if false, proves the existence of the idea. Ramses II, two hundred years later, did certainly obtain Amon's oracle before elevating the high priest of the provincial towns of Dendera and This to the immensely more important high priesthood of Amon of Karnak: as this was one of the first independent acts of a very young king, we can readily imagine why the oracle was thought necessary. Humbler men of Ramses II's generation and later often submitted their affairs to various major and minor Theban deities, and the oracular responses obtained in such cases seem to have had legal effect. But in the Twenty-first to Twenty-third Dynasties, kings, generals, and high priests seem to have resorted to oracles for almost every important decision. Possibly they found the device helpful in ruling an Egyptian populace which may still have resented the rule of upstart soldiers like Herihor, or of "Libyans" who made their foreign origin a point of honor.

Another development of the "Libyan" period is the elevation of the "god's wife" of Amon of Karnak to the headship of the sacerdotal principality of Thebes, displacing the "chief god-servant" or high priest. Under the Eighteenth Dynasty, the "god's wife" was the queen, a reflection of the state fiction that the god Amon became the actual father of each successive Pharaoh. Under Dynasties Twenty-three to Twenty-six the god's wife was always a king's daughter; she did not marry, but each in turn eventually adopted a later king's daughter as her "daughter" and successor. In this way among others, successive dynasties, Egyptian and Nubian, gained or maintained control over what remained of the Theban principality.[24]

From 730 to 663 B.C. the history of Egypt is dominated by Nubian and Assyrian conquerors. Of the Egyptian princelings who maintained a precarious existence through this period, the most important were those of Sais: Tefnakhte who resisted Piankhi, Tefnakhte's son Bokkhoris who appears in tradition as the sole king of the Twenty-fourth Dynasty, Bokkhoris's son Necho who was carried captive to Nineveh by Ashurbanipal but later restored to his principality by the same Assyrian king, and Necho's son Psammetichos who in 663 B.C. proclaimed himself King of Upper and Lower Egypt and who did in fact reunite the country, founding the Twenty-sixth Dynasty which ruled

[24] See Sander-Hansen, "Das Gottesweib des Amun," Det Kongelige Danske Videnskabernes Selskab, *Historisk-filologiske Skrifter*, I, No. I (Copenhagen, 1940).

until conquered by Cambyses in 525 B.C. The class of "warriors" which arose in the "Libyan" period seems to have survived long enough to be observed by Greek writers, though the kings of the Twenty-sixth Dynasty relied much on Greek and other non-Egyptian mercenaries. As for the hereditary priesthood, we saw that priestly birth was considered important in the Twelfth Dynasty (Hepzefi) and it certainly was important in the Twenty-sixth Dynasty and under Persian rule, but I would not venture to suggest that an outsider might not have been able to buy a priestly office. At no time did the warriors, the priests, or any other class of persons in ancient Egypt constitute a "caste" in the Indian sense.

VII · FEUDALISM IN INDIA

BY DANIEL THORNER

Source material for most of India's history is sparse, hard to handle, and quite removed from the facts of everyday life. Historians of India have had their hands full trying to make this refractory material tell us simply what happened and when. Their books provide meager fare for social scientists interested in delineating the chief phases or patterns in India's development.

To the present writer's knowledge there is no single work solely devoted to feudalism in India; nor is there even a single article on the place of feudalism in the historical evolution of India. To say whether there have existed in India any feudal ages—in the sense described in the introductory chapter of this book—would require a fresh examination of all the phases of India's history since invaders speaking Indo-Aryan languages made their way into the country from the northwest some thirty-three centuries ago. As an alternative, however, to a task of this magnitude, we can pick out for discussion the two regimes to which the term "feudal" has occasionally been applied: the Rajput rule in western India, and the Muslim regimes of northern India. We can begin by reviewing the work of two important writers who have looked at these phases of India's history in terms of feudalism, and then consider the extent to which the periods and institutions which they describe can justly be characterized as feudal ages.

1. The Rajput States

"Sketch of a Feudal System in Rajasthan" is the title of one of the early sections in the magnificent work which James Tod published in 1829 on the *Annals and Antiquities of Rajasthan.*[1] Such discussion of feudalism in India as has taken place stems more from this than from any other single source. At the age of sixteen Tod was named a cadet in the army of the East India Company and about 1800 sailed from England to India. There he served for two dozen years, in both military and political capacities, principally in Central India and Rajputana. In the course of this work Tod developed a marked sympathy

[1] James Tod, *Annals and Antiquities of Rajasthan, or the Central and Western Rajput States of India*, ed. with Introduction and Notes by William Crooke, 3 vols. (London, 1920).

for the Rajput style of life, became a partisan of the Rajput princes, and gained their confidence to such an extent that some gave him access to the letters and records stored in their palaces.[2]

Tod himself tells us that early in his career he began to study the Rajputs as an avocation; and he came to suspect that the Rajput "martial system" and "traditional theory of government" bore striking analogies to the "ancient feudal system of Europe," at least "with reference to a period when the latter was yet imperfect." When Hallam's account of medieval feudalism was published in his *View of the State of Europe during the Middle Ages* (London, 1818), Tod examined it and his doubts were resolved.[3] He concluded that the Rajput system was so strikingly analogous to the European as to be truly feudal. If Tod's view had been confirmed by subsequent investigators, then his conclusion would have had profound significance for the present study, for Rajputana is an area of exceptional importance to the analyst of social history. There are grounds for believing that from the eleventh to the eighteenth centuries the Rajput states preserved more of their antique structure than any other basic region of India. As one of the later writers on Rajputana, A. C. Lyall, put it in 1875, these states constituted "perhaps the best specimens of early institutions that can now be found within the purview of comparatively settled civilisation"; they were "the only ancient political institutions now surviving upon any considerable scale in India. . . ."[4]

Tod believed he saw characteristically feudal relationships wherever he turned in Rajputana. What, according to Tod, were their chief features? First, the hierarchical structure of society, at the top of which stood the several dozen leading princes of Rajputana. The superior houses each had the colorful regalia of feudalism: armorial bearing, banner, palladium, kettle-drum, silver mace, as well as a bard to spread its fame. The great chiefs had under them vassals of higher or lower rank, according to the size of the landed estates which they held as fiefs. The obligations of the vassals included military service, attendance on the person of the prince for varying periods, and a number of payments, such as reliefs, escheats, aids, and wardships. The lower houses rested upon subdivision of the great grants, subdivisions which Tod explicitly termed subinfeudation; this process he considered to have

[2] The remarks on Tod's career follow those in Crooke's Introduction to his edition of Tod's *Annals*, I, i-xliv.

[3] *Annals*, I, 154.

[4] *Asiatic Studies: Religious and Social*, 2nd edn., I (London, 1907), 219-220.

extended to the lowest subdenomination, the *charsa*, or "hide of land," sufficient to furnish one equipped knight.[5]

Tod called the class of tenures which we have just sketched feudal—the lord (*thakur*) holds (*giras*) by grant (*patta*) of the prince. But these were not the only tenures in Rajputana. Alongside of them existed *bhumia*, freehold tenures which Tod considered the counterpart of European allodial tenures. *Bhumia* was "a most expressive and comprehensive name, importing absolute identity with the soil. . . ." Lands so held were exempt from payment of the customary share of the crops owed to the local ruler; the chieftain's revenue officers could not measure *bhumia* holdings, nor could they assess them. *Bhumia* tenures thus were highly esteemed. The holders considered themselves scions of the earliest princes in Rajputana. The *bhumia* paid no fine for investiture, for their grants did not have to be renewed, since they rested on prescriptive possession. All that they were liable for were small annual quit-rents and local service, say as frontier guards or as a sort of irregular feudal militia. "So cherished," Tod tells us, was "this tenure of Bhum, that the greatest chiefs are always solicitous to obtain it, even in the villages wholly dependent on their authority: a decided proof of its durability above common grants." Because of *bhumia's* advantages, in fact, a great object of ambition was to serve without a *patta* or grant. A favorite phrase on the lips of the Rajput nobility was *ma ka bhum*, "my land."[6]

In the Rajput states the lands held under these *bhumia* tenures typically were greatly inferior in extent to the lands held as grants. To illustrate the distribution of various types of land, Tod describes the case of Mewar (or Udaipur), the premier state of Rajputana and the one in which ancient institutions presumably persisted in purest form. Except for the central part of the state surrounding the capital city of Udaipur (named after its putative founder, Udai Singh), the great bulk of the land, roughly three-quarters, was usually held as estates by the chiefs. Each of these estates contained something like fifty to one hundred villages and towns. In the heart of the country lay the best and richest land which formed the crown demesne of the ruler or Maharana of Mewar. This tract, some twenty-five miles in circumference, was the *khalisa* or fisc. "To obtain any portion thereof," Tod stated, "was the reward of important services; to have a grant of a few acres near the capital for a garden was deemed a high favour; and a

[5] *Annals*, I, 201; I, Book III, passim.

[6] *Annals*, I, 190-197, 576-577.

village in the amphitheatre or valley, in which the present capital is situated, was the *ne plus ultra* of recompense." *Bhumia* tenures, by contrast, appeared in the parts of Mewar settled since remotest antiquity, "where they were defended from oppression by the rocks and wilds in which they obtained a footing; as in Kumbhalmer, the wilds of Chappan, or plains of Mandalgarh, long under the kings, and where their agricultural pursuits maintained them." In the latter area as many as four thousand *bhumias* persisted. "They held and maintained without support the important fortress of that district, during [the past] half a century of turmoil, for their prince."[7]

What were the relationships among the prince, chieftains, lesser vassals, and *bhumias*? Here we must be on our guard against the danger of portraying the functioning of "government" in a more precise or organized fashion than ever in fact existed. Tod's own description of the "feudal system in Rajasthan" begins with the sentence: "It is more than doubtful whether any code or civil or criminal jurisprudence ever existed in any of these principalities; though it is certain that none is at this day [1829] discoverable in their archives." Subject to this reservation we may offer the following oversimplified outline of the governmental structure. Its mainspring was the prince. "The character and welfare of the States depend on that of the sovereign. . . ." Legislative authority, to the extent that it was more than a purely local phenomenon, emanated from the prince, his civil council and his four chief ministers and their deputies. In practice, however the principal concerns of the prince's council were the grand question of general peace and threats to the tranquillity of the government. When these subjects were before the council, Tod tells us, the chieftains themselves constituted that body, in association with the prince. In quieter times it would appear that the principal business of the council was to supervise the collection of the revenues due to the crown and to administer justice in the crown demesne.[8]

The authority of the prince, insofar as it was exercised in the outlying districts, was wielded by two sets of officials: heads of garrisons manning border posts, and "resident rulers" (a civil officer and a military officer conjoined) of the constituent districts of the principality. The headquarters of the latter generally were in the principal place of each district. The civil power of these resident rulers usually was weak since the chiefs were extremely jealous of their own prerogatives. Thus

[7] *Annals*, I, 166, 196-197.
[8] *Annals*, I, 174, 170, 172.

Tod tells us, "in cases regarding the distribution of justice or the internal economy of the chief's estates, the government officers seldom interfere." In all cases involving property, the ancient, self-constituted tribunals, the *panchayats*, sat in judgment. In criminal cases the chiefs were not supposed to act without the special sanction of the crown, but in fact, Tod concedes, justice "has long been left to work its own way. . . ." The courts of justice of the princes always sat in the *khalisa* or crown demesne. "It was deemed a humiliating intrusion if they sat within the bounds of a chief. To 'erect the flag' within his limits, whether for the formation of defensive posts or the collection of duties, is deemed a gross breach of his privileged independence, as to establish them within the walls of his residence would be deemed equal to sequestration."[9]

Sequestration raises the crucial question of the mutual relations of the chiefs and their vassals. Under what conditions could a prince or a chief resume a grant made to a vassal? What was the term of these grants? Under what conditions could a vassal renounce his obligations to his lord? Tod's handling of these questions is decisive for the applicability or non-applicability to Rajputana of feudalism and its terminology. Following him, we may at once classify the *bhumia* land in a special category. Those who possessed land of this sort had a stronger and more valid right in the soil than grants from the sovereign himself. (Otherwise, Tod queries, "What should induce a chieftain, when inducted into a perpetual [sic] fief, to establish through the ryot [peasant] a right to a few acres in bhum, but the knowledge that although the vicissitudes of fortune or of favour may deprive him of his aggregate signiorial rights, his claims, derived from the spontaneous favour of the commune, can never be set aside; and when he ceases to be the lord, he becomes a member of the commonwealth, merging his title of Thakur, or Signior, into the more humble one of Bhumia. . . ."[10]

Our real concern is with what Tod called fiefs of the crown, particularly in the state of Mewar, where they long persisted in their purest form. Tod believed that in the first phase of the conquest by the Rajputs of the lands to which they have given their name (Rajputana or Rajasthan), fiefs were not grants in perpetuity but were transferable. But, as in Europe, so in Rajputana, during the evolution of the feudal system, fiefs changed from movable to perpetual to hereditary. In its developed form, the grant of an estate was "for the life of the holder,

[9] *Annals*, I, 167, 172, 167n, 171-172.
[10] *Annals*, I, 575.

with inheritance for his offspring in lineal descent or adoption, with the sanction of the prince, and resumable for crime or incapacity: this reversion and power of resumption being marked by the usual ceremonies on each lapse of the grantee, or sequestration (*zabti*), of relief (*nazarana*), of homage and investiture of the heir." In characterizing these tenures, Tod emphasized the crucial importance of ties by blood. Typically a vassal was a kinsman of his chief, his lord. Where this was not the case, where chiefs had vassals (Rajputs to be sure) who were of different blood and from another Rajput tribe, then the estates of the latter were of inferior title. These "foreign" grants bore the epithet *kala patta*, "black grant." Such foreigners did not have the kinsman's "strength in the soil," even though they continued to hold the same estate for "twenty generations' duration."[11]

In fact, consideration of the role of blood ties in that society leads to the conclusion that Rajput society was truly patriarchal. The greater portion of the vassal chiefs, Tod states, "from the highest of the sixteen peers to the holders of a *charsa* [hide] of land, claim affinity in blood to the sovereign." Further, "only those of pure blood in both lines can hold [true or hereditary] fiefs of the crown." The greatest prince among the Rajputs could wed the daughter of a Rajput father so poor that he possessed only one *charsa* of land, and not be degraded at all by such a marriage. In Mewar two great clans, Chondawat and Saktawat, formed the "blood royal," the Kula Sesodia, foremost tribe of the Rajputs; scions of subdivisions of these two clans composed the chief "vassalage" of Mewar. Such blood ties underlined the dangers to the prince in trying to resume a long-established grant. "Though in all these estates there is a mixture of foreign Rajputs, yet the blood of the chief predominates; and these [estates?] must have a leader of their own, or be incorporated in the estates of the nearest of kin. This increase might not be desirable for the crown, but the sub-vassals cannot be turned adrift; a resumption therefore in these countries is widely felt, as it involves many. If crime or incapacity render it necessary, the prince inducts a new head of that blood; and it is their pride, as well as the prince's interest, that a proper choice should be made."[12]

Critics of Tod, in fact, have raised the question whether in Rajputana the basic relationship actually was that of lord and vassal and have asserted rather that it was that of tribal chieftain and his blood kin. Tod himself furnishes us materials for probing this question. As an

[11] *Annals*, I, 192-195.

[12] *Annals*, I, 155-156, 165, 193, 195.

appendix to his "Sketch of the Feudal System in Rajasthan" he printed twenty documents, dating chiefly from the period between 1750 and 1820. This was the age following the disintegration of the Mughal empire. The older order of Rajput society was attacked from without and challenged by adventurers and ambitious warlords within. Those who embodied and benefited from the older, long-established arrangements of society protested and eventually sought outside aid. One of the chief forms which their protests took was a restatement of the antique arrangements of society and the way in which they were being defiled. Chief among the recipients of their appeals for aid was Tod himself, during the years from 1818 to 1822, when he was the East India Company's Political Agent to the Western Rajput States.[13]

The principal theme of these protests and appeals was that ancient usages were being set aside and land usurpations were taking place. In particular they complained that the great princes and chieftains were not maintaining the dignities due to the lesser chiefs and other Rajputs, and that the peasantry were being oppressed by exactions and arbitrary fines. The chiefs of Mārwār made a particularly clear statement to this effect, while describing in 1821 the process by which their prince, the Maharaja of Jodhpur, had dispossessed them. The Maharaja and themselves, they declared, were all of one stock of Rajputs, all Rathors. "He is our head, we his servants: but now anger has seized him and we are dispossessed of our country. Of the estates, our patrimony and our dwelling, some have been made khalisa [added to the fisc], and those who endeavour to keep aloof expect the same fate. . . . Such a spirit has possessed his mind as never was known to any former prince of Jodhpur. His forefathers have reigned for generations; our forefathers were their ministers and advisers, and whatever was performed was by the collective wisdom of the council of our chiefs. . . . Now, men of no consideration are in our prince's presence; hence this reverse." The first part of this terse pronouncement concluded with the following declaration about the mutual relations of the prince and the Mārwār chiefs: *"When our services are acceptable, then is he our lord; when not, we are again his brothers and kindred, claimants and laying claim to the land"* (Tod's italics).[14]

Far from being couched in terms of vassals and their lord, this sounds more like the language of tribal brethren, men of the same stock, equal to one another. This would fit a tribe whose outstanding prince could

[13] *Annals*, I, xxvi.
[14] *Annals*, I, 228-229.

marry with impunity the daughter of the poorest landed Rajput. Lest we seem to be making too much of what might be simply an isolated statement, here is a related declaration of 1819 from Deogarh, a district in Mewar, some miles north of the capital, Udaipur. In remonstrating with their chief, the Maharaja Gokuldas, the sub-chiefs of Deogarh began with the accusation that "he respects not the privileges or customs established of old." For our purposes the most relevant passage is one voicing the same sentiments as those expressed by the Mārwār chiefs about the Maharaja of Jodhpur: *"When Deogarh was established, at the same time were our allotments: as is his patrimony, so is our patrimony"* (Tod's italics). Both the subchiefs who made this statement, and the kinsman and chief about whom they made it, belonged to the same branch of the main stock of the Sesodia clan, the head of which ruled Mewar. It is therefore significant that in their concluding passage the sub-chiefs declare: "Our rights and privilege in his family are the same as his in the family of the Presence [i.e., equality in the presence of the ruler of Mewar, the Maharana]."[15]

We have now to face directly the question: Are the holdings, described by Tod in terms of feudal relations of lords and vassals, basically and primarily tribal holdings by blood and birthright of the clan? We must state at once that the editor of the best edition of Tod's *Annals* William Crooke, took the latter position. Crooke, himself an outstanding authority on tribal organization in northern India, had little patience or use for Tod's comparisons of Rajput phenomena with those of medieval feudalism in Western Europe. Crooke wrote:

"While it is possible to trace, as Tod has done, certain analogies between the tribal institutions of the Rajputs and the social organization of medieval Europe—analogies of feudal incidents connected with Reliefs, Fines upon alienation, Escheats, Aids, Wardship, and Marriage —these analogies, when more closely examined, are found to be in the main superficial. If we desire to undertake a comparative study of the Rajput tribal system, it is unnecessary to travel to medieval Europe while we have close at hand the social organization of more or less kindred tribes on the Indian borderland, Pathans, Afghans, or Baloch or, in a more primitive stage, those of the Kandhs, Gonds, Mundas or Oraons [of the central highlands of India]. It is of little service to compare two systems of which only the nucleus is common to both and to place side by side institutions which present only a factitious

[15] *Annals*, I, 230-232.

similitude, because the social development of each has progressed on different lines."[16]

Crooke's dismissal of Tod's feudal analogies might have been less summary, had not A. C. Lyall contributed in 1875 a masterly essay centered on the political institutions of "The Rajput States of India."[17] Lyall himself had an intimate knowledge of Rajputana, since he had served there as British Chief Commissioner in the 1870's. Also, as a friend and close student of Sir Henry Maine, he shared the latter's wide-ranging interest in comparative political institutions.[18] Early in his analysis of Rajputana, Lyall emphasized that the term "Rajputana" did not so much mean "Land of the Rajputs," as "Lands Ruled by the Rajputs." (There were and are many more Rajputs outside of Rajputana than within it.) He urged his readers to think not so much of France, the country of the French, as of Lombard Italy, the country taken by the Lombards. To Lyall, in the western states of Rajputana, at least, "the conquering clans are still very much in the position which they took up on first entry upon the lands."[19] The Rajput clans he saw as a political and military overlay upon the cultivating classes, composed mainly of castes and clans whom the Rajputs subdued when they first took possession. They were a conquering tribal settlement, the lords of the soil, and in each Rajput state the governing authority vested in the hands of the hereditary chief of the dominant clan. The chief was "supposed to be the nearest legitimate descendant in direct male line from the founder of the State. . . , and the heads of the branches from this main stock are the leading Rajput nobles, the pillars of his State."[20]

What was it, Lyall asks, that suggested the analogy with feudalism? He answers, the interior constitution of a complete Rajput state. The chief of the dominant clan normally possessed the largest single portion, the rest by and large being divided up among the branch families and their offshoots. Where the clan organization was strongest, there the territory ruled directly by the chief was likely to be the smallest; where the chief lately has been particularly strong, there his direct dominion is likely to be largest. Hereditary heads of the

[16] Introduction to *Annals*, I, xxxix. [17] *Asiatic Studies*, I, 203-264.

[18] See the paper, "Sir Henry Maine," which I contributed to *Some Modern Historians of Britain: Essays in Honor of R. L. Schuyler*, ed. Herman Ausubel et al. (New York, 1951), pp. 66-84.

[19] *Asiatic Studies*, I, 224. The remarks in this and the succeeding three paragraphs follow closely the language of Lyall, as cited above, pp. 225-245.

[20] *Asiatic Studies*, I, 228.

branch septs may possess large tracts of land and act like chiefs in miniature. The lesser chiefs pay certain duties to the state chiefs; they must render military service against the foreigner or against rebels; their lands are rated in terms of the number of horsemen they are to furnish. At every succession the heirs of the lesser chiefs are bound to render homage to the state chief and pay a certain fine to his treasury. These acts are essential to his entry into legal possession of his inheritance. He also pays some other customary dues which Lyall does not cavil at calling "of a feudal nature." Alongside these services and payments "their jealousy of his power never sleeps." But "disobedience to a lawful summons or refusal to do homage involves sequestration of the lands, if the Chief can enforce it, *bien entendu*. . . ."[21]

Such a society, Lyall wrote, bore a resemblance to feudal society which was at first sight striking enough. It misled Tod into missing "the radical distinction between the two forms of society, tribal and feudal. Although he clearly understands the connection of those whom he calls 'vassals' with their suzerain to be affinity of blood, still he insists that the working system of Rajputana is feudal."[22] But, in truth, declared Lyall, nowhere in western Rajputana had the system become entirely feudal, i.e., nowhere had "military tenure entirely obliterated the original tenure by blood and birthright of the clan." Land tenure in Rajputana, he wrote, had not become the basis of the Rajput "noblesse"; rather, "their pure blood is the origin of their land tenure. . . ." This fact lay behind the protests of the Mārwār chiefs and the Deogarh subchiefs. These protests took "their stand on rights far beyond the feudal conception; and indeed it is universally assumed in every clan of Rajputana, that the Chief and ruler of the State is only *primus inter pares*."[23]

In his final appraisal of Tod, Lyall saw him as one who had made an unprecedentedly exhaustive special study, founded on a knowledge of Rajputana unequalled in its intimacy; "and perhaps we should not blame him for failing to see that his Rajput feudalism was not the basis of the society, but an incomplete superstructure, and that Raj putana, as he surveyed it, was a group of tribal suzerainties rapidl passing into the feudal stage, which we now know to have been largel built up in Europe over the tribal foundations."[24] Thus, in conclusion Lyall leaves us with the impression that feudalism might really hav

[21] *Asiatic Studies*, I, 240.
[22] *Asiatic Studies*, I, 243.
[23] *Asiatic Studies*, I, 245.
[24] *Asiatic Studies*, I, 244.

evolved in Rajputana had not British power overlaid the whole subcontinent in the century after 1750.

II. The Muslim Regimes of Northern India

The most explicit characterization of early Muslim and Mughal institutions in India as feudal was made by the dean of Russian social and economic historians before World War I, Maxim M. Kovalevski.[25] One of the abiding interests of Kovalevski's long and distinguished career was the "historical-comparative study of the process of development of landed property." India attracted him because of its extraordinary richness in archaic forms of land tenure; and because of the opportunity to study the way in which those tenures were dissolving under the impact of British agrarian policy. While still a neophyte, Kovalevski came to enjoy the friendship of the man who in the 1870's and 1880's was the foremost British authority on these subjects, Sir Henry Maine. To Maine's writings and conversations he credited the impetus for launching his own work in the same field; Maine undoubtedly helped to give him entree to the archives of the India Office in London, and their "voluminous and priceless materials. . . ."[26] Kovalevski found in London much of the material for his monograph, the sixth chapter of which deals with Muslim India.

According to Kovalevski the decisive influence in the direction of the "feudalization" of India was the series of Muslim conquests, particularly in northwestern India from the eleventh century onward. He developed his position by first outlining India's agrarian structure under the "Native Rajas" (i.e., chiefly Hindu), and then he analyzed the impact of the Muslim conquerors' policies upon the older institutions. Our presentation of his views will follow the same order.

In his analysis of agrarian structure under the "Native Rajas" Kovalevski did not find any characteristically feudal relations. He did discern two major kinds of property (*sobstv'ennost'*), communal

[25] See Kovalevski, *Obshchinnoye Zyemlevladyenie, Prichini, Khod i Posled'stviya ego Razlozheniya* [Communal Landholding: Causes, Course, and Results of Its Disintegration] (Moscow, 1879). The translation of the chapters in it bearing on India would not have been possible without the encouragement and support of the Chairman of the South Asia Regional Studies Department at the University of Pennsylvania, Dr. W. Norman Brown. The translators of these chapters were Drs. Leigh Lisker and Surendra J. Patel.

[26] Kovalevski, Preface.

landholding and individual. The basic, underlying and most typical he considered to have always been communal.[27] In the course of time communal holding by kinsmen gave way, Kovalevski believed, to common holdings by villagers who were not necessarily kinsmen. This in turn gave way to joint, indivisible family property; and finally there appeared, relatively late, individual land tenure. The process of individualization of property Kovalevski considered to have been a very slow one, extending over many centuries. He did call attention to two pressures which tended to decompose communal tenures into individual tenures: (1) pressure from the tribal chiefs, who strove to turn themselves into a sort of supreme proprietors of the territory occupied by their people; they tried in particular to claim special rights of granting unoccupied lands as private property to individuals or groups willing to bring them under cultivation; (2) pressure from the priestly caste, the Brahmans. To sustain their activities—religious observances, temple building, charity, and the like—the Brahmans desired gifts, especially land and its revenues. A serious obstacle in their path was the prevailing inalienability and indivisibility of village community and family land. It was to the interest of the Brahmans to accelerate the change from group holding to individual tenure. In analyzing successive legal codes in India Kovalevski called attention to what he considered to have been the results of pressure of this sort.

Kovalevski's central thesis was that the land policy of the Muslim conquerors of northern India, primarily from the eleventh century onward, set in motion a process of feudalization of this older structure. The distinctive feature of the Muslim land policy was the granting of *iqtas,*[28] that is, the Sultans distributed villages and districts to their followers on condition that they furnish upon demand a stipulated number of troops. In return for this military service the *iqtadar* (holders of the *iqtas*) turned to their own use the land revenue raised from the villages or district granted to them. (Kovalevski equated the *iqta* with the benefice of Western Europe.) Meanwhile the village population continued to hold the land either communally or individ

[27] This is not the place to discuss in detail the various categories of commun landholding listed and analyzed by Kovalevski: "gentile" communes (based o kinsmen), village communes (based on territorial co-habitants, rather than kin men), and familial group holding (indivisible "property" of the joint family Suffice it to say that in the formidable body of literature on the nature and histo of landed property, Kovalevski's views and many writings occupy a centr position.

[28] Kovalevski believed the *iqta* to have been of Persian origin, dating back pre-Mohammedan times.

ually, as before, but without the same personal status. In time, however, by a process of commendation, free proprietors "lost their independence, and therewith their allodial tenure became feudal." According to Kovalevski, this "feudalization" process had two phases: the first, from the twelfth to the fifteenth century (the "Turk" and "Afghan" conquests), and the second, under the Mughals ("Moguls" or "Mongols"), from the sixteenth to the eighteenth century.

The core of the feudalization process from the twelfth to the fifteenth century, according to Kovalevski, was the effort of the holders of *iqtas* to make their prerogatives hereditary and independent of the Sultan of Delhi's will. Thus an incident is recorded in the middle of the thirteenth century of many *iqtadars* refusing to perform military service on the ground that their grants were not conditional but hereditary and unconditional. In this case, at least, the effort failed. The Sultan struck back hard by ordering those *iqtadars* who were incapable of bearing military service deprived of their holdings. He also resumed those grants which, upon the death of *iqtadars*, had passed into the hands of minors. The same conflict between Sultan and *iqtadars* marked the fourteenth century. Upon ascending the throne, successive Sultans of Delhi, although claiming the right to resume *iqtas*, generally confirmed the position of the existing *iqtadars*. In the reign of Firuz Shah (1351-1388), according to Kovalevski, hereditability received legislative acknowledgement. Firuz, we are told, "took active steps to assure an indisputable transfer of an *iqta* from the individual originally granted it to his heir." He also enlarged the sphere in which "benefices" operated by admitting not only officers but also soldiers to the usufruct of *iqtas*. Besides these steps in the military sphere, Firuz Shah also endeavored to extend hereditability in the sphere of secular affairs. Thus, during his reign, Kovalevski held, "there was completed in India the same transformation in the feudal system as in the Carolingian, the monarchy connected with the name of Charles the Bald. Like the benefices, the iktas became hereditary."[29]

The outstanding feature of the fifteenth century and the first part of the sixteenth, Kovalevski held, was the weakness of the central authorities and the struggle for power of minor officials and holders of *iqtas*. The empire of Delhi fell apart and the system of "beneficial tenure" became entrenched; and alongside these there grew up, "to the detriment of administrative and political unity," the system of leasing tax collections. In this setting Northern India offered weak resistance

[29] Kovalevski, Chap. VI.

to invaders from Central Asia, and a bold adventurer like Babur, with only a few companions, was able to gather supporters in the middle of the sixteenth century and found the Mughal empire.

In their land policy the Mughal rulers followed in the footsteps of their Muslim predecessors. They granted *iqtas* to the military classes. The *iqtadars* had exclusive rights to payments in money or in kind from the districts which they held. "Their sole obligation was one of personally rendering military service and of furnishing at their own expense a specified number of infantry and cavalry soldiers." They were not required to make payments to the government treasury. In addition to these *iqtadars*, Kovalevski stated, whole districts in outlying parts of the realm were left in the hands of Hindu princely houses which had persisted through the earlier centuries of Muslim rule. They took the designation of *zamindars* (landholders) and undertook tc collect land taxes and transmit them to the imperial government. Fo their service they received the right to levy and retain an additiona assessment upon the local population. The holdings of these *zamindar* and of the *iqtadars* were not hereditary. The emperors and their pro vincial rulers insisted that they all had to be renewed at the beginnin of each new reign and also retained the right to deprive at will holder of grants. But, as a matter of fact, "they did in most cases pass fron the father to his oldest son."

In short, the Mughal rulers did not alter basically the land systen which they found in India. In their regimes, however, basic change did occur, in a gradual fashion. One cause of this was the vagueness and broadness of the rights granted the benefice-holders (*iqtadars*) an tax-officials (*zamindars*, in Kovalevski's terminology). Crushing taxe persecution, and violence often caused "small owners" to abandon the land, whereupon the *zamindars* absorbed them as personal holding Alternatively the small holders might cede their rights to the larg magnates and become their dependents, on condition that they retai its hereditary use. This arrangement, which Kovalevski termed stril ingly similar to medieval commendation, bore the name of *iqbalda* It spread with particular rapidity as the Mughal regime weakened; tl last strong emperor was Aurangzeb, who died in 1707. Simultaneousl the holders of benefices and the *zamindars* (in practice, these grou tended to merge) strove to make their positions hereditary. As the power grew, they found it more advantageous not to collect the lar revenue themselves, but to lease out that right to third parties. In tin these tax-farmers themselves claimed hereditary rights, and sublet their rights to still another class of subordinate intermediaries.

Kovalevski concluded his account with an endeavor to state what was and what was not feudal in India, on the eve of the British conquest. For this purpose he listed four criteria of feudalism: system of benefices, commendation, leasing of offices, and patrimonial justice.[30] The first three of these, he held, had clearly existed in India under the Muslims. The fourth and last of these, private jurisdiction, was clearly not present. The local courts (usually formed and conducted by the villagers themselves, in the form of *panchayats*, councils of five), handled most criminal matters and all civil matters, especially property suits. To this virtual autonomy in the sphere of justice Kovalevski attributed the principal difference between the less intense process of feudalization in India and the more intense one in Western Europe. The autonomy of the civil courts, in turn, he explained by the fact that "the leasing of offices did not take place by any means throughout the entire country. Whole districts were subordinated directly to the treasury and to tax officials by an arbitrarily appointed and removable administration. This system was in force not only in the Empire of the Great Mughals, but also in the monarchies dependent upon it to a greater or lesser extent. It alone was known to the Marathas, who step by step gathered into their hands [in the eighteenth century] the power over all of central and western India." The power of the central government, in short, explained both the limited development of feudal relations and the persistence of communal landholding and popular, rather than feudal, justice:

"While in the West the tenure of land together with the exercise of supreme rights within the limits of individual communities and districts becomes in the end the property of the former benefice holders and local officials, whose offices become hereditary by law, in India toward the end of Muslim sovereignty this same result was attained in only a few districts; in the others communal and individual property remained, as before, in the hands of the native holders, but the exercise of governmental functions was entrusted to officials appointed by the central administration. . . . India's process of feudalization at the time the English conquered her was still far from completion. . . ."[31]

[30] Kovalevski himself did not accept these as valid criteria of feudalism, but used them because they were widely employed in Europe at the time when he was writing in the late 1870's.

[31] Kovalevski, concluding paragraphs of Chap. VI.

Views such as those of Kovalevski on feudal elements in Muslim India have been subjected to criticism almost as sharp as that given to Tod's sketch of Rajput feudalism. W. H. Moreland, in his major study of the *Agrarian System of Moslem India*, furnished perhaps the bluntest statement of this type for the era of the Sultans of Delhi. Moreland began his analysis by pointing out the need to distinguish between two types of *iqta*: mere "troopers" whose holdings were small, and great nobles charged with the administration of substantial tracts. The latter, Moreland discussed in terms of the name they usually bore in the thirteenth or fourteenth century, *muqti*. He pointed out first that for the thirteenth century many of the outstanding *muqti* early in their lives had been slaves who later rose to royal favor; in fact, several of the kings themselves were of slave origin, as a result of which the thirteenth-century dynasty has often been referred to as that of the "Slave Kings." For this reason alone Moreland regarded it as "quite impossible to think of such a nobility in terms of a feudal system with a king merely first among his territorial vassals: what we see is a royal household full of slaves, who could rise, by merit or favour, from servile duties to the charge of a province, or even of a kingdom—essentially a bureaucracy of the normal Asiatic type."[32]

Just as the origin of the early *muqtis* led Moreland to reject the term feudal, so did his analysis of their position and duties. "A muqti had no territorial position of his own. . . ." The king could post him anywhere, at any time, and remove or transfer him, for any or no reason. "Such arrangements are the antithesis of anything which can properly be described as a feudal system." The *muqti's* post was purely that of an administrator; his duties were to govern; if he failed, he could be fined or dismissed. Among his duties was that of maintaining a body of troops, whose strength and pay were set by the king. The *muqti* paid the troops out of the revenues raised in the area under his charge; after deducting this and other sanctioned expenditure, he had to forward the surplus to the King's treasury. The *muqti's* receipts and expenditures were subject to audit by the King's revenue ministry. If he was short, he sometimes had to pay with his own person, and not merely a pound of flesh; some defalcators were flayed alive. Some kings were less severe than others, but the auditing of accounts continued to be customary. On the basis of this analysis Moreland utterly

[32] W. H. Moreland, *Agrarian System of Moslem India* (Cambridge, Eng. 1929), p. 218.

and emphatically rejected the idea of applying feudal terminology to the Kingdom of Delhi:

"We have officers posted to their charges by the King, and transferred, removed, or punished, at his pleasure, administering their charges under his orders, and subjected to the strict financial control of the Revenue Ministry. None of these features has any counterpart in the feudal system of Europe; and, as a student of European history to whom I showed the foregoing summary observed, the analogy is not with the feudal organisation, but with the bureaucracies which rulers like Henry II of England attempted to set up as an alternative to feudalism. The use of feudal terminology was presumably inspired by the fact that some of the nobles of the Delhi kingdom occasionally behaved like feudal barons, that is to say, they rebelled, or took sides in disputed successions to the throne; but, in Asia at least, bureaucrats can rebel as well as barons, and the analogy is much too slight and superficial to justify the importation of feudal terms and all the misleading ideas which they connote. The kingdom was not a mixture of bureaucracy with feudalism: its administration was bureaucratic throughout."[33]

It would appear that the same kind of analysis which Moreland made of the Kingdom of Delhi can be extended to the Mughal regime which followed. Lyall, in his discussion of Rajput States, which was quoted earlier, referred to the levelling action of the Mughal emperors upon the older native aristocracy of India. Everywhere that their power reached, Lyall observed, the Mughals completely flattened the local aristocracy; while "the only aristocracy which they set up consisted of a few lucky individuals who managed to hold and transmit for a few generations the grants of land obtained as rewards for service, often as bigots, lackeys, or panders."[34] In support of this view Lyall quoted a striking passage from the celebrated *Travels* of François Bernier, a French physician who served at the Court of the last of the great Mughals, Aurangzeb:

"It must not be imagined that the omrahs or lords of the Mogul's court are members of ancient families, as our nobility in France. The king being proprietor of all the lands in the empire, there can exist neither dukedoms nor marquisates; nor can any family be found possessed of wealth arising from a domain and living upon its own patrimony. The courtiers are often not even descendants of omrahs,

[33] *Agrarian System*, pp. 218-219, 221.

[34] *Asiatic Studies*, 1, 248-249.

because the king, being heir of all their possessions, no family can long maintain its distinction, but, after the omrah's death, is soon extinguished, and the sons, or at least the grandsons, reduced generally to a state bordering on mendicity, and compelled to enlist as common men in the cavalry of some omrah. The king, however, usually bestows a small pension on the widow, and often on the family; and if the omrah's life be sufficiently prolonged, he may obtain the advancement of his children by royal favour, particularly if their persons be well formed, and their complexions sufficiently fair to enable them to pass for genuine Moguls. But this advancement through special favour proceeds slowly, for it is an almost invariable custom to pass gradually from small salaries and inconsiderable offices to situations of greater trust and emolument. The omrahs, therefore, mostly consist of adventurers from different nations, who entice one another to the court, and are generally persons of low descent, some having been originally slaves, and the majority being destitute of education. The Mogul raises them to dignities, or degrades them to obscurity, according to his own pleasure and caprice."[35]

Using feudalism, then, in the sense of a method of government, as indicated in the Introductory Essay, we have to conclude that neither the Rajput States nor the Muslim regimes of northern India were feudal. Whether, without the coming of the British, feudalism would actually have developed in eighteenth-century northern India, or in nineteenth-century Rajputana, is at best a speculative question.

[35] François Bernier, *Travels in the Mogul Empire*, ed. Archibald Constable (London, 1891), pp. 211-212.

VIII · "FEUDALISM" IN THE BYZANTINE EMPIRE[1]

BY ERNST H. KANTOROWICZ

1. Introduction

THERE is general reluctance among historians to transfer, freely and without specification, institutional terminology from one cycle of culture to another or to apply modern notions to the conditions of the past. The historian might object to the application of the Augustinian notion of "City of God," even though it derives from Philo of Alexandria, to Eastern religious thought or to the Byzantine Church in general. Also, he would probably refrain from calling the medieval guilds "trade unions" and hesitate to talk about "socialism" in antiquity.

Analogies of that kind are almost certain to do injustice to both the original and the simile. The original becomes too easily a mere abstraction, severed from its genuine surroundings in time and space, and therefore in danger of forfeiting its own color values; and the simile is in danger of being forced into a framework of conditions and of mind unwarranted by its proper setting.

To avoid confusion, therefore, the historian will be inclined to use contemporaneous notions which really belong to the time and cultural orbit he intends to discuss. And he will gain very much by that procedure. For example, instead of talking about "Renaissances" during the Middle Ages he may prefer to speak of medieval *Renovatio* movements; and by using that term, which the Carolingians themselves used, the whole historical development becomes clear: the Carolingian *Renovatio* suddenly appears in the perspective of the Roman imperial *renovatio* coins while, on the other hand, the features distinguishing the medieval *renovatio* from the Italian Renaissance stand out as clearly as those which both movements have in common.

[1] This essay, written down hastily, was submitted in the fall of 1950 for the purpose of serving as a starting point for general discussion at the conference on feudalism, held then by the American Council of Learned Societies, which led to the writing of the present volume. It was not the author's intention to have this sketch published, for it does no more than render a digest of what scholars such as A. A. Vasiliev, Georg Ostrogorsky, and others have said about a highly disputed subject. The author does not claim any opinions of his own, while he admits he may have misunderstood those of others. It is at the editor's request that the essay is published.

All this holds good also with regard to feudalism. When the historian talks about Western feudalism, he thinks of a form of military, social, political, and administrative organization determined, not by the ownership of land, but by man's temporary relationship to land. He knows that man's relationship to land defined man's social status, and that through the medium of land or feudal tenure very many human relations—services and duties as well as privileges, pensions, and prerogatives—were expressed which had nothing to do with the soil itself and even less with the performance of military service in return for holding a patch of land. It is easily forgotten that parliamentary representation is just as much an offshoot from feudal concepts as the sovereignty of petty German princes, or that at least fifty per cent of modern common law is based upon feudal thought. Again, the historian, when discussing feudalism may visualize a decentralized, fragmented, and personal government, or a feudal hierarchy interpreted, by contemporaries, in terms and as a mirror of the angelic hierarchies, or a feudal universalism as a political ideology. Feudalism, in the West, actually formed Western Society, formed that "feudal society" into which the church too, was integrated.

Western feudalism actually reflects, and is synonymous with, a peculiar conception of the world; and if we bear the complexity of Western feudal society in mind, we may say *a priori* that nothing comparable to such complexity ever existed in the Byantine Empire, except when and where the Empire became Frankish.

The term feudalism, therefore, in the sense of a complex organization of feudal society, does not seem applicable to Byzantine conditions. If, however, we forget about that complex feudal society and the feudal conception of the world, and simply ask whether some isolated feudal features can be detected in the Byzantine orbit, the answer would be in the affirmative. Military tenure, independent magnates, immunities, private armies and taxation as well as other feudal features are found in Byzantium, too. In this respect we may recall Anglo-Saxon England where certain feudal features and principles had been developed before 1066, though without forming a feudal system; for not before the time of the Norman Conquest did England change into a feudally organized realm. And, in a similar fashion, it was not before the Frankish conquest of 1204 that Byzantine territories were really feudally organized, even though some Byzantine institutions may have favored that new organization.

The Frankish rule in the East was merely an episode which will not demand consideration here. One thing is clear: feudal features and principles existed in the Byzantine Empire, but they were never tied together to form an articulated whole consistent in itself. Nor was political or legal thought ever determined by a feudal conception of the world. Feudalism never became an ideal; the "day-dream" of feudal structure as expressed in the famous *nulle terre sans seigneur* was completely absent from the Byzantine East. On the contrary, what feudal features did exist were always somewhat isolated and accidental, and they were "deviations" from the normal pattern of state organization, the ideal of which was always a state governed centrally by the Christ-like basileus and his heliocentrically working officials.

The isolated feudal features which will be discussed here are closely interlocked with Byzantine history in general, with territorial gains and losses, with military needs and the solution of defense problems, and with the problems of the rural population of the empire. Our sources are scattered. There is, needless to say, no codification of feudal law and customs comparable to the Western *coutumiers* or the Frankish colonial codes of Jerusalem and Morea. We have to rely upon observations made here and there and analyzed by modern scholars. Their investigations are as yet anything but definite, and the disagreements are often very considerable. Certain facts, however, stand out clearly.

Both the social and military history of Byzantium were determined by the polarity of peasant militia and latifundia-owning nobility. Both systems derived from late Roman conditions. During the middle-Byzantine period, from the seventh to the eleventh century, the system of peasant militia prevailed owing to the theme organization. From the eleventh century onward the landowning nobility became again the most important factor of Byzantine society. In the thirteenth century, it is true, the peasant militia came to the fore again when the Byzantine Empire was reduced to the small realm of Nicaea. But it was eclipsed once more by the great landowning lords after the fall of the Latin Empire, in 1261. And those lords remained the most powerful element throughout the late-Byzantine period.

The feudal features are particularly strong whenever the great nobility rules. But certain feudal elements are found also in the militia system; nor are they absent from the church.

I shall start with a discussion of the system of peasant soldiers. I shall then turn to the lords of the latifundia. And I shall conclude with a few remarks on the church. The nature of the problem will make it necessary to discuss feudal features largely within the frame of military history.

II. The Army and Forms of Dependent Tenure

During the early-Byzantine period, which extends well beyond Justinian I until the beginning of the seventh century, the army was a motley congeries of many elements. The nucleus was still the old mobile army, the professional soldiers (*stratiotai*) who were either volunteers or drafted men. These units were reinforced by the *buccellarii*, the private guards of the great landowners (*dynatoi*), which belonged also to the mobile army. The frontiers of the empire were guarded by the *limitanei*, called *ripariенses* before A.D. 363, peasants with military obligations settled on the frontier. Finally there were the *symmachoi* or *foederati*, barbarian client tribes which had received land within the empire, sometimes straddling the frontier line and formed semi-independent vassal states under the Roman protectorate. It is well known that those barbarian tribal auxiliaries, which had been settled as tribes and not as individuals on the frontiers, were of the greatest importance during the early Byzantine period and the age of the migrations. The empire, by utilizing the manpower of Goths, Huns, Alans, Lombards, and others, secured itself against the attacks of those as well as of other tribes; but it required all the skill of Byzantine diplomacy to play those tribes off successfully against each other or, when they grew dangerous as allies, to march them off to the western parts of the empire.

The question may be raised whether those tribal frontier states, which were formed on the Rhine and the Danube as well as on the Euphrates, should be considered "feudatories" of the empire. For when, around A.D. 1000, Otto III organized Poland, Bohemia, and Hungary in a somewhat comparable fashion as *amici imperii Romanorum* those frontier neighbors appeared often as feudally dependent kingdoms. However, neither in early Byzantine times nor in later centuries did Byzantium avail herself of a feudal ideology to designate relations with tributary neighbors, although in effect the tributary relationship may not have been very different from that of vassalage. The relations of Byzantium with other states were expressed in terms of a complicated spiritual kinship, and it had a very specific meaning if, for example, the Frankish kings or emperors were addressed as *pneumatikos adelphos* (spiritual brother), whereas the Tsar of the Bulgarians was styled *pneumatikon teknon* (spiritual son). Also it meant one thing when the Prince (*archon*) of Russia received, like the princes of the Turks or Patzinaks, imperial letters (*grammata*), and another when the princes of Croatia, Serbia, Naples, Amalfi, and also the Doge of Venice received an order (*keleusis*), for *grammata* were sent by the basileus, and a *keleusis* by the *despotes*, the "lord." It is, however, obvious that the dependency implied in these modes of address was not conceived in feudal terms.[2]

Besides the frontier tribes and states, the frontier militia is of great importance to our subject.

During the third century, allegedly under Severus Alexander, a bipartition of the Roman army was effected. The mobile army, which could be sent to any of the four corners of the world, was relieved by an immobile army stationed as garrisons along the *limes,* the *limitanei milites.* These frontier guards were genuine peasant-soldiers. They received from the government farmsteads which were inheritable and were owned, or held, on condition of performing military service. Here, then, we find a frontier militia of small landowners, a clear case of the combination of grants of land with military service. The soldier-settlers doing this service were more often than not barbarians, individual barbarians as distinguished from the barbarians settled as whole tribes along the frontiers, which have been discussed above.

That this system of frontier peasant-soldiers survived in Byzantine times is a fact evidenced even in the law. Justinian, in his Code (XI, 60, 3) repeats a novel of Theodosius II of the first half of the fifth century (*Nov. Theodos.*, XXIV, 4) in which the emperor proclaims that military service as *limitaneus* is the necessary condition for possessing land on the frontiers of the empire; and Theodosius remarks that by his decree he is merely continuing old practices and old laws.

The peasant militia which composed the *limitanei* was to become of the greatest importance in the middle period of Byzantine history. During the fifth and sixth centuries the professional army, weakened by unreliable barbarian components, was gradually decaying, and the wars of Justinian whittled down its strength. At any rate, the mobile army was not able to ward off the Slavs when they occupied the Balkan Peninsula, nor could it stem effectively the Persian attacks or, finally those of the Arabs who occupied Egypt and Syria and, in the latter half

[2] Georg Ostrogorsky in *Semin. Kondakovianum,* VIII (1936), 41ff.; A. A. Vasiliev in *Speculum,* VII (1932), 350ff.

of the seventh century, pushed forward to the very capital of the empire. The frontiers of the Byzantine state had moved from the Danube and the Euphrates to the outskirts of Constantinople, that is, to Asia Minor.

In that emergency a complete reorganization of the army, and indeed the state, became imperative. If in former days the frontiers had been guarded by the *limitanei*, a hereditary peasant soldiery, why not apply that system to the central provinces of the empire, to Asia Minor which now had become the frontier? In fact, the application of the *limitanei* system to the heart of the empire was synonymous with the introduction of the theme organization.

The administrative reorganization of the surviving parts of the empire, which was started by the Emperor Heraclius (610-641) and carried through by his immediate successors, is not the subject of our discussion here. It amounted to a militarization at large in that the regimental or army districts (*themata*) first superseded, and later replaced, the former provincial divisions as instituted by Diocletian. Moreover, the *themata* no longer were ruled by civilians, as had been the case with the provinces, but by military governors, called *strategoi*, to whom the full military, civil, and jurisdictional power was delegated. Their *merum et mixtum imperium* resembled that of the two exarchs, of Ravenna and Carthage, as established by Justinian.

The greatest changes resulting from the theme organization, however, were those which affected the social stratification of the empire. The former professional army composed of barbarian mercenaries disappeared, if we except the imperial bodyguards in Constantinople, and in its place a new army of peasant-soldiers was created. The change started with the quartering of certain regiments permanently in certain districts of Asia Minor, now the glacis of the fortress Byzantium, instead of moving the outfits about, from one frontier to another. That is, the regiments were settled down like the former *limitanei* units, and the tendency to settle would probably have arisen anyhow among the soldiers themselves. This settling of the soldiers was now carried through systematically by the government. There was more than enough land to settle an army. After the Persian and Arab invasions of Asia Minor, after the occupation of those territories by the invaders, and after the reconquest of the devastated provinces, the government had plenty of unoccupied soil at its disposal. This land was parcelled out in the form of farmsteads (*stratiotika ktemata*) to individual soldiers, large enough for the maintenance of a family. The farmsteads were owned hereditarily on the condition that the tenant performed military service.

The peasant-soldier, of course, could own more land than he needed for his maintenance provided that he, or his family, were able to cultivate the land. The minimum, however, which he had to have was an estate of the value of four pounds gold. This minimum could not be alienated, sold, or given away, whereas the excess land owned above the four pounds margin was saleable. Normally, the eldest son of the peasant-soldier would inherit the estate with the incumbent military duties, whereas the younger sons would settle as free peasants and normal taxpayers without military duties attached to the soil.

The change that had taken place was considerable. In former days the professional soldiers were called *stratiotai*; now, however, the word *stratiotes* designated the farmer settled within the theme and holding, or rather owning, land of a size comparable to the Western knight's fee. From later sources we may gather that the new *stratiotes* was obliged to appear, when called to active duty, fully equipped with a horse, that he had to pay some taxes for his little estate, but that during active service he received a certain, though small, amount of pay. From the Western knight's fee the *stratiotikon ktema* differed in that it was not conferred for a limited time only, but was given as hereditary property to the *stratiotes*. Moreover, the *stratiotai* did not form an aristocracy—at least, not in the classical period—but remained small peasant holders.

The effect of the theme organization was to make it possible to recruit the army from within the empire instead of hiring barbarians or other mercenaries. As a result, the government's expenses for the army and for the defense of the empire in general were reduced considerably. In addition to being more economical, the theme system created a reliable peasant militia which was willing to defend its property, which drew from the soil both its livelihood and the means for waging war, and which, on top of all that, even paid some taxes to the state.

Whereas in Western feudal institutions military duties were attached to the person, they were attached to the soil in the Byzantine theme system. And this is significant because the theme system was the direct continuation, or the revival, of the Roman system of *limitanei* which, in Byzantium, had moved from the frontier to the heart of the empire when, so to speak, the suburbicarian districts of the capital became identical with the "frontier."

The *stratiotai* themselves were not all of Greek stock; many of them were foreigners, often barbarians. Armenian settlers abounded, but there were also many Slavs among the peasant-soldiers. This Slavic colonization has led Russian scholars in particular to the assumption that Slavic influence was largely responsible for the theme system, above all on the ground that the peasants sometimes were organized into taxation communities which coincided with village communities. Others, however, prefer to think of the model of Persia and assume that both Persia and Byzantium were affected by the practices of Turanian tribes—Huns, Avars, Protomagyars, Turks, and others. However that may be, the theme system was, in the first place, a development of the Roman *limitanei.*

The theme organization remained effective for three centuries and a half, and it was not by chance that the age of peasant militia coincided with the best centuries of Byzantine history. The theme system not only activated Byzantium's military power, but socially, too, had most wholesome effects, for it goes almost without saying that a strong peasant militia and a healthy peasantry as represented by the younger sons of the *stratiotai* was the best means of checking the power and curbing the greed of the great landowners, the *dynatoi.*

Ever since late Roman times, the government had tried to stop the development of the latifundia and to check the increasing power of the great landlords who, as a result of Rome's Hellenistic heritage, had transformed the economic life even of Italy, a typical peasant country. At the same time, however, the government depended on the great landowners to whom the free peasants had been turned over for fiscal military purposes, the collection of taxes and the recruitment of soldiers. The peasants thus became serfs, *coloni*, men legally bound to the soil—*glebae adscriptitii*—and practically bound to the ownership of their lords. We know the organization of the latifundia from all parts of the empire, in greatest detail, however, from Egypt where the Oxyrhynchus papyri have yielded the papers of the Apion family. The Apion were lords of large parts of Middle Egypt in the time of Justinian and they were, at the same time, holders of the highest imperial offices. Their huge estates, which resembled privately owned principalities, were administered on the model of the imperial administration. Like other landlords, the Apion had their private army of hired soldiers (*buccellarii*), including men of Germanic extraction, which formed a military reserve badly needed by the government for the reinforcement of the professional army.

These landowning magnates, called *dynatoi* in Byzantium, tended there, as everywhere else, to expand their estates by absorbing the smal farmers and bringing the free peasantry into quasi-feudal dependency. The Byzantine emperors tried to stop that development, and, although Justinian I as well as Justinian II legislated against the expansion of the latifundia at the cost of the peasants, it was nevertheless only through the theme system that a countermovement became effective. Not only did the government-protected system of military estates begin to develop its own dynamics, but the landlords were also strictly forbidden to bring the *stratiotai* and the military estates into their possession; and wherever the great lords had actually bought, or otherwise acquired, *stratiotika ktemata* they were obliged to return them to the former owners, often without compensation. Moreover, through the inroads of Persians and Arabs the great landowners had suffered terrific losses so that the establishment of the theme peasantry coincided with a state of weakness of the *dynatoi*.

Under these conditions, which lasted until the middle of the eleventh century, the empire began to gather strength. The new system of peasant militia, together with the general militarization of the theme government and the generally healthy condition of the state, enabled Byzantium to reconquer great parts of the lost provinces. In the south and east, Syria returned to the fold, the Euphrates was reached again, and even Aleppo was taken for a while. Most spectacular were the final victories of Basil II (976-1025) over the Bulgars. The Balkan provinces returned to the empire and once more the Danube formed the frontier of the Byzantine power. But the recovery was not decisive, for a vicious circle was in operation and it led on to a nearer approach to feudalization of Byzantium than the earlier changes had done.

III. The Later, Quasi-Feudal Regime

The greater extension of the empire brought about changes of the army organization. Frontier soldiers of the pattern of *limitanei* within the central provinces appeared less important, a consideration which strongly affected the theme militia. Instead, a professional army was needed which could be moved about quickly. This new permanent army developed from the nucleus of the imperial guard regiments stationed in and around Constantinople, and by the tenth century the garrison of the capital became almost coincident with the "mobile army." We find that those guard regiments, the *tagmata*, became as important as the *themata*, the agrarian militia, and that finally the themes were completely eclipsed by the army of professional mercenaries composed of Normans, Russo-Varangians, Anglo-Saxons, and others.

The formerly quite wholesome militarization of the government now began to show a different aspect. The *strategoi*, that is, provincial commanders and governors of the themes, showed an increasing interest in the permanent professional army which could be utilized for the exercise of political power and against the emperor far more conveniently than the militia of the themes. The generals of the victorious wars had been drawn from the great landowning families, whose influence began to increase as the increased security of the empire gave new value to the possession of land as a source of wealth. In other words, generals and great estate-owners, here as everywhere, began to line up and soon became a menace to the central government and to the emperors themselves. The emperors of the tenth century—Romanus I, Constantine VII Porphyrogennetos, Basil II—legislated against the increasing power of the landed aristocracy and tried to keep the theme organization intact. At the same time, they had to fight rebellious generals aspiring to the crown. Finally, the emperors of the Ducas Dynasty (1059-1081), after the Macedonians, changed the tactics. Supported by the church, they began to build up a civilian aristocracy of scholars and great officials within the capital (Michael Psellus belonged to that category) and to play off that new aristocracy against the military aristocracy of the generals who were supported by the great landowners.

In short, the eleventh-century rulers tried to demilitarize and to civilianize the administration and to reduce the power of the military class. This policy is clearly reflected in the decay of the theme organization. The *strategos* as governor of a province began to disappear at that time, and his place was taken by the *praetor*, formerly the supreme justice on the staff of the *strategos*. The *praetor*, of course, was a civilian, and thus the former primacy of the military command in the themes was replaced by the primacy of a civilian administration based upon the new aristocracy of scholars and civilians in the capital.

But the preponderance of the civilian aristocracy in the capital did not entail a strengthening of the central power in the rural districts. Generals and great landowners outweighed the civilians, and with the accession of Alexius Comnenus (1081-1118) the military party conquered the state anyhow. But even before the time of Alexius and his military supporters, the emperors of the Ducas Dynasty had been compelled to give great privileges both to their civilian adherents and to their military or landowning adversaries. And it was under those civilian-minded rulers that the *pronoia* system was first developed, a system which approached quasi-feudalization of Byzantium.

Theologically, *pronoia* means "providence"; otherwise it means "foresight" or "care." To give lands to a person *eis pronoian* means, accordingly, to give lands into the care of a person. In practice, it meant that estates were given both to high officers of the state or army and to monasteries and private persons also. They were given in permanent administration as a reward for services. The grants differed from simple donations in that the *pronoia* land was absolutely bound to the recipient, the *pronoetes*; that he received it for a definite period only, usually for life; that he could not sell the *pronoia* estate; and that it was not hereditary.

It is significant that the first *pronoetes* that we know of was a member of the civilian aristocracy of the capital, Constantine Lichudes, a great scholar and friend of Michael Psellus, whom Constantine Monomachus (1042-1055) had chosen responsible minister in his government. When the power of the civilian aristocracy was reduced, the *pronoetai* came to belong more or less to the landed or fighting aristocracy. Already Alexius I (1081-1118) availed himself of the rapidly developing *pronoia* system for military purposes. The old *stratiotika ktemata* of the peasant militia under the theme system had become unimportant. The former legislation forbidding any person to buy, or otherwise acquire, the military farmsteads was revoked under the Ducas emperors. The result was that the *dynatoi* now were able to expand and bring the former *stratiotai* into dependency. In any case the *stratiotai* themselves had often changed from the status of poor peasant soldiers to that of petty nobility or gentry. Under Heraclius, the founder of the theme system, the minimum value of a military estate had been four pounds gold, the quantity of land which could not be sold by the *stratiotes*. By the end of the tenth century, the minimum value of those knights' fees was raised to twelve pounds gold, due not to a devaluation of the money but to the heavy armor which the *stratiotes* now was expected to own. But an estate worth twelve pounds gold no longer was a peasant estate fit for the poor; it was an estate fit for the mailed knight of the landowning gentry. And this new class of gentry was likewise found among the *pronoetai*, the owners of *pronoia* estates.

Moreover, the new class of *pronoia* owners replaced, in liability to military service, the former class of peasant soldiers of the decaying theme organization. The owner of a *pronoia* estate had to serve as a heavily mailed knight of the caliber of *kataphraktes*, and, when summoned, he had to appear with a certain number of horsemen, likewise mailed, according to the size of his *pronoia* estate. It is true, of course, that other landowners, too, had to serve; nor were the landowning monasteries and churches exempt. But their contingents were lightly armed infantrymen and not heavy cavalrymen. It is probable that the government, in order to get more mailed knights, expanded the *pronoia* system enormously during the twelfth century with the result that a military aristocracy rapidly developed; they stood between the government and large sectors of the rural population, peasants and small landowners who had become dependent on them.

Certain parallels between the Byzantine *pronoia* lords and the Western feudal lords cannot be denied, and those parallels become all the more striking when we consider the "immunities" which the *pronoia* lords enjoyed. Immunity—in Greek *exkousseia* (from *excusare*, excuse)—had existed before the times of the Comneni. Churches and monasteries had not infrequently enjoyed, for certain parts of their property, the revenues of taxation. In fact, they were allowed to collect for themselves the ordinary taxes and keep them as so-called *solemnia*, a practice which tended to undercut the emperor's prerogative of collecting taxes. But those ecclesiastical exemptions were not the rule, though they were not rare. At any rate, they do not compare with the immunities granted to the *pronoia* lords.

It had, of course, been common practice in late Roman and early Byzantine times for great landowners to enjoy immunities. This practice had not disappeared, but had become relatively unimportant, during the middle period of Byzantine history in which the theme organization, then the favorite child of the government, had flourished; in the interests of the themes the emperors of the tenth century had tried to restrict the *dynatoi* in every way. With the decay of the themes and the peasant militia in the eleventh century, however, *exkusseiai*, immunities, began to mushroom everywhere. Immunity privileges included partial or total exemption from taxes of the *pronoia* lord within his estate; exemption usually from public works also; and exclusion of the imperial officials from entry upon the lands of the *pronoia*. Since the formerly free peasants within the *pronoia* district had become *paroikoi*, more or less serfs, of the *pronoetes*, they came under his jurisdiction although that jurisdiction was restricted. At the same time the bad custom of farming out taxes began to develop. The central government thus jeopardized its most important prerogative in the rural parts of the country, including the right of direct taxation, for either there was a *pronoetes* who was tax-free or was granted the taxes, or else a tax-farmer, replacing the former imperial collectors, imposed and collected the dues to his own advantage.

Under these circumstances the *pronoetai* became great magnates within the empire, and their large estates appeared, like those of the Apion family of sixth-century Egypt, as little empires within the empire. The magnates had their own soldiers; they held land in return for military service (personal as well as with their retainers), and the number of their liverymen was fixed according to the size and value of their estates; they held land for a restricted time only and not as property; they enjoyed immunities and exemptions; they had some jurisdiction within their estates; and they encroached upon and absorbed the former *stratiotika ktemata* insofar as the former *stratiotai* did not themselves become *pronoetai.*

It goes without saying that the crown became more and more dependent on the magnates, all the more so as financial problems of keeping a professional mobile army became almost insurmountable. Pay and provisions for that mobile army became so expensive that the maintenance of the mercenaries devoured the greater part of the budget, then as ever. The army had to be paid mainly from the urban revenues and from the rents paid by the rural tax-farmers. Throughout the late Byzantine period the costs of the mobile army remained the crucial financial burden, since the upkeep of mercenaries was as ruinously expensive in the East as it was in the West. Hence, the contingents of the *pronoia* lords were, apparently, the only cheap element in the late Byzantine army. But the indirect losses involved in the form of immunities and alienated taxes made the new system in fact far less advantageous for the government than the old theme organization of Byzantium's golden age. Nor was the military service of the *pronoia* lords a reliable resort, for a tendency arose to allow it to be replaced by the payment of a sum of money. This, of course, corresponds to the Western scutage. The favor of commuting the military obligations was granted above all to the monasteries owing to the peculiar position of the church; this is something which occurred both in the East and the West. The surviving peasant soldiery were usually allowed to pay money instead of serving, and in late Byzantine times scutage must have been almost the general custom. This is indicated by the strong opposition to special taxation for the hiring of mercenaries maintained by Gemistos Plethon, the statesman who was well known in the West for his discussions of Plato at the Council of Florence.

Thus there were in the later Byzantine period, beginning with the Comneni, a great number of feudal features, isolated and not integrated into a general feudal conception of the state or the world. It was this situation which the Franks encountered when they conquered Constantinople and the greater part of the empire—the empire which they divided and subdivided according to a regular feudal pattern such as hardly existed in the West. The conquerors found the Byzantine *pronoia* system so similar to their own feudal organization, and the Greeks found the new feudal system so much like their own, that the words *pronoia* and *feudum* became interchangeable. *Pronoia* was actually used as a translation of *feudum*, and vice versa.

It remains true that before 1204 the feudal features never amounted to anything comparable with the complex feudal totality of the West. Feudal tendencies there were in Byzantium, but the empire—except under the Franks—remained a centrally governed state of imperial officials. Even the weakened Byzantine administration was vastly more a centralized bureaucracy, and far less a feudal state, than France around 1300 under Philip IV or England under Edward I. The Byzantine Empire remained essentially bureaucratic in its last two centuries as before. Nor should we overestimate the Frankish influence which was lasting only in Greece (Morea) and Thessalonica.

Further, the oscillation between the theme system and the *pronoia* system was not ended by those events. There was an interlude when the little Empire of Nicaea under the Lascarides returned, during the Frankish occupation of the Latin Empire, to the system of a peasant militia. After the reconquest of Constantinople by Michael Palaeologue in 1261, however, the *pronoia* system acquired new strength. It was then that the *pronoia* estates became hereditary and began to resemble feudal principalities of Western pattern.

IV. The Church and Feudalistic Tendencies

Finally, a few words about the church and some feudal features within the ecclesiastical orbit.

Needless to say, an ecclesiastical feudal edifice, independent of the state, never had a chance to develop in the East. It is quite inconceivable that the Patriarch of Constantinople should ever have exercised the rights of a supreme feudal lord over secular vassal princes, comparable to those which his Roman colleague claimed over Dalmati and Sicily, Aragon and England as well as over other kingdoms and principalities and over all islands. Nor was there in the East a Patrimony of St. Andrew comparable to the Western Patrimony of St. Peter, a state teeming with counts and barons who, as lords of the Campagna, were direct vassals of the pope, recognizing him as their sovereign lord.

Also unknown in the East were those great spiritual princes of the West who were not only bishops of the church but also great feudatories and officers of the crown; who, being vassals themselves and having vassals, were integrated into the general feudal nexus, and were equal in importance and in some regions in number with the secular feudal princes. In the Holy Roman Empire around 1500 we find 127 spiritual princes standing beside 159 secular princes. Nothing of the kind existed in Byzantium. Yet the Byzantine Church was affected by those feudal tendencies which have been mentioned above —immunities and the duty of raising foot soldiers from its estates. Also, monasteries could be granted lands *eis pronoian.* Above all there is one institution which must be considered because its Western equivalent profoundly influenced the whole development of feudalism: this is the *charistikion.*

Charistikion is the literal translation of the Latin *beneficium* which, in the West, came to mean, and to be synonymous with, "fief." The benefice was a special kind of lease or of the Roman *precarium*, a lease given for temporary use or for life on conditions so favorable that the *precarium* appeared to the recipient as a *beneficium.*

The Byzantine *charistikion* was not an institution taken over from the West, but it derived from the same late Roman conditions as the *beneficium.* Both in the West and in the East the system served, above all, the needs of the church whose landed property was inalienable and had to be leased in one way or another if it was to yield a rent. But whereas in the West the *beneficium* was fused with vassalage, especially after the secularization of church property by Charles Martel, the Eastern *charistikion* had, from the very beginning, a different function. It was applied mainly, though not exclusively, upon monastic property. The owner of a monastery—he might be the emperor, a bishop, or any other person—would give the monastic lands in tenure, usually to a layman who had to administer the property, take care of the buildings, and provide for the maintenance of the monks. Since church property was never tax-free in Byzantium, the tenant (*charistikarios*) had to pay the public taxes from the revenues, but he could keep, once all his expenses were covered, the excess of the revenues.

That this administration through *charistikarioi* was often oppressive cannot be denied. But the *charistikion* was not altogether an anti-monastic institution, as has sometimes been assumed, or even a result of the iconoclastic struggles and the anti-monastic feelings of the iconoclasts. The system was much older than iconoclasm. It can be traced back to the fifth century when the Fathers of the Council of Chalcedon sharply censured the practice; the censure was often repeated in later times. Some churchmen thought less unfavorably of the *charistikion*, however, and in earlier times it had usually been the church authorities themselves who handled appointments of *charistikarioi*. The quasi-feudal appearance of the *charistikion* belongs to the early period of the Comneni, for then the emperor—Alexius I began it—assumed the right to appoint the *charistikarioi*, and he began to invest his supporters freely with good *charistikia*, usually for life. It was, of course, a convenient method of rewarding them.

It is to be noted that the *pronoia* and imperial *charistikion* appeared simultaneously; there was a parallelism between the two institutions, and Alexius I was chief promoter of both. Nothing prevented the emperor from giving the same man a *pronoia* estate and a *charistikion* as well. In the West, the advowson, which in a number of respects was reminiscent of the *charistikion*, became feudalized, and the parallelism of *charistikion* and *pronoia* was reflected in the parallelism of advowson and fief; but, whereas the former were of limited term, the latter were not.

In ecclesiastical as in lay institutions in the East feudalistic developments remained sporadic and unsystematic; they were never integrated. The involved mechanism of Western feudalism with its hierarchies of vassals, its divided jurisdictions, and its fragmentation of power had no more chance of engulfing the Byzantine Church than it had of superseding the bureaucracy of the Byzantine state.

IX · ASPECTS OF FEUDALISM IN RUSSIAN HISTORY

BY MARC SZEFTEL

1. Definitions

A SEARCH for the feudal aspects of Russian institutions must begin with a definition of feudalism and a delimitation of the historical and geographical area to study. As to the latter, it will cover European Great Russia. It is Great Russia which has supplied the unity and continuity of Russian history since the thirteenth century, and the history of Great Russia can be carried back further than that. Asiatic Russia is excluded, for Great Russian feudal institutions (truly feudal or not) did not spread there.[1] Although Great Russian in population, the city-dominated republics of Novgorod and Pskov are not relevant to our subject prior to their annexation by Muscovy.[2] Thus delimited, the area of our study is a historically composite unit consisting roughly of three main regions, each with a different background: the lands on the upper and middle course of the Volga and on its tributary, the Oka, which formed the Grand Principality of Moscow as of 1462; lands to the west, north, and northeast of the Grand Principality, forming the territories formerly belonging to the Republic of Novgorod and the tiny Republic of Pskov, which the Grand Principality absorbed respectively in 1478 and 1510; and, lands in the southeast, originally non-Russian, which became a part of the Grand Principality after 1552 under Ivan the Terrible and were shortly settled by Great Russians.[3]

[1] There are excluded the "feudal states of central Asia and Transcaucasia" (a term customary among Soviet historians), and the Tartar khanates of the Volga, Crimea, and Siberia. If any of these were feudal, they are not in the historic Great Russian descent.

[2] Kievan-Novgorodian Russia will be considered only as historical background. Feudal institutions developed in the western territories of that part of Russia which fell under the Lithuanian or Polish rule for a part or all of the period from the thirteenth to the eighteenth centuries. Those institutions, for the most part in the Polish tradition, are, however, distinct from Great Russian institutions.

[3] The frontiers of the Great Russian area under our study run about as follows: the European coast of the Arctic Ocean as far west as the border of Finland; from there southward to Leningrad, and from there irregularly southward and a little eastward to the mouth of the River Don; then to the mouth of the River Terek on the Caspian Sea, and thence to the Ural Mountains which separate Europe from Asia; finally along the line of the Urals to the Arctic Ocean.

As to the meaning of feudalism, it happens that we are excused here from the task of making a definition since one has been provided already in the Introductory Essay.[4] That definition, with its emphasis upon the primacy of the political facet of feudalism, will serve as criterion, when we come to determine finally the extent and character of feudalism in Russia. Meanwhile, since it is not an inflexible definition, it will not inhibit the use of the term quite freely in analytical inquiry. The inquiry falls naturally into two parts both on chronological and on substantive grounds: from origins until the rise of Moscow, and under Muscovite and modern Russian regimes. The change from the one to the other is not, of course, momentary; it is a gradual transition, occurring as Muscovy spreads over Great Russia and the character of the Muscovite regime unfolds itself.

II. Historical Background: Feudal Aspects in Central Russian Principalities

Before the invasion of the Tartars the region around Moscow formed a part of one state with the Novgorodian regions and the territories of the basin of the Dnieper. It had been founded by a Scandinavian dynasty in the middle of the ninth century, but subsequently hac suffered many strains upon its unity; the Tartar invasion was the fina blow. In this Kievo-Novgorodian Russia trade with Byzantium and th Middle East was very important, and this gave political predominanc to the big cities and the merchant population within those cities. Th country as a whole offered the picture of a federation of regions witl a common dynasty as a link, every region being ruled by the sovereig assembly of its biggest city. No prince could maintain his power agains the will of this assembly in which all chiefs of families of the cit participated. Institutions were influenced very strongly by this pr eminence of urban life, and the documents of this period, such a "Russian Justice," a code of laws whose most ancient provisions g back to the beginning of the eleventh century, are witnesses thereo Agriculture, certainly, was important, but until the middle of tl twelfth century there were no big landed properties outside of tho of the church, and one can assume that the rural population did n yet come into a relation of dependence on landlords, lay or ecclesiastica Slaves were numerous, but they chiefly represented an item of inte national trade, if they did not belong to the church. In the latter cas they were employed as manpower on ecclesiastical estates.

[4] Above, pp. 4ff.

The situation changed altogether by the middle of the twelfth century. An economic crisis connected with a basic change of the commercial relationships between Western and Eastern Europe made external trade little profitable in the aforesaid territory. An evolution began which toward the second quarter of the thirteenth century resulted in a transformation of Russian economic and social life. With the deterioration of external trade, and finally of the cities, the urban factor ceased to play its former role. The cities lost much of their economic power and lost population. Those of the merchants—or of the military class associated with merchant activity—who had great numbers of slaves found it more profitable to employ them as manpower on the estates which appear in ever greater number beginning with the middle of the twelfth century. The agricultural population living around these estates, facing an ever greater economic plight, aggravated by constant invasions of the nomads, fell into a dependence on ecclesiastical and lay landlords which did not exist formerly. The former political unity of the Russian Federation, conditioned by common interest in the same external trade, gave way to ever more centrifugal tendencies, and the princes of the dynasty of Rïurik localized their interests, centering them upon their growing landed possessions first of all. Their military men followed their example. These considerations do not apply to the Novgorodian part of pre-Tartar Russia, farther north and nearer to the Baltic. Novgorod still remained a merchant republic, and even after the Tartar invasion did not lose this basic character. The rest of the territory underwent changes both in its political and its agrarian life which have been thought feudal and were certainly of a character in several ways analogous to feudalism.

At the time of the invasion, both in the basin of the Dnieper and in Central Russia this evolution was pretty much advanced. There was, however, a growing difference between the two regions in the form of a major demographic change: the population was moving from the now dangerous area on the Dnieper to the more secure Central Russian area. In the latter territory this settlers' movement, on the one hand, acted as a stimulus to political feudalization, or at any rate to fragmentation of political authority, but, on the other hand, slowed down the evolution toward greater dependence of the rural population on the owners of the big estates.

Thus, in Central Russia there had been little population in the first half of the twelfth century and few important cities. Then, around the middle of the century, suddenly population began to flow into this region in great numbers. The princes took advantage of this situation. They organized the movement of the settlers, and a relationship became established from the beginning in which the settler accepted the condition that the land on which he lived was the local prince's land, on which the prince had a *dominium eminens*. In this region far from the main water-lanes of Russia, commercial interests never loomed as large as agricultural ones, and cities were not very powerful. It was not difficult for the prince to assert his pre-eminence over the cities in this region, while at the same time local agricultural interests tended rather to separate than to unite the numerous princes. Each prince, settling population in his territory, faced the task of administering it and providing for its defense. For these functions he needed a special personnel. But money was scarce and trade was poor so that he could not, as in the past of Kievan Russia, attract administrative and fighting men by offering money or a share in commercial profit; the only thing he could offer them was possession of land—land was indeed inexhaustible. Hence land became the counterpart for service. Yet the great quantity of the land and the shortage of military and administrative servants (plur. *boïare, vol'nye slugi*)[5] constituted two very specia conditions whose effect upon institutional development was profound

It soon became evident that the relation of the prince with his servan and also of the landlord with the settler could not lead under the circumstances to a very strict dependence of the servant on the princ or of the settler on the landlord (prince himself, military servant, o ecclesiastical institution). The country was enormous in territory an

[5] These are very usual terms in Russian historiography, and in fact they ar actually historic terms. The need for them marks one of the conspicuous di ferences between Russian history and the history of the West. At a later perio under Muscovy, "military and administrative servants" were often endowed wit a status in some respects not greatly different from that of the feudal vassals the West, as will appear in the text below. But in earlier times, including th time here under discussion, the sharp separation between land tenure and person service necessitated words to denote the "servants." Because of the continuity the character of the service from the time it was unconnected with land tenu into the time when it became so connected, the same words continue to be use with varying epithets up till Peter the Great's reorganization both of the servi to the state and of the regime of landed property. It is necessary to transla *literally* into Western terminology since the term "vassal" would be incorre more often than it would be correct. A strict etymological equivalence migh however, be misleading: the term *serjeant* in Western languages, *serviens* medieval Latin, is a fairly near translation of *sluga*, but it fails to convey the hi status of the *vol'nye slugi* or, in Muscovite times, *sluzhilye lïudi* (plur.), and refers to a comparatively small class in Western feudal society.—Ed.

hardly cultivated as yet; the number of princes was great, and their power more or less equal (an average principality was actually not bigger than the valley of a small river). Competition was great among the princes for military servants and among landlords for settlers at a time when work mattered more than land itself. The result was that freedom both for military servants and for settlers to change their masters became the rule. With regard to the military servant, the relation amounted to a unilateral commitment binding the prince only; at any time, the military servant could change his allegiance *without losing his landed property* situated in the principality of his former prince.[6] This right of "departure" of the prince's "free servant" (*vol'nyĭ sluga*) implies for his landed possession (*votchina*, patrimony) a non-conditional character. It was an allod, not a fief, whatever its origin—whether the outright grant of the prince or the acknowledged fact of first occupancy. It is true that a *parallelism* existed as a rule between the personnel in the prince's service and that holding big landed property in his principality, but there was no *legal* connection between the two functions; a "free servant" might also be a big landlord and, if so, he was not only servant (*sluga*), but also was called boyar (*boĭarin*). With regard to the rural settler, there is no trace of serfdom in Central Russia before the middle of the fifteenth century; the settler had complete freedom to relinquish his tenure and to change his master.

There were two other important features of this evolution. First, the master of an estate with settlers on it, ecclesiastical or lay, came to enjoy a privilege to judge the population of his estate and to collect taxes from it in certain cases. These *immunities*[7] can be explained as a

[6] According to Pavlov-Sil'vansky (*Gosudarevy sluzhilye lïudi* [The Sovereign's Serving People] St. Petersburg, 1898, pp. 24-25), in the beginning, as long as the prince's power was weak and the boyar's independence very great, the "departure" to another prince meant also in most cases a territorial expansion for the latter, his *dominium eminens* extending to his new servant's landed property in the principality of the former master. There is no direct evidence, however, for this assumption of "free commendation" in the 13th and 14th centuries. From the end of the 14th century on sources are available, but they stress a different rule: The boyar may serve whomever he wants, but his landed property not only remains in the *dominium eminens* of the local prince; it is also submitted to his justice and gives him the princely tribute.

[7] The oldest known lay charter of immunity (given by the Grand Prince Ivan Danilovich Kalita of Moscow, 1325-40, but preserved only as a confirmation to Ivan Petelin by Basil II in 1450; cf. trans. into French, A. Eck, *Moyen âge russe*, Brussels and Paris, 1933, pp. 492-493) contains cases reserved to the prince's jurisdiction: ". . . and my *volostel's* [district chiefs] and their *tiun's* [judges] . . . do not judge them [i.e., Ivan and all his people] for anything excepting murder, brigand-

result of the necessity to organize police and justice in the only feasible manner under existing conditions, namely that, on the one hand, military servants were scarce, and, on the other, territories were little accessible. Second, with every generation the number of princes grew and their principalities decreased in area, while their interests were being widely concentrated on local, economic, non-political problems. This means that gradually many a principality approached the type of a princely estate.[8] Thus two important tendencies toward feudalism or some analogous political structure mark the condition of Central Russia at the time of the Tartar invasion: the pulverization of public authority,

---

age, and theft with material evidence." We have no earlier charters, but many elements in the charters of immunity available indicate that they did not create a new state of things; on the contrary, they confirmed an ancient and well-established custom. It was only with the growth of power of the Prince of Moscow that the old, very extensive immunities received limitations, such as reservation for the prince's judges of the three cases mentioned in the quoted charter. It seems that in earlier times the *votchinnik's* prerogatives in his *votchina* did not have such limitations, and practically his administrative and judiciary power rooted in custom was largely the same as the prince's in his principality.

This theory is advanced by K. Nevolin in his *Istoriia Rossiiskikh grazhdanskikh zakonov* [History of Russian Civil Law] (St. Petersburg, 1851), II, par. 272, and accepted by several Russian historians, e.g., Pavlov-Sil'vansky (*Gosudarevy sluzhilye liudi*, pp. 18-20), Eck (*Moyen âge russe*, pp. 235-254), and V. Storozhev ("*Votchina*" in Brockhaus-Efron, *Entsiklopedicheskii Slovar'* [Encyclopedic Dictionary], XIII [1892], 321). There is strong evidence in its support.

Another theory interprets the regime of immunities restrictively, considering it not as an expression of an old custom but as privileges established for the grantees by the prince in order to create for them an exceptional situation. Such was S. Solov'ev's opinion (*Istoriia Rossii s drevnêishikh vremen* [History of Russia from Most Ancient Times], 2nd edn., St. Petersburg, 1897, Book I, p. 1213) followed by V. Kliuchevsky (*Kurs russkoi istorii* [Lectures on Russian History], Moscow 1937, I, 375-377) and others. Recently, V. B. El'iashevich has emphasized this interpretation very strongly in the chapter of his book, *Istoriia prava pozemel'noi sobstvennosti v Rossii* [Legal History of Land Ownership in Russia], I (Paris 1948), on the boyars' lands (pp. 249-266).

[8] The term *udêl* which in the Kievan period meant only "share" in the common property of the princely family of Riurik now evolves in the sense of patrimony thus covering the dual quality of "principality" and "estate." Some writers use this term adjectivally to characterize this period of political fragmentation. Eck (*Moyen âge russe*, p. 569) rightly translates it as *principauté patrimoniale*. Cf. also p. 43: "*Udêl* is generally translated as 'appanage,' *udêlinyj knjazi* [Eck's transliteration] as 'appanaged prince' which is completely erroneous, *udêl* being hereditary property not reverting at all to the crown after the proprietor's death while an appanage reverts." This objection is valid, but foreign historians have simply followed, anachronistically, the use of the term *udêl* as appanage in modern Russian legislation since Paul I's *Uchrezhdenie o Imperatorskoi familii* [Establishment concerning the Imperial Family] of April 5, 1797. See *Stolêtie Udêlov* [Centenary of the Appanages], 1797-1897 (St. Petersburg, 1897).

and its connection with landed property. Above the multitude of princes, entirely independent in their principalities, big or small, theoretically there was a higher power, that of the Grand Prince of Vladimir. However, it did not amount to very much at the time of the invasion.

When the invasion came and ravaged all of Central Russia and of the Dnieper region (it did not go as far as Novgorod), its results were to promote a final territorial split between Novgorod, remaining practically independent, Russia of the Dnieper region (soon absorbed by the growing Principality of Lithuania and the Kingdom of Poland), and, finally, Central Russia. With regard to Central Russia, the Tartars not only organized the material exploitation of this region, since most of all they were interested in material gains, but they also gave substance to the authority of the Grand Prince of Vladimir, who from 1328 became their farmer-general for the over-all collection of the tribute. At the same time, from that moment they normally invested the Prince of Moscow with the dignity of the Grand Prince of Vladimir and the functions it involved; in this way the Prince of Moscow gained authority over the other princes.

This is the beginning of the rise of Moscow. Within two and a half centuries its power was to grow like a snowball, aided by the extreme pulverization of Central Russia. The story of this rise represents a chapter of Russian history which cannot be studied merely in a footnote. Here we need only mention a movement resulting from this pulverization, namely the general rush of military servants and the patrimonial princes themselves in ever greater numbers into the service of the Prince of Moscow. In doing this, the military servants were exercising their customary right of free departure while the patrimonial princes were voluntarily seeking a dependent position by commending themselves to the Prince of Moscow. The power of the latter could easily be used to make out of the acceptance of a new boyar a pretext for annexation of his landed property in another principality, and thus, by and by, not only a great host of military servants, but more and more territory became concentrated in the hands of the Prince of Moscow. By 1462, the beginning of Ivan III's reign, this process of concentration had been completed for almost all Central Russian territory. As this concentration proceeded, however, with one Grand Prince superseding numerous princes, the old custom of free change of service ceased to be feasible. Old local interests yielding to one major national interest represented by the Grand Prince of Moscow, the service to him became national service; and free departure, change of national allegiance, or breach of loyalty to the sovereign was punishable by loss of patrimony, whether principality or non-princely landed property. Thus, toward the end of the fifteenth century a connection developed between patrimony and the sovereign's service, a new customary law replacing the old law of free service, and imparting to hereditary landed property a conditional character, either directly,[9] or more often, indirectly by means of a suspended threat of confiscation.

At the same time new developments set in as a result of the annexation of the Novgorodian territory, which was the last step in the rise of Moscow, practically completing the unification under the same power of all then existing territories of Great Russia. New tasks faced Muscovy from that moment on, nationally, militarily, and administratively, and to cope with them reforms were necessary which led to the disappearance of old relationships and the creation of new ones; whether the new ones were feudal raises new questions. The basic reform was that of military organization whereby the system of benefices (*pomêstnaĭa sistema*) came into existence. For the Russian peasantry this led to the loss of its medieval freedom. This process began under Ivan III and was accomplished in the middle of the seventeenth century.

III. Feudal Aspects in Muscovy
(and Their Aftermath in Modern Russia)

As long as Central Russia was not unified, conflicts between its numerous independent princes did not involve the participation of great military forces. Military servants organized the population of their estates for war, and, whenever necessary, mustered and led it in the service of the prince with whom a link of free service connected them. This service was parallel to the possession of land in practice, but the latter was unconditional in law and did not have the character of military tenure.

[9] ". . . And what I have granted to my boyars, Prince Andrei Fedorovich and Prince Peter Mikitich, the patrimony I have given to them to replace their [own] patrimonies [follow the names of the new patrimonies] . . . as long as they and their children serve me and my children; if their children continue to serve my son, this belongs to them, and if they do not serve my son, then their patrimonies [go] to my son. And if God calls to Him my son Fedor, then this grant of mine will be their patrimony to replace their [own] patrimony. . . ." (Will of Prince Boris Vasil'evich of Volok, 1477, *Dukhovnye i dogovornye gramoty velikikh udel'nykh kniazeĭ* [Wills and Treaties of the Grand and Patrimonial Princes XIV-XVI c., Moscow and Leningrad, 1950, p. 251.)

When an enormous Muscovite state was built on the whole territory of Great Russia its increased needs led to the creation of a new military system. It did not have to fight its Russian neighbors any more, but foreign powers: Sweden, the Livonian Order, the Grand Principality of Lithuania, and its former masters, the Tartars, still powerful in the southeast even after Muscovy had rejected its centuries old allegiance in 1480. More extensive borders had to be defended, and more skillful military forces had to be faced, numbering tens and even hundreds of thousands of well-trained and well-armed warriors. A special mobile and numerous military class became an urgent necessity. Muscovy began to organize it in the last quarter of the fifteenth century, utilizing different social elements for the purpose. Some of them were the heritage of the preceding epoch, such as *dêti boĭarskiĭa* (junior boyars), i.e., junior members of families of military (and administrative) servants; *dvorĭane*, people holding offices at the court (*dvor*) of formerly independent princes or boyars; Novgorodian *svoezemtsy* (landowners), i.e., townspeople who had land with agriculturists on it outside of the city. This was not enough, however. From abroad, especially from Lithuania and the Tartar countries, military people in considerable numbers came to Muscovy to serve the Grand Prince. Later on, other warriors came in, recruited from the Cossacks (people who looked for a free life in the no man's land, the Russian "frontier" on the margin of the Muscovite territory). All those elements served to build a militia of cavalry; at the same time, a small, permanent, mercenary army was formed in Muscovy, consisting of infantry and special technical troops.[10]

There was not enough money to insure the existence of this numerous militia. For this purpose the Grand Prince of Moscow created the *pomêst'e* (benefice, military holding) which was given to the new military servant personally and conditionally, as long as his service continued. In the beginning, this tenure was not hereditary, either in law or in practice. But already in the beginning of the sixteenth century, military service now being more and more connected with the *votchina*, the hereditary principle began to extend also to the *pomêst'e*. After the

[10] During the Livonian War (1558-83) the Muscovite army consisted of 75,000 cavalry (*dvorĭane, dêti boĭarskiĭa* and their men), 20,000 infantry (arquebusiers) and Cossacks (both on horseback and on foot), and, finally, 14,000 Tartars, other allogenes and some foreigners (Dutch, Scottish, Greek, Danish, etc.), in all about [illegible]0,000 men (S. M. Seredonin, *Sochinenie Giles'a Fletcher's kak istoricheskiĭ istochnik* [Giles Fletcher's Work as Source of History], St. Petersburg, 1891, pp. 337-338, 349, 359).

Time of Troubles it became law, all distinction disappearing in practice between the *votchina* and the *pomêst'e* at the same time, both finally becoming hereditary landownership burdened with military service. As a result of this development, the class of landowners became identified with the class of public servants (*sluzhilye lĭudi*, i.e., primarily military servants). A semantic evolution corresponded tc this process: the word *pomêshchik*, which originally meant military tenant, has established itself in the Russian language down to our day with the general meaning of "landlord." By the middle of the seventeenth century this evolution was completed. From 1649 to 1762 th feature of landowning—hereditary landowning—gradually prevailec over the feature of military service, and this led to the actual reversa of the feudalizing process whereby land tenure had become conditiona upon service: thus the landowning class, called generally *dvorĭane* in th seventeenth century, obtained freedom from all service to the state an kept, nevertheless, its landed privileges. Peter the Great's legislatio called only a temporary halt to this development.

The rise of military tenure had enormous consequences for Russia agricultural population. On the one hand, military fiefs were very ofte created in territories which had been settled by free peasant commun ties, and these now suddenly found themselves under a master wh had to be fed in order to enable him to give all his time to public servic On the other hand, constant distribution of new lands to military ter ants greatly restricted the possibilities for free rural existence. Whe this development was already considerably under way in the midd of the sixteenth century, under Ivan the Terrible, suddenly the who of the southeast became Russian territory, and soon afterwards, towa the end of the century, the borders of Muscovy began to move acro the Urals in the direction of the Pacific. New possibilities for settleme opened up, and the population began to leave the old Great Russi territory in order to look for a better life elsewhere. This happened a time when Muscovy became involved in a major war for the co of the Baltic (1558-1583) and was interested more than ever in assuri the existence of its army of military tenants and the continuance sources of taxation. With the population running far away into t southeastern space, military tenants were losing their manpower a the government its taxpayers. In order to keep both, restrictions peasant liberty to move were introduced. After the Time of Troubl the premises of this situation did not change, and it appeared that t only way to have national defense insured and the treasury satisfy needs was to restrict still more the right of the peasant to leave his landlord, so that by 1649 the rural population became permanently attached to its place of residence. In the meantime, all difference between allodial property and military fiefs disappeared, and the rule prohibiting the voluntary change of landlord became law for all kinds of privately owned populated property.

Between 1649 and 1762 a development was accomplished whereby serfdom[11] came close to actual slavery, though not identical with it. Serfs were sold, separately and without land even, in spite of timid attempts on the part of the imperial government to react against it. In law, however, there was nothing to justify this custom; it resulted from the absolute dependence into which serfs fell upon their landlords who during this time became their judges (except in major cases), their ax collectors (for the state), and their police. As a matter of fact, peasants on privately owned estates as well as elsewhere in theory remained itizens to the same extent as any other subjects of the Tsar; they took normally the oath of allegiance at every advent of a new sovereign. But heir actual situation involved them in the exigencies of a very rigid ystem of dependence, in many respects paralleling the system of immunities of old pre-Muscovite days so far as the interests of the nobility were concerned; for them, as peasants tied to one and the same master, his system brought with it a virtual loss of liberty which the former ystem of immunities had not implied for their class.

Thus, by 1762, on the one hand the landlords were dispensed from n obligation which was originally the very condition of their tenure or the major part of their ancestors; on the other hand, the peasantry eached a status coming close to slavery in many of its features. As the ussian peasantry—and Great Russian institutions in the course of enturies spread to some of the annexed territories, while other territories had developed a serfdom of their own before the time of their nnexation—kept the historic memory of the circumstances under hich their loss of liberty became possible, they expected from every ew sovereign a charter establishing "peasant liberty" as a natural ounterpart of their masters' freedom not to serve the state any more. easant liberty meant for them their liberation from bondage, but it so meant more, namely their getting back the land the state had taken way from them to give to military tenants. Another century elapsed

[11] This was not the official term; the legal term for serfs in Russia was *poddanye*, ., subjects. Customarily the peasants' status was defined as *krêpostnoe pravo*, ., a status governed by law of bondage.

before peasant liberty was granted by the Emperor Alexander II in 1861: the whole of the Russian privately owned peasantry received not only personal freedom, but four-fifths of the soil they used to till. As a consequence of this reform, reforms of the local administration and of the judiciary in 1864 did away with all privileges connected with centuries of serfdom. One can safely conclude that feudalism, in all its aspects and ramifications, came to an end in Russia at this date.

IV. Conclusions

If one now takes the specific points of the definition of feudalism as given in the Introductory Essay and applies them to the Russian development, both conformity and disconformity will appear.

The regime of the *udêl* (patrimonial principality) coupled with that of immunity connects *political authority* with *private possession of land* in pre-Muscovite Central Russia. This connection survives, in a certain sense, in Muscovy and even in modern Russia in the privileges given to military tenants or, later, to landlords over the agricultural population. The connection became firmly established because of the importance of military functions in local politics in pre-Muscovite Centra Russia and its national importance in Muscovy. Whenever possessior of land is hereditary, the authority connected with it also is hereditary this *heredity* was the normal regime in pre-Muscovite times, and i again became general in the seventeenth century, the non-hereditar *pomêst'e* being merely a historical interlude, even if rather a long one

However, in pre-Muscovite Russia the *essential* relation is not tha between lord and vassal, but that between the *votchinnik* and the population of his *votchina*, coming close to that of ruler and subject. Ther was no link between the prince's service and possession of land, and, i there was heredity of landholding, there was no heredity of the prince' service itself; there was also freedom of departure, and no concept o felony at all. Can one speak of vassalage under these circumstances Pavlov-Sil'vansky and Eck answer affirmatively, but Kliuchevsky denie categorically the existence of a feudal relationship, discounting a external similarity. Kliuchevsky readily grants that the patrimoni prince, who is at the same time ruler of his principality and *dominu eminens* of its land, recalls the Western lord, "but his boyars and fre servants certainly are not vassals." Carrying his argument further, h points out that, "if it is true that in the fifteenth century some Gran Princes of Moscow aimed at creating between patrimonial princ and themselves a link of vassalage, it was not a manifestation of a feudal fragmentation of power, but a forerunning sign and a lever of its national concentration."[12]

Can one recognize a lord-vassal relationship in the Muscovite military tenure? Here, there is a connection between military function and possession of land, even though the *pomêst'e* is not hereditary. It is not, however, based on a feudal contract which involves *mutual* fealty between a suzerain and a vassal. Its source is the absolute sovereignty of the Tsar *requiring* service from his subject and *granting* a *pomêst'e* in return for service. There is compulsion in this service, first of all, in the interest of the community, and Peter Struve defines it as a feature of a "liturgical" regime (cf. *Leitourgia*, as consecrated by Max Weber), "a kind of state feudalism, but in its legal aspect . . . in some ways the direct opposite of classical Western feudalism."[13]

It is not surprising then that the Russian Middle Ages did not evolve an ideal of chivalry comparable to that of the West. There were elements of it in Kievan times, reflected in the epic tales, but neither the long centuries of Tartar rule nor the Muscovite concept of the Tsar's service created a favorable climate for the ideas of chivalry. In the case of Russia, barbarian influence (if the Tartars may be called barbarians) acted as a vehicle rather of ideas of personal subordination than of personal rights as expressed in the Western lord-vassal relationship.

How did Russian medieval institutions originate? Both the technique of fighting and military organization were largely the same in pre-Muscovite Central Russia as in earlier, Kievan times: neither new expensive military equipment, nor monopolization of military service by a new, smaller group of persons occurred. What happened was that the military man grew in importance as a local center of defense both from outside and from inside dangers; he became also a source of material aid. In this regard one should emphasize that during the period of settlement the local boyar generally was not a strong man risen from the bottom, but an organizer of colonization who came from the south with his retinue and numerous slaves, i.e., resources of both physical and economic power of peculiar value in an extremely isolated forest region where primitive agriculture offered the only available means for existence. Only in Muscovite times more expensive military equipment (use of more numerous and better armed cavalry) may be quoted as a reason for the monopolization of military service by a special, newly

[12] *Kurs russkoĭ istorii*, I, 375-377.

[13] *Cambridge Economic History of Europe*, I (Cambridge, 1941), 419.

created class; this reform, however, was an instrument of growing centralization, and not a beginning of fragmentation of political power.

Considered dynamically, the Russian "feudal age" immediately followed a period of higher political organization, the Kievan-Novgorodian federation. The principle of unity survived as a theoretical linkage between the numerous patrimonial princes the more easily in that they all belonged to the same family of Rĭurik. This memory served as an instrument of centralization in the hands of one of them, the Prince of Moscow; the rise of the Principality of Moscow to the Tsardom of Muscovy was the combined result of the tenacity of this memory and the extreme pulverization of political power in Central Russia. The term "Russian Middle Ages" largely covers the period when this process was being accomplished.

This term applies to a somewhat longer period, from the thirteenth to the end of the seventeenth century, if attention is focused on the history of Russian culture. Kievan-Novgorodian Russia had a higher level of culture than pre-Muscovite Central Russia and even Muscovy itself; until the twelfth century it was at least as high as that of contemporary Western Europe, with which steady relations were cultivated. The influence of the Christian Church was great, but the culture was secular in many important ways. Especially from the Tartar invasion on, Central Russia became largely isolated from Western Europe, and isolation remained when it became Muscovy; in this culturally self-sufficient, but also backward, region, all intellectual life became dominated by the church. Only with Peter the Great did Russia fully emerge from its cultural middle ages to a renewed contact with Europe and a new, brilliant, worldly culture.

To sum up, the Russian "feudal age" fits the analysis of the Introductory Essay only partially. There certainly was a system of government based on immunities and the pre-eminence of military functions but neither vassalage as a bilateral contract, nor fief developed in Russia and there was neither consistent heredity of military or administrative function nor code of chivalry. On the other hand, if the Russian "feudal age" was one of a mainly agricultural society and was essentially a period of transition (*moyen âge*) from one highly organized political system to a still higher centralized government, and from one period of high culture to another higher period of culture; if furthermore it was an "age of faith": nevertheless its origin cannot be traced either to barbarian invasions or to a new military technique and new military organization, though commendation again represents a common feature with Western Europe and so also does manorial economic and social organization.

If such is the discrepancy, is one authorized to speak of Russian feudalism at all? It would be dogmatic to answer with a simple negative. It is clear that feudalism as an all-inclusive system, a "total culture," did not develop in any period of Russian history, and, if we say with Strayer and Coulborn that the lord-vassal relationship is the crux of the matter, then even that scarcely reached full development in Russia. Nevertheless, there were unquestionably important feudal *aspects* in Russian institutional development. Should they be defined as semi-feudalism, quasi-feudalism, para-feudalism, or abortive feudalism? Abortive feudalism would be the best, but whatever the definition, it will hardly cover the manifold historical reality and will still leave unsolved the problem of its full understanding.

With an eye to this understanding particular attention should be called to the resettlement movement in medieval Central Russia, and the important differences between Russian and Western development which may be related to that movement. If the movement produced feudal aspects in Russian life, it was also the source of instability in social relationships. It arose fundamentally from the mobility of the rural population caused by the rapid exhaustion of the not too fertile soil under conditions of primitive, extensive agriculture.[14] Here is one of the sharp contrasts between Russia and the West, for in the West "the freeman to protect his freedom surrounded himself with a chain of stable hereditary relationships, as if it were a castle wall; he was becoming the most important center of local community, a stable, even permanent social unit led by him and backing him."[15] In Russia the shifting local population did not provide the "free servant" with elements to rely upon, and there was no other protection for his liberty than the temporary character of his service and the right of free departure. The mobility of rural population thus stimulating the mobility of the military class, no lord-vassal relationship of the Western European type could develop in pre-Muscovite Russia, no code of chivalry based on it, and no consistent heredity of functions.

[14] "The forest is cleared or burnt; after a year or two of cultivation the lands are abandoned and the cultivators push further on. The annual fallow land with manure appears only at the end of the 15th century, and the triennial rotation of crops with fallow lands has been known from only the second half of the 16th century" (Eck, *Moyen âge russe*, p. 59).

[15] Klĭuchevsky, *Kurs russkoĭ istorii*, I, 377.

In the Muscovite period the institutional development was determined, on the contrary, by a strenuous desire to stabilize the population. Here, the military reform affected institutions powerfully, and on the surface there can be noted a certain parallelism with the early feudal development of the West; the parallelism extends both to origins in military need and to the resemblance of the *pomêst'e* to the Western benefice.[16] However, the context being different, this similarity is not more than superficial. All Muscovite institutional changes were results of the action *from above* of a "liturgical" state; they represent not steppingstones in the direction of a feudal system, but as many measures leading from it toward an extreme centralization of all national life.

[16] This is not the only resemblance. The *pomêst'e* system very closely recalls the Byzantine *pronoia* and the Moslem *iqta* and the idea has been expressed that the two developments, the Muscovite and the Oriental-Byzantine, influenced each other (P. Miliukov, in his article on feudalism in Russia in *Entsik. Slovar'*, LXX [1902], 549) or even that the Byzantine pattern might have influenced the *pomêst'e* directly and, possibly, through the Ottoman military fief, the *timar* (Vernadsky, "On Some Parallel Trends in Russian and Turkish History," *Trans. of the Conn. Academy of Arts and Sciences*, XXXVI, July, 1945, 33-34). There is, however, no direct evidence to prove this influence.

PART THREE

A COMPARATIVE STUDY OF FEUDALISM

BY RUSHTON COULBORN

1. A CLASSIFICATION

The aim of this essay is to test feudalism as a developmental uniformity; that is to say, to find out to what extent feudalism has passed through similar stages of development in the different times and places of its occurrence in history, and to what extent it has recurred with similar antecedent, concomitant, and consequent political forms. The ground covered is in the main the same as covered in the eight essays by specialists which precede this essay in the present volume, but I have to say at once, with due apology, that I differ in some matters from the judgments made by my colleagues—an ordinary occurrence in scholarship, and one which must finally contribute the more to knowledge. There comes first, therefore, a summary classification of the twelve cases of possible feudalism which have been studied, for that discloses immediately what my main judgments are.

There are only two fully proven cases of feudalism, those of Western Europe and of Japan. In two other cases, Chou China to about 700 B.C. and Mesopotamia in the five or six hundred years after Hammurabi, there is a probability of feudalism. For Chou China the probability is large, for in that case almost all the evidence necessary to prove feudal conditions is found except the crucial evidence of the forms of dependency of vassal upon lord. In two more cases, Egypt under the Libyan Pharaohs and the Rajput states of northern India, alien forces from outside the respective societies intervened and deflected the course of political development away from the direction it was taking. In Egypt up to that juncture there were most of the signs of movement towards feudalism. In India the process was very complex and the evidence is both scanty and confusing, but the possibility that a feudal order would have arisen if it had not been for Muslim and European intervention cannot be ruled out.

These six cases contain all the positive evidence found in this book for feudalism as a uniformity. It is enough, I think, to justify the rather precise definition adopted in the Introductory Essay and the extension of that definition in the present essay into an abstract historical outline approximately applicable to all cases. There is also negative evidence which serves in the usual manner to confirm the definition; it confirms the extension of the definition as well. One thing the negative evidence happens to establish is another uniformity, a recurring course of events which in an abstract sense parallels feudal development, but is in sharp contrast with it, and concretely actually precedes or is contemporary with feudal development in a neighboring territory. The negative evidence also establishes special cases which differ both from feudal development and from the contrasted development of the other uniformity. They appear to arise in somewhat unusual circumstances.

The other uniformity is one of break-up of a great empire into two or more fairly large states ruled not very differently from the empire itself, followed by restoration of the empire. This course of events happened in Egypt between the Fifth Dynasty and the Twelfth, in China from the Posterior Han Dynasty to the T'ang Dynasty, and in the eastern part of the Roman Empire from about the fifth century A.D. to the eleventh century when the Byzantine Empire was firmly established. The rise of the Byzantine Empire was earlier than and contemporary with the rise of feudalism in Western Europe. The establishment of the T'ang Dynasty in China was achieved several centuries before the emergence of feudalism in Japan, but the dynasty was contemporary with the direct antecedents of Japanese feudalism. And it is possible that political forms which could be antecedent to feudalism arose in Palestine in the time of the Twelfth Dynasty in Egypt. These three periods in the history of Egypt, China, and Byzantium have sometimes been described as feudal, and some doubt in the cases of Egypt and Byzantium remains in the special essays dealing with them above, but it will be shown here decisively that they were not feudal.

There remain the special cases of Iran-Mesopotamia in the time of the Arsacid and Sassanid rulers, Byzantium in its later career, and Russia, the two latter being intimately connected. It is worth saying here only that some of the complications arising in these three cases are historical complications: they have to do with special influences from a complex past. None of the three is feudal although the study of feudalism throws light upon them—is necessary even to an understanding of them. Since they are unalike, their occurrence does not suggest a third uniformity Nor does any of them approach feudal form closely enough to make i profitable to broaden or loosen the definition of feudalism used here

The dozen cases, half of feudalism, half not of feudalism, treated i this volume[1] are not the only possible cases of feudalism in history, bu they are the great majority of cases we know anything worth knowin

[1] Numbers are not really important, but for those much concerned with th quantitative the negative Russian case could be split into at least two, possib three, cases occurring at different dates.

about. Of other possible occasions of feudal developments, four deserve notice. The earliest is the one, already mentioned, in the countries neighboring Egypt after the early empire in Egypt collapsed in the time of the Sixth Dynasty. The second is in India, probably in the Ganges Valley, after the Indo-European invasions. The third is also in India and eastward across the Indian Ocean in the peninsulas and East Indian islands after the fall of the Maurya Empire. The fourth is in regions other than Japan and Korea after the fall of the Han Empire. Korea had the one certainly feudal regime which is not treated in this book. Of all the rest it is my opinion that at present there are not enough data available to show whether feudal developments occurred or not. They are not treated in this essay.

Finally, it is possible that feudalism occurred at the rise of civilization in the valleys of the Nile, the Tigris and Euphrates, and the Indus and Great Mihrab, also that there was an earlier feudal period in the Yellow River Valley than that of the Chou Dynasty; nor must the possibility of feudalism in pre-Columbian America be forgotten. The question of feudalism at the rise of civilization in the river valleys of the Old World is an interesting and important subject for speculation; it is considered in the Conclusion of this essay.

2. THE ORIGIN AND EARLY DEVELOPMENT OF FEUDALISM IN JAPAN AND WESTERN EUROPE

THE idea that feudalism originated with barbarians is as old as the concept of feudalism itself. True, it has been hotly disputed in its application to Western Europe—often from other than scientific motives—but leading opinion now is that the idea is sound. The particular opinion advocated here is that, while other characteristic events and conditions are necessary to the origin of feudalism, the barbarian is the key man. There will therefore be a description of the barbarian before the other events and conditions are outlined.

The Greek word *barbaros* meant alien, non-Greek. It did not matter whether the people in question were highly civilized Persians or Egyptians, or wild fellows from the tribal societies of central Europe and Russia. The word was most often applied to those the Greeks encountered most often, the peoples on their frontiers, who inevitably became affected in some degree by the attractive culture of Greece. The typical barbarian came more and more to be a frontiersman. In the time of the Roman Empire the frontier had become a very important political fact, and the frontier barbarian had become eligible to serve the empire as a fighting man. In fact, he had become one of the empire's best soldiers, and as such was admitted to the civilized world. It was this barbarian who contributed at a later time to the origin and growth of Western European feudalism, and what he contributed he first learned in the frontier world, the world of the heroic age, which was part Roman, part barbarian. That world had its own quite special characteristics:

"Now it deserves to be remarked [says Chadwick] that these characteristics are in no sense primitive. In social organisation the distinguishing feature of the Heroic Age is in the nature of a revolt or emancipation from those tribal obligations and ideas by which the society of primitive peoples is everywhere governed. The same remark applies in principle to political organisation; the princes of the Heroic Age appear to have freed themselves to a large extent from any public control on the part of the tribe or community. . . . The force formerly exercised by the kindred is now largely transferred to the comitatus, a body of chosen adherents pledged to personal loyalty to their chief. So also in government the council of the tribe or community has come to be nothing more than a comitatus or court. The result of the change is that the man who possesses a comitatus becomes largely free from the control of his kindred, while the chief similarly becomes free from control within his community."[1]

It was the attachment of leader and follower in the comitatus, or war-band, which came to serve as the central ethic of feudal society in Western Europe. The attachment was extremely strong, close, and personal. If it was not primitive, it certainly reproduced the simplicity, fervor, and durability of primitive relationships. Loyalty, courage, and personal honor were thus brought to a jaded imperial world, to be worked in time into a new system of cohesion. We shall find that essentially the same ethic came to prevail in other feudal societies, but that in some the sharp institutional break between tribe and war-band, found by Chadwick for Western Europe,[2] did not occur. A society moving in a feudal direction is one in which the personal relations of loyalty between leader and follower, or lord and vassal, come to serve as a political system and to take the place of the political system operating through officials serving the state. When (and if) the old state has become nothing but a vestige and its personnel converted into feudal magnates, the feudal polity may be said to have arrived. Just how small a vestige the old state must be, no authority has sought to define closely.

But many things must have happened in the rise of feudalism before the old state is superseded. The old state must first weaken, and go on weakening for a long time. At an early stage in its weakening great magnates arise—landlords, generals, officials, sometimes chieftains of tribes or clans—who take over some of the state's powers upon a local basis. The great magnates must acquire the character of leaders of barbarian war-bands; the enduring lord and vassal relation must become established between them and their followers. Tribal chieftains acquire that character fairly easily, since it is at first for them only the substitution of one set of personal relationships for another. Hence, where the society consists at all largely of tribes, the passage from tribal relations to war-band relations to feudal relations is likely to be continuous and uninterrupted, except by the vicissitudes of internecine warfare and of the break-up of the old state. Where the majority of magnates are officials of the old bureaucratic state or great noblemen or military

[1] H. M. Chadwick, *The Heroic Age* (Cambridge, Eng., 1912), p. 443.

[2] Also for Greece in the heroic age recorded by Homer.

officers of such a state, the barbarians in their war-bands come in as invaders from outside the society, having already made the break with their tribal organizations which Chadwick describes, and there follows a merging of the barbarian and the civilized types of magnate. In those societies which thereafter proceed to feudal conditions the barbarian type comes to predominate.

There may come a time in a society whose leadership is changing in this manner when political reformers seek to restore the disintegrating state by calling to its aid the personal vassalage relations which have come to permeate its upper ranks, thus tightening up or replacing the loosened relations within the official hierarchy. Wherever a movement of this sort occurs, it is a well-marked innovation. It occurs in every case of feudalization studied here, and I call it the "proto-feudal" stage of those movements. It would be incorrect, I think, to suppose that a society which reaches the proto-feudal stage must necessarily continue into a fully feudal stage, but a likelihood that it will do so must be admitted.

After the proto-feudal stage there follows the early feudal stage, dramatically described for Western Europe by Mr. Strayer.[3] The transition between the two stages is probably the most disorderly and violent period in the whole development of feudalism. The disorders and violence continue into the early feudal stage for perhaps a century or two, but in a spasmodically diminishing extent. It would be an exaggeration, however, to describe conditions in that stage, or even at the transition before it, as anarchic. In the Introductory Essay the doctrine that anarchy is a normal feature of feudalism was called in question. Here the doctrine is rejected and we begin now to show in what way, to what extent, and when fighting and the lack of functioning political institutions really are a part of the feudal system. I rather suspect that real anarchy could inhibit, perhaps prevent, the formation of a feudal system.[4]

The arrival of the early stage of feudalism is announced by the emergence of the elemental, small, strong fief, that immensely tough little political unit headed by a feudal lord with his band of personal retainers, and populated by the lord, his retainers, his other vassals scattered over the fief, some rear-vassals probably,[5] and all the simple people

[3] Above, pp. 18-19.

[4] For a possible case of the kind, see pp. 225-226, 304-306, 323-324 below.

[5] Probably there was some hierarchical development from a very early, formative stage in the rise of fiefs, for feudalism is by its very nature a series of arrangements

tending to become praedial and menial dependents. The elemental, strong fief is the characteristic product of the disorders attendant upon the collapse of the proto-feudal regime and the beginning of the true feudal regime. The disorders are the price paid for the elemental, strong fief; it is indeed probably correct to say that they are the necessary milieu in which the fief arises. Perhaps that is the chief reason for the notion that feudalism is essentially violent and anarchic. Yet, apart from the fact that in most of its later stages feudalism is far more orderly, the elemental, strong fief is an area of peace internally, a small state which is the very opposite of anarchic, for it is characteristically well-governed, often even governed with the active consent and cooperation of its members.

The elemental, strong fief results from survival of the fittest; it is a true exemplar, I believe, of the Darwinian doctrine, which is a rare thing in the evolution of society. Historians do not appear to have noticed hitherto that the elemental, strong fief also exemplifies another famous doctrine: it is an "in-group" arrayed against all "out-groups" after the manner conceived by Sumner. Feudal society in its early stage, in fact, seems to approximate quite closely to primitive society, as Sumner describes it. Here are some of Sumner's remarks:

"The conception of 'primitive society' which we ought to form is that of small groups scattered over a territory. . . . A group of groups may have some relation to each other (kin, neighborhood, alliance, connubium and commercium) which draws them together and differentiates them from others. Thus a differentiation arises between ourselves, the we-group, or in-group, and everybody else, or the others-groups, out-groups. The insiders in a we-group are in a relation of peace, order, law, government, and industry, to each other. Their relation to all outsiders, or others-groups, is one of war and plunder, except so far as agreements have modified it. . . .

"The relation of comradeship and peace in the we-group and that of hostility and war towards others-groups are correlative to each other. The exigencies of war with outsiders are what make peace inside, lest internal discord should weaken the we-group for war. These exigencies also make government and law in the in-group, in order to prevent quarrels and enforce discipline. Thus war and peace have reacted on

---

for mutual support between greater and lesser persons. But anything like the European hierarchy to the seventh degree of infeudation (legally recognized, further unrecognized) must have been a later development. I doubt too that such development occurred widely, or even at all, in other societies.

each other and developed each other, one within the group, the other in the inter-group relation. The closer the neighbors, and the stronger they are, the intenser is the warfare, and then the intenser is the internal organization and discipline of each. Sentiments are produced to correspond. Loyalty to the group, sacrifice for it, hatred and contempt for outsiders, brotherhood within, warlikeness without,—all grow together, common products of the same situation. These relations and sentiments constitute a social philosophy."[6]

This is a strikingly accurate description also of a feudal society, especially in an early stage of its development, with the fiefs all struggling against one another and being hammered in the course of the struggle into tougher and tougher little associations. Is a feudal society a primitive society, then? The question seems easy to answer in the affirmative until we recollect Chadwick's opinion. The primitive society is broken up in the heroic age. If the barbarians, leaders in that age and key men in the rise of feudalism, are not primitives, how comes it that the feudal society they form seems so nearly primitive? We can answer this question, and find a useful guide to the place of feudalism in the rise of civilized societies if we call in anthropological and sociological authority.

Redfield and Tönnies offer the two most serviceable analytical distinctions for these purposes, and Durkheim has an important principle which may be applied. Redfield shifts the distinction between the two kinds of society away from the categories civilized and primitive, and contrasts instead the "folk society" and the "urban society."[7] The new distinction first facilitates abstraction, offering a theoretical picture of a society composed purely of folk features. But then Redfield returns to fact, pointing out that actual societies are combinations of folk and urban features, and that there are many possible combinations.[8] A feudal society, then, is perhaps one of the combinations of folk and urban, or primitive and civilized features—I prefer the latter terms for reasons which will shortly appear.

This sounds elementary, and it is so, but it leads to particulars of the feudal combination—if it is a combination—and for the historian it raises the question how the proposed combination came into existence, something which is not elementary. Tönnies' distinction between *Ge-*

[6] W. G. Sumner, *Folkways* (3rd edn.; Boston, 1940), pp. 12-13.

[7] Robert Redfield, "The Folk Society," *American Journal of Sociology*, LII (1947), 293-308.

[8] pp. 306-308.

meinschaft and *Gesellschaft*[9] throws some light on the matter. A fief at its formation is unquestionably a *Gesellschaft*, an association consciously formed by men for a certain purpose, to wit, mutual defense. Such things are not unknown in primitive societies, but they are certainly rare there; they are usually, always perhaps, *ad hoc* arrangements made between different primitive societies for purposes they have in common. They may produce a rudimentary superstructure based upon a number of primitive societies. Certainly the *Gesellschaft* type of association is not the basis of a primitive society as it is of the feudal society. Redfield, again, says that relations in a folk society are not contractual; they are tacit and traditional.[10] But relations in a feudal society are, precisely, contractual. A feudal society, therefore, is not a primitive society.

And yet a feudal society undeniably shares many characters with a primitive society. Not only are both of them constructed of alternate in-group out-group relations, but their entire mentalities are similar. Redfield, yet again, suggests that the men of the folk society, like medieval men, think in terms of association of symbols, not in terms of cause and effect.[11] Behavior in a feudal society is largely spontaneous and uncritical. It is strongly patterned. What Bagehot called the "cake of custom"[12] settles easily and strongly over a feudal society. A feudal society's power to meet crises effectively is dependent more upon common understanding of what is important than it is upon discipline exerted by force.[13] The original *Gesellschaft* tends to turn into a *Ge-*

[9] Ferdinand Tönnies, "Gesellschaft und Gemeinschaft (Theorem der Kulturphilosophie): Entwurf von 1880/81," *Soziologische Studien und Kritiken*, 1 (Jena, 1925), 1-33.

[10] p. 300.

[11] p. 305. "Association of symbols" is my phrase, not Redfield's. Actually, I think there is some misapprehension here. Redfield cites Lévy-Brühl and is, it would appear, somewhat misled by him. I think all people, not merely primitives and medievals, think in association of symbols instead of in cause and effect as soon as familiarity with the causal sequence has habituated them to the association. Hence the illusion today among certain scholars that causality is falling out of fashion in science and can even be deliberately evaded. Cf. Ch. 10, n. 26 below. It remains perfectly true that men in folk societies become set enough in their ways to think in association of symbols and that the same habit in the Middle Ages affords a well authenticated historical parallel.

[12] Walter Bagehot, *Physics and Politics; or, Thoughts on the Application of the Principles of "Natural Selection" and "Inheritance" to Political Society* (New York, 1875), p. 27 and *passim*. What Bagehot said on this subject is still enlightening.

[13] Redfield, p. 299. In this sentence I borrow some of Redfield's words about the folk society and alter them a little to change the meaning and make it fit the

meinschaft, an association men enter by birth or by circumstance, accepting its purposes unthinkingly, as of the nature of things.[14] A feudal society is the product of no theory; it happens. So does a primitive society, but the feudal society happens by human agency in a sense that the primitive society does not.

Durkheim has shown how the division of labor, as a principle in operation at various junctures in the development of a society, enters into the changes through which a society may pass.[15] In the feudal society there is one very conspicuous division of labor which is almost completely missing in a primitive society.[16] It is the division between fighting man and farming man, or between political man and economic man, in Western Europe between noble and simple. If we look for the sources of this division, it will lead us to the historic process whereby a feudal society gets its special compromise between primitive and civilized characters. In the particular societies Chadwick thought about there is little to help, for there the primitive is, seemingly at any rate, suddenly cut off. The fighter is the barbarian, and the farmer must be the civilized peasant the fighter brings under his authority. But we get to know more about the peasant and about the barbarian fighter too if we study them in the places where the transition from primitive conditions was not sudden. Such places are Japan, Central and Northern Europe which had not been in the Roman Empire and to which feudalism was brought slowly after it had germinated in France, probably large parts or even all of Chou China, and other places—if we knew enough about China and the other places to be sure.

The actual history in those parts of Europe and in Japan will be treated below. Here we may by anticipation give a few of the findings of that history. It is very clear in the case of Japan that clan relations were quite gradually replaced by feudal relations, that the fighting man differentiated slowly from the farming man, that the division of labor between them evolved.[17] The kinship relations which, as Chadwick

feudal society. His words are: ". . . [a folk society's] power to meet crises effectively is not dependent upon discipline exerted by force or upon devotion to some single principle of action but to the concurrence and consistency of many or all of the actions and conceptions which make up the whole round of life."

[14] I think there is a tendency for any *Gesellschaft* to do this, but that the tendency is stronger in some societies than in others. In a feudal society it is strong.

[15] Emil Durkheim, *De la division du travail social* (Paris, 1893), pp. 50-72 and passim.

[16] Redfield notes that there is not much division of labor in a folk society; p. 297.

[17] These things are perfectly clear even though there is an unknown in the transition in Japan; see below, pp. 200-202.

says, are everywhere a large part of the substance of primitive social relations gave place to specifically feudal relations of lord and man. At first the new type of relation and the old stood side by side: an individual might be both a cousin and a vassal of a landed magnate, but gradually cousinship lost its importance, the old, the primitive faded out, and only the feudal type remained. But we need not be surprised if the new, feudal type still resembled the old, primitive type even after the transition was fully accomplished. Habits of mind and of life survive transitions, especially gradual transitions. The *Gemeinschaft* of kinship relations was changed bit by bit in a long and widespread series of conscious, purposeful agreements, but, when the change had been accomplished, when in particular the object of the change, the restoration of some political stability, had been accomplished,[18] it is natural that the whole society should be found to have returned to a fair extent to *gemeinschaftlich* character.

Elucidation of the place of feudalism in the rise of civilized societies is not yet complete, but we must pause to notice the profound importance of the substitution of something different for kinship relations. Tylor, Bachofen, Morgan, and others of their time saw the evolution of society beginning in the relations of the family and spreading out into clan, sept, tribe, and whatnot, all of them forms of kinship. There are, as a matter of fact, scores of examples in history, far more than those scholars knew, of the extension-distention of kinship relations.[19] But extension of kinship relations will not explain the whole evolution of human society. If that is well known, I do not think anthropologists have ever envisaged a clear and definite process of transition away from kinship. The *Gemeinschaft-Gesellschaft* distinction is an important theoretical conception. A *Gemeinschaft* could consist entirely of kin relations. It could transcend kin relations to include others which seem as "natural," almost as independent of human invention. But the making of feudal contracts, besides exhibiting the theoretical distinction between *Gemeinschaft* and *Gesellschaft*, gives a historic occasion on which the distinction came about. I propose that there have been other such historic occasions, or, alternatively, that all occasions of the rise of civilized societies out of primitive societies have been of the setting

[18] The extent of stability reached in a feudal society is not to be supposed to be great. It is surely less than in a primitive society, but neither is completely stable as a whole. It is only the interior of clan or tribe which exhibits stability, and, relatively, the interior of an elemental fief does so too. See text below.

[19] Rather a good one occurs in this essay in the relations of the princes descended from Riurik in Kievan-Novgorodian Russia; see below pp. 349, 353.

up of feudal relations, or relations quite similar. Whichever is the fact, I think it is clear that civilization, within the meaning assigned to it in this essay, was not constructed on its political side out of kin relations but out of escape from kin relations.

But that is a matter which does not concern the body of this essay; it will be taken up again briefly in the Conclusion.[20] If, meanwhile, the escape from kin relations into feudal relations was a change of great moment, the vast difference between the development of a feudal society and of a primitive society, which has not yet been taken into account, may be explained. The generic difference, extending to all other kinds of civilized society besides feudal societies, is the broad viability of relations: in principle relations are not limited to kin; they are universally possible, and universality, even as something potential, is not a small matter in the development of societies. Shifting of relations between individuals is to be expected in civilized societies, then, and consequently far more frequent and more rapid change than in primitive societies.

Nevertheless, the elemental fief, historic successor to clan or tribe, does not lose all the solidarity and durability of the primitive society. Primitive societies can remain in existence and recognizable over thousands of years, possibly over tens of thousands. The elemental fief presumably cannot do that. Being, like the primitive society, a product of in-group out-group struggle, however, it does show notable toughness. As an association it can outlast a great number of large changes in the history of a civilized society; in Europe, in Japan and in Egypt we shall encounter important examples of this. And yet with its very endurance it couples change: what was an elemental fief characteristically loses its feudal quality, while it keeps its individuality as an association with a geographic location and always a distinct local culture; as such, it ordinarily becomes a unit in the administrative structure of a large state.

In its notable propensity toward change, both the change in the quality of its elemental fiefs and the great changes in its higher structure, a feudal society displays its power of growth. And that must be taken to proceed from its civilized past—if and where it has one.[21] Perhaps some of that power derives from the desire of men to restore the empire of the past which, as we shall observe, is always witnessed in a feudal society by the existence there of what I call the "ghost empire." Certainly much of the power resides in the influence of religion

[20] pp. 374ff. [21] See previous note.

The beginnings of political growth are probably always present within the elemental fief itself, as vestigial survivals from the civilized past.

A feudal society is not, in fact, in any particular a primitive society. It does not grow like a primitive society. It embodies a marked division of labor. It is based on contract. It is not based on kinship. It proves not to be a combination of primitive and civilized, or folk and urban features. The term urban is quite wrong as applied to feudalism; the term folk, applicable perhaps in Redfield's usage, only obscures the important historic change whereby the primitive is changed for something else. That something must be called civilized even though, of things civilized, it is most like the primitive. There is, in fact, suggestive historical evidence of the difference between a primitive and a feudal society: it is that a civilized society in decline has never, so far as I know, lapsed to primitive status; civilized societies in decline have always been caught at the feudal level, if not earlier, and have recovered from that. It appears that there is some sort of barrier between the primitive and the feudal which can be crossed upwards but not downwards—or, at any rate, never has been crossed downwards.

A feudal society newly formed after a decline is therefore at rock-bottom in the scale to which the word civilized applies. In its initial moment it is a new beginning, not quite from nothing political at all, but from the elemental, the simplest, of relations dictated by necessity for survival. The elemental fief is a special form of those simplest relations; it is the specifically feudal form of the in-group, having at least the toughness of primitive in-groups, probably rather more than most of them since neighbors in a feudal society are near and pressing. The elemental fief is at once the most characteristic and the most valuable product of feudalism. If feudalism is a nursery of politics, it is within the elemental fief that its lessons are best learned. That fief remains the most important and effective institution in a society until the emergence of the nation, and from the fief to the nation there occurs a complex transition, the next fundamentally important transition after that from the proto-feudal to the feudal polity.

The most evident difference between our two proven cases of feudalism is the geographical one we have already noticed. In Western Europe the barbarians moved into the old empire; in Japan the empire moved in upon the barbarians. Yet the essential process was the same in the two cases: feudalism, we must suppose, arose from contact between the barbarians and the disintegrating empire; it does not seem to have mattered where or how the contact occurred, or which of the two, barbarians or empire, moved to bring the contact about.

But this is somewhat of a simplification. In the earliest stages of the process, before the two empires began to disintegrate, the one, the Roman Empire, expanded, moving its frontiers outward to make contact with Teutonic and other tribesmen. The other, the Han Empire in China, expanded further as an idea than as a physical fact so that it was an idea and not an imperial frontier which reached Japan. The Japanese Empire was thus a reflection of the Chinese original, not an extension of it. The early Japanese Empire was always a weak reflection of the original, and it would be hard to say just how early the struggle to get it established became a struggle to prevent it from disintegrating. It is clear, however, that its struggles disturbed the clan organization of the Japanese, just as the struggles of the Roman Empire, especially when it began to go to pieces, disturbed the tribal organizations of the Germans. Japanese clansmen and German tribesmen thus both became barbarians, within our meaning of that word, for the same reasons.

At this point there is a divergence. In the frontier world of the Roman Empire, a vague area which grew up on both sides of the frontier line when that line faded out, the development of the warband was rapid, rather desperate, and a prelude to migration into the supposed El Dorado in the body of the empire—although, as has already been noticed, the tribal system of the primitives long survived east of the frontier world in Germany, in other parts of central Europe, and in northern Europe. In Japan the frontier world was the whole area the feeble Japanese Empire sought to rule. It stretched from the region of the empire's early capitals, Nara and Kyoto, to include the western one third of the main island, Hondo, and the islands of Kyushu and Shikoku, south and west of Hondo. The Japanese clans did not migrate. Hence their clan organization survived and was only slowly transformed into a feudal organization. The feudal society in Japan thus originated in this same area, whereas in Europe it originated in a special region of the old empire, northern France, where the invading barbarians effected a very strong lodgment.

The great majority of the peoples of central and northern Europe outside the frontiers of the old empire, both Germans and others beyond them, long remained in their tribal systems, as the Japanese did, and, again as happened to the Japanese, the empire was brought to them and imposed upon them, breaking down their tribal relations and giving rise to feudal relations. The empire which was brought to central Europe was Charlemagne's empire, and that was not quite like the Sinic empire which was brought to Japan. Yet the difference was certainly not great enough to annul the significance of the comparison between the feudalization of the people of central Europe and of the people of Japan.[22]

Among the cases of feudalization and possible feudalization of which we know, probably rather more peoples were feudalized *in situ*, having their tribes and clans transformed from truly primitive to feudal paraprimitive, than were overrun by barbarians and converted from subjection to an empire. In Chou China the majority were transformed *in situ* from clan to what were probably feudal relations. In Japan, as we have seen, all were transformed *in situ* from clan to feudal relations, while in Europe a substantial minority were so transformed. Only in Mesopotamia post-Hammurabi had almost all the peoples affected een subjects of the empire, but many of them were its subjects for nly a short time, and there is reason to think that the incursion of arbarians there was an unusually large one. It must be remembered oo that more societies which were overrun by barbarian invaders did ıot become feudal than did become feudal.[23]

It may be that this is the reason why, on the whole, the Japanese case erves better as the classic case of feudalism than the Western European ase does. That feudalization was more usual among tribesmen who emained *in situ* and less usual in societies which were invaded by bararians from the outside signifies, I believe, the importance of barbarans in feudalization. It is easier to make a barbarian out of a tribesman han out of the civilized subject of an empire. Hence feudalism will rise fairly readily among formerly tribal peoples, given the necessary olitical forces to cause the change. In a civilized society feudalism, if arises at all, will originate where the invading barbarians are conentrated, or where they become especially important politically—but, course, that is not the only cause operative; another has to do with

[22] The elements among the Japanese people whose experience came nearest to at of the peoples of central Europe were those who lived in northeastern Japan d were not affected by the empire until it was in extreme disintegration; see 207 below.

[23] Early Byzantium was overrun; Egypt between the Fifth and Twelfth ynasties and China from Han to T'ang were invaded, but scarcely overrun: none the three became feudal. Egypt under the Libyan dynasties was infiltrated her thoroughly by barbarians, and then gave every sign of becoming feudal.

extent of disintegration of the civilized society, a subject which is studied in Chapter 5 below.[24]

It has been thought that in the history of Western Europe the formation of war-bands and the formation of feudal relations were distinct and discontinuous. I think the argument was always a very poor one, and perhaps now there are few scholars who pay much attention to it.[25] Certain remnants of it will be considered on their merits shortly, but first the analogous transition in Japan will be reviewed for the general probabilities it suggests.

Finance seems to have been crucial in the failure of the early Japanese Empire. As the empire's organs grew, it became more expensive and its taxation was extended. This hit small men, who would seek and often obtain immunity for their lands. Through that process, in the main, there grew up the *sho*, estates largely immune from taxation. But the empire, short of money, could not enforce the peace, and the proprietor of *sho*, thus needing protection, would turn to the nearest strong man, whether or not that man was of his own clan. The heads of the great clans remained for a considerable time the strongest men in Japan, and vast numbers of persons commended themselves directly to them. Lesser strong men to whom small proprietors commended themselves would eventually come into dependence directly or indirectly on clan leaders. In the tenth century clan leaders found their military function increasing in importance because of the failure of the peace. In the eleventh century clan structure remained visible, but the clan was ceasing to be simply a clan because so many persons not of it had commended themselves to its chief and to others of its leading members. In the proto-feudal thirteenth century the idea of the clan and fragments of actual clans persisted, but the idea was by then nearly a fiction. And yet even with the advent of true feudalism there survived from the past a strong clannishness.

To make his protection effective, the leader of the clan-clique formed a war-band—a comitatus. It is of importance here to find out how this was done, but unfortunately it is not completely clear. It is likely that there was from the first a nucleus of men personally attached to the leader. Takekoshi thinks that there was such a nuclear body, but supposes that its members, like all other fighting men, were formerly

[24] pp. 254-269.

[25] It was conscientiously examined by Carl Stephenson twelve years ago; "T[he] Origin and Significance of Feudalism," *American Historical Review*, XLVI (194[1]) 788-812.

farmers.[26] I think that is probably so, but it may be that the clan, or fragments of disintegrating clans, produced a class of small administrators, and that it was from these that new members of the war-band were chiefly drawn. But, whether or not a class of administrators was involved in the transition, it seems to me obvious that the war-band developed directly out of the clan warriors, probably at first by addition from whatever source of new persons to the original body. As the war-band had to fight more, it must have become necessary for the leader to support its members, old and new. This was done in a way peculiar to Japan. The leader received *shiki*, shares of revenue (presumably chiefly in rice) arising in their lands, from proprietors who commended themselves to him. These shares he could use to keep his men in his household, about his person, and usually under arms. It is sure that, wherever the original members of the war-band came from, they were gradually converted into retainers on the basis of support, and the conversion I take to have been the inner institutional part of the transition from a clan to a feudal system. These retainers were not the only forces the lord of a war-band acquired. In the twelfth century, when the new military system was in full operation, there were men on the land who were called into service by their lords when they were needed. They were not necessarily, and probably not often, the proprietors of the land who had commended themselves to the lords, but rather leading farmers, or else administrators of the kind considered above. They received *shiki*, other than those the lord received, arising in the land as pay for the occasional military service they now did and for the administrative duties they certainly now undertook if they had not had those duties before.[27]

Undoubtedly, the retainers remained the chief fighting men, and they became increasingly numerous. They came to form a special class, the *samurai*, "those who serve." These men's attachment to their leaders was in every way the equivalent of the attachment of the Teutonic barbarian to his war-leader, and the ethic of this attachment came to penetrate Japanese society as conspicuously as that of the Teutonic barbarian's attachment came to penetrate Western European society. In Japan the ethic was descended directly from clan ethics, as is seen clearly in the heroic literature which arose. The *Heike Monogatari*, for example, written about 1240, describes the rise and fall of the Taira,

[26] Yosoburo Takekoshi, *The Economic Aspects of the History of the Civilization of Japan*, I (London, 1930), 127-128.

[27] Mr. Reischauer (above, p. 31) gives the opinion that most fighting men of the time were local *shiki* holders.

ostensibly a great clan, but in fact a great feudal clique; as a clan it could not have had the meteoric military career the romance narrates so that the very occasion for the story would not have arisen, and yet clan traditions, prejudices, and loyalties form a constant part of the theme, and the devotion to the clan of heroes who were only attached to it as feudal vassals is taken for granted. Nevertheless the ethic of the story is feudal: it is narrowed somewhat to a military expression, and shows an exaggerated emotional intensity. That intensity of emotion became generally characteristic of the *samurai*, and is well shown in the increasing importance of the cult of the war-god, Hachiman.

In Europe it was a long time from the first formation of the Teutonic war-bands and their penetration into the Roman polity until the emergence of feudalism. That perhaps is the one objective difficulty in the problem of the connection between the war-band and the rise of the feudal relation in Europe. The rest of it seems to be man-made, arising out of the old controversy as to whether feudalism was of German or Roman origin, a controversy deeply tinged with the national prejudices of Frenchmen against Germans and Germans against Frenchmen, and with class prejudices also. This controversy is too remote from the realities of history, as understood today, to be of interest, but various matters originally incidental to it must be noticed. Thus, it would appear advisable to avoid the idea that the spirit of the war-band was forgotten, or forgotten in some regions, for a long period of time and then somehow or other recovered.[28] Bloch has observed that the barbarian immigrants did not abandon their comitatus relations as they settled into the unstable society of latter-day Rome.[29] Why on earth should they? There was no important difference between conditions in that society and the frontier conditions in which comitatus had first been formed; the one was continuous with the other in time and place.

It is conceivable that Dopsch discerns something real when he suggests that the war-band spirit was not to be found in the Merovingian king's bodyguard, but rather between the king and his landed personal dependents.[30] There could be some truth in this. Institutions of the Merovingian government were very Roman in intention, and perhaps

[28] Cf. the awful difficulties of Paul Guilhiermoz (*Essai sur l'origine de la noblesse en France au moyen âge*, Paris, 1902, p. 86 and *passim*).

[29] Marc Bloch, *La société féodale* (Paris, 1939), p. 238.

[30] Alfons Dopsch, *Mitteilungen des österreichischen Instituts für Geschichtsforschung*, XLI (1926), 35ff. I take it that that is what Dopsch means, but I confess that I find it difficult to put trust in an argument part of which depends upon the exact meaning of a word, *leudes*, in Merovingian times.

the barbarian sense of personal honor became rather thin in such an environment. Yet it seems doubtful that a sharp contrast between what was Roman and what was barbarian was at all widespread either in Merovingian Gaul or anywhere in the late empire itself. We have been taught that *scholares, pueri, buccellarii* in the service of late Roman magnates were something very different from German *comites*. Were they? Vinogradoff thought that the buccellary relation itself was some sort of approximation to the Teutonic war-band relation, pointing out that the *buccella* was a roll or biscuit, superior to the bread the ordinary imperial soldier received, hence marking the retainer of a Roman magnate as a privileged person.[31] His idea is that, even as it occurred in Roman society, the spirit of the personal dependency relation was substantially of barbarian origin, for most such dependent soldiers were barbarians. This seems to be more sensible than most views on the subject. I see no reason to think that personal relations of this sort ever fell into disuse in the society from the third century to the eighth. They do not appear to have left very much record in that period, it is true. That may be partly because they were illegal some of the time. The more likely explanation is more general, namely that late Roman and post-Roman government, with a few partial exceptions such as Theodoric's government, still was or professed to be Roman, and did not take any official account of personal relations as the barbarians saw them, but only as Roman law saw them. The Roman legal descriptions seem to have misled historians as to the underlying facts.

The classic character of Japanese feudalization is well illustrated in the proto-feudal stage. In Japan this was the first shogunate, the Kamakura Shogunate, which was so successful that it lasted for about a century and a half and put off full feudalization for that length of time. The main feature of the Kamakura regime was the building up of a great vassalage structure on the elementary and partial basis of his clan relations by Yoritomo Minamoto and his application of that structure to shore up the tottering empire. The most important aspect of the regime for present purposes is its resemblance to the Carolingian regime in Europe, and that will be investigated in a moment. But in certain ways the Kamakura regime can best be compared with a twelfth- or thirteenth-century government in Europe. Thus the *Bakufu*, the central organ of government in Kamakura, had some formidable de-

[31] P. Vinogradoff in *Cambridge Medieval History*, II (2nd edn., Cambridge, 1926), 641-642.

partments, the *Man-dokoro* (administrative secretariat), the *Monchu-jo* (central court), and the *Samurai-dokoro* which controlled the vassals and served as a central police organ. These cannot be paralleled in Europe until the administrative innovations of Henry II of England, or, better, Philip Augustus of France and his successors. But, of course, whereas those European feudal governments set up institutions which were destined to grow more or less steadily, the *Bakufu's* machinery reached its best development almost as soon as it was set up and afterwards declined.

Most local officials established by the shogunate were at once officials and vassals. Thus *jito*, stewards, were appointed to many *sho*. They were vassals of the shogun, and they collected taxes to supply the shogun's military forces, including a new tax, the "commissariat rice," which fell, significantly, on the landlord, not on the farmer as such. Some of the taxes collected they paid to the local officials of the empire, so strengthening for a time the old institution. The establishment of the *Bakufu* involved a duality of government which is unique. The effect on the state was not divisive, for the *Bakufu* took control over vassals who had slipped out from under the authority of the imperial officials, fitted its own administrative structure almost into the interstices of the imperial administration, and did not at first seek to break down any old institutions which would function; moreover the shogun often dictated the policy carried on through the old institutions themselves.

The Carolingian regime was the proto-feudal stage in Europe. It resembles the Kamakura Shogunate remarkably. The main resemblance is in the use of feudal relations to strengthen the old state, but it went further, for both regimes sought also to improve the non-feudal side of government. In the latter, the Carolingians reconstructed the old state, whereas the shogunate used bureaucratic as well as feudal methods in the construction of the *Bakufu*, leaving the imperial administration much as it had been. The shogunate and the Carolingian state both had their methods of ulterior supervision: the local official of the shogunate was the shogun's vassal, or "house-man"; the Carolingian local official became the vassal of his own administrative superior, usually a count, but the count and his vassal-subordinate were both inspected by the *missi dominici*.

There is a contrast in the way the two regimes came into existence. The European one was slowly built up, beginning, I think significantly, with a duality not wholly unlike that of empire and shogunate. Th was in the earlier eighth century, chiefly under the rule of Carl Martel, who was mayor of the palace, not king. He began the characteristic policy of applying vassalage to strengthen the state. Pepin, at the mid-century, did away with the duality and assumed the crown, thereafter carrying on the feudalizing policy. Even then it remained for Charlemagne to complete the proto-feudal structure. As against this, the shogunate was, all of it virtually, Yoritomo's work, though it was certainly not built in a day. The greater rapidity with which the shogunate, mainly the *Bakufu*, was constructed is matched by the great effectiveness of the *Bakufu* as an institution. The Carolingians never achieved anything to compare with it, doubtless because the fundamental social conditions of Europe in their time rendered such an institution impossible. It is logical that the Carolingian structure, built up so laboriously, began to crack almost from the moment of its completion, whereas Yoritomo was able to pass to his successors, the Hojo Regents, a polity which lasted for more than a century.

In the absence of any important organism such as the *Bakufu*, Carolingian vassalage has looked to some scholars like a mere device to strengthen the army. Moreover, the need for strengthening the army has sometimes been ascribed to the occurrence of a second series of barbarian invasions, those of the Saracens, Norsemen, and Magyars. So, a general theory has tended to develop that two separate series of barbarian invasions, successive in time, are required in the rise of a feudal order, and the theory has been applied to other cases besides the European one. I do not find that a second series of barbarian invasions is a necessary stage of feudalization, but there is good ground, I believe, for thinking that a second body of barbarians, distinguishable from the first one which formed the original war-bands, becomes involved in feudalization in the proto-feudal and the early feudal stages. This will be shown below, but first the militarization of government may be studied as an important general characteristic of a proto-feudal regime.

The militarizing of government was very clearly a vital feature both of the Carolingian and the Kamakura regimes, for the *Bakufu* produced an army too, a new one and one which proved reliable over a longer time than the Carolingian army. The two regimes were alike also in using material already to hand for that purpose, the *samurai* in Japan and the knights in Europe. Knights may perhaps have become more numerous in Europe as the Carolingians developed their policy, but there is probably no substance in the idea that their arms and equipment underwent a great change at the time. That change must have happened centuries earlier at the time when the old Roman army was being replaced by the private forces of great magnates. Those forces were already mounted men and barbarians for the most part, using armor, the stirrup, and other novel devices.[32] In fact, all things considered, it seems that the knight, with his horse and arms, his personal attachment to his leader, his membership in a band, and his quality as an aristocrat, arrived in Europe in late Roman times and continued substantially unchanged as a member of the transitional society until feudal times: the simplest explanation of his origin is the best. It was only the knight's political position which was changed with the advent of the proto-feudal regime, and changed again later when that regime broke down and was succeeded by the fully feudal regime. As vassal or subvassal in either regime, the knight served as a fighting man. When he served the Carolingian kings, it was part of his duty to suppress rebellion, banditry, and private warfare, which were rife. But that was not his whole duty; there must have been times and places when it was not his main duty, for he had also to administer—and the feudal contract itself provided for that as well as for military service. Since it was always the aim of the Carolingians, though they never succeeded in it, to restore the internal peace of society, the administrative duties of their vassals were the more fundamental even if their military duties were often the more immediately pressing.

The Carolingian rulers fought many foreign wars, both of expansion and of defense, and their vassals served them in those wars. Having regard to the endemic disorders of eighth-century European society however, we cannot think that service in foreign wars was as frequent as police service in internal wars. For this reason and for others, the idea that the invasions of the Saracens and of the barbarian Norsemen and Magyars played a formative part in evoking feudal institutions cannot easily be entertained.[33] One of the other reasons for not entertaining the idea is chronological: the formative proto-feudal period falls neatly in between the Saracen assaults on southern Europe and the Norse raids on the European coasts. The Norse raids did not become

[32] Cf. Bloch, *La société féodale*, pp. 234-237. Contrast H. Brunner, *Forschungen zur Geschichte des deutschen und französischen Rechts* (Stuttgart, 1894), pp. 39-41; Guilhiermoz, *Essai sur l'origine de la noblesse*, pp. 450-451; Carl Stephenson, *AHR*, XLVI, 807.

[33] The formative part sometimes ascribed to the invasions is that of necessitating the development of the knight. I prefer the opinion of Bloch (see previous note) that the knight had long been present.

serious until about the moment when the Carolingian experiment collapsed; in fact, there is no doubt that the raids became gravely destructive because the Carolingian organization of defense was no longer there. It is not excluded that the Saracen invasions influenced Carl Martel in developing the vassalage policy, but the peak of the invasions—the battle of Tours, which Carl won—was passed a considerable time before vassals had become a substantial support to the state. Moreover, Carl and Pepin had more trouble in the south of France with great vassals, such as the Count of Toulouse, who were really independent rulers, than they had there with the Saracen invaders. As for the Magyar invasions, those did not begin until the very end of the ninth century, and they took effect mainly in Germany. Nevertheless, Norse and Magyar raids had a minor place at a later time in the promotion of feudal development in Europe, as we shall shortly see.

Japan's experience of barbarian invasions in proto-feudal times was far more restricted and special than Europe's, but Japan did in those times have the experience of bringing within its polity a new body of barbarians. These were the peoples of the northeastern part of the main Japanese island, Hondo. They had scarcely been affected by the rise of a Sinic high culture in western Japan, they were still known in the twelfth century as the *Azuma-Ebisu*, eastern barbarians, and the empire had never ruled them.[34] They bulked large in the political impasse which the establishment of the shogunate for the time being broke through, as is shown by the choice of Kamakura as the seat of the shogunate; for Kamakura lies at the base of northeastern Hondo and from it Yoritomo could conveniently control his own vassals in the new country and bring under his authority other substantial magnates who had acquired vassals there. Why should new barbarians be drawn into the society in its proto-feudal stage? I think because the society was naturally expansive then: the great clan-cliques, the Taira, the Abe, above all the Minamoto themselves, competing with one another and seeking strength to resist the claims of the empire, extended themselves into the outer territory by feudal means.

Western Europe in the proto-feudal and in the fully feudal period was similarly expansive, a fact which puts the Norse and Magyar attacks in a special light. The feudalization of Japan has been compared above with that of Germany east of the Rhine. If that comparison be

[34] Takekoshi compares their relation to the empire with "that of barbarian Germany to the old Roman Empire" (I, 158). The comparison is permissible, but it would be better to put the Merovingian kingdom in the place of the old Roman Empire.

made precise, the great Japanese feudal families can be compared wit the German feudal families of the middle and later centuries of th Middle Ages, the Minamoto with the Welfs, for example: the Germa families were also engaged in competitive expansion; they were eve trying to loosen imperial authority over themselves. Wends, Sorbs Pomeranians, Moravians, and a variety of other new barbarians wer thus brought into feudal Europe. But that was the later part of th European movement. It had begun, and indeed had been forcefull advanced, in Charlemagne's time, and Charlemagne, like Yoritomo had made great conquests. Charlemagne had encountered one remark ably tough group of barbarians in the course of his conquests, th Saxons, and Toynbee makes the interesting suggestion that the Nors invasions of Western Europe should be regarded as *ripostes* for Charle magne's crushing subjection of the Saxons.[35] There is obvious substanc in this, for in the course of his Saxon wars Charlemagne came in con tact with the Norse king Gudröd, ruler of a large territory in Denmar and southern Norway and Sweden, and Gudröd actually contemplate a counterattack on Charlemagne. But provocation was not the whol cause of the barbarian attacks. There were internal causes which drov the Norsemen to expand out of Scandinavia[36] and other causes whic drove the Magyars out of their lands between the Don and the Dniep and brought them to central Europe. Nevertheless, Charlemagne stirre up all the peoples on the northern and eastern borders of his realm, n indeed only by his military conquests but also by his promotion Christian missionizing.

Charlemagne's own successes after a time overawed the barbaria neighbors, and they remained fairly quiet during the reign of Lou the Pious also. Once it became clear, however, that the great power the West was gone, barbarian attacks multiplied, and they were stim lated by Western pressure of a less dramatic, but far more lasting kin This was the steady encroachment of the great baronial families, whic as we saw, got their start with Charlemagne's conquests. They were a the freer after the Carolingian "empire" fell in pieces to pursue the private aims, and they brought to central Europe the new politic system, coupled with Western ideas of land tenure, which transform

[35] *A Study of History*, II (2nd edn., London, 1935), 344-345.

[36] But we do not know what they were. If they were to any large extent t penetration into Scandinavia of European ideas of government and land tenu then they were not ultimately internal causes, and the explanation by Europe provocation can be enlarged. This, however, should not be done unless and un the necessary evidence is found to back it.

the German tribes, as similar influences in Japan transformed the clans at the corresponding juncture of Japanese history. German magnates developed the characteristic land hunger of magnates turning feudal, matched by a hunger for converts on the part of churchmen, who indeed shared in the land hunger. Expansion of the now Christian and Westernized Saxons brought on ravages by Danes and other Norsemen on the Frisian coast. As the weight of the internal pressure in Scandinavia got behind this movement, the coasts and river valleys of all Western Europe were assailed, and eventually there were Norse migrations into Normandy and England.[37] The Magyar raids began as an ncident in the career of Arnulf of Carinthia, last of the Carolingians, whose personal possessions lay out in the new territory far to the east, adjacent to the land of the Moravians and to Hungary which the Magyars had occupied.

We may here digress to consider a notion put forward by Tarn about he history of Parthian Iran, a society which is to be studied in a later part of this essay.[38] The original Parthians were barbarians who invaded ran from the steppe. Tarn's notion proposes—in a deftly tentative manner—a change in modes of armament and in tactics in connection with a second series of barbarian invasions at a crucial time in the development of the Parthian state. He says:

"At some period unknown—it is difficult to dissociate the process rom the Saca invasion—the Parthians abandoned the mixed Hellenistic ype of army for the horse-archer; they used no more mercenaries and ardly any footmen, and had no standing army. Their horse archers, ke the Achaemenid cavalry, consisted of the landowners and nobles, who followed their lords to battle; the Parthian innovation was to bolish javelin and short spear alike, and arrange that the whole nobility, Parthian and Iranian, should arm their retainers with the bow. rom youth up they were trained in shooting; and their method, rought from the desert, of pretending to fly and firing back over the upper—the 'Parthian shot'—became famous."[39]

Clearly, there is here a hypothesis modelled directly on the hypothesis at the Norsemen and Magyars invaded Europe, caused a change in

[37] It is a nice speculation whether England would have suffered the Danish vasions, or would have suffered them in such force, had it not been for Charlemagne's conquest of the Saxons, Nordalbingians, and Frisians, and the further essure of feudal Europe northward which followed.

[38] Below, Ch. 8, pp. 325-343. The question whether Iran was feudal is treated ere.

[39] W. W. Tarn in *Cambridge Ancient History*, IX, 601-602.

European fighting methods, and a consequential change to feudalism in the European social and political structure. Knowing the hypothesis for Europe to be false, we are not surprised to find the one for Iran to be groundless. The "period unknown" when the Parthians made the innovation in methods of warfare is much more likely to have been the third century B.C., when the Parthians themselves invaded Iran, than the last quarter of the second century B.C., when the Sacas did so—just as in Europe the cavalryman using stirrups came in with the first wave of barbarians and not with the second wave. In short, the Parthians never used the mixed Hellenistic type of army at all, and the Parthian shot came with them from the desert and was not copied from the Sacas as would be more probable if Tarn's hypothesis were upheld. It is likely that the expansion of the Parthian dominions by Mithradates II (124-87 B.C.) out into the steppe country provoked the Saca invasions, as Western European expansion provoked Norse and Magyar invasions, but we need not pursue that question here; it can be left for the time when Iran is to be studied.

To return to our present concerns, the expansion of proto-feudal and feudal Europe may be summed up as follows: proto-feudal and feudal Europe expanded to take in great numbers of new barbarians, as proto feudal and feudal Japan did, because it is in the nature of such political systems to expand. The Norse invasions and the Magyar invasions were incidents of the European expansion, reinforced by special conditions external to the expanding European society. The eastern barbarians in Japan were possibly less formidable, but there were plenty of tough peoples among them too, and the absorption of the more distant of them was postponed far into the Ashikaga period, just as the absorption into feudal Europe of Scandinavians, Lithuanians, and Poles was long postponed. Thus, it proves that barbarians can be involved in the rise of feudalism in two different ways and at different, though overlapping times. One lot enters the society in the early days of the disintegration of the old state and comes after a time to take a prominent position in the transitional society. As the feudal regime actually takes shape, political authority devolves into the hands of the successors of the first lot of barbarians, and at that same time new barbarians are drawn into the society as it expands. This is as true of Europe as it is of Japan, and the occurrence of certain complicating external events together with the larger scale and greater variety of internal events in Europe ought not to be allowed to obscure their ultimate character.

There is a possibility that invasion did play a certain part, both in Europe and in Japan, in the ruin of the proto-feudal regime and the consequent advent of fully feudal conditions, and that matter must have attention as we proceed to consider the early stage of the full development of feudalism. It does not look as if the effects of invasion were at all important. For one thing, the invasions in the two cases were very different: in Japan they were the Mongol invasions, powerful attacks aimed at conquest in short order; the Norse invasions in Europe were a long series of raids, first for booty, later for settlement, lasting for more than a century, while the Mongol menace to Japan was all over within less than seven years. For another thing, the invasions took place at slightly, but crucially, different junctures in the two cases: the Mongol invasions dealt a blow to the Kamakura Shogunate while it was still a prosperous, going concern, and thereafter it wobbled on weakly for another half century; the Norse invasions, as we have seen, did not begin until the Carolingian regime had decisively broken down. The real cause of the movement over from the proto-feudal to the eudal regime was a continuation and development of the cause of all najor changes society had been undergoing, namely the struggle for ecurity or for gain in a society not sufficiently controlled from the top —a society which, for profound reasons we do not understand, was going into dissolution and soon could no longer be controlled at all.

The breakdown of the proto-feudal polities led to the onset of the ravest disorders which had yet occurred, both in Europe and in Japan. There is a certain logic in that, for the old state was then at last almost ompletely destroyed and what remained were but vestiges and recol-ections. A bitter and profound irony attended that final tragedy. Whereas feudal loyalty as between the barons and the shogun or the ing had been intended to stabilize the society, and had even done so n part and for a time, now the feudal loyalty of their vassals to the arons gave the barons the armies which broke to pieces the remaining ructure of the state, and destroyed more life and wealth than ever efore. Indignation at breaches of faith, at the flagrant betrayal by the upper class of its own ideals, rings through the records both of Japan nd of Europe at this juncture. In Japan the struggles covered about the tter two thirds of the fourteenth century, the period when the Ashi-aga Shogunate became established after the destruction of the Kama-ura Shogunate and of the remains of the empire which it had stained. In Western Europe the period began before the middle of e ninth century, and had no very clear term. Furthermore, it is rather in northern France, the nuclear feudal area, than elsewhere in Europe that the chronology applies; developments in Germany and regions beyond lagged behind those of northern France, while in southern Europe and in the British Isles special influences varied the course of events.[40]

The first two thirds of the fifteenth century in Japan were somewhat quieter, but far from peaceable: feudal warfare was common still. Then followed a decade of frightful destruction, the Onin War from 1467 to 1477, and such outbursts were renewed spasmodically during the remaining century of the Ashikaga period. The fourteenth to the sixteenth century was the era of "high feudalism" in Japan.[41] In France the corresponding era began perhaps in the later tenth century and lasted until some time in the twelfth. In England it began suddenly with the Norman Conquest in 1066 and lasted into Henry II's reign. But the notable feature of the era is not the spasmodic feudal warfare, which in Europe became less as time went on, in Japan followed no clear pattern; it is the emergence of the elemental, strong fiefs, the first political entities which belonged completely and in their essence to the rising civilization and were neither attempts to restore institutions of the old society nor attempts to blend the new with the old. These were the in-groups of the feudal society. They were truly new in that they were the earliest political formations which could survive in that society.

It is natural that these fiefs exemplified no theory. They were not the embodiment of any idea, even of the simplest. They were merely the strongest units which could be put together. And they were extremely strong: the war that was the normal external relation between them enforced peace, order, discipline, close cooperation, within each of them. They were all strictly local, the work of local strong men. Thus

[40] The special influences in southern Europe were the outside influence of Isla and the stronger survival there of old institutions, the latter coupled with th influence of Byzantium which was not at any time completely severed cultural from Italy. Ireland, Scotland, and northernmost England lagged behind much a Scandinavia did. All of these regions, north and south, followed northern Franc and were not only late in feudal development, but also less completely feudalize in a few special cases, such as the highlands of Scotland and patches of Italy, the were not feudalized at all.

Southern, central, and part of northern England and south Wales were anoth kind of special case. In late Anglo-Saxon times the usual feudal drift was evidence, but the Norman Conquest suddenly brought feudalism, fully and rath specially developed, to the country. Whether the disorders of Stephen's reig ought to be classified as a belated version of the troubles of very early feudalis is anybody's guess—but those disorders look in detail very much of that kind.

[41] Above, p. 34.

in Japan the elaborate *sho-shiki* system was swept away and power was dissipated and then reconstituted in the hands of the *daimyo*. They occupied the same positions as the early great barons of Europe, and among both there were persons who had been major local officials, or their forebears had, in the old state, counts in Europe, *shugo* (provincial constables) in Japan. In their novelty, both in Europe and in Japan, they were notably free from restraint of old law and custom. There were to be new law and custom in the future, but these were beginning to be created anew out of the order and discipline required within the fiefs. At the moment of their creation, custom and law remained malleable, amenable to the practical and pressing needs of the struggle for survival.

In feudal France the fiefs were on a larger scale than in Japan. Normandy, Flanders, Anjou, Poitou, Burgundy, etc., the great provinces, were the important fiefs of France. Japanese fiefs were destined also to long survival as administrative units of the monarchy but they were smaller. Bungo, Izumo, Aki, Owaro, Echizen, were all seats of important *daimyo*; they were on an average about the size of such small French counties as Maine, Perche, or La Marche in the twelfth century. Most larger Japanese fiefs were unstable and did not appear until the disorders of the sixteenth century; they were not elemental fiefs. The few large ones that arose earlier and may be called elemental were in the far north or the southwest, such as Satsuma on the island of Kyushu, property of the Shimazu. It is hardly reasonable to bring the English fiefs, which about equalled the Japanese in size, into the comparison, for the English ones were kept small, artificially as it were, by the policy of the powerful Norman kings.

Perhaps there were initial moments in the two societies when the emergent fiefs were purely feudal, but probably there were not; "purity" is a rare thing in history. It is more probable that there was always a rudimentary officialdom. When we get to know them, French fiefs had developed such officers as the vicomte, bailli, and seneschal, and there were courts in which vassals met their lord and one another for common business and to reach agreement in disputes and probably on policy. English constitutional historians and French institutional historians have laid great emphasis on these institutions, but it was not the institutions as such which were the original and fundamental source of the fiefs' strength; it was essentially the feudal bond which was. The great French fiefs, Normandy, Anjou, Flanders, the Ile de France, in which good government was provided, in some cases for many generations in succession, were profoundly feudal and personal feudal ties continued to be made anew in them all through the high feudal period and beyond. The administrative personnel and institutions were secondary to the personal feudal relations; they were results, not causes. But they were extremely important results. Mr. Strayer finds that those parts of Europe which were most fully feudalized contributed most to the later development of European institutions.[42] The institutions in question began their growth within the great fiefs of France and England. It is easy to suppose that this is cause and effect: because they were constructed first in those strong political units, the institutions were useful and durable.

The feudal relationship, undertaken amid the pressing dangers of ninth- to tenth-century France or fourteenth-century Japan, was easily and fully understood. So understood, it forced subordinates to learn and carry out their political functions,[43] and taught superiors the more difficult lesson that their survival and fortune depended on discharging their own political duty to their subordinates. The personal feudal relation may be regarded, in fact, as one of the ultimate, completely simple elements with which a political system can be put together. Simple though it is, it is not actually primitive, but it produces in-groups of a strength and durability comparable with the in-groups of primitive society. In the two cases studied above the durability of its products, the elemental, strong fiefs, is witnessed by their long survival on the map even when their internal structure had been changed. The fiefs which matured in France, Western Germany, and some parts of Italy in the eleventh and twelfth centuries almost all existed as provinces at the time of the French Revolution. Similarly, many of the fiefs of fifteenth-century Japan were still there in 1868. Long before those critical dates, the feudal relation itself in Europe and in Japan had undergone a subtle transposition and enlargement to become the ethical foundation of the nations.

42 Above, pp. 23-25.

43 Cf. A. B. White, *Self-Government by the King's Command* (London, 1933), where this principle is found by detailed study of the archives to have informed the government of England in the first quarter of the thirteenth century.

3. POSSIBLE FEUDALISM IN CHOU CHINA, MESOPOTAMIA, EGYPT, AND INDIA

WE pass to the second and third groups in our classification, the second of societies which may have been feudal, the third of societies which might have been feudal. The latter group, Egypt in the time of the Libyan dynasties and Rajput India, might have become feudal if conquest or penetration of influences from other civilized societies had not supervened and altered the course of events. The former group, Chou China and Mesopotamia, may in fact have become feudal, but the final proof is lacking. Mr. Bodde, however, thinks that Chou China was feudal.

In all four cases the barbarians were present—the barbarians of the first series, that is to say; there is no record of any second wave of barbarian invaders,[1] except, not very significantly, in the case of China. In Egypt and Mesopotamia the barbarians were invaders, as in Western Europe; in Mesopotamia the invasions were possibly almost continuous right through the period we should expect between the first and second waves. In India, some of the barbarians were invaders, but at a time which fits with a certain difficulty the pattern of chronology we expect from other cases; other barbarians were perhaps indigenous. In Chou China there were indigenous barbarians and possibly some invaders.

We encounter first in all four cases the old political system going into disintegration before the rise of conditions which look feudal. In the case of the old system in China we shall limit ourselves in this chapter as far as possible to what we know for sure about it: that is not a great deal, and it relates only to the narrow period before and after the Chou conquest of the Shang regime. A full discussion of the character of the Shang state is left for Chapter 4. Great pre-feudal magnates turn up sporadically in all four cases, and they tend to divide into the two main types we know, great officials of the old regime and tribal leaders. Libyan Egypt had a regime which was quite possibly proto-feudal, Rajputana may or may not have had such a regime, Chou China almost certainly did, and Mesopotamia did also. Information is lacking in the cases of Chou China and Mesopotamia for the elemental strong fief, and our inability to prove the occurrence of the elemental fief is a fur-

[1] The Muslim and Europeans in India, and the Assyrians, Persians, and Greeks in Egypt were aliens, but not barbarians within our definition; nor did they behave in the least like barbarians in the part they played in the affairs of the two societies.

ther reason, additional to the lack of particulars about actual vassalage relations, for refusing to recognize those two societies as having certainly had feudal periods.

Egypt and Rajputana can be treated more shortly than Mesopotamia and Chou China since the history of their development was cut short by outside interference. Egypt will be considered first.

Late Ramesside and post-Ramesside Egypt experienced the weakening of the central government and the rise of powerful local magnates which are usual historic developments as great empires break down. In Egypt of the "Empire" a professional army had been created by the Eighteenth Dynasty itself. This became a special class in the state—though only one of several, for the entire population was organized in classes—some of its members having land. Under the Twentieth Dynasty (1200-1090) this army came to consist almost entirely of barbarians, the great majority of them so-called Libyans who were in fact ex-tribesmen, who had descended on Libya from Europe during the movement of the "peoples of the sea" at the break-up of the Cretan Sea Empire. After abortive attempts to break into Egypt by force of arms, these barbarians had infiltrated by hiring themselves out as mercenaries under their own leaders, and had thereupon been established on the land, entering on some basis into the Egyptian military class. Some of them were important people under the late Twentieth Dynasty and the regime of the Twenty-first (1090-945) when the Pharaoh ruled only in the Delta and the High Priest of Amon in Thebes was ruler in Upper Egypt. On the obscure ending of the Twenty-first Dynasty, a Libyan lord became Pharaoh as Sheshonk I. This is a series of events much like events in the late days of the Roman Empire.

The Libyans were barbarians, "wearers of the two feathers"; they were the Meshwesh, remembering always their tribal origins, and their best men were of the blood of Buyuwawa. We have no actual record of the personal relations of chieftain and follower, lord and man, among them, but it is likely enough that they were the honorific relations of the war-band, for the Libyans were certainly organized in war-bands. The regime of the Libyan Twenty-second Dynasty had many of the features we have found in the proto-feudal regimes in Japan and Western Europe. Sheshonk was, for example, an energetic ruler who conquered territory—previously lost territory, in this instance—and put the government at first on a stronger basis than it had had since the early Twentieth Dynasty. His power rested on the support of the "chief of the Me" (i.e., Meshwesh), who were Libyan magnates established in most of the large cities and commanding the garrison troops there. They conducted or supervised the civil administration also. In certain cities high priests ruled, but these also were Libyans and ordinarily were members of the royal family. The heir was usually High Priest of Amon at Thebes, the most important of those posts. Another important one was that of High Priest of Harsaphes at Heracleopolis, and this post had been in the hands of the royal family ever since they had first settled in Egypt, more than a century before Sheshonk. If we may trust Herodotus, the garrisons were military colonies, each man being provided with a small plot of land.[2] We do not know the form of the attachment of the chiefs of the Me to the Libyan Pharaoh, but this surely was a system like those of Yoritomo and of the Carolingian kings in that it brought the special relations of the Libyan magnates to the support of the fabric of the old state. It was possibly more like that of Yoritomo if the crown made provision in land directly for all the military forces.

There is no strong reason to think that the rule of the Twenty-second Dynasty was seriously weakened in its first century. After that dynastic troubles became serious, and then the local lords began usurpation of royal powers; the period is often known as that of the "dynasts" by reason of the number of claimants to the style of royalty. This was preliminary to the commencement of serious internecine wars, which look like the sort of wars out of which a true feudal regime can arise. But it is sure that matters never got as far as that in Egypt; this is the point at which alien influences changed the course of events. Neither the first Ethiopian conquest, that of Piankhi (751-716), nor the conquests by Esarhaddon (681-669) and Ashurbanipal (669-626) of Assyria did more than introduce a new element into the disorders which had arisen. Bocchoris, lord of Sais (720-715), and the fourth Ethiopian Pharaoh, Taharqa (690-664), both attempted policies aimed at weakening the landed position of the Libyan lords by legal means, but it was apparently Psamtik I (663-609), founder of the main Saite line, the Twenty-sixth Dynasty (663-525), who inaugurated the policy that was

[2] Herodotus speaks only of garrisons in the Delta and in Thebes, and he is most interested in the forces of the Delta known as Calasiries and Hermotybies, which served particularly under the king himself (II, 164-166). It is, therefore, possible that only they were provided with small holdings, and that the other garrisons were otherwise provided for. It is also possible that the Delta troops were a survival of pre-Libyan rule and that the garrison troops in other towns were quite differently organized.

to eradicate them and turn the history of Egypt aside from a possible feudal development. A feudal regime rests upon a military basis, and Psamtik cut the ground from under the Libyan dynasts by introducing Greek mercenaries who were militarily the Libyans' superiors.[3] The Libyans seem quite rapidly to have been reduced to political nullity. Thereafter they continued to exist as large landowners, but in the course of various land reforms their numbers were reduced and eventually they were merged in the general population. The Persian conquest in 525, a far more effective change than the Assyrian, by continuing the provision of a powerful alien military force, ensured that there should be no reaction.

For Rajputana Mr. Thorner's verdict on Tod's views must be accepted as correct in the main. Essentially Mr. Thorner is for Crooke's opinion, that eighteenth-century Rajputana was tribal, not feudal. The opinion will be tested.

It must be observed to begin with that the Rajputs were not tribesmen who entered India during the decline of the Mogul Empire; they came, those of them who were immigrants, during the decline of the Gupta Empire in the sixth century A.D. or earlier, and were established in India all through the period of Muslim penetration. They were of various different peoples, and were not recognized as Rajputs for some time after their immigration, for the term Rajput is an Indian term and the formation of the Rajput communities was a series of little known events which took place within the Indian social system. Some of those taken into the Rajput communities were not immigrants, but Gonds and other tribesmen who had long been established in India without being caught up into the development of the high culture. About the middle of the ninth century we hear of the Pratihara Empire, a state covering northern India. It was ruled probably by Gurjara invaders, a people from whom some of the Rajputs were drawn, and it lasted as an effective institution for less than a century. It is easy to suggest that the Pratihara Empire was a proto-feudal regime, but the only grounds for such an assertion are that it was ruled by invaders, that it arose after the fall of the Gupta Empire at about the time a proto-feudal regime might be expected to arise, and that it lasted the sort of length of time such regimes usually last. Since we know nothing whatever about its

[3] The effectiveness of this kind of military change in a society in the proto feudal stage is to be contrasted with the limited effect of the breakdown of the feudal army in late feudal times. See pp. 308-310, below.

form of government, it is impossible to maintain that it was proto-feudal. It is just as likely that it was some other kind of a barbarian successor state to the Gupta Empire. As it broke up in the tenth century, the Rajput states emerged.

Presumably, all Rajputs, whether immigrants or surviving indigenous primitives, underwent Indianization under the Pratihara Empire and perhaps before that, for they developed city life and some participation in the arts India had practiced earlier.[4] This Indianization must have been comparatively superficial, perhaps about like the sinification of the Japanese between the sixth and eleventh centuries, for otherwise tribal institutions could not have survived so substantially as they did when Tod observed them in the early nineteenth century.

Meanwhile, soon after the Pratihara Empire began to break up, the Muslim invasions began; Mahmud of Ghazni, in fact, finished the empire off. It must be borne in mind that these were no ordinary invasions. They were the intrusion into India of a series of peoples belonging to another civilization, Islam; most of them, including the Moguls, belonged to the Persian variety of Islam. Against Islam the Rajputs became the first natural Indian champions. It is probable, I consider, that the strong conservatism which the Rajputs developed as a defense against Islam played a part in the preservation of tribal institutions. Only the constructive policy of Akbar (1556-1605) did much to reconcile the Rajputs to Mogul overlordship, and that policy belongs to a time when the Rajputs had been resisting the Muslim by one means or another for five and a half centuries. Akbar's policy was maintained for a bare century, but seems to have been effective during that time. It was then followed by the insensate Islamization of Aurangzeb (1658-1707), which restored the anti-Muslim tradition of the Rajputs to full vigor at the moment the Mogul Empire was ruined and began to go to pieces.

That the main basis of eighteenth- and nineteenth-century Rajput ociety was still tribal is made sure by Tod's insistence on the imporance in it of blood relationships. It is hardly possible that the whole xplanation of this is the one suggested above, conservatism developed s a defense against Islam, unless Rajput conservatism had a very special uality. But there is some ground for thinking that it did have a very pecial quality, established upon the peculiar character of the Indian

[4] A Puranic legend records the admission of the Rajputs to the Kshatriya caste y Brahmans, who were always agents of Indianization; see H. G. Rawlinson, *ndia: A Short Cultural History* (London and New York, 1938), p. 200.

social system. In that system the state is often of secondary importance and the main fabric is supplied by caste and religion directed from the top by the Brahmans. We know so little about the history of this remarkable social fabric that it is feasible to suggest here that much of it was actually built up in the frame of Rajput tribalism by the Brahmans as a defense for religion and for Indian culture generally against the Muslim. There is evidence supporting this in the existence of various groups of outcasts reported by al-Biruni, the eleventh century Muslim writer.[5] Since political authority had fallen to the Muslim, a social system in which political authority was made less important would be a logical defense for the Hindus. Al-Biruni's account of India in his time affords other significant data also: he remarks, for example, that no very great distance separated the Vaiçyas from the Çudras.[6] The remark suggests important changes in the structure of Indian society, for the Vaiçyas had been the free, yeoman, agrarian class, the Çudras vastly below them performing the meaner functions assigned in al-Biruni's account to lesser castes. The Çudras have become personal dependents of the Brahmans,[7] the Brahmans and Kshatriyas, but especially the Brahmans, having all power, prestige, and authority. The general picture is, in fact, one in which a gulf had opened between the two topmost classes and the rest, the Brahmans having so complete a hold on moral and religious leadership as to ensure that the Kshatriyas must have become their pupils and followers. A society of this sort was certainly one of a powerful conservatism, devoted under Brahman direction to the defense of Indian culture against Islam.

Rajput tribal organization may well have been preserved as an integral part of the culture.[8] There is, however, no explanation yet of the actual origin of the tribal organization. Moreover, the military mentality of the Rajputs, which is witnessed by all outsiders who have known them, Tod included, is something which also needs explanation. It is far more quixotically heroic than is normal in tribal leaders. It is, in fact, the mentality of the heroic age, having all the devoted loyalty and exaggerated martial ardor of the typical barbarian mind.

[5] E. S. Sachau, *Alberuni's India* (London, 1888), I, 101-102.

[6] Sachau, I, 101. [7] Sachau, II, 136.

[8] Al-Biruni does not record any features of Indian society which must have been tribal and could not have been anything else. That, however, is not very surprising since Tod recognizes only one such feature. Al-Biruni, however, was mainly concerned with Indian intellectual culture; his remarks referred to above are incidental to his main theme.

The easiest explanation of the origin of Rajput tribal organization is that it is the organization of the indigenous Gond and other tribes who were drawn into the Rajput communities as they were formed. Alternatively, the Gurjara invaders, who also became Rajputs, may have brought their tribal organizations with them.[9] They can only have done this if the Gupta Empire at the time of their invasion was so feeble as to have offered them almost no resistance. It is possible that it was as feeble as that, and there are precedents for primitives preserving their tribal organization on migration into the territory of a defunct empire, for example the Chaldaean tribes which settled in Kassite times in southern Mesopotamia.[10] On this assumption, it would follow that the militarism of the Rajputs was developed in the course of their struggles in India against the Muslim, which, again, is quite possible.

The main difficulty with this is the Pratihara Empire. Tribal leaders do not set up empires, or any large states, until they have been transformed into barbarians, within our special meaning of the word.[11] The greater probability seems to be, then, that, however feeble the Gupta Empire when the Gurjaras entered its territory, they were met by resistance and were formed into war-bands of the kind we know well. It would be natural for the leaders of the war-bands to set up a state when power fell to them, just as Theodoric, Clovis, and others did in Europe. And when that state fell, and the Rajputs found themselves under constant attack from Muslim invaders, their mentality would retain and develop its heroic quality perhaps like the mentality of European crusaders did. The tribal organization must, then, be that of indigenous peoples, and perhaps we may think that the Brahmans favored its preservation since Hinduism provides a place for tribal practices in its general system.

Hence the Rajputs, as we know them, are basically tribal, but have been Indianized in religion and in the high culture generally, and in

[9] Crooke's suggestion (Tod, *Annals*, I, xxxix, Introduction), that Rajput tribalism is comparable with Pathan, Afghan, and Baloch tribalism, tends to support this second alternative, but it is possible that indigenous tribalism in northern India was also similar.

[10] Such tribes must be presumed not to have lived on the frontier of the empire in its vigorous period, but to have migrated from a long distance beyond it. This is improbable in the case of the Gurjaras, but a known fact in the case of the Huns.

[11] Tribal leaders who are not migrants may be stirred by the example of a neighboring civilized state to try to copy its forms, but, if the early Japanese are any guide, such tribal leaders become transformed virtually into civilized people before they attempt to set up a civilized state.

the course of Indianization have been urbanized in places to a small extent. The Rajput aristocracy, however, also still shows the signs of a heroic age of barbarian migrations in time gone by. The case of Rajputana is thus a most unusual example of arrested or diverted feudalization, consequent essentially upon the usual weakness of Indian political institutions and the intrusion of an alien high culture into India. Its most remarkable quality is that it is part primitive, part civilized. Of course, this verdict is speculative, but it has the merit of allowing fully for the scanty and confusing evidence.

With Mesopotamia post-Hammurabi and Chou China the position is not at all as it is with Egypt and India. There is a real possibility that there was a feudal period in Mesopotamia and a probability that there was one in China.

Mesopotamia can best be discussed in three parts: Babylonia, the middle and southern part of the valleys of the Tigris and Euphrates, together with Elam, the Land of the Sea, etc.; the northern part of the valley, most of it ruled by Mitanni in the sixteenth and fifteenth centuries, but by Assyria in the thirteenth century and perhaps already in the fourteenth, together with half-barbarian Urartu in the northern mountains; and Hatti, eastern Asia Minor, where the Mesopotamian colony of Kanis had once been, and a number of other cities of Mesopotamian type had grown up. The barbarians flooded into the two latter territories, but they were different barbarians, and they perhaps came from different directions. The Hittites may have come from the west across the Hellespont or the Bosporus. Vast numbers of others moved from north and east over Assyria-Mitanni-Urartu, an exceptional inundation whose occurrence probably has much to do with the subsequent militant character of Assyrian policy. Babylonia possibly had few barbarians, but it did have the Kassites, and it had tribesmen from Arabia, as did Syria and perhaps parts of Mitanni.

The best information for the seventeenth to about the thirteenth centuries concerns Hatti—but it is best in a very bad total fund. It permits some firm statements about Hatti down to some time in the fifteenth century, the time of the "Old Kingdom," but not between the "Old Kingdom" and the "New Kingdom." For reasons which will appear, I make a bold guess about the course of political development in Hatti: that Hatti was proto-feudal in the main period of the Old Kingdom, and then that something like fully feudal conditions, as in the early stage of feudalism, emerged in the disorderly times toward the end of the Old Kingdom and before the appearance of the New Kingdom.

The Old Kingdom, with "King's sons" (were they actually king's sons, or were they so described as an honor?) established on various lands as hereditary dependents of the crown, with "Great Ones" and warriors each having their respective privileges, was unquestionably a barbarian state established in what had been imperial territory. Possibly the territory had not been ruled by the empire for some time, but that is not important; it is sure that a Mesopotamian political system with the cities as centers existed there, together with the rest of the Mesopotamian culture, when the Hittites arrived, for the Hittites used the system as the basis of their own government.[12] Thus the personal relations of the Hittite monarch with his aristocracy and his warriors were evidently applied as a support to the old political system in the manner we have called proto-feudal. If the warrior was the *ḫipparas* man, with a small holding granted directly by the crown, then the military system is reminiscent of those of the Libyan regime in Egypt and of the Kamakura Shogunate in Japan.

So far the hypothesis is not at all badly supported. But to say then that the interval from about the reign of Mursilis (c.1555—post 1530[13]) of the Old Kingdom to that of Suppiluliumas (c.1360) of the New Kingdom was the early feudal period is more speculative. Disorders are certainly authenticated in the interval, with weak monarchs, some recovery under one Telepinus,[14] and then a complete blank which can well have been a time of still worse disorders. But this is not enough to prove a feudal regime, for we have nothing at all about institutions. Yet the New Kingdom which followed shows the character of a late feudal regime[15] as clearly as the Old Kingdom shows that of a proto-feudal regime so that the guess that Hatti had an early feudal regime is worth making.

The Hittites overflowed into Syria from time to time, and other peoples moved in there as well, notably the Hurrians. There seem to have been many small principalities, great disorders and destruction,

[12] R. S. Hardy, "The Old Hittite Kingdom: A Political History," *American Journal of Semitic Languages and Literatures*, LVIII (1941), 178-179; L. Delaporte, *Les Hittites* (Paris, 1936), p. 176.

[13] The dates for Mursilis are from Hardy corrected according to W. F. Albright, "A Third Revision of the Early Chronology of Western Asia," *Bulletin of the American Schools of Oriental Research*, No. 88 (December 1942), 28-36, table p. 32, which latter I use for all other dates relating to Mesopotamia.

[14] Hardy, pp. 201-210. [15] Below, Ch. 6.

and princelings with their dependent lords and warriors—two kinds of dependents. Mr. Brundage thinks the picture one of a heroic age rather than of a feudal age—the age in question being on both sides of 1500—for the dependents were "clustered retainer-fashion" about the prince, and were "not a landed aristocracy."[16] But there is, as a matter of fact, no evidence that they were *not* landed; there is only a lack of evidence that they were landed. Apart from that, if the prince had land, he could have been a feudal prince even though his retainers had no land and were maintained in his household. It is nevertheless true that the scanty evidence will fit a heroic age or an early feudal age equally well, a proto-feudal age perhaps somewhat less well. But, since we have ventured to guess that Hatti proper was early feudal at the time, and since we happen to know that Mursilis sacked Aleppo in Syria in the late sixteenth century,[17] it seems better to extend the guess to include Syria with Hatti in the early feudal region of that time.

All or most of Babylonia and some of Mitanni-Assyria had been ruled directly by Hammurabi and perhaps other emperors of the first Dynasty of Babylon. With Mr. Brundage's argument that Hammurabi's rule was not feudal[18] I am in full agreement; neither was it proto-feudal. There were magnates who held large estates, but that does not necessarily make it even pre-feudal. The fifteenth century, when most of the northern part of the valleys was ruled or claimed by kings of Mitanni, was the period of the Nuzu tablets, which throw some light on land tenure. The forms of that tenure are in dispute among specialists but it would seem that some of them were the same as forms defined in Hammurabi's Laws; these were forms whereby farmers held land of various magnates, including perhaps the crown. The tablets also show that royal judges functioned in litigation concerning such tenures as had been the case under Hammurabi.[19] So far, there is not a thing to suggest feudalism, but instead a government like that of Hammurabi. We must remember, however, that the tenures in question were those

[16] Above, p. 105. [17] Hardy, p. 203. [18] Above, pp. 95-96.

[19] On these points the specialists do not appear to be in dispute. For the arguments: H. Lewy, "The Nuzian Feudal System," *Orientalia*, XI n.s. (1942), 1-4 209-250, 297-349; F. R. Steele, *Nuzi Real Estate Transactions*, American Oriental Series, No. 17 (New Haven, 1943); P. M. Purves, "Commentary on Nuzi Real Property in the Light of Recent Studies," *Journal of Near Eastern Studies*, I (1945), 68-86. I am disposed to think that Purves' view of "false adoption prevails over Mrs. Lewy's—that she is in error in seeing feudal conditions under that form; feudal conditions, if any, existed higher up in the social scale. I am indebted to Professor E. A. Speiser for his advice in these matters; he bears no responsibility for the opinions I have reached about them.

of humble farmers, giving no evidence one way or the other about the position of the upper classes. As to the latter, we know that the Mitannian monarchy was supported by an aristocracy, the *maryannu*, and that there were times when the monarchy was weak and members of the *maryannu* could assert their independence.

Assyria became the chief power in the northern valleys in the course of the fourteenth and thirteenth centuries, and it then acquired most of the land which had been Mitannian, probably other land from the tribes to the north, and certainly some from Babylon. Assyrian power was maintained, probably extended somewhat, in the twelfth century, but thereafter it seems to have collapsed. The fourteenth to twelfth centuries have been called the time of the first Assyrian empire, but the term empire can scarcely mean anything much. Two things we know about the territory in the period: there was almost constant fighting, and there were a good many political units of tribal or tribally derived character. What we do not know are also two things in the main: what the character of the political units derived from tribes actually was, and whether many Mesopotamian city-polities survived in the land. There is, as Mr. Brundage says,[20] an *a priori* likelihood of feudal conditions arising, and, while we must remember that there is scarcely a thing that can be called evidence for this, the general conditions are substantially of the kind which have in other cases produced feudalism. I retain one important reservation, however, about this theoretical argument: it is that the disorders may have been excessive—too devastating to permit the formation even of elemental fiefs.

This last introduces a new consideration into our general theory, and it must at once be said that there are no cases in which an excessive amount of fighting can be shown to have prevented the formation of elemental fiefs; the suggestion rests only on the present case. It receives a little support, however, from the evident fact that in the whole region the Assyrian monarchy sought to control from the fourteenth to the twelfth centuries there were an immense number of primitives or barbarians either actually in migration or quite insecurely settled. The many "kings" whom Tiglath-Pileser I (1114-1102 B.C.) conquered and reconquered may well have been pre-feudal barbarians. They may, of course, have already been feudal lords, or some of them may have been, and the Assyrian King of Kings may have established himself as their overlord. But, if he did, he almost certainly did so only temporarily. That is the most reasonable explanation of the two dark centuries

[20] See above, p. 106.

which follow Tiglath-Pileser. It is indeed hard to think that feudal relations did not arise in those centuries, the eleventh and tenth—unless, as already suggested, chaos was too great to permit that. When information is again available, for the ninth century, Assyria was still—or again—an unstable monarchy, but the *mar banuti*, the nobility, as known to us then, look very much like a post-feudal nobility: they had become courtiers, the greatest of them a body of ministers who constantly tended to become an oligarchy displacing the monarch, but each of them at the same time was ruler of a province, probably also owner or holder of it, in some sort of tenure from the crown.[21]

It would seem fairly probable, then, that the northern part of the valleys was not yet feudal in the fifteenth century B.C. when it was ruled by Mitanni. But it may have become proto-feudal under the Mitannian regime; the relation between the king and the *maryannu* could have been used in the proto-feudal manner. A certain disjunction occurred in the fourteenth century as power passed from the Mitannian to the Assyrian monarchy. With the change there almost certainly came a more military kind of government, probably cruder political methods in every way. There is also a probability, though a lesser one, that the whole structure of society deteriorated with the influx of more primitives and barbarians so that the northern part of the valleys and the mountain territory farther to the north were somewhat assimilated to each other. Whether between the fourteenth and tenth centuries actual feudal conditions were at all largely developed, it is not possible to say, but, if they were not, it is most likely that the failure resulted from the extreme degree of violence and disorder which the barbarians brought into the country.[22]

The southern part of Mesopotamia came under the rule of the Kassite monarchs, who, like all the other barbarian rulers of the Mesopotamian area, had under them an aristocracy. But about the aristocracy we know

[21] Quite possibly this description of a supposed post-feudal nobility in Assyria describes equally well the nobility of Urartu in the next century, the eighth. Adontz, however, inclines to the view that Urartu had provincial prefects, who were presumably appointive officials, in its main territory, as distinct from the post-feudal nobility, the *rabuti*—the latter indeed Adontz calls feudal (*Histoire de l'Arménie*, pp. 217-219). Such a variation in Urartu is eminently possible, and the similarity to Hittite institutions is significant. I think the evidence for Urartu, for what it is worth, strengthens the assumption that feudal periods occurred at an earlier time both in Assyria and (earlier still) in Hatti, but I must add that I do not think the evidence for Urartu is worth a great deal, for much of it is from Assyrian sources and could well be colored by Assyrian preconceptions.

[22] See below, pp. 304-306, 323-324, for further development of this argument.

less than about the others. In all likelihood most Kassite monarchs were feeble, and noblemen were able to flout their authority. There was still a state of Elam, whose inroads perhaps damaged Babylonia more than those of other enemies; but it was Mursilis of Hatti who had actually sacked Babylon in the late sixteenth century, and ended the then flimsy rule of the First Dynasty of Babylon. Tribesmen got established in some parts of the country and cities took over large estates. It is often said that the tenures recorded in the *kudurrus* were feudal. The benefices they define had large immunities so that private government obtained in them, but it does not look at all like feudal government, for a number of administrative functions were discharged by paid officials. This would seem to imply that the same kind of administration by an officialdom existed directly under the crown, and that at a time when it possibly did not in Mitanni-Assyria and Hatti. The institution of the *kudurru* holdings looks, in fact, like a policy for bringing back under the usual Babylonian administration territory which had got into the hands of cities or of tribes, for the crown in some instances had bought the land from tribal chieftains and their fellow-tribesmen just before granting it under *kudurru*. Nor can I see any evidence that holders under *kudurru* rendered military service for their holdings.

Certain deductions about Mesopotamia may now be made by comparing the three areas into which it has been divided for discussion here. First, if the suggestions about conditions in Mitanni-Assyria be accepted, then those conditions were less feudal—whether actually feudal to any extent or not—than conditions in Hatti, and such feudal tendencies as there were in Assyria were in operation far later than those in Hatti. And then—if the suggestions in the paragraph last above be accepted—there was no truly feudal period in Babylonia at all. Such a gradation from one region of the society to another is very reminiscent of feudal Europe. There was only a minor development of feudalism in Italy, which, like Babylonia, had been the old center of civilization. The central feudal area of Europe, northern France, had been colonial territory of the old society, Rome, from a fairly early time, and then it received an infusion of barbarian immigrants when the Roman Empire broke down; the description fits Hatti quite well also. But, of course, there are also the dissimilarities which always accompany historic similarities. Thus, Assyria was colonial territory of the old society, just as Hatti was; yet our hypothesis puts Assyria rather in the position Germany occupied in feudal Europe, for it seems to have been less feudal than Hatti, just as Germany was less feudal than France, and Germany was not to any extent a Roman colony. And, considered as a whole, Mesopotamia was probably less feudal than medieval Europe: Hatti less than France perhaps, though that is quite unsure; Babylonia even less feudal than Italy, probably; Mitanni-Assyria-Urartu less feudal than Germany and parts beyond if my very special supposition that the Assyrian area was submerged excessively with barbarians is correct.

A second observation to be made about Mesopotamia is that cities played a part in its political system. Ashur seems at some time in the earlier part of the period to have been a city-state. Cities were important in Hatti even after the establishment of the Hittite Kingdom with its feudal or feudalistic institutions. Mesopotamia had been a society of cities before the great empires of the Dynasty of Akkad and the Third Dynasty of Ur were established, and in the new age, with those empires gone, city polities evidently showed signs of recrudescence. There has been in some societies a certain antinomy between feudalism and cities, while in others city and feudality have developed in a special relation to one another. Mesopotamia was perhaps among the latter. Conceivably, some sort of "city-feudality," a minor modification of true feudalism, developed there. This could explain why we do not find the characteristic elemental fiefs in Mesopotamia; cities may have served in that capacity. It happens that a city-feudality is also a possibility in Chou China, to which we now turn.

It is probable that Chou China was feudal at one time. If it was not, it must have had a regime closely parallel to a feudal regime. The barbarians are much in evidence. The sinologists offer a picture of surviving primitives living in less favored places, such as mountains, swampy country, and the like, in among the civilized "Chinese," the two distinguished basically by the different levels of their agricultural practice, and the Chinese gradually ousting or absorbing the primitives. Central European primitives were similarly absorbed into feudal Europe, one of the chief changes which occurred in their condition also being their conversion to the relatively high standard of European agriculture. The European primitives were not scattered about within the society, but it is not certain that the Chinese ones were scattered evenly through the society's territory either. I suspect that there were not many of these "inner barbarians" left in the Great Plain region of China in the period with which we are concerned;[23] there may have been substantial numbers in the loess highlands to the west.

There were plenty of outer barbarians, probably a ring of them all round the society, and these were certainly formed out of tribesmen. The I were in the east, the Man to the south, and to the west the Jung and, perhaps not until a later date, the Ti. It is likely that the outer barbarians of the west were more numerous and perhaps more aggressive than the others, just as the inner barbarians were more numerous in the western, highland part of China than they were elsewhere; the inner and outer barbarians were, in fact, continuous. Not long before the Chou conquest the Chou themselves had been barbarians living somewhere westward. Their arrival in the valley of the River Wei, however, was probably the occasion of a change in their condition, for the Wei was an important tributary of the Yellow River, and the Chou when based in the Wei Valley could adopt the irrigation methods used by the Shang in the Yellow River Valley itself. This would provide the material basis for an urban society like that of the Shang, and it is clear that the Chou were busily absorbing what they could of the Shang culture in the generations before the conquest.

Among the Chinese themselves tribal, or, more probably, clan relations remained strong, and therefore, on the precedent of our study of Japan, we may suppose that, if there was a movement in a feudal direction, it was preceded and mediated by the formation of war-bands out of the bands of clan warriors. Thus the Chinese themselves would have become barbarians. If China was invaded by the outer barbarians at the outset of the changes with which we are concerned, then it showed from the very outset both kinds of barbarian participation in the feudal movement, the invaders as in Europe and Mesopotamia, and the large population of clansmen changing *in situ* as in Japan. Europe had the latter only from the proto-feudal stage onward, so that the

[23] It is usually supposed that there were, but this rests on a view of the probable order of events in the rise of Chinese civilization which I cannot accept. That view sees the development of irrigation and water control on the Yellow River itself as a climax coming fairly late in the story. I hold, on the contrary, that, as in all the great river valleys, it was the initial achievement and that no large-scale civilized society was possible without it. (Cf. my "Concept of the Conglomerate Myth," *Proceedings of the Tenth International Congress of Philosophy*, ed. Beth, Pos, and Hollak, I, Amsterdam, 1949, 74-81.) On this assumption, the spread of the water control system over the Plain would surely follow next, for it is an almost inevitable consequence. I think, therefore, that there can have been few primitives left in that region in Chou times. For the opposite opinion, see Owen Lattimore, *Inner Asian Frontiers of China* (London and New York, 1940), pp. 312-319, and *passim.*

case of China, if it is correctly diagnosed, would alone bridge the two alternatives evenly.[24] The Chou conquest was not a barbarian invasion within the meaning required; it occupies another place in the feudal movement, as will be shown below. There is some small reason to suppose, however, that, well before the Chou conquest, barbarian invasions from the west did occur. But the reason is inferential, namely that invasion from that direction was severe in later times also, and that some kind of political collapse at the beginning of the era of change must be presumed.

The breakdown of the Chinese political system must have begun a good time before the Chou conquest, probably in the thirteenth or twelfth century B.C.[25] What were the Chinese society and polity like before the trouble began? Obviously tribal or clan relations were very important in it, but it cannot possibly have been purely tribal. According to Maspero, the "feudal lords" were served by various official functionaries at the time of the settlement after the Chou conquest.[26] The predecessors of those lords (who were certainly not feudal) before the conquest were presumably served by similar officials. The officials' duties seem to have been management not only of estates but of the affairs of merchants and others. We have to conclude, therefore, that territorial states had descended from the original tribal organizations, probably in the same sort of way in which in India the Rajputs became established in territorial states and kept most of their tribal characters.[27] Was this the entire political order of Shang China? Possibly, but there is also a possibility that there was something else—a general hegemony exercised by the Shang king. This is a matter subject to so much con-

[24] Possibly the difference proposed here between China and Europe is nugatory.

[25] The Chou were at war in western territory for a long time before their conquest of the Shang, possibly for a century. The Shang themselves were involved in serious campaigns against the I before the Chou conquest. The capital of Shang was moved to the "great city Shang" in the reign of Pan Kêng in the thirteenth century (the fourteenth century in the traditional Chinese chronology; H. G. Creel, *Studies in Early Chinese Culture*, 1st series, Baltimore, 1937, pp. 133-140), and it is possible that that event marked a degenerative change. Maspero thinks that the process of colonization by the Chinese among the barbarians began "toward the middle or end of the Yin [Shang] dynasty." (*Annual Report of the Smithsonian Institution, 1927*, Washington, 1928, p. 446.)

[26] "Le régime féodal et la propriété foncière dans la Chine antique," *Revue de l'Institut de Sociologie*, XVI (1936), 43-49, which is reprinted in *Mélanges posthumes sur les religions et l'histoire de la Chine*, III, *Etudes historiques* (Paris, 1950), pp. 118-124. Cf. Bodde, above, pp. 51-52.

[27] Not necessarily through intervention of a priestly influence, such as that of the Brahmans. Nevertheless, the influence of religion is very probable so that the Indian parallel is a good one.

troversy among sinologists that it will have to be specially investigated below.[28] Such a hegemony could have provided in ordinary times for maintenance of general peace, but it is likely that, if it existed at all, it was at some times a good deal more fragile than the structure of the individual states.

What caused the breakdown of this political system? Lattimore suggests that, as other groups, notably the Chou, learned some of the Shang culture there was bound to come a time when they would be militarily stronger than the Shang because they would have "fewer slaves and more free warriors."[29] It has already been assumed above that the breakdown began long before the Chou conquest, so that Lattimore's view could explain only the Chou conquest itself and not the whole transition of the period. If the Shang exercised a hegemony, then the breakdown of the hegemony would be a natural starting point for change, if not a sufficient explanation of its cause.[30]

Whatever the form of the Chinese political system in Shang times, and whatever the cause of its breakdown, there is no doubt that it changed, and that within a century or so after the Chou conquest of Shang a new order, customarily called feudal, had come into existence. Whether or not the new order must finally be described as feudal, we know some of the factors and at least one stage in its development far better than we know the political system of Shang times. This knowledge is carefully and rather thoroughly described in Mr. Bodde's essay in this volume. Much, but not all, of it shows a process of change like that we know in the societies which went feudal.

Two things of major importance are the practice of commendation whereby a man entrusted himself by solemn oath to a patron so that "each great lord thus had his bands of followers. . . ,"[31] and an elaborate system of ethics, the *li*, by which the aristocracy lived. Our authority warns us that the evidence for the practice of commendation is not good, but the existence of the *li* may be taken to strengthen it since the two things very often go together in other cases. The *li* as known to us belong to a much later time and are something different from the European and Japanese ethical systems we know, for alone of the three the Chinese system was taken up by a great thinker at the moment when it might have been expected to lapse into archaism and

[28] Ch. 4, pp. 248-252. [29] *Inner Asian Frontiers*, p. 305.

[30] For what makes societies and their culture decline, see below, pp. 364-365.

[31] Above, pp. 55-62. The words in quotations are actually those of Maspero, *Revue de l'Institut de Sociologie*, XVI, 68: *Mélanges posthumes*, III, 144.

worked into a code to suit a highly sophisticated society. In the face of the *li* as restated by Confucius and his successors, it is the more difficult to deduce the character of the earlier *li* of feudal society. But at least it may be deduced that a system Confucius in the sixth century thought worth redeveloping had had a very strong hold on society before that. The number of the tales of correct conduct as conceived in feudal times confirms the hold the system had had.

Chou society had a sharply marked aristocracy, the *chün-tzu*, with a basic class of *shih* comparable with European knights and Japanese *samurai*. An even more strongly marked survival of clan practices is found among the Chinese aristocracy than among the Japanese. Possibly the strength of those practices is explained by the fact that they had religious sanction; they were almost the whole outward manifestation of ancestor worship. Since ancestor worship is amply shown by archaeological evidence to have been the religion of the Shang, it can be deduced that the *li* and the war-band organization which arose out of commendation were developed by the civilized Chinese population itself in the course of the transition from the old order to the new. This does not at all exclude the barbarians—other barbarians if the Chinese themselves should also be so described. Presumably both the inner barbarians and the outer barbarians, whose existence we have noticed above, were involved. Since they must have produced war-bands earlier than the settled Chinese did, they may have played an originating part in their formation as the invading barbarians in Europe did, but the continuity of the practices of ancestor worship ensures that the settled population had an active part in developing the new ethic and the new society and was not merely led into them by the barbarians.

Mr. Bodde is at some pains to point out that the Chou were not barbarians in the sense of being near-primitives at the time of their conquest of China.[32] They certainly were at least as respectable claimants to leadership of the civilized society as, say, the Franks were in Western Europe. And the function of the Chou leaders in the movement toward feudalism was almost certainly the same as that of the Carolingian rulers: they set up a proto-feudal polity. There is no mistaking this quality in the regime King Wu and the Duke of Chou set up. Maspero's study of the personal and tenurial relations of the regime makes it plain that those relations—whatever they actually were—were used to strengthen the state, to become, in fact, a part of its structure

[32] Above, p. 52.

in the characteristic proto-feudal manner, and it shows equally plainly that an old administrative system survived also in the total structure.[33] An important part of the policy of the Duke of Chou was, without a doubt, to apply ethical sanctions to support the political edifice he was building. By contrast, he did not attempt to set up any important centralizing agency such as the *Bakufu*, and it is surely to be presumed that no such thing was possible in China at the time. As far as is known, there was not even as much central government as the Carolingians achieved.

The Chou conquest had been planned a generation before it was actually undertaken. If the part in the planning traditionally ascribed to King Wen of Chou is a fact, then Wen was a man of wide vision and great capacity. About King Wu, the conqueror, we do not know a great deal, but the Duke of Chou, who took part in the conquest and afterwards served as regent for the infant King Ch'êng, was one of the greatest figures in Chinese history. He compares well with Yoritomo and with Charlemagne. If his actual achievement was less than Yoritomo's, it was as great as Charlemagne's. But these great men are not fairly judged by their achievements. Not even Yoritomo could establish a permanent regime, and Charlemagne's and the Duke of Chou's work fell to pieces soon after it had been done; it was beyond the power of men to make proto-feudal governments stable and lasting in Chou China, Japan, or Western Europe; there is, in fact, no such thing as a stable and lasting proto-feudal government in history. It is by the nobility of their aims and the magnitude of their temporary achievements that these men should be judged. According to Chou tradition, the Duke's avowed aims were to unite—or reunite[34]—the whole civilized world, to reestablish peace, and to rule in accordance with the will of a moral Heaven. Like Charlemagne, he momentarily realized his aims. He completed the projected conquests and brought together a huge and rickety state which, in the opinion of some, was larger than any China had had before.

Half a century later a large new expansion southward toward the

[33] Maspero's material on this subject is mostly concerned with the internal administration of the *kuo* (principality—? fief). He deals with the duties of the prince to the king by collecting examples of service done, giving no contracts, and admitting that the information is vague; he says nothing about the obligations of the king to the prince. He also gives an account of the investiture ceremony. (*Revue de l'Institut de Sociologie*, XVI, 58-67: *Mélanges posthumes*, III, 134-143.) Cf. Bodde (above, pp. 53-54) who has used Maspero and other authority also.

[34] To reunite if there had been a Shang hegemony.

valleys of the Han and the Yangtze set in.[35] This sounds like the typical expansion of a feudal society. If it was, it betokens also the breakdown of the temporary, proto-feudal equilibrium, for that kind of expansion is the work of feudatories seeking new territory to strengthen themselves in their struggles with one another and with their overlord, the king. The breakdown of the proto-feudal regime did occur, for this we know otherwise, and, though we do not know when it began, a half century after the establishment of the regime is a very likely date. Maspero finds that local administrative officials of the proto-feudal government soon began to convert themselves into barons,[36] which probably signifies the final disintegration of the old state and the advent or imminence of the early feudal regime or of something like it. But there is no record of the emergence of the elemental strong fief. There is no doubt that power became fragmented and distributed to local centers, as occurs in a feudal system, but it remains possible that the local units were not the elemental strong fiefs we expect to find in an early feudal regime, even that they were not true fiefs of any sort.

Of the first known local units Mr. Bodde says: ". . . there came into being a host of small states or principalities—at least one hundred are known to have existed in the eighth century B.C.—each consisting of a walled capital, surrounded by tilled lands from which it derived its sustenance."[37] The walled capital was a city, and the prominence of the city in this political order compels us to consider whether it was really a feudal order, as so readily appears, or whether it was an order of city-states with a city aristocracy in the commanding political position. The European feudal baron was never a city man, the Japanese *daimyo* only in a limited sense and in a late period. It is as compatible with our small knowledge of Assyria and Hatti that Assyrian and Hittite lords became absorbed into cities as that they became true feudal barons. All we know about actual tenures in Chou China is inferred from services done by lords to the king and from the ceremony of in-

[35] Maspero, *La Chine antique* (Paris, 1927), pp. 57-58.

[36] Actually Maspero says they did so towards the end of the Chou Dynasty and had probably done the same "dès l'antiquité"—a sufficiently vague statement. (*Revue de l'Institut de Sociologie*, XVI, 57: *Mélanges posthumes*, III, 133.) Cf. Bodde, above, p. 58.

[37] Above, p. 53. Cf. Maspero, *La Chine antique*, pp. 24-25; K. Wittfogel, "The Society of Prehistoric China," *Zeitschrift für Sozialforschung*, VIII (1939), 182-183; Lattimore, *Inner Asian Frontiers*, pp. 394-395. I feel some doubt of the importance of irrigation control in the formation of the "city-and-country cell," as Lattimore calls it, but the idea is very interesting and well worth considering.

vestiture; we know nothing at all about tenure directly from contracts or from other forms of agreement. One thing which may be said of the Chou aristocracy, whether it was a feudal or a city oligarchical aristocracy, is that its sharp distinction from the common folk, the *min*, must have come about in the period of formation of the new feudal or city polity; class divisions of that kind are foreign to a tribal society. This class division is unfortunately no help with the problem whether city or feudality predominated. It is true that every society we know of which went feudal developed sharp class distinctions as it did so, but cities, as they were formed, seem to have done the same, as witness the Greek cities and Rome.[38] We have no choice, therefore, but to leave open the decision as to whether Chou China developed a feudal system or a system of city states as its first enduring polity.

I think there is no doubt that the question whether a rising civilized society will develop a city system or a feudal system is a real and a very important question. To realize this, it is necessary only to glance at the classic case of the Greek cities, at Mesopotamia in the first cycle of its history in the fourth and third millennia, and then by contrast at feudal Europe and feudal Japan. In Chapter 9 of this essay we shall encounter the case of Kievan Russia in which there were city-states, barbarian leaders with war-bands, but no feudality.[39] The circumstances of Russian history are too unusual to permit the Kievan polity to be put forward as an example of compromise between a city and a feudal system; and it was hardly a compromise anyhow, for the feudalistic side of the polity was utterly stunted. I do not feel convinced, however, that feudality and city are necessarily incompatible, and that they must always be conflicting alternatives. The little we know about Chou China would be consistent with a "city-feudality" more or less harmoniously organized within each city-feudal unit. And, if such a combination did in fact develop, its place in society and the course of its history must have been closely analogous to those of a true feudality, for so much of the small external evidence there is points in the direction of feudality. Neither do we know that Greece did not at one time have city-feudality; it would ease some of the difficulties about its early history if it did have.[40]

[38] But cf. the opinion of Zimmern; see p. 379.
[39] Below, pp. 347-350.
[40] The relation of cities to feudalities and the possibility of city-feudalities is discussed further in the concluding chapter; see pp. 378-383 below.

4. OLD EMPIRES AND THEIR GHOSTS*

IN this chapter history will be written backwards. Most of the societies treated in the last two chapters contained strange reflections of great empires which had existed in their past. The reflections, called ghosts here, will be considered first since they concern feudalism more directly. Afterwards, the foregoing great empires will receive attention, and, in particular, certain anomalous cases in which, although ghosts occurred, great empires perhaps did not, or are found in unexpected places.

Proto-feudal states always occupy an important place in the succession of ghosts to great empires, and also in those peculiar successions in which the great empire is hard to find. Proto-feudal states are, in most of the cases we know, the last endeavors to restore the empires but, if there really are cases without great empires in the historic background, then proto-feudal states can only be attempts to bolster up the flimsy polities which immediately precede the proto-feudal states. Certainly, proto-feudal states always are in an immediate sense attempts to bolster up such flimsy polities, and for the moment we should allow ourselves to consider feudalism only as a political system which follow upon the disintegration of flimsy old states ruled in some manner, no necessarily very direct, by a central authority.[1]

The ghost empire of Western Europe presents a problem. It is no difficult to find a ghost empire in that society: the Holy Roman Empir is an obvious ghost; in fact, its ghostly quality gives the type very wel But the Holy Roman Empire was not of simple origin historically, an the complications of its origin have had important consequences. I is the German Holy Roman Empire, set up by Otto the Great and Pop John XII in the tenth century, which is ordinarily meant by the nam Holy Roman Empire, but the German empire was not a direct reviva of the old empire of the past. It was a revival of an earlier reviva and the earlier revival was the empire set up by Charlemagne and Pop Leo III in the year 800. Both revivals were intended to confer upo their respective principal actors, Charles and Otto, an imperial authorit and dignity effective in all Europe, in all Christendom perhaps—ove

* The term "ghost" was first applied to polities of the kind intended here b Toynbee, *A Study of History*, I, 342-343 and *passim*.

[1] The importance of so restricting the concept of the place of feudalism history, at least provisionally, emerged in discussions between Mr. Bodde an myself.

all the peoples of European, or Western culture, to use a modern concept.

Charlemagne's authority was indeed quite general except where barbarians resisted it, or where it came into conflict with that of another emperor, him of Byzantium, who was undeniably the legitimate and direct successor of the emperors of the old empire. Some of the barbarians Charlemagne subjected by force, thereby asserting his claim and setting a precedent his successors might follow with all other barbarians. With the Byzantine Emperor Charlemagne negotiated, and the result was a formal division of empire so that a Western Empire and an Eastern Empire came into existence as coordinates. This was the full realization of a tendency which had first been shown in Diocletian's time more than five centuries earlier.

Otto the Great gained recognition of his title from the Byzantine Emperor, but within his own "empire" he met resistance more formidable than that which Charlemagne had met. Barbarians he met as Charlemagne did; and vassalage became in his empire a means to educe them to a sort of order as it had in Charlemagne's empire. But Otto and his successors met another problem, resistance to their auhority on the part of the less barbarous of their subjects. These did not deny them the imperial dignity, but their chief lords very soon egan to claim that their "kingship" excluded the emperor from effective power over them.[2] It eventuated that Holy Roman Emperors had "dominion" over Germany and parts of Italy, but not over Western or northern Europe. There were thus at least two kinds of ghostly imperial dignity in Europe, the kind which gave some functioning power, dominion, and was limited to Germany and Italy, and the kind which extended to all Europe, all Latin Christendom, but gave no dominion, not even suzerainty. Both were held by the same person.

Not since Bagehot and Bryce have scholars paid much attention to istinctions of this sort; they are somewhat vague distinctions perhaps, ifficult to understand, and so they have been neglected. We are going o find, however, that they have some importance, that in certain ways entral Europe and Western Europe became systematically different om one another, that they may be said to have been distinct societies,

[2] Otto was, possibly, a usurper, having displaced Berengar of Italy. Twenty-five ears after that episode the French displaced their Carolingian puppet and set emselves up, not an emperor, but a king, Hugh Capet. Otto's and his successors' mewhat equivocal position in France and other countries of the west and north ay have to do with the French transaction.

and that some historic events are explained by the difference between them.[3] There is another distinction of the same vague sort which is better known because its results have been far more obtrusive. This is the distinction between the authority and dignity of pope and of emperor in Europe, the distinction which we describe in a rough way as that between church and state. But, in fact, popes especially, and churchmen in general, had authority and dignity which can easily be confounded with that of lay magnates, and often was so confounded—if that is the right word—in the early centuries of the Western society. Leo III and John XII accepted the necessity of lay empire, but not all popes did so by any means, and a number believed that imperial power resided in some primary way in the papal office. Nor was the Caesaro-papist idea of the imperial office confined to Byzantium; in the West too the imperial dignity carried priestly quality. The emperor was in some mysterious way pope, the pope in some mysterious way emperor.

This last is well known, and the dichotomy of church and state in Europe is usually taken for granted. It should not be; it is a strange and remarkable thing.[4] The dichotomy is not wholly unknown in other societies, but the Western case of it is an extreme one. That we can best appreciate by contrasting the West with China, for China, especially in the Chou period with which we are, so far, chiefly concerned, produced an extreme case in the other direction: there was virtually no dichotomy of church and state in Chou China. The Chou *wang* was pope as well as emperor, and his noble subordinates were priests as well as barons; the noble and clerical estates were one. The Chou monarchy was, like the Holy Roman Empire, a ghost, but, unlike the Holy Roman Empire, it was a single ghost. No separate papacy competed with it, and, so far as we know, the *wang*, while he retained dominion at all, retained it everywhere.

But we do not know what the ghostly Chou monarchy reflected; that will be considered at the end of this chapter. We may say meanwhile that the Chou monarchy was a ghost of itself, or of something still flimsier which had preceded it. It is hard to say just when the Chou monarchy lapsed into powerlessness, but the time was, of course, the same as that of the rise of the feudal or city-feudal regime. Certainly it was powerless after 771 B.C. when it suffered a disastrous defeat at

[3] See pp. 297-300, 313-314 below.

[4] On this matter cf. Bagehot and Thomas Arnold as reported by Bagehot, *Physics and Politics*, pp. 26ff. For an effect of the dichotomy of church and state in Europe not hitherto noticed, see pp. 310-314 below.

the hands of barbarians and moved its capital from the vicinity of Sian to Loyang. The Chou monarch remained a venerable figure, however, titular ruler of the world, more clearly so than the Holy Roman Emperor, for, as has been remarked, his dignity and authority were the same everywhere: other monarchs who arose in China for a long time admitted his suzerainty, as the other chief monarchs of the West did not admit the Holy Roman Emperor's suzerainty.

Like the Chou monarchy, the Japanese Empire became a ghost, directly at any rate, of itself. It was going into dissolution at the time, in the twelfth century, when the Kamakura Shogunate was set up. For a century and a half the empire lived a half-life under the protection of the shogunate. Then under the Ashikaga Shogunate it lost even that substance and became a mere simulacrum—a ghost; the court existed barely and nothing more. Nor under the strong Tokugawa Shogunate did the imperial government return to political life. And yet when in the nineteenth century a complete reconstitution of the Japanese polity was planned and the feudal structure was at last to be suppressed, the imperial court could be brought back to life to crown the new structure of the state and to confer upon it the most venerable, sacred legitimacy.

It has been shown above that the dichotomy of empire and shogunate in Japan has a short-lived analogy in Western Europe in the rise of the mayoralty of the palace beside the Merovingian monarchy. The analogy is enough to show that the empire-shogunate dichotomy is not a church-state dichotomy. But it is not a thing of an entirely different kind, for the division of function is somewhat similar in the two instances. Thus, the nominee of deity, whether he was pope, Sinic emperor, or Merovingian king, had difficulty in dealing with brutal political realities: a pope like Leo III, therefore, set up an emperor to deal with them; a cloistered ex-emperor of Japan gave recognition to the office of shogun; and monkish Merovingian monarchs allowed real power to fall to their mayors. Differences are, of course, that mayors wanted dignity as well as power, and soon got it; shoguns may have wanted dignity, or they may not have, and anyhow they never got it; nor did European emperors try to become popes—although Napoleon might have liked to become son of Re. It is not an accident that the first revival of empire in Europe followed hard upon the displacement of Merovingian king by his mayor. It is not an accident that all these transactions happened in proto-feudal societies, for it was the brutal political realities of such societies that old-fashioned dignitaries could not face. In the event only feudal barons could deal with them. It may be—I think it is—because old dignitaries could not descend to the political methods required in feudal societies that those old dignitaries, the emperors, became sacred, and their ghost empires sacred institutions. Every one of them had this quality in a far more marked and explicit sense than its predecessor, the old empire, and I think it is likely that its existence was preserved by possession of sacred quality, for it could not have survived in the feudal world by virtue of its feeble political power alone.

In Mesopotamia a number of magnates were ready to claim imperial dignity but they all had the same difficulty as the kings, emperors, and popes of other societies in coping with brutal political realities. The number of them in Mesopotamia introduces some confusion, and makes it hard to spot which one was the true ghost emperor. His identity comes out, however, in such episodes as the claim of Burnaburiash of Babylon to overlordship over Ashuruballit of Assyria in the fourteenth century B.C.: the king of Babylon was rightful ghost emperor. It may be that all Mesopotamian monarchs claimed imperial dignity, for all of them, even the Achaemenid monarch of a much later date than the others, used an imperial title, usually the title "King of Kings."[5] The conflicting claims should probably be attributed ultimately to instability and incoherence of the old empire which the *soi-disants* ghosts affected to succeed; that matter will be examined below when old empires are considered. We may, however, take note here of the immediate basis of the Babylonian claim, and of the Assyrian claim which, as we happen to know, was deduced from the Babylonian.

This had to do with the sacred quality of empire—in this instance the sacred quality of all political authority. In Mesopotamia this rested on the theory of tenure from deity, each ruler being "tenant-farmer" of some god. All the gods had their home cities and political theory had been worked out in theological-cosmological terms to justify earthly empire by erecting one or another god to authority over all the others. Thus the imperial authority of Babylon was secured by the exaltation of Marduk, the city god, to supremacy over the rest of the pantheon. But that event had happened during the brief earthly supremacy of Hammurabi, an episodic restoration of the old empire i

[5] Before Hammurabi various different titles, all denoting broad and som universal authority, had been used by emperors, and probably more than on survived in Babylonia and Assyria in the later period. The term "King of Kings seems to have become the usual, if not the only title in Assyria, however, and t have passed from that nation to others, including Persia. See H. Frankfor *Kingship and the Gods* (Chicago, 1949), pp. 223-230.

the midst of its disintegration. It seems rather probable that so ephemeral an episode was not enough to establish Babylon's claim to empire to the exclusion of other claims. Assyria in Hammurabi's time was some sort of an ally, a subject-ally perhaps, of Babylon, and it took part in Hammurabi's short-lived restoration of the empire. It looks as if some Assyrian monarch during the disorders which followed the breakup of Hammurabi's state tried to salvage the debris and put the empire together again, for there exists an inscription whereby Marduk grants from all eternity to Ashur, god of the first capital of Assyria, "the gods of the four regions to honour him so that none might escape."[6] We do not know what Assyrian monarch contrived this nor when precisely he did so, but it must have been fairly soon after Hammurabi.

Whether other Mesopotamian monarchs besides the king of Assyria intended by assumption of imperial style to compete with the Babylonian monarch for empire, we scarcely know. If only the king of Assyria did so, the Mesopotamian case could be paralleled in the European, for the Byzantine and Holy Roman Emperors remained competitors for succession to the real Roman emperors even though they recognized each other's rights. If all Mesopotamian monarchs were competitors, then the only parallels are to be found in predominantly non-feudal societies.[7]

The ghost empire in and after the Libyan period in Egypt is perhaps a little problematical; it was the monarchy of Napata, which soon moved its center to Meroë and there lasted not far short of a thousand years. All things considered, it seems right to regard it as a ghost, for it was derived directly from the Egyptian Empire proper via the regime of the Chief Priest of Amon at Thebes, and certainly the Napata-Meroë regime was but a reflection of the great empire. Yet the quality of the tombs left at Meroë[8] suggests that it may have been rather more substantial than some ghosts. The strongly sacred character of the regime recalls the sacred character of all the other ghosts. Napata-Meroë was not entirely without a bifurcation of church and state, but, as in Egypt proper, it was very slight. Of course, the really odd thing about Napata-Meroë is that, during the main part of its career, it was not in Egypt. That its rulers felt it ought to be there is shown by their

[6] Quoted by L. Delaporte, *Mesopotamia*, trans. V. Gordon Childe (London, 1925), p. 309, from *Musée du Louvre: Département des antiquités orientales*, II, fig. 315.

[7] See below, pp. 301-302.

[8] Dows Dunham, "Notes on the History of Kush, 850 B.C.-A.D. 350," *American Journal of Archaeology*, L (1946), 378-388.

conquest of Egypt almost as soon as the regime had been established in Napata—Napata itself was in Egypt at that time. With its capital in Meroë, however, the ghost was what we may call a "refugee ghost." It seems quite likely that the occasion for its rulers seeking refuge in Meroë was the threat of Persian conquest of Egypt.[9]

As a refugee ghost, the Meroë regime is not alone in history. We shall consider in a moment whether there was such a regime in the history of India. There certainly was one in the somewhat unusual history of Byzantium-Russia, that is to say, in the later history of Byzantium and its extension in Russia. "Moscow, the Third Rome," was a ghost of the Byzantine Empire, set up in explicit imitation of the Byzantine Empire because Byzantium had been conquered and the empire suppressed by the infidel: Rome was a refugee from Byzantium in Moscow. And the new Moscow was a highly sacred regime, brought into existence largely through the agency of the church, which became an important institution in Russia for the first time as the Moscow regime emerged. Thus, Moscow received as a part of its heritage the Caesaropapist system of church-state relations invented in Byzantium. This bears a relation to the Western system, but puts the state, or, to be more accurate, the monarchy, decisively above the church.

As to India, there may or may not have been a ghost of the Gupta Empire, and then later there may or may not have been a refugee ghost. Harsha's state was rather a revival of the Gupta Empire itself, but the Pratihara Empire, from the ninth century to the eleventh, was a very feeble affair for most of its career, and there seems to be at least some reason to regard it as a ghost. There then comes a very obscure period of a couple of centuries in which perhaps, retreating before the Muslim invaders through various shadowy regimes in the east, the Deccan, and the south, empire came to Vijayanagar in the fourteenth century. If that is sound, this retreat resembles the retreat of the Egyptian empire to Meroë, though it was slow, and passed through a number of stages. We should then consider Vijayanagar as a refugee empire. But it is not sure that the hypothesis is sound. While the Pratihara Empire and the Empire of Vijaynagar certainly stand out, they are

[9] Chronology is as follows. Cambyses conquered Egypt in 525 B.C., and it is possible that the threat of Persian conquest was abroad twenty years earlier when Amasis, next to last Pharaoh of the Saite line (Twenty-sixth Dynasty), allied with Croesus of Lydia and gave him some sort of support against Cyrus. On the side of Napata-Meroë, Dunham gives the definitive movement of the capital to Meroë in 538.

obscured to some extent by the maze of ephemeral lesser states all over India and in the colonial lands of Further India. The Pratihara Empire may have had the same sacred quality the Brahmans succeeded in giving to the Rajput states, but that we do not know. Neither do we know that even the Pratihara Empire was considered by its rulers or its subjects to be a continuation or revival of the Gupta Empire. This is not to say that Vijayanagar, at any rate, does not represent as true an assertion of Hindu civilization against Muslim-Persian as Meroë does of Egyptian civilization against Persian and Greek, but that is not really the point; what we are looking for is precisely a political reflection of the past and one consciously held to continue the old empire. Vijayanagar lasted only until the early seventeenth century, and after that there was nothing which can be regarded even tentatively as a ghost of the Gupta Empire. Even if Vijayanagar be regarded as such, then, it ended several centuries earlier than the shortest-lived of the other ghosts. The occurrence of a ghost empire in India must, therefore, remain problematical.

Some of the old empires in the six societies we have at the moment under observation are as obvious as some of the ghosts are, but the obvious ghosts and the obvious empires occur in the same society in only a single case, Western Europe: the Roman Empire was the great empire preceding the rise of that society as surely as the Holy Roman Empire was the real Roman Empire's ghost, or one of the real Roman Empire's ghosts. Egypt under the Libyans and India have obvious great empires, or fairly obvious ones. The Egyptian one was that of the Eighteenth and Nineteenth Dynasties, and the Indian one, as we have seen, was the Gupta Empire, not the Mogul, which makes it rather less obvious. We have already considered complications in these two successions, but we may notice that there was no break in the Egyptian succession: the various empires were direct continuations of one another.

There follow then Mesopotamia, Japan, and Chou China, in which cases problems arise, problems of difficulty increasing in that order. For Mesopotamia, least problematic of the three, the chief difficulty is the long break in the unity of the empire between its two main dynasties. Those dynasties were the Dynasty of Akkad and the Third Dynasty of Ur. The rule of the Dynasty of Akkad lasted for a little under two centuries, from about 2360 to 2180 B.C., the period of breakdown between dynasties, with disorder and barbarian rule, a little over a century, and the rule of the Third Dynasty of Ur also for a little over a century, about 2070 to 1960.[10] Other empires have also suffered interruption, for example, the Roman Empire during a substantial part of the third century, and the Egyptian Empire at the transition from the Eighteenth to the Nineteenth Dynasty. The interruption in the case of Mesopotamia was only greater in degree than what happened in other cases.

After the Third Dynasty of Ur the decline and disintegration of the empire began. It was of long duration, about three and a half centuries until the appearance of the possibly proto-feudal regime, a little shorter than the corresponding period of decline of the Roman Empire. The disintegration was gradual, the first hundred years not yet very bad dominion then being divided between two main states, Isin and Larsa The First Dynasty of Babylon turned up about 1830, but it ruled only a local state except during a part of the reign of Hammurabi (1728-1686)[11] and possibly also of that of his successor, Samsu-Iluna (1686-?) Hammurabi's career was one much like that of Justinian, both in it temporary reconquest of a large part of the empire and in its administrative reform, including the laws. The Kassites were already attacking before Hammurabi's death, and the debacle followed with the Firs Dynasty staggering on for over a century, but local powers, many o them of invading barbarians, conducting their own disorderly rule

The verdict upon this empire is that centripetal forces never becam as strong in it as they have done in some other empires. It is quite usua for an empire to be a comparatively loose organization in its earl stages, as the Mesopotamian empire was in its first phase under th Dynasty of Akkad. After that, usually an empire develops more an more effective centralizing institutions.[12] Nor did the Mesopotamia Empire wholly fail to do this: the Third Dynasty of Ur built up a effective bureaucratic state, and the empire then reached the climax o its political achievement. That achievement was remarkably short-live

[10] All dates for Mesopotamia according to Albright's 1942 chronology: "A Thi Revision of the Early Chronology of Western Asia," pp. 28-36; table, p. 32.

[11] Albright has drawn attention to the disintegration prevailing in the ear part of Hammurabi's reign with contemporary evidence: Itur-Asdu, an official Zimri-Lim, King of Mari, says in a letter that ten or fifteen kings follow Har murabi, as many Rim-Sin of Larsa, as many again Ibal-pi-el of Eshnunnak, many yet again Amut-pi-el of Qatna, and ten Yarim-Lim of Yamkhad (Aleppo "there is not a single king who is really powerful by himself" ("Western Asia the Twentieth Century B.C." [Eighteenth, on the 1942 chronology], *Bulletin the American Schools of Oriental Research*, No. 67, Oct. 1937, pp. 26-30).

[12] Cf. Toynbee, *A Study of History*, VI, 36-37 and 37 n.

however, for it lasted little, if any, more than two generations. The explanation is no doubt concerned with the long break between the two dynasties, and, not improbably, with the incursion of barbarians which then occurred. The Amorites, one of the groups of barbarians who then moved into Mesopotamian territory, very probably continued to move in even in the days of the Third Dynasty. In fact, the twenty-second and twenty-first centuries seem to have witnessed a sort of tussle between the barbarians with their way of life and the civilized society with its way. The dominion of the Third Dynasty was a notable assertion of the vigor of the civilization. Another assertion was the effective conversion to Mesopotamian ideas of many of the Amorites, perhaps the majority of them, such that it was they who contributed most to prolongation of the old society's career after the fall of the Third Dynasty. Thus, the Dynasty of Isin was an Amorite dynasty which ruled essentially on the lines of the Third Dynasty's rule, and the First Dynasty of Babylon was also Amorite so that Hammurabi's egregious achievement was that of an Amorite ruler. There were besides a good many other Amorite dynasties, which upheld Mesopotamian culture locally to some extent in the bad days of the nineteenth century and later.

How far excessive incursions of barbarians explain the weakness of the Mesopotamian empire in its later career, we cannot finally decide; no doubt there are other factors in the explanation also. But the vast inundations of Hurrians, Hittites, and others, which may have been continuous in the period of decisive breakdown of the empire with the earlier incursions, support the idea that repeated barbarian dilution of the culture cut down the society's achievements.

In such unstable conditions it may be doubted that the very idea of imperial unity became as firmly rooted in Mesopotamian tradition as it did in the tradition of most civilized societies. The political situation after the fall of the Third Dynasty of Ur was probably the proximate origin of the claims to universal authority (if that is what they were) of all national rulers in later periods of Mesopotamian history. In that situation the usual practice of a would-be King of Kings was to form a following of lesser kings, and two such combinations existed already in the Isin-Larsa period immediately after the fall of the Third Dynasty. There were usually more than two later on. Hammurabi may temporarily have suppressed all rival combinations, but if he did, his success did not prevent the rapid return of a multiplicity of claimants to imperial authority. In turn, the duality of the days of Isin and Larsa can well be traced back to the days of division between the Third Dynasty and the Dynasty of Akkad, and then back to the time before there was any empire. The only long period of unity was the first one, that of the Dynasty of Akkad, and that may not have been long enough, nor the unity of the time close enough, to have fixed the ideal of the single empire effectively in Mesopotamian tradition.

It is the Japanese case which has a great empire in an unexpected place—not in Japan at all, but in China. The significance of this may be appreciated by observing two things, that Japan was a single nation of the Chinese society, and that the greater part of that society did not go feudal at all, but instead was restored to unity some three and a half centuries after the breakdown of its great empire. As a single nation of the Chinese society, Japan resembled any of the nations of Europe[13] in relation to the whole Western European society, and resembled most the Scandinavian nations which had never been parts of the Roman Empire any more than Japan had been of the Chinese Empire. With the exception of Japan and Rajputana we have to do in this book with whole societies, or at least with large parts of societies containing several nations, and even Rajputana stands in a special place in the development of India as a whole.[14] Thus, the other ghost empires we are concerned with covered, or aspired to cover, whole societies, or large parts of them; the Japanese ghost empire was peculiar in being on the parochial scale of a single nation.

The extent of analogy between Japanese and other ghost empires is suggested by the circumstance, referred to above, that China proper, the major part of the society, was formed again into a very real and solid empire only a few centuries after the breakdown of its old empire. If, then, a ghost empire is something which necessarily accompanies feudalism, Japan had to have its own private ghost empire since the main part of the society had an empire of different quality. This is not a unique development even if it is perhaps unusual. As a matter of fact a somewhat similar development happened in Europe, and the com

[13] Russia is excluded, for it is not a nation of Europe in the sense that other nations are; see Ch. 9 below.

[14] If, as is probable, Rajputana was originally the remnants of the Pratihara Empire, then it fills a place like the remnants of Charlemagne's empire in European history. Not all of Europe had been included in Charlemagne's empire but a very large nucleus had been, and most political institutions within and without the nucleus were derived from those of Charlemagne's time. How far Rajputana served similarly as a vehicle for later (non-Muslim) Indian institutions we do not know, but it must have done so to some extent.

parison serves to clarify the analogy further. In Europe too the old empire was restored, and that at least as rapidly as in China, but only in a relatively small area, namely Byzantium, whereas the European feudal area was very large and covered many nations, and its ghost empire, though not as extensive as its feudal area, covered more than one nation.

In Europe the originators of the Holy Roman Empire did not seek to model that institution closely upon the revived Roman Empire of the east—although it would be quite an error to think that they did not do so at all. They professed to be reviving the old western part of the empire which was its original central territory and so could claim a legitimacy of its own, a greater legitimacy than Byzantium had. But the Japanese Empire, having no local roots of its own, was quite new. It was modelled, therefore, very closely indeed on the restored old empire, its contemporary, the T'ang Empire, rather than upon the ancient institution, the Han Empire, which lay in the historic background both of Japan and of China. In fact, in the mid-seventh century an ambitious plan of reform, the Taikwa Reform, was undertaken in Japan with the express purpose of setting up there a replica of contemporary T'ang institutions.

How different does this render the Japanese ghost empire from others? Not fundamentally different. The T'ang Empire was in so many ways a revival of the Han Empire that the Japanese Empire was probably little affected by the predominantly indirect manner of its derivation. In particular, no dilution of the strong, fully civilized quality of the exemplar was involved, for the T'ang Empire, at least before the rebellion of An Lu-shan, was a larger and stronger political institution than the Han Empire had been. The ultimate relation with the Han Empire did subsist too otherwise than through the T'ang Empire. The earliest persistent Chinese influence on Japan goes back indeed to Han times: it had been exercised through the Han colony established in Korea in the first century A.D. Another mode of the relation is found, not in externals, but in the fundamental matter of Confucian doctrine which lies at the basis of all Sinic institutions: the Japanese for centuries relied mainly upon the Han commentaries on Confucianism, rather than on those of the T'ang,[15] in their attempts to assimilate it.

The most significant thing about the Japanese in their pre-feudal

[15] G. Sansom, *Japan: A Short Cultural History* (London, 1931), pp. 225-227. The Han commentaries gave an "orthodox" version of Confucianism which the T'ang writings did not.

and their long feudal age is that these attempts were failures: they could neither assimilate Confucianism nor create a real empire to embody it. That they had the contemporary T'ang Empire, which carried for them the whole prestige of tradition, to copy did not render them any better able to create a true empire than the Europeans were with the small and rather secondary Byzantine Empire. The Japanese and the Europeans, each with some sort of contemporary model, could do no better than the Mesopotamians and the Chinese of Chou times without any. All of them produced only ghosts. The mode of derivation does not seem to have affected their solidity.[16]

Finally on the subject of foregoing empires comes the most important single problem of them all, that of the nature of the polity or polities which preceded the Chou regime in China. It is well to say at the outset that there is at present no solution for this problem. There are opinions, two at least, but it cannot be too strongly emphasized that all judgments based on presently available data are speculative. Those data are very few and somewhat uncertain, whereas there remains a source of new data which has as yet been only slightly used. This is the archaeological resources of the Yellow River Valley. Excavation which has been done is little compared with what can be done there, and until the valley has been dug over as systematically as, say, Mesopotamia, no opinion about the early history of China is worth much. It is to be remembered that before 1920 the history of India was thought to begin with the invasion of Aryan-speaking peoples some time in the latter part of the second millennium B.C. Since the work of Marshall Mackay, Majumdar, and others in the Indus Valley it is clear that i began at the latest about 3000 B.C., probably nearer 4000 B.C., and that th earliest chapter runs fairly closely parallel with the history of ancien Mesopotamia and Egypt. In almost any kind of a general study excep the present one there would be much to be said for ending inquiry int the early chapter of Chinese history which precedes the possibly feuda age right here. Our comparative aim compels a review of available data however, for we must try to get what idea we can as to whether great empire necessarily precedes a feudal society or not.

The polity which preceded the Chou polity in China was the Shan polity whose dates were c.1500-1000 B.C.[17] If there was an empire befor

[16] For further consideration of ghost and more solid re-creations of empire, s pp. 254-256 below.

[17] The traditional dates are 1765-1123 B.C., but these are known to be a litt too high.

feudal times in China, then, it presumably existed in Shang times—I shall henceforward use the term feudal of Chou China without prejudice to the question whether it deviated at all from true feudal type. The leading evidence for the character of the Shang state is found in two portions of the *Shu Ching*,[18] one of those most difficult ancient documents on which, together with meager archaeological evidence, the early history of China is so shakily founded; the portions are the *To Shih* (The Numerous Officers) and the *To Fang* (The Numerous Regions).[19] It cannot be said for certain that these books are genuine, but I rely on the opinion of Professor H. G. Creel that they are,[20] and use them as genuine below. The books are exhortations addressed by the Duke of Chou, with whom we are already acquainted, to the Shang people after the Chou conquest urging the Shang people to accept the Chou regime. The exhortations embody the doctrine of the Decree of Heaven (T'ien Ming), afterwards developed into classical political theory by Mencius. According to that doctrine, Heaven selected the ruler for his virtues and he and his descendants then ruled until and unless one of them displayed such vice that Heaven would "change the Decree"; Heaven did this by revealing to another person, one of transcendent virtue, that he was to take the place of the evil ruler; thus a new dynasty was installed. The Duke of Chou, of course, so explained the overthrow of the Shang by the Chou, and included in his argument the point that T'ang the Victorious, one of the early rulers of the Shang house, had similarly overthrown a degenerate ruler of the house of Hsia, the predecessors of the Shang. Since there is no doubt that the Duke of Chou was in process of building up an empire, his arguments plainly require that the Shang monarchs had ruled over an empire at some time before the Chou conquest.

Mr. Creel has made a study of these portions of the *Shu Ching* and

[18] James Legge, trans., *The Chinese Classics*, III: *The Shoo King* (London, 1865).

[19] pp. 452-463 and 492-507.

[20] I am most grateful to Professor Creel for furnishing me with excerpts from his private notes to this effect. His decision is based on linguistic evidence, namely that the language of the two books resembles that of Western Chou (early Chou) bronze inscriptions. Professor Creel has conferred with Professor Ku Chieh-kang on this question, and Professor Ku is in agreement. (Professor Creel's letter to me of May 26, 1953; in my files.) I draw attention of sinologists to the fact that I do not rely upon *The Great Declaration* (*The Shoo King*, pp. 281-297), and I am grateful both to Professor Creel and to the late Professor J. J. L. Duyvendak for warning me off that book.

other materials which bear upon the problem.[21] He is rightly suspicious of the Duke of Chou's arguments as propaganda, but I am inclined to think that he carries his criticisms a little beyond what the evidence will support. He finds that T'ang had indeed been a conqueror, even that he had conquered the Hsia state, but denies that the Hsia had ruled over an empire or that T'ang by his conquest of Hsia had acquired that empire.[22] It may be, as Creel argues, that the Duke, or some adviser, knowingly inflated the tale about T'ang's conquests, but it does not follow necessarily that it was "fiction that the wide empire, embracing many tribes and states . . . had actually been in existence for centuries or millennia," still less that this "fiction" "was dreamed of for the first time by the Chou chieftains."[23] Surely, propaganda is of much more use if it is plausible than if it is not, and an appeal in the name of empire would scarcely have been very persuasive if there had not already been in men's minds the knowledge that an empire had existed, and perhaps that in some way it ought to exist. That seems to me a far more likely explanation of this part of the Duke of Chou's speeches than that it was pure invention except for the bare fact that T'ang had conquered Hsia and other states. Perhaps T'ang had not really been the originator of the Shang "empire"; perhaps that dominion or hegemony had come rather gradually into existence, and perhaps the Duke dramatized its origin for his own special purposes. But it seems much more likely that it was in existence when the Chou conquered the Shang than that it had never before been dreamed of, and perhaps still more likely that it had been in existence not very long before the conquest and that recent Shang kings had been losing it.

As a matter of fact, I do not think Creel's general view of the early Chou and previous periods really requires this hypercritical argument, and he has in another place boldly suggested that the Shang state was similar to that of Sargon of Akkad, a union of petty kingdoms and never a centralized empire.[24] It is to be observed that Hu Hou-hsüan's gleanings from the oracle bones support this rather well,[25] and there is besides, as Creel has pointed out, a later tradition supporting the early

[21] *Studies in Early Chinese Culture*, pp. 50-63 and passim.

[22] pp. 97-131. But contrast Lattimore, *Inner Asian Frontiers*, pp. 298-306.

[23] p. 51.

[24] *The Birth of China* (New York, 1937), p. 136. Creel quotes Rostovtzeff a authority for Sargon's empire (*A History of the Ancient World*, I, Oxford, 1926 27).

[25] Above, pp. 51-52.

existence of such a polity.[26] But it is of crucial importance here to consider whether there can have existed at some early time a more or less centralized empire, whose decline and fall led eventually, as in other cases we know, to feudalism. Two authorities have negatived the idea. Maspero, quoted above with approval by Mr. Bodde,[27] says: "Chinese feudalism does not emerge from the decomposition of an antecedent regime more or less strongly centralized."[28] Lattimore says: "There was no process of devolution from a higher but decayed society to combine with the process of evolution from primitive society."[29] Lattimore's opinion is essentially the result of his theory, and I should say that this particular opinion puts more weight upon the theory than it ought to carry. Both Lattimore and Maspero rely upon the idea that agriculture in Chou times remained very simple, but for more than one reason I doubt that.[30]

Against this view there is little but a rather clear indication of decline of the aesthetic culture from late Shang to middle Chou times.[31] That, however, is as much relevant to the issue as the level of agriculture is, and it would seem to upset the general remark made by Lattimore, though it cannot be taken to indicate anything about centralization. As to this, a loosely organized dominion like Sargon's empire can lead on to a centralized state; Sargon's empire was in fact followed after an interval by the empire of the Third Dynasty of Ur, whose first two rulers effectively centralized it. Again, a loosely united dominion may, as we know in a number of cases, occur during the decline of an empire. Hu Hou-hsüan's material could indicate a successor state of that sort

[26] This is contained in the *Shang Sung*, a book of the *Shih Ching*, another of the ancient Chinese documents (James Legge, *The She King; or, The Book of Ancient Poetry*, London, 1876, pp. 384-391). The book is a product of the local Shang state long after the Chou conquest, namely in the seventh century B.C., and is therefore hardly of value as an authority for events before the conquest, though it is an interesting repository of tradition. Cf. Creel, *Studies*, p. 54.

[27] Above, p. 73.

[28] *Revue de l'Institut de Sociologie*, XVI (1936), 68: *Mélanges posthumes*, III (Paris, 1950), 144.

[29] *Inner Asian Frontiers*, p. 370.

[30] The main reason is that I hold a competing theory of larger generality (see Ch. 3, n. 23 above) which requires a highly developed agriculture in the riverine civilizations from an early time. Also, the "simple" agriculture of Chou times is supposed to have involved exhaustion of one set of fields after a few years and preparation of a new set by burning off the brush, but now Bodde reports that the word in the Shang inscriptions which had been thought to refer to this "fire farming" is conclusively shown to refer to burning over the fields as a preparation for hunting; see above, p. 65 and n. 25 on the same page.

[31] Below, p. 373.

just as well as a state which had never been centralized. But these are mere possibilities.

Chinese tradition is that the "empires" of the Chou, the Shang, and the Hsia were a series of empires as solid, civilized, and powerful as the empires of the Han, the T'ang, the Sung, and the rest of the dynasties. There seem at the moment to be reasons for rejecting this idea, but they are mainly negative reasons, and I am not quite satisfied that Chinese tradition is to be disposed of by ingenious theories and a dead minimum of solid evidence. It is worth remembering that up till 1928, when the digging at Anyang began, the pundits pooh-poohed the idea that "Shang vases" could date from so early a time as the Shang period; they must be of Han date. But Shang vases were then dug up in the Shang remains at Anyang. My guess, for the moment, is that of Creel when he compares the Shang regime with Sargon's regime as a loose federation of petty kingdoms with the Shang king as suzerain. But it is necessary to maintain a sense of proportion about "knowledge" of this sort. It is better than nothing perhaps, but not much better.

The failure of information about early Chinese history is a great pity because it prevents a satisfactory working generalization about the antecedents of feudalism. We cannot get much further than the observation made in the second paragraph of this chapter, that feudalism is a political system which may follow upon the disintegration of a flimsy state, or of a congeries of such states, ruled through some sort of functionaries by a central authority.[32]

Our ignorance of what must precede the flimsy state or states leaves one of the most important questions about the place of feudalism in history with, at best, two alternative answers. If a true empire, centrally ruled by an effective officialdom and with a highly developed civilization, must always precede the flimsy state, then feudalism is a phenomenon which may occur in the general course of history between phases —cycles, we may call them[33]—of high civilization; feudalism could thus have no place at the origins of civilized societies, for those societies did not spring, fully developed with centralized empires, from the head

[32] Above, p. 236.

[33] Such are: Mesopotamia from origins to the decline after the Third Dynasty of Ur; and from the latter juncture to the decline towards the end of the Achaemenian Empire; Egypt from origins to the decline between the Fifth and Twelfth Dynasties; and from the latter juncture to the decline of the Nineteenth Dynasty; etc. No mechanism, or other special doctrine, is implied in the use of the word cycle; for full explanation of the use see pp. 364-365 and n. 1 on p. 365.

of Jove. If, on the contrary, feudalism can follow upon the disintegration of flimsy states which themselves have been brought together on a basis of groups of primitive societies, then feudalism could be a vital stage in the development of civilized out of primitive societies, and its place in history would be a very different one. No answer to this large question has been found in this study. A few more data, scattered and some of them obscure, will be turned up, and the question will be considered as fully as is profitable in the concluding chapter.[34]

[34] Below, pp. 374-383.

5. AN ALTERNATIVE TO FEUDALISM

THE assumption which ended the last chapter requires that feudalism, during the main course of history, follows the disintegration of a great empire. But that does not mean that the disintegration of an empire must always lead on to feudalism. As a matter of fact, doubts have already arisen as to the extension of feudalism in Mesopotamia after Hammurabi: if it be granted that Hatti and perhaps Urartu and Assyria had a feudal period, the probability is that Babylonia, the old civilized center of the society, did not. Europe seems to have had a feudal period everywhere, but not everywhere at the same time. Nor was all of Western Europe feudalized to the same extent; in Germany many non-feudal institutions remained throughout the feudal period, and in most of Italy feudalism was but a thin and temporary veneer.[1]

What developed in China after the fall of the Han Empire was certainly not a feudal regime by the definition of feudalism used here. Yet we have found that the early Japanese Empire was a ghost of the Chinese Empire and that Japanese feudalism was something which followed failure to create a Sinic type of civilized polity in Japan. In China itself, though nothing like true feudalism was ever realized in the period after Han times, certain minor feudalistic tendencies are discernible for a time and then followed a new empire which was in many respects the old empire restored; this was the T'ang Empire. If, therefore, the whole Chinese world be considered together during this period, it may be said that some of it, Japan for example, was very fully feudalized, while the rest of it was feudalized very little and only for a short time. Hence, as we have already seen, the whole Chines world of the period is comparable with the whole European worl after the fall of the Roman Empire. The comparison exists even between the Chinese and the Western European worlds, but it is close if Byzantium be included in Europe, as it obviously ought to be if the two things compared are both to be made as inclusive as possible. Th comparison then shows a difference in degree: a large Chinese territor —China proper—in which feudalism virtually did not occur, and relatively small European territory—Byzantium and parts of Italy— in which it did not; and, conversely, probably rather a small Chines

[1] We do not know whether Chou China was equally feudalized everywher but we do not know either whether the Chou regime followed a great empire s that Chou China cannot be useful in the present discussion.

territory—Japan, Korea, perhaps nowhere else[2]—in which feudalization did occur and a rather large European territory in which it did; in both worlds ghost empires arose in the feudalized territory and real empires in the territory not feudalized.

There is one more case which enters usefully into this comparison. This is Egypt between the Fifth and Twelfth Dynasties, after the "Old Kingdom." The Old Kingdom was, in fact, an empire, but its disintegration was not followed anywhere in Egypt by feudal developments and a ghost empire; instead there followed after a relatively short period of disintegration a new empire, that of the Eleventh and Twelfth Dynasties, as real an empire as the T'ang Empire in China and as the Byzantine Empire in Europe. But there were regions nearby Egypt in which there may have been feudalization and certainly there were nomads and perhaps other barbarians.[3] These are Palestine-Syria, Libya and Upper Nubia, which belonged then to the Egyptian society just as Japan, Korea, and other regions belonged to the Chinese society from the time of the Han Empire; that is to say, Egyptian culture had spread to Palestine-Syria, Libya, and Upper Nubia, as Chinese culture had spread to Korea and Japan. The spread of the culture is a feature of all these transitions from an old empire either to a new empire or to a feudal regime, and it occurred throughout the periods in question, beginning before the fall of the old empire.[4] We have already seen its dynamics in operation in Europe and Japan in proto-feudal and feudal times.[5]

When great empires break down it naturally becomes the aim of statesmen to restore them. The recollection of the good old days when the empire still stood becomes strong. To the extent that they have been unsuccessful feudalism has ultimately arisen, being the last resort for holding the society together, but so great has the reputation of the empire been that in feudal societies a ghost empire is maintained in the belief that it is necessary or right that an empire should exist. There are thus two alternatives for a civilized society whose political edifice breaks

[2] Possibly territories in Manchuria, Tibet, and Indo-China also, but I hardly think so.

[3] N. Glueck, "The Civilization of the Moabites," *American Journal of Archaeology*, XXXVIII (1934), 212-218; W. F. Albright, "The Excavation of Tell Beit Mirsim, II: The Bronze Age," *Annual of the American Schools of Oriental Research*, XVII (1936-1937), 16; N. Glueck, "Explorations in Eastern Palestine, III," *Annual of the American Schools of Oriental Research*, XVII-XIX (1937-1939), 90-92, 268-269.

[4] Cf. Toynbee, *A Study of History*, III, 128ff.

[5] Ch. 2, pp. 207-211, above.

down, restoration of the edifice and feudalism—and we find no true compromise between them, no third, middle type.[6] In all cases the culture has spread to new peoples during these transitions, and the restored empire has taken in some of the new peoples as well as all the old, but, wherever any of the new peoples have been left out, there feudalism and a ghost empire have arisen. We do not know of a society entirely without a restored real empire unless we choose arbitrarily to say, for example, that there had been an empire in Shang China which was not restored in its reality, or, equally arbitrarily, that the Western society and the Byzantine society were entirely separate and distinct. It would be not only arbitrary, however, but actually erroneous to separate the two latter in this connection, for in fact they both succeeded to the Roman Empire. Similarly, T'ang China, Japan, Korea, and other territories all succeeded to the Han Empire, all later Mesopotamia succeeded to the Empire of the Third Dynasty of Ur, and all of Egypt, Palestine-Syria, Libya, and Nubia to the empire of the First to Sixth Dynasties.[7]

But it has quite usually been said that Egypt from the Fifth Dynasty to the Twelfth, China from the Han to the T'ang Dynasty, and early Byzantium were all feudalized. It must now therefore be shown, in justification of statements made above, that they were not. The contrast between the process of feudalization and the process of restoration of the empire will be amplified in the course of the demonstration.

Feudalization is not a simple process which depends upon one causal factor to the exclusion of all others for its realization. The earliest constructive phenomenon in the disintegration of an empire is the emer-

[6] Whether there was a middle type must be considered again for the case of Iran, but it will be decided that Iran was not such a type; see p. 342 below. If there were such things as "city-feudalities" at times after the breakdown of empires, it is likely that they varied only in a minor way from true feudalities. For city-feudalities, see pp. 234-235 above and pp. 378-383 below.

[7] Neighboring social-political formations are never wholly separate; it is of the nature of human society that it is always continuous geographically even when its parts actually seek to break connections, as in the extreme case of separate sovereign nations. Nevertheless, processes of development—of growth and decline—unquestionably cohere about certain centers and become tenuous as they extend away from their nuclear areas. The student must, therefore, proceed pragmatically. It is perfectly correct to limit study to one nation provided that the matters studied really occurred substantially within the boundaries of the nation. It is equally legitimate to study China and Japan, Byzantium and Western Europe as separate social entities if the matters studied were confined in the main within those entities. But the present matter is not one in which they were respectively separate.

gence of the great local magnate with land and a private army and other dependents. There is then the barbarian with his war-band. He plays a vital part in feudalization, and yet his appearance is no guarantee that feudalism will follow. If the barbarian leader and his war-band become largely merged as types with the great local magnate and his dependents, then feudalization is advancing, but it still may never be achieved. The old empire must fall utterly to pieces, its administrative machine survive in nothing but ineffective vestiges, and the local magnate, having acquired certain important attributes of the barbarian leader, must have become the only effective government before there is true feudalism. This last and crucial part of the process of feudalization occurs in two stages, the proto-feudal stage, when the local magnate has been brought to the aid of the old political system, and the early feudal stage, marked by the emergence of the elemental strong fief and its lord. Let us search for the local magnate, the barbarians, the utter collapse of the old empire, the proto-feudal polity, and the elemental strong fief in Egypt, China, and Byzantium in the periods in question.

The great local magnate appeared early, as is usual, in all three societies. In Egypt he was the nomarch, ruler of those ancient local divisions in Egypt called nomes. Nomarchs had been appointive, salaried officials, but under the Fifth Dynasty, especially in Upper and Middle Egypt (the Valley as distinct from the Delta), they entered on the career which led ultimately to their becoming hereditary lords of their nomes, having many of the powers the central government had once had over them: they gained large immunities. In China, characteristically, the great magnates were members of clans—the extended Chinese family—which acquired large landed establishments in the south with dependents, the *k'o*, who were probably about like serfs. The families of magnates got control of local offices on a class basis, but the central government still retained some powers, more than it did in Egypt, and there was no rounding off of local territorial units. Much of the southern country of China was newly acquired, and it could have no venerable ancient local units such as Egypt had. The great magnate in the late Roman Empire is well known. In the east he was the *dynatos*, and it is thought by some that his estate, the *latifundium*, was a Hellenistic institution which spread from the east to the west of the empire. There were plenty of ancient administrative divisions in the Byzantine end of the Roman Empire, but, unlike the Egyptian ones, they were falling into uselessness and were being replaced by new ones constructed by the central government and closely controlled by it. There was only occasional approximation of the estates of the *dynatoi* to local government units, those estates being of the same general type as the estates of the Chinese families. The Byzantine government was, however, stronger through the transition period than the Chinese or the Egyptian.

The Balkan territories of Byzantium were flooded with barbarians of many kinds. The early ones, Goths, Gepids, and Alans, the government managed to get rid of, passing them on to the West where they had interesting careers. The later ones came to stay. They were mostly Slavs, who probably changed the ethnic basis of the Balkan regions largely. They even passed on to a few regions in Asia Minor, where they formed a new element. The Bulgars arrived as conquerors and played a part which will be considered below. It is to be noted that it was not the Balkan Peninsula in which the *dynatoi* were really important; Asia Minor and parts beyond were their stronghold—Asia Minor alone during most of Byzantine history since the parts beyond were soon lost to Islam. In Egypt, Asiatic tribesmen infiltrated into the Delta and settled down there. Possibly some of their leaders usurped Pharaonic dignities, but the best authorities do not regard the irruptions as anything very formidable; Wilson suggests that they may have constituted a "police problem" for the pharaohs ruling then from Heracleopolis.[8] On the other hand, it was, as remarked above, in the Valley mainly that nomarchs set themselves up as powerful local lords. In China, while the great families were established chiefly in the south, the barbarians entered in the north. There they were far more than a police problem: they did become the government, setting up dynasties, some of which were ephemeral and some fairly lasting. But they did not usually try for long to alter the established pattern of Chinese life; on the contrary, they were absorbed into it, as the Asiatics were absorbed into the Egyptian way of life.

The repeated pattern of barbarian intrusion in one region and ris of local magnates in another is certainly significant, and it may not b wrong to say that, since the barbarians and the magnates did not com intimately enough into contact, the usual feudalistic merging of th two types could not follow. In Egypt and China, however, there wer also other barbarians, for both societies expanded southward and too in barbarians *in situ*. These became subjects and dependents respectivel of nomarchs and of Chinese families, but did not anywhere constitut

[8] John A. Wilson, *The Burden of Egypt* (Chicago, 1951), p. 106.

the whole base of the social structure, for Egyptian and Chinese peasants entered the respective new southern regions also.[9] The humble barbarians of the south, like the formidable ones of the north, were soon absorbed, becoming Egyptianized or Sinified. On the whole, therefore, it would seem safest to conclude that another factor besides that of insufficient contact between local magnates and barbarians was in operation in all three cases to forestall feudalization; that factor indeed probably prevented sufficient contact between barbarians and local magnates as a part of its forestallment of feudalization. There is no doubt that this other factor was the surviving vigor of the old culture, whether expressed through political or other processes.[10]

Thus, in Byzantium it did not matter that barbarian war-bands appeared in the service of the *dynatoi*; the imperial government could even let its own paid forces dwindle and hire the war-bands of the *dynatoi* to fight for it without ultimately collapsing before them, while the *dynatoi* themselves and their entourages remained conspicuously of the Latinized Greek culture—just as much as the nomarchs remained of Egyptian culture. Neither was it of avail to the Tartar and other invaders of north China to seek to keep their barbarian organization and culture.[11] In no case in which they did so did their rule last for more than decades; to survive in authority they had to become Sinified. In short, in all three cases barbarian habits and ethics either had to be abandoned or had to take a very minor place subordinate to habits and

[9] In both cases a part of the southern territory was old territory without barbarians, but this made no appreciable difference to the social-political pattern.

[10] For the other processes, cf. pp. 366ff. below. Why societies and their cultures sometimes have more power of recovery than at other times is the most difficult problem in history. It has been known to scholars ever since Gibbon began investigation of the reasons for the fall of the Roman Empire. Since the publication of Mr. Kroeber's *Configurations of Culture Growth* (Berkeley, 1944), I have felt convinced that questions of the vigor of culture are real questions. The answer given in that book is in terms of exhaustion of pattern. Although the answer leads to the further question as to what exhausts a culture pattern, I think the pattern is shown to be a reality.

[11] Their organization and culture were nomadic, and nomadic organization may be defined as a combination of the characteristic war-band organization of the frontier of a civilized society with a special herding practice and usually other, minor practices suited to steppe physical conditions. This is no surprise in view of the origin of nomadism on the frontier of the civilized society of China; Lattimore's account of this (*Inner Asian Frontiers*, pp. 53-70, 326-334) should be compared with Chadwick's account of the rise of the war-bands of the Teutonic and Greek heroic ages (*The Heroic Age*, pp. 432-463). Hence invasion by nomads has much the same effect in civilized societies as invasion by barbarians; nomads are barbarians within the particular meaning of the word used here.

ethics of the old society and government. Proto-feudal conditions were never approached even remotely in Egypt or China. In Byzantium the state's reliance on the private forces of the *dynatoi* constitutes an approach to proto-feudal conditions, as does its use of the *dynatoi* for a few administrative purposes, but the essential proto-feudal nexus was lacking, for the *dynatoi* never became vassals of the emperor. The empire never needed the special support feudal vassalage can give; its bureaucracy remained effective enough without that.

Since no proto-feudal stage was reached in any of the three societies, there was no subsequent struggle leading to the emergence of strong fiefs. The theory of Jacques Pirenne, that the Egyptian nomes were formed into fiefs *pari passu* with the Pharaoh's loss of power[12] mistakes the very nature of feudalism. Prolonged disorder and the virtually complete dissolution of the old government are required before the elemental strong fief is formed—or else some other process equivalent would presumably be required, and Pirenne offers no suggestion whatever of anything we could consider equivalent. Neither in Egypt, nor in the other two societies did the old administration break down more than temporarily, and in Egypt it was the nomes in which the old administration was most effectively preserved. In China and Byzantium, as has been noticed, no local units of any particular stability were formed. Such units in those two societies, whether private estates or administrative units, remained malleable, to be changed at the will of the central government if they were administrative units, or in accordance with transfer by inheritance or otherwise if they were private estates. The nomes were something exceptional. They may have been fiefs a thousand years before the time here in question and so have acquired their exceptional strength.[13] Again, they were probably connected in origin with irrigation and control of the river, which were vital to the existence of Egypt and had to be done on some sort of cooperative or authoritative basis; the basis of the elemental strong fief would have been quite appropriate. But, if once, long previously, the nomes had been fiefs, they had afterwards shed their feudal quality and had retained

[12] *Histoire des institutions et du droit privé*, I, 248-249 and passim; "La féodalitié en Egypte," *Revue de l'Institut de Sociologie*, Instituts Solvay, Brussels, XVI (1936), 15-36. Pirenne's misunderstanding of the nature of feudalism does not invite confidence in his view of the mechanism of devolution in Fifth and Sixth Dynasty Egypt, whereby the Pharaoh's *imakhu*, a word meaning something like intimates, became priests of the cult of the Pharaoh as a god, and thereby acquired the large local powers they came to dispose of as nomarchs.

[13] Below, pp. 376-377 and n. 16 on p. 377.

only their strength. That very strength rendered them in the age of disintegration between the Fifth and Twelfth Dynasties an effective obstacle to feudalization.

It is now demonstrated that Egypt, China, and Byzantium did not go feudal after the break-up of the Egyptian Old Kingdom, the Han Empire, and the Roman Empire. The regions which did go feudal showed a tendency to divide up into larger territories, such units as northern France, southern France, Burgundy, etc. in Western Europe, and such as Hatti, Mitanni, etc. in Mesopotamia. These divisions were mostly superseded by others at later dates, and the early divisions were unstable and not very conspicuous by comparison with the feudalization process. The non-feudal regions also divided up into large units, three main ones in China, two in Egypt and Byzantium, and that process of political fission was more conspicuous than what went on at the lesser local level, except in Egypt where the nomes were powerful.

The process of fission followed physiography, ethnography, and history, together with special influences of the moment in a few times and places. Byzantium as a whole was one of the states which emerged at the break-up of the Roman Empire, but thereafter, in the seventh century, it split apart, the Bulgar Khanate becoming separate from the Byzantine Empire itself. The loss to Islam of all territory east and south of Asia Minor was not, of course, one of those fissions with which we are here concerned; that was the product of conflict between two separate societies which were not even cognate. The lines of division between Byzantium proper and Bulgaria manifest clearly both ethnographical and physiographical determinants; ethnographically, the Khanate was Bulgar-Slav as against the empire which was Greek-Slav; physiographically, one of the east-west ranges of the Balkans usually marked the fluctuating border.

In China, the three territories which emerged at the downfall of the Han Empire were distinct both physiographically and ethnographically, and although Shu-han, modern Szechuan more or less, did not survive the historical vicissitudes of the period, the other two, the North and the South, did. Divided by the watershed between the Yellow River and the Yangtze valleys, the North took in Tartars and Turks, while the South was engaged in absorbing the barbarians *in situ.* Obviously, the divisions of Egypt were determined more by physiography than by anything else, delta country in the north, valley in the south. The infiltration of Asiatics into the Delta was unimportant, as we have noticed above. Between the Sixth Dynasty and the Eleventh Egypt was for the most part divided between the Theban and the Heracleopolitan states. The frontier lay, however, at Siut, two hundred miles south of the Delta. While it was by no means a fixed frontier, it illustrates rather well how particular circumstances may vary the effects of environment; that the frontier lay so far south is probably in the main the measure of the relative strength of the Delta and the Valley when the Delta was united. The Delta was not always united, however. It was probably disunity there which enabled the Eleventh Dynasty, from the southern Valley, to reunite the whole country by force of arms. Had that failed, there might have been, not two states, but three or even more, as there possibly had been for a short time at the breakdown of empire in the time of the Sixth Dynasty.

The short-lived states at the breakdown of the rule of the Sixth Dynasty were, however, of little significance, and the same is true of some short-lived states which arose in the North of China when the North broke up in the fourth century. There were small, impermanent states also in the new territories beyond China in Korea and Manchuria, and the same is true of Palestine-Syria beyond Egypt. Korea and Japan, however, were before long formed into single states as coherent as the two main Chinese states themselves, and as clearly divided from one another physiographically. This does not seem to have happened until a later era in Palestine-Syria, for the city-monarchies, like Kadesh, which appeared in inland Syria were the products of penetration there of Mesopotamian culture which began to crowd out Egyptian.

These fairly durable states—North China, South China, Shu-han perhaps, Korea and Japan, the Delta and the Valley in Egypt, the Byzantine Empire and the Bulgar Khanate—are to be considered as nations. Indeed, the physiographic, ethnographic, historical, and other lines of division between them will serve as a part of the main means for defining what a nation is.[14] These nations are different in certain important ways from the nations which eventually arise in territory which has gone feudal, but both should be called nations, for they are similarly determined geographically and in certain other ways. One of those ways is in the imitation by their rulers of the style of emperors and, in some cases, the imitation in the national government of the methods of imperial government. Thus in feudal Europe kings copied the titles and actual powers of the Holy Roman Emperor, or even those

[14] See also pp. 273-274 below.

of the Roman Emperor himself together with Roman modes of government so far as those could be seen in Roman law. Rulers of the various nations of China proper carried on the government and assumed the dignities of the Chinese Emperor. In the same way the Bulgar Khan acquired powers and dignities the Byzantine Emperor had. The kingdoms of the regions which went feudal did not emerge until late feudal times or later. It is not that these nations were not always there potentially, but rather that feudal development for a long time prevented their taking form. That matter will be examined in the next chapter.

Certain features of the actual reintegration of the three empires we have been studying are instructive for their likeness or unlikeness to developments in feudal regimes.

The new Chinese Empire, as it emerged, presents the sharpest of contrasts with a feudal regime. For a century the T'ang government undertook a powerful centralization,[15] and there was even a relatively strong development of law,[16] characteristic only of the most energetic governments China has had. The practice of redistributing and equalizing peasant landholding,[17] which had arisen soon after the downfall of the Han, may quite possibly have been used against the great families. Whether it was or not, it is evidence of vigor in Chinese governments, both the T'ang government and earlier ones. The T'ang regime was fairly similar to the Han regime, but there were differences. One was the closer reliance of the T'ang upon the army: the military *tu-tu* supervised or even possibly conducted local civil government on the frontiers and in strategic regions of the interior of the empire.[18] This has its significance for comparison with feudal rule, which is also military. We shall return to it shortly.

The Byzantine case exhibits the restoration of the empire most clearly as alternative to feudalization, for, not only did Byzantium face police problems like those in regions which went feudal, but the bifurcation

[15] R. des Rotours, "Les grands fonctionnaires des provinces en Chine sous la dynastie des T'ang," *T'oung Pao*, XXV (1927), 220; *idem*, *Traité des fonctionnaires et traité de l'armée traduits de la nouvelle histoire des T'ang* (Chap. XLVI-L), I (Leyden, 1947), lxvii-lxxi.

[16] K. Bünger, *Quellen zur Rechtsgeschichte der T'ang-Zeit* (Peiping, 1946), Monumenta Serica, Monograph II. This law was essentially criminal law—"punishments," as the Chinese call it.

[17] Des Rotours, *T'oung Pao*, XXV, 321-323.

[18] Des Rotours, *T'oung Pao*, XXV, 235; *Traité des fonctionnaires*, II (Leyden, 1948), 684, n. 2; 707, n. 2.

of the Roman Empire into East and West actually offers the student the contrast of two developments from the same early disintegration, the one to a feudal system, the other to reconstitution of the empire. The first sign of new life in the East came with the financial reforms of Anastasius I at the turn of the fifth and sixth centuries. It was a long time since the imperial government had been able to relieve its subjects' condition by improvements in the system of taxation, and it looks as if this had been made possible when the government of Constantinople ceased to be responsible for the West. At any rate, one result of Anastasius's reforms was that town curials were released from the burden of collecting and making good the land tax of their districts, which had been an extreme measure by which Aurelian, Diocletian, and Constantine had sought to keep the crazy structure of the whole empire together.[19]

With the reign of Justinian other significant events followed. Apart from his momentary restoration of the whole empire, which will be considered below, his ferocious attack upon the *dynatoi* and certain methods he used in his renewed government were important for the future. While great magnates went from strength to strength in the West and eventually became feudal, in the East Justinian attempted to destroy their power. Many of his successors continued the policy so that in the seventh and eighth centuries the magnates were for the time somewhat effaced. On the positive side there was the development o the new structure of the empire, later called the theme system. It wa a military system—more clearly so than the T'ang system in China— and it was almost certainly begun by Justinian's practice of giving th provinces of the empire, usually before they had been fully recon quered, into the hands of *magistri militum* and subordinating the civi administration to them. At the end of the sixth century the exarchate of Ravenna and Carthage were organized on this basis, and the em peror Heraclius, after his final victory over Persia, generalized th organization throughout the empire. Thereafter every dynasty unt and including the Macedonian Dynasty added something to this cha acteristic frame of the rejuvenated imperial structure.[20] It is scarcel too much to say that the theme system *was* the Byzantine Empire.

[19] J. B. Bury, *History of the Later Roman Empire*, I (London, 1923), 441-44 It is possible that curials were not completely released from their burden, or th there was a partial return to the old system later, but at least a part of wh Anastasius did was permanent.

[20] A. A. Vasiliev, *History of the Byzantine Empire*, I (Madison, 1928), 275-27

This militarized government served some of the crucial purposes of feudalism. From Justinian to Heraclius and spasmodically thereafter Byzantium was beset by enemies, internal and external. Slavs, Bulgars, and uprooted natives constituted an internal police problem of the very greatest magnitude; Persians and then Arabs assailed the empire from the southeast. Whereas in feudal societies such dangers were met by the local magnate and his retainers, Byzantium met them with the full resources of a militarized imperial state. A fundamental feature of the system was the peasant soldier, settled on his *stratiotikon ktēma*, his "soldier's property," which he held in return for military service and could not alienate. The system is comparable to the old Roman frontier settlements, but it became general throughout the empire in Byzantium. It has sometimes been described as feudal, but it was not that. Like feudalism, it was a way of making the land yield fighting men a-plenty, but, unlike feudalism, it was a way by which a strong bureaucratic empire could make the land do so, and not one by which political authority fell into the hands of local magnates.

So viewed, the strength of the Byzantine Empire is impressive, and so is that of the restored Chinese Empire. Nevertheless, there was one task too great for either of them to accomplish. The task was the completion of the unification of the territory of the society, greatly enlarged as it was in both cases by the spread of the high culture to new peoples during and after the time of the old empire. The Chinese accomplishment in this matter was much greater than the Byzantine, for the Sui and T'ang empires exceeded the Han quite largely in extent, and it was the lesser part of the territory of Sinic culture, all of it newly civilized, which was left out of the re-unification. In Europe, on the contrary, the major part was left out, and that included not merely newly civilized country, but even the old center of the empire, Rome, and all the western territories except parts of Sicily and Italy.

The magnitude of the efforts exerted by both new regimes to extend their authority to the whole civilized society is impressive. That in Europe was the heroic effort of Justinian, which in the end was a disaster, bringing back permanently under Byzantine rule only Sicily and those parts of Italy mentioned above. Although the success of the effort in China was much greater than in Europe, the actual effort required was less; a far larger part of China than of Europe tended to cohere.

05-306, 423-426; II (Madison, 1929), 147-158, 237-241; cf. C. Diehl, trans. G. B. ves, *History of the Byzantine Empire* (Princeton, 1925), pp. 46-50.

Yet in China also there came a point at which resistance to incorporation in the empire became formidable, and the attempt to break the resistance led to a disaster. Yang Ti, second Sui emperor, sought to add to his predecessor's exploits the conquest of Korea. He failed so disastrously that the re-unification already accomplished was momentarily undone, the Sui fell, and authority passed to the T'ang Dynasty which repeated the unification of Yang Chien, first Sui emperor. This was not the end of all attempts to extend the territory of the T'ang empire, and when, rather more than a half century later, the state of Silla unified Korea, it did so with the aid of T'ang troops, and Korea became nominally a dependency of China.

It is unfortunate that we are in doubt about the corresponding achievement of the restored Egyptian Empire. To be sure, the uncertainty is only a matter of date and details: the Twelfth Dynasty, which accomplished the main restoration, may later have gone on to conquer Palestine and Syria,[21] but, whether it did so or not, the Eighteenth Dynasty did. Hence, although it did not last as long, the Egyptian achievement in restoring the empire was, for a time, greater than either the Chinese or the Byzantine.[22]

The main work of restoration in Egypt had been done differently from the way in which it was done in China and in Byzantium. It was not done by militarizing administration; instead, there was a relatively simple process, conducted apparently by civil means, of withdrawal of the independent powers of the nomarchs. But the restoration, though a simple process administratively, was not an easy one: there was constant resistance to it, and it is probably a good guess[23] that the Eleventh Dynasty was overthrown and replaced by the Twelfth because the

[21] For an affirmative view of this: W. F. Albright, "New Egyptian Data on Palestine in the Patriarchal Age," *Bulletin of the American Schools of Oriental Research*, No. 81 (February 1941), pp. 16-21; Albright, "The Land of Damascus between 1850 and 1750 B.C.," *Bulletin of the American Schools of Oriental Research*, No. 83 (October 1941), pp. 30-36; J. A. Wilson, "The Egyptian Middle Kingdom at Megiddo," *American Journal of Semitic Languages and Literatures* LVIII (1941), 225-236. But Wilson gives a negative view ten years later: *The Burden of Egypt*, pp. 134, 136.

[22] The collapse of Egypt before the Hyksos, which interrupted Egyptian incorporation of Syria-Palestine if the Twelfth Dynasty conquered that territory and preceded it if the Twelfth Dynasty did not, suggests the limits of the restored regime's strength, but this has not great significance because the military strength of the Hyksos was that of Mesopotamia so that its application against Egypt means nothing in purely Egyptian terms.

[23] By Drioton and Vandier (*Les peuples de l'orient Méditerranéen*: II. *L'Egypte* Paris, 1938, pp. 247-248).

Eleventh sought to suppress nomarchic power too drastically. The Twelfth, on the other hand, dragged the process out until the reign of Senusert III, a period of over a century. It is obvious that the special character of the nomes was the reason for the slow, cautious policy, so different from policy in China and Byzantium. There is a striking resemblance between this Egyptian policy and the policy of certain late feudal monarchies, the French monarchy for example. As we shall see in the next chapter, these gradually and cunningly got the better of their great feudatories largely by legal and administrative means. However obviously unfeudal the acquisition of power by nomarchs under the Fifth and Sixth Dynasties, then, a scholar who knew nothing about that could be forgiven for thinking he had to do with a late feudal or post-feudal regime under the Twelfth Dynasty. There is no contrast here, but a marked resemblance.

Was there, then, any real similarity between these three restored empires? On the surface, not much between Egypt and the other two, for Egyptian government was civilian government and Byzantine government and Chinese government were militarized. Even between Byzantine and Chinese there was a difference of degree of militarization. But these differences are not fundamental. In their imperial expansiveness all three empires were alike, and the differing degree of success each had is accounted for at least as much by external causes as by internal. The new Chinese and Egyptian empires were larger than the old to a similar extent and the newly incorporated lands were similarly related in the two cases to the old lands. That Egypt conquered Syria-Palestine may have been a reaction against the Hyksos conquest of Egypt if the first Egyptian conquest of Syria-Palestine was that of the Eighteenth Dynasty;[24] China, which did not conquer Korea and Japan, was never itself threatened with conquest from those countries. Byzantium, beset by enemies on all sides and inundated with an almost overwhelming flood of barbarians, may well have been unable, for reasons of sheer physical force, to equal the expansion of China and and Egypt; it is clear that Byzantium would have incorporated Kievan Russia if it had had the force to do so. Yet the fundamental dualism of Greece and Rome constituted repulsive forces as between the two, which must also be taken into account in judging the lesser expansion

[24] So, among others, Wilson, *The Burden of Egypt*, pp. 166-167. The difference between Egypt and China in this matter is, again, that between a civilized society with a neighboring civilized society pressing on its frontiers and one without.

of Byzantium: Byzantium was Greek, and it was not Roman except in the limited sense that Greece had been Romanized politically.

In spite of the expansiveness of the three new empires, all of them were in danger of local particularist movements, and that fact is quite fundamental to their characters. A century and a half after the restoration in China, a barbarian military man, An Lu-shan, who was in a position to seduce the military officers concerned with local government, raised a calamitous rebellion. After it, military men got control of local territories and the authority of the emperor was greatly damaged. Eventually, the T'ang Dynasty was, in fact, overthrown by a mutiny, and there followed half a century of struggle between military adventurers, many of them barbarians, with their power based in local units of territory. If this was worse than what happened in Egypt and Byzantium, the local magnate nevertheless remained a danger there too. The *dynatoi* were somewhat effaced in the sixth and seventh centuries, but they were still there, and there was a danger that they might get control over the soldiers of the theme system, for they constantly attempted to do so. And in Egypt the nomarch was always to be reckoned with—although the essentially non-military government of Egypt was probably the safest of the three, for Senusert III succeeded in withdrawing the last powers of the nomarchs.

For comparison with feudal polities the particularist tendency of these imperial polities is significant. It is the more so since the origin of the local units was quite different in the three cases, in Egypt the time-honored nome, in Byzantium the estate of the *dynatos* which was not a fixed unit but was an ancient social institution, in China mere *ad hoc* areas hacked out by military adventurers. The basic fief in a feudal society could in origin have any or all of these characters and was bound to have the last. The particularist tendency was, then, common both to the parts of the societies which went feudal and to the parts which did not; it was not because the tendency was absent in the latter that they did not go feudal: the two diverged from a common base in this respect. Feudalism was a necessary resort when the bureaucratic structure became too weak to overcome the particularist tendency. Even in the case of China, in which quite a serious breakdown occurred after the restoration, the prevalence of local powers lasted for only two centuries. Moreover, it was only the last half century of that period in which conditions approached anarchy: before that the later rulers of the T'ang Dynasty succeeded most of the time in holding the state together, even though uneasily, against ambitions of local rulers; afterwards came new restoration by the Sung, and, although there were intrusions from the steppe in later centuries, the frame of empire was never seriously shaken again between the tenth century and the twentieth. The other great empires did not last as long, but their endurance was impressive also. The Egyptian Empire did not always hold Palestine-Syria, but it lasted in all the Nile Valley just under a thousand years and then began to disintegrate slowly of its own intrinsic degeneration. The Byzantine Empire lasted about as long from the time of Anastasius I until it was brought to an end by conquest.

6. LATER FEUDALISM AND THE NATIONS

THE political evolution of the societies we have been dealing with in this book has in general followed much the same course: it has moved from the collapse of an old empire to the establishment of a new empire. Perhaps there is one case, Chou China, without an old empire at the beginning, but, if so, Chou China entered the usual evolutionary course at a fairly early juncture, the one we have called the proto-feudal stage, or a little earlier than that. And there are two cases in which no new empire has yet been established, Western Europe and the present Chinese society, but they each look as if they had reached a stage approaching that of empire.

Between the old empire and the new there were always nations. In the last chapter, we have followed cases of societies, or parts of societies, in which the evolution was simply from the old empire to nations and then to a new empire, which, though usually become larger, was in most ways a re-creation of the old empire. We must now consider the later stages of the evolution of those parts of societies in which disintegration went much further than that and had to be remedied by feudal means—for that is essentially what feudalism does: it takes from the barbarians, who come into, or into contact with, the civilized society during the breakdown of the old empire, a version of the old, primitive in-group formation for defense against out-groups, and through that as means recreates the elemental basis of society, almost as it were *ex nihilo*.

But, if there is really almost nothing then at the basis of society, there is always the recollection of the empire at the top of it, embodied most of the time in the ghost empire—if a ghost may be called a body. Often there are adumbrations of nations too, for, when the old empire breaks down, it usually gives place at first to large units even if it subsequently disintegrates further. Such nations bring no new idea to the society they have not the elemental principle of strength which early fiefs have; neither have they the grand, universalistic principle the empire has—even if they attempt to usurp it. Ghost empire and feudality are left facing each other across the seemingly unbridgeable gulf between localism and universalism: "even while they seemed to blend," says

Bryce, "there remained between the genius of imperialism and that of feudalism a deep and lasting hostility."[1]

How deep it was may be illustrated with the spectacle of an Otto III who moved from the land of German barbarians and established himself in Rome, the imperial city, drew up and installed there a new body of dignitaries for the city, commanded his judges to rule both the city and the world only by Roman law, appointed popes, created kings, and set a policy of return to the past which was not really abandoned until the great disasters which befell the Hohenstaufen emperors two centuries later. Otto was one of those emperors known as "stupor mundi," and the fierce German barons, denizens of that astonished and uncomprehending world, busily seized the land and established themselves on it by feudal means against all comers, including the emperor. The Lombard barons did the same and developed the ambition to have a king of their own, one of themselves, who should not threaten them with subjection to a renovated Roman Empire.

And there was the Emperor Daigo II of Japan who, beginning in pursuit of dynastic ambitions, affected to overthrow the then tottering Kamakura Shogunate and to restore the imperial regime. Here again was an array of ministers seeking to draw the center of power away from the land of the barbarians and back to the imperial city. The result was disaster: the proto-feudal regime finally collapsed; the imperial authority was divided between two claimants, each with his court and dignitaries. They were but puppets: behind them stood the reality, cliques of ambitious barons who pushed their ostensible leaders about for a couple of generations as suited their aims. And their aims were to get the land, which they did by feudal means.

The struggle of feudalism with the ghost of imperialism went to feudalism every time, for the age of resort to feudalism was become one of extreme material simplicity in which the great structures of empire were impossible. But thereafter feudalism gradually developed its own structures, bigger and bigger, better and better fiefs. The method was essentially simple: fiefs got bigger when they were aggregated together, chiefly by hierarchical development of overlordship, and they got better by a twofold process, the withdrawal of power from rear-vassals all the way down the hierarchy, and its redeployment by the paramount lord, who got it, through a growing service of functionaries.

[1] James Bryce, *The Holy Roman Empire*, rev. edn. (London and New York, 1921), p. 130.

Some remarkable structures were built up. In Europe as early as the twelfth century Henry of Anjou got together French territory equal to about half of modern France. To his own patrimony he added the immense fief of Aquitaine by marrying its heiress, and then he acquired Normandy and overlordship of Brittany. Besides all this he had, by interpretation of his mother's claim and by conquest, the English crown. In Japan conquest figured more largely than dynastic marriages and converging inheritance, and the magnates who benefited by it were more often than in Europe upstarts. Neither did the process continue so long in Japan, not much more than a century, as against about three centuries in Europe. In sixteenth-century Japan the size of the agglomerations rose rapidly until it culminated through the conquests of Oda Nobunaga and Toyotomo Hideyoshi almost in the logical limit of a fief covering all Japan. Still more remarkable in some ways was the great agglomeration of the Habsburgs in Europe, for that agglomeration came finally to include two minor kingdoms, Bohemia and Hungary, and even temporarily the kingdom of Spain, together with a mass of counties, duchies, margraviates, principalities, and the Archduchy of Austria.

But discrepancies between quantity and quality tended to arise in the great agglomerative fief. The hierarchy of lordship rendered the dynast at the apex remote from the small vassals at the base, and feudal bonds in chain formation were apt to loosen if only because their combined strength was not more than that of the weakest link. And then the service of functionaries necessary to counterbalance the loosening feudal relations would usually come into conflict with the fief's agglomerative frame. But, if the fief was to remain a feudal structure, its frame must be preserved. Thus the conflict would become endemic and the administration of the fief be inhibited from the necessary development. Vast feudal structures could nevertheless endure for a long time in favorable circumstances, but sufficiently favorable circumstances were not very common, and an alternative to the great fief was needed.

This was the opportunity for growth of the nation. Nations and fiefs are based in part upon the same and in part upon different principles of cohesion. The nation in a feudal society is, in fact, based upon a sort of Hegelian synthesis, a combination and consolidation of opposites. The opposites are the conflicting principles of feudalism and empire, and the period of the nations appears to be, is probably, a necessary stage in a feudal society between the feudal period and the return to empire. Thus the monarch who heads most nations in their earlier da is a paramount feudal lord, but he is also the ordained of heaven, as the emperor is. The principle of national cohesion, then, becomes on the one hand a transmutation of the feudal bond into the personal loyalty of the subject to the monarch and of the monarch to his subjects, and on the other hand the subject's adulation of the monarch as if he were supreme earthly ruler. This is a remarkable convergence of spiritual forces, which together make of these nations the nations *par excellence* of history. They have vastly more cultural individuality and more sheer material power than the nations of non-feudal societies. Their culture includes a political ideology, always distinctive for their society, often distinctive for the particular nation.

These nations are the first strong and stable political units to emerge after the elemental, strong fiefs, and the strength and coherence of nation and fief are akin in that both are in-groups. They are the only two types of in-group in the history of civilized societies.[2] Even though the nations are modelled in important ways upon empires, they show a coherence which empires, not being in-groups, do not show. And the nations vastly excel the great agglomerative fiefs in stability and coherence, for most of the latter are little more than transitional forms. As in-groups, naturally, the nations are in rivalry and armed conflict with one another. Their struggles, in fact, tend to enlarge and increase until they culminate in great and terrible wars, the greatest armed conflicts man has so far experienced. The process of enlargement of those conflicts has a significance of which we must take account below.

Some nations have developed out of great fiefs, but that is not usual. More often nations are formed territorially in a different manner from fiefs. Ordinarily the nation is larger, much larger, than the great fief, and the territorial division of a society into nations is governed by the

[2] Sumner takes note of European nations as in-groups (p. 15). He considers the failure of the medieval Christian church, of Islam, and of certain empires to become in-groups (pp. 15, 503-505), and he shows how the amalgamation of groups leads to syncretism of folkways with those of the group dominant in the amalgamation enjoying the advantage (pp. 115-117), a process which is important in the formation of nations.

Not any or all of this gives warrant for the idea that the nation is some sort of an ultimate achievement as a social and cultural unit, as intended, for example, in this remark: "Europe presents particular nations, constituting a unity in their very nature, and having the absolute tendency to form a state" (G. W. F. Hegel, *The Philosophy of History*, trans. J. Sibree, rev. edn., New York, 1900, p. 400). To me an "absolute tendency to form a state" is either the product of superstition or it is meaningless. Cf. O. Spengler, *Decline of the West*, trans. C. F. Atkinson (New York, 1932), II, 170-186, for an example of the wilder consequences of this kind of thinking.

same large determinants in a feudal as in a non-feudal region. These determinants are physiographic, historic, and ethnographic. Islands and peninsulas are the most obvious physically determined national territories. Seacoasts are one of the common kinds of frontier and large mountain ranges another. In a continental area earlier history usually explains why some mountain ranges, dense forests, desert stretches, etc. form national frontiers, and others do not. History usually explains too why some frontiers run where no physical barrier exists; for example, Babylonia was divided from Assyria along a line which was roughly the northern boundary of the ancient Akkad, one of the original civilized territories of Mesopotamia; what became Assyria had begun as colonial territory in the later days of Akkad. Ethnography alone has probably never determined a frontier, but it frequently strengthen a physical frontier and sometimes ethnic distinctions have been adde to historic distinctions between nations.

These determinants all precede the development of feudalism i time, but cannot become effective in the formation of nations in countr which has been much disintegrated until feudalization has remedie the disintegration. Fiefs, great and small, have usually been constraine within frontiers so determined. But on the rather rare occasions whe such determination was weak or lacking feudal processes could deter mine national territory. Two regions in which this has happene largely are Germany and the North China Plain. In regions of tha kind aggregation of fiefs could determine the main extent of the terr tory, and the actual frontiers would then probably be settled by th formation of "marches." The march is a simple feudal device whereb a baron is given a frontier fief with very broad powers, especiall immunities, on condition of defending it against those on the oth side. Most marches have been mere reinforcements of physically dete mined frontiers, but the Germans used marcher lordships in mediev north Germany actually to conquer and convert to the German, fe dal way of life the Slavs who lay eastward of them. In this case t march overrode ethnic distinctions. It seems likely that in Chou Chin where the great majority of national frontiers ran in the plain, son form of march was used. We know that the lack of any sort of natur barrier was felt there as a danger, for at one period the nations too to fortifying their frontiers with walls.[3]

Nation and fief, then, usually of different origin territorially, found in part upon different political principles, were likely to come into co

[3] Lattimore, *Inner Asian Frontiers of China*, pp. 390, 403-404, 429-430.

flict. The later history of feudalism is concerned with that conflict, the conflict of crown and baronage. But that is not all it is concerned with, for in the political principle the two share, there is a continuity from fief to nation which is in contrast with the discontinuity signalized by the struggles of crown and baronage. Continuity and discontinuity are intimately bound up together since the nations of feudal societies are on one side of their descent feudal. It is, in fact, quite erroneous to see the passage from feudality to nation as a simple transition in which the feudality and all things feudal come to an end and are succeeded by the nation and things national. Perhaps it is true that feudalism is always eradicated eventually as the nation matures, but there have certainly been occasions in which barons won important victories which greatly weakened the monarchy and long postponed the emergence of the strong nation; those are questions for the next chapter. In this chapter the intimate relation of feudalism with nations is the subject. It will be treated in two steps. The first step shows the continuity between the two, the second the discontinuity. Strong though the continuity is, the discontinuity is strong also, often strong enough to manifest itself in revolution.

The continuity from fief to nation is always shown in political forms, but not usually in geography. There is, however, the unusual case of Chou China which, as we have just noticed, occupied chiefly the North China Plain, and whose nations were transformations of some of the larger agglomerated fiefs. That development seems to simplify the whole connection of fief and nation—somewhat delusively, as will appear. The Chou *wang's* power virtually withered away, probably in the eighth century B.C., which left the rulers of the states only nominally his vassals and in effect sovereign princes. In some of the states which thus emerged there were reforms about the seventh century which reduced the power of the nobility, brought local government directly under authority of the central government, and divided civil from military power. These changes were the first steps in elimination of feudalism, and, as they were also steps which strengthened the states and made them begin to look like nations, it would appear that in Chou China the elimination of feudalism and the rise of nations were successive parts of the same transition. Yet some feudal forms survived for a long time, at least in some states. This is shown by the fact that one state, Chin, broke up in the fifth century into three parts, each of them before the break-up a large fief.

It is not of great importance at what time it is said that the states of Chou China ceased to be fiefs and became nations, but, if a time must be chosen, the best would seem to be the eighth or seventh century B.C., when the *wang's* power ceased and the state rulers became in effect sovereign. At that juncture they acquired both strength and independence, and that is the same juncture at which it will be decided below that nations emerged in other societies.[4] Certainly it is an error to think, as has been usual in sinological studies, that the mere existence of distinct states, each with its prince in nominal dependence on the *wang*, in the period from the seventh century to the third constituted a kind of feudalism.

The advent of nationality in Chou China is shown most evidently in ideology, in this case a consciously formulated ideology which sought to mediate and guide the transition from the old society to the new. This is the ideology of the "Hundred Schools" of Chinese thought in which the school of Confucius was the greatest. It is most unusual to find the transition shown primarily in the ideological change, for it is very rarely that the ideological change is so clearly and directly formulated in theory. The formulation in Chou China covered the whole intellectual and aesthetic culture, but it is very significant of what was most important in the age that it was heavily weighted on the ethical and political side. It is, of course, the ethical and political doctrines which concern us here. Among them there is a clear statement of the proper relationship between monarch and subject which was quite evidently a transmutation of that between lord and vassal. It is Confucius' statement: he described the relationship of monarch and subject as one o the three cardinal relationships of society, and approximated it to an other one of the three, that of father and son. From the subject wa required respect and obedience, from the monarch the most auster practice of virtue both as an example to the subject and as a contro over his own actions; control was expanded into severe restraint as caution against abuse of authority. Restraint of authority is a matter o special importance. It witnesses to the fact that government was gettin stronger—the rise of the strong monarchy. It is also important in itsel for it had profound effect upon Chinese polities, a fact which is cor firmed by the diametrical reaction against it to be found in Legalisr

[4] Lattimore was the first, so far as I know, to see that the separate states of late Chou China were nations, comparable with those of Europe; see *Inner Asia Frontiers*, pp. 392-393. For a consideration of similarity and dissimilarity Chinese, European, and other nations, see below, pp. 297-302.

(*Fa chia*), another school of thought: the Legalists advocated instead something like totalitarian despotism, but their influence, while important, was far less profound than that of Confucianism. In our discovery of the emergence of strong monarchy, therefore, it is to be observed that, although Chinese national monarchies emerged strong, the strength of most of them was restrained in application under Confucianist influence. That that restraint was the source of the durability of the Chinese society and of the system of ethics on which it was founded is a plausible thesis, but it cannot be pursued here.[5]

In Germany fief and nation were in most cases geographically continuous as they were in Chou China, and the same is true in a few cases in Italy also. No doubt will arise about this in the case of Brandenburg-Prussia, but it may appear to some scholars unusual to describe other states of the Holy Roman Empire as nations. Certainly, they were nations of a somewhat different sort from the great European nations outside the empire; Brandenburg-Prussia shows the difference by having transformed itself from the one sort into the other. The manner and meaning of the difference will not be considered yet, but will come up in the next chapter when the courses of evolution of the different societies are analyzed comparatively.[6] Meanwhile, it is to be noted that the German states got almost as free in practice of their ghost emperor as the Chinese states did, the German states by the decisions of the Diet of Augsburg in 1555; that it is easier in the German case than in the Chinese to discern the persistence of feudalism in the national institutions —perhaps only because we have more knowledge; and that there was in Germany no doctrine in the least like Confucianism, but, on the contrary, a tendency on the one hand to a rather crude absolutism and on the other to a very crude, reactionary gentleman's particularism.

The other nations of Europe, the great nations, were different. Neither England, nor France, nor any of the other conspicuously feudal nations of the west began its career as a fief, or ever was one in any serious sense.[7] And these nations also show that it is a delusion to de-

[5] I suspect that it has to do with the relatively minor extent of the decline of the society between Han and T'ang, and the comparatively small change in the fundamental character of the culture in the revived society. The actual occurrence of a decline between Han and T'ang I take to be due to independent causes.

[6] See pp. 297-300 below; cf. also pp. 238-239 above.

[7] John's agreement to hold England as a fief of Pope Innocent III was an obviously exceptional, and quite unreasonable, episode, and the English never took his action seriously. The acceptance of the English crown's overlordship by Scotland temporarily and by Gwynedd more or less permanently as a result of

duce from the geographic continuity of fief and nation in Chou China that nationhood is acquired by supersession of feudal with other methods of government: they do this by their thoroughly feudal character at the time when they first emerge into palpable existence with the rise of their strong monarchies. A medieval European king relied always upon his vassals. His ascent to effective power might begin with success in war against some of his vassals. It usually did, and that success might have to be repeated from time to time. But, even when fighting some of his vassals, he was supported by others, and a successful feudal king was able to extend and consolidate his "peace," fighting less and less, and counting more and more on his vassals' loyalty. It paid the vassal to support a king who was doing well for himself in this way, and it got more and more dangerous for the vassal to rebel. Nor is it correct to think that loyalty ensured by fear of punishment was worth little. In the practical world that is precisely the kind of loyalty which is valuable. It had been the basis of the elemental strong fief. The lord of such a fief and the feudal king were alike ruined if they failed to do their respective jobs. Ruin faced the vassals too if they failed in their loyalty—ruin at the hands of the external enemy as much as of their lord in the case of the elemental strong fief, ruin wholly at the hands of the king in the case of the strong monarchy. The strong feudal monarchy embodied, in fact, a transitional political equilibrium between the enduring stability of the elemental strong fief and the enduring stability of the nation.

It was feudal lords who made the earliest non-feudal administrative reforms, the lords of the earlier strong fiefs. There was no discontinuity between the government of fief and of nation, then, when the strong feudal king resorted to similar practices. As had been the case with the reforming feudatory, so with the king, such reforms came in in close connection with feudal reforms, for there was no consciousness of any fundamental difference between the two. But, if there was no discontinuity between the administrative reforms of fief and of nation, there was important novelty in those of the nation. There was novelty in the extent to which national monarchs moved away from feudal practice and in the special devices they invented as they did so. Yet the special devices were always modifications and developments out of practice

Edward I's campaigns might be considered exceptions of greater significance, but neither principality had begun its existence as a fief of the English crown, and the significance is, I think, rather of the approaching unification of the island as a kind of triune nationality than of the building up of an agglomerative fief.

or institutions already in operation in feudal government. In Europe, the most important of these developments were those which brought out of the feudal court, on the one hand more complex bodies of a parliamentary character, and on the other courts of professional lawyers. But the appearance of such bodies as these, in the thirteenth century, was a sign of the passage of leadership from fief to nation, for the feudatories were not able to keep up with the monarchs by inventing similar bodies to develop their fiefs. Preservation of the old framework of the fiefs and sheer conservatism in other ways inhibited the great feudatories from keeping up. Political solidarity, therefore, developed much more on the basis of the nation than of the fiefs; the new sentiment of loyalty of subject to monarch could grow up unobtrusively, but most effectively, in the operation of the new national political organs even though those organs were still largely feudal or of close feudal derivation.

France, Aragon, Castile, and Portugal were monarchies whose early strength was feudally based. Their institutions consequently show the continuity of strong fief and strong monarchy. Anglo Saxon monarchies, Scandinavian monarchies, German monarchies large and small, and monarchies on the eastern fringe of central Europe show it less because they were less feudal. But the Norman conquest of England, which swept away the last Anglo-Saxon monarchy, shows the continuity more forcefully than any other event in history, for England was made, not less feudal, but far more feudal than it had been before by that revolutionary event. William the Conqueror's great strength exemplifies admirably the general thesis stated above. He was, that is to say, always well supported by the majority of his vassals, and with their aid suppressed small minorities who rebelled. The non-feudal practices he introduced together with the feudal practices were important, the reform of the function of the English sheriff on the lines of that of the Norman *vicomte*, for example. His withholding of immunities from his vassals was something specially bold and effective, as was also the huge domain he kept in hand.

The history of Japan also offers a conspicuous example of the continuity of strong fief and strong monarchy. The reestablishment of the power of the shogunate through the conquests of the sixteenth century was done on a completely feudal basis. In fact, the Tokugawa Shogunate, when set up, was a great fief covering a little less than the whole territory of the nation. It was a monarchy, for the Shogun was a single ruler set over the whole country. It remained a fief also, however, and it employed the feudal method of knitting the country together, namely making all *daimyo* vassals of the Shogun. But too much is made sometimes of the exclusively feudal character of the new shogunate. It included a revitalized Bakufu, which, as a central bureaucracy, had never been exclusively feudal; the Bakufu was an elaborate secretariat, such as strong feudal monarchies in Europe also developed, and in Japan, as in Europe, such an institution was mainly non-feudal even when functioning at the center of a predominantly feudal regime. It remains true that the Tokugawa Shogunate was very feudal: the *daimyo* governed their own fiefs without any regular intervention of the officers of the shogunate; there was no taxation of the *daimyo* by the new shogunate even though the Ashikaga Shogunate before it had at least claimed the right to tax them; there was resort to the legal jurisdiction of the Bakufu; but the only inspectorate for the central government was one of spies. The peace was secured, as it was in strong feudal nations in Europe, by strategically placed garrisons and the maintenance of a large force of fighting men analogous to knights in demesne. It is to be noted that this force was not at any time replaced, as it was in the so-called bastard feudalism of Europe in the fourteenth and fifteenth centuries, by mercenaries.

In exhibiting the element of continuity between fief and nation, the Tokugawa Shogunate and the Norman government of England were for the most part typical strong feudal monarchies. But the Norman conquest was a revolution and so, in a slightly lesser measure, were the conquests of Oda Nobunaga and Toyotomi Hideyoshi which led to the establishment of the Tokugawa Shogunate in Japan. Hence there were aspects and episodes of the continuity in both cases which were exceptional and not typical. The urgent efforts of the Tokugawa regime to preserve the feudal system and fix it as the conquests had left it, together with the regime's restriction of the non-feudal side of government to minimum development, were something very special. They are to be explained by reference to the curious supersession of the imperial by the shogunal power in Japan, for what was feudal belonged of right to the shogun, and, when all power ran through feudal channels, the emperor could have no part in it.[8] Again, the introduction by the Normans of feudal institutions fully developed into England was also very special. It was made possible by the existence of the English Channel which was barrier enough to permit England to lag behind the

[8] Cf. remarks of Sir George Sansom, *Japan: A Short Cultural History* (New York, 1938), p. 433.

development of northern France for a certain time, but not barrier enough to prevent the new institutions from suddenly crossing it when the lag reached crucial magnitude. These two special developments in Japan and England, intrinsically of entirely different characters, made the new governments of the two countries more feudal than they would otherwise have been and more feudal than the governments which had preceded them. But it would be quite fallacious to deduce from this that when a strong feudal government on a national scale is set up, it must necessarily be more feudal than what had preceded it. The normal process was for the strong national monarchy to begin no more and no less feudal than the great fiefs, its contemporaries.

In Mesopotamia strong monarchies are known to have emerged about the fifteenth or fourteenth century B.C., and continuity between them and the regimes which preceded them is not hard to establish. There is no evidence for this period about Assyrian institutions, but for Hatti, which was also feudal, or city-feudal, the strong monarchy was the "New Kingdom" (or "New Empire").

That kingdom first emerged in the late fifteenth century B.C. in the reign of Telepinus.[9] Telepinus made a considerable number of innovations and modifications in the nation's institutions, and it was probably he who made the chief local magnates into governors removable at the king's will instead of hereditary dependents of the crown. If that change did away with a feudal institution, it probably does not imply any sweeping elimination of feudalism, for the old system continued in newly conquered frontier territories, and there it looks very like a system of marcher lordships. Telepinus's marcher lordships were in ex-barbarian territory, and they therefore recall those of the eastern frontier of medieval Germany. But not all marcher lordships in Mesopotamia were against barbarians, for Mr. Brundage notices one set up by Nebuchadnezzar I of Babylon on the Elamite frontier about the mid-twelfth century. Under Nebuchadnezzar's dynasty and under the last Kassite rulers before it Babylonia had become a strong nation.

These marcher lordships are suggestive in more than one way. They certainly mean in each case continuity with earlier forms of government and they almost certainly mean that the earlier forms were forms involving delegation of power, whether feudally or not, to local magnates by the central government; we know they mean this in the case of Hatti. Very possibly the resumption of these powers for dependencies

[9] Hardy in *American Journal of Semitic Languages and Literatures*, LVIII, 209-210. Hardy does not give a date for Telepinus.

other than marches, which was happening in Hatti, happened elsewhere in Mesopotamia too as the strong monarchy emerged. Continuing marcher dependencies do not negative that possibility, for marcher dependencies have outlasted other feudal forms in most feudal societies. But the Mesopotamian marcher lordships must not be construed as evidence of feudalism—for Hatti, and similarly for Urartu, there are other evidences of feudalism and for Assyria a large general probability—for the form of a frontier province under military rule by a strong lord is too general a political form to give evidence by association for feudal forms.[10]

The discontinuity between fief and nation which accompanies the continuity between feudal and national institutions is the product of the differing elements of principle in the origins of fief and nation. And those are chiefly, if not exclusively, the profound difference in principle between fief and empire. The resulting discontinuity was not infrequently sharp enough to produce revolutionary changes, some great, some small. In fact, that is the main clear evidence of the discontinuity that we have. Not that the emergence of a nation in a feudal society must always be marked by revolution; it is important not to be led into exaggeration about this by the inevitable conspicuousness of the cases in which major revolutions occurred. The majority of nations in feudal societies emerged in a slow, predominantly gradual, evolutionary manner—which obscures, but in no wise annuls, the discontinuity between their emergence and the growth of feudal institutions which preceded and accompanied it. Thus France may be said to have taken three centuries to emerge, the twelfth to the fifteenth, Aragon and Castile about the same, the Scandinavian nations longer. For other societies than Western Europe we are less sure of the time taken, and sometimes also of the incidence of revolution; the latter may in some cases have been greater than we know. The nations of Chou China perhaps took two to three centuries, the eighth or seventh century B.C. to the sixth or fifth, to emerge. Mesopotamian chronology for this matter may have been longer, beginning not earlier than the late fifteenth century.

The tendency toward revolution is shown intruding upon the slow evolution of many of the nations. It appears, for example, in the alter

[10] It could be said that the Habsburgs after 1908 made Bosnia and Herzegovina into a march, and, while the outer form of the Habsburg dominions—Austria-Hungary—at that time still had a feudal flavor, and indeed some of the inner forms too, clearly the Bosnia-Herzegovina march was not truly a feudal institution

nating ascendancy of the great barons and the crown which was characteristic of the later days of feudalism. If the two could develop side by side, there also came times when there must be conflict between them, for they represented different forces, and, when one prospered, the other might languish. Most such episodes of which we know occurred in Europe. In Japan there was only the one when the momentarily strong regime of the shogun Yoshimitsu interrupted the growth of baronial power at the turn of the fourteenth and fifteenth centuries. Of the European cases there were some which became almost major revolutions: these were all cases of the final suppression of baronial power by the crown at the end of the alternation process. But France, always the leading feudal country in Europe, scarcely had such an episode: Charles VII and Louis XI delivered serious blows to baronial power after the struggles of the Burgundians and Armagnacs and the last events of the Hundred Years' War, and yet Henry IV in the sixteenth century and even Richelieu in the seventeenth had to take measures to reduce the local power of the nobility.[11]

Sharpest and most decisive of the revolutionary episodes which ended baronial power in Europe were the acts of Henry VII of England and of Juan II (1481-1495) of Portugal. Henry VII put an end to the Wars of the Roses and installed the English monarchy in the most powerful position it has ever held. His method was largely that of arbitrary courts and strong military commissions, a method which had, as a matter of fact, been tried already by his predecessor, Edward IV. On the very eve of Henry VII's revolution, Juan II had accomplished an even greater one although, of course, in so small a country as Portugal it was on a smaller scale. Again, predecessors, Duarte (1433-1443) and Pedro of Coimbra, first minister of Alfonso V (1443-1481), had pointed the way. Juan, however, carried out the policy, which consisted mainly in greatly increasing the power of the crown's local officials, the *corregidores*, in a bold seizure of baronial land, and a strong treatment of persons much in the manner Henry VII of England also used. Another episode which may have been as great a change as any in Europe was Tiglath-Pileser III's (747-727 B.C.) restoration of the power of the crown in Assyria after a century of aristocratic faction. The monarchy had collapsed in the reign of Shalmaneser III (859-824 B.C.) after several centuries of growing strength. The domination of the great lords which followed had the usual features, such as increasing immunities, private warfare,

[11] Even Richelieu's apparently final measures did not prove actually final, for the French nobility could still rebel against the regime of Mazarin.

and the like. They vied for control of weak monarchs, and eventually, as in England, the crown itself was dragged into the arena. This proved the route to monarchical revival, for Tiglath-Pileser III was in fact the usurper Pulu, one of the greatest of the great lords. Like Henry VII's and Juan II's revolutions, Tiglath-Pileser's was one which finally overthrew baronial power.

There were, however, yet greater revolutions than any of these. They occurred in several different societies and not always at a similar juncture in their political development. One of them, the conquest of all Japan by Nobunaga and Hideyoshi in the sixteenth century, was an episode quite like those just considered, for it was the final overthrow of baronial power. But it was a greater change than the European revolutions in that it so suddenly raised the size of the strongly governed, efficient political unit. In Japan the size of such a unit had previously been some two or three provinces agglomerated together under the rule of a *daimyo*; in the space of a generation the conquerors raised it to that of all Japan. In this the Japanese revolution resembled the Norman conquest of England. That was an even greater revolution, for in less than a decade it raised the size of the effectively governed political unit in Europe from that of Normandy to that of all England. It is instructive that these two prominent historic changes illustrate the discontinuity between the growth of fief and nation as markedly as they illustrate the continuity, the discontinuity by their revolutionary character, the continuity by the feudal methods of government the conquerors used: this shows how intimately connected continuity and discontinuity are in the total process of the emergence of the nation in a feudal society. In the case of Japan, it also shows a difference between the sixteenth-century conquests and the revolutions in Europe which brought baronial power to an end, for Henry VII of England did not rule to any extent by feudal methods and Juan II of Portugal only in a few ways, whereas it is one of the conspicuous features of the Tokugawa Shogunate, which followed the conquests in Japan, that it did.[12]

Why the Tokugawa Shogunate stuck so obstinately to feudal methods of government is a subject which must be postponed until the next chapter. That it did so, however, was the immediate reason for a later revolution in the history of Japan—another very plain illustration of the discontinuity between feudal and national development. This revolu-

[12] Tiglath-Pileser III probably ruled to some extent through the nobility even though he effectively repressed their independent powers, but that does not constitute rule by feudal methods.

tion was the recent one in 1868 when the shogunate and its then worn-out feudal paraphernalia were suppressed and a national state of a new and highly imperialistic character was set up in their place. Another revolution of the same general kind as the Japanese revolution of 1868 was the revolution of the fourth century B.C. in the state of Ch'in in China. Both of these revolutions brought as great changes to their respective nations as the Norman settlement did to England, and greater ones undoubtedly than the Japanese revolution of the sixteenth century brought. But the changes in Ch'in and in nineteenth-century Japan were very different from those in England and in sixteenth-century Japan: the former did not raise the size of the effectively governed state at all, but instead set up in each case a new kind of monarchy which had greater power than the respective earlier strong monarchies had had.[13] In Chapter 8 we shall come upon the remarkable conquest of all Iran by Ardashir and Shahpuhr I, the first two rulers of the Sassanid house. That was a revolution in certain important ways like the conquests of England in the eleventh and of Japan in the sixteenth century even though it did not lead to the establishment of a national government, and it occurred in a society which was probably not truly feudal.

There were certain differences, to be investigated shortly, between the English and the Japanese revolutions, but, on the whole, they were more alike than different. Both of them brought strong feudal governments on the national scale into existence, and the two governments were the first strong feudal governments on that scale in their respective societies. Feudalism was not much more mature in sixteenth-century Japan than it was in eleventh-century Europe, and the revolutions of those dates in Japan and England may be said, both of them, to have occurred at about the height of feudal development in their respective societies.[14]

The revolutionary process was, I think, about as follows in the two cases. The size of territory which could be effectively governed was steadily increased through the experience accumulated by a long series of able feudal lords.[15] The competition among the many lords not

[13] See below, pp. 308-309, for classification of the Ch'in and nineteenth-century Japanese revolutions.

[14] In 1066 the feudal regime in northern France was rather more than two centuries old, the Japanese in 1590, the date when Hideyoshi finally established his authority, just about two and a half centuries old. The institutions of both were fully developed at the respective times.

[15] E.g., the houses of Anjou, Normandy, Champagne and Blois, and Flanders in Europe and in Japan those of Hojo (Kwanto province), Otomo (Kyushu),

only eliminated the incompetent ones, so indicating which methods of government were effective and which not, but it also restrained the expansion of the fiefs to something less than it would have been had they not all been constantly pressing upon one another. There thus accumulated a fund of political skill which might be put to larger use than it had had before the crucial revolutionary movement occurred, and at the same time a condition of political compression, so to speak, which tended to bring the revolution about. When the revolution did occur, it was as if the determinants of the extent of the nation were suddenly released and brought into effect. There was nothing to arrest the expansion of the size of the effectively governed unit of territory, once the large fief had been transcended, until the limits of the nation were reached. Those limits, physiographically determined, had already been sketched in beforehand by earlier historical events, the events which produced respectively the Ashikaga Shogunate and the dominion of the house of Cerdic, but they had little practical importance until the new, strong governments were set up.

The limits of territory were not reached with the same degree of revolutionary rapidity in the two cases. In Japan the expansion, though rapid, was less rapid than in England. In Japan it was accomplished in a series of successive and very hard fought conquests, not in a single, decisive campaign. The single, decisive campaign of William the Conqueror could occur by reason of a special geographic circumstance, the barrier of the English Channel, which, as we noticed above, was instrumental in postponing the diffusion of political advance from France to England until a crucial disparity between the two countries had accumulated.

Now, the geographic circumstance was another cause of revolution,[16] independent of the political advance itself, and the magnitude of the English revolution, proceeding from the two causes together, is witnessed by the reaction which followed it. The first three Norman kings were capable men who successfully maintained William the Conqueror's revolutionary regime. But the minute a more ordinary ruler succeeded, the reaction occurred: under Stephen's easy-going rule England experienced something like the initial disorder which usually occurs at passage from the proto-feudal to the early feudal stage of political

Oda (Owari), Mori (Suwo), Takeda (Kai) and Imagawa (Suruga); for the Japanese cases, Takekoshi, I, 329-331.

[16] In 1789 it was again a cause of revolution. On that occasion political institutions leaped the barrier also, but in the opposite direction.

development; it was the stage which had, for the time, been missed out as a result of the revolution. After Stephen, there were a few more jolts, such as the violent oppression of John, and then England fell into the usual European pattern of alternating royal and baronial ascendancy which manifests in a minor way the discontinuity of development of fief and nation. Japan's major revolution did not lead to a noticeable reaction like that which followed the English revolution. The Japanese revolution, in fact, merely permitted the country to catch up with what its own political experience could sustain; it did not force the country forward to a stage it could not sustain, as the English revolution did because of the disparity at the time between the political development of England and that of northern France. It follows that the Japanese revolution is the better example of a revolution on the grand scale caused by the shift over from predominance of the fief to predominance of the nation in political development.

7. THE END OF FEUDALISM

SINCE fief and nation were both continuous and discontinuous, it is clear that the elimination of feudalism was not a simple change. Indeed, in the literature about feudalism its ending is a somewhat elusive subject. Most authors mention the policy of certain kings and the rise of commerce, cities, and the middle class as concerned in it. The first of these we have already noticed. Yet the struggles of king and barons did not necessarily lead, even when the king was victorious, to elimination of the feudal basis of barons' power. Conscious movements to eliminate feudalism, where we know of them, were both rare and of late date, aimed at feudal survivals rather than at major feudal institutions. This is a puzzle which requires some theoretical analysis before we proceed to trace its history.

There is the beginning of enlightenment about it in the remark in the Introductory Essay that the idea of feudalism is an abstraction fully developed only by eighteenth-century thinkers to describe certain institutions whose remains survived in their time. This applies to Europe only, but it suggests a reason why conscious movements to eliminate feudalism in that society did not occur at earlier dates: people at earlier dates were not conscious of feudalism as a general category of political relations. Kings were often opposed to particular feudal persons, or even to particular feudal practices, and the rising middle classes often objected—much more often than not—both to persons and to practices, and would support kings who proposed to suppress them; but no notion of eradicating feudal institutions in general arose out of these antipathies. The rise of the middle classes and the increasing quantity and liquidity of wealth were instruments in the attenuation of feudalism; they were not agents of its destruction.

But the European case is peculiar in that feudalism began to break down there so very long before people became aware of it as a system. The time of the breakdown was about the fourteenth to the seventeenth centuries, earlier in the west, later in the east. Yet at the very time it was breaking down both governments and people were very much aware of another change which was going on, the overthrow of ecclesiastical power. And that certainly is a reason why Europe remained so little conscious of the change from feudal political relations for so long: attention was directed elsewhere. In Chou China, on the contrary, it appears that consciousness of the corresponding political change fo lowed the event much more closely and perhaps even caught up with it; for, to a large extent, the political thought of the Hundred Schools was concerned in just that. Chou China had no such phenomenon as the European dichotomy and conflict of church and state to divert attention from the political change.

Even in Chou China, however, the change began somewhat before there was understanding of it; the elimination of feudalism was not a political change planned beforehand there any more than it was in Europe. In both societies it was the creation of something new which necessitated the transformation of feudalism, which was then something old. Neither was the connection between the new and the old very direct, or logically continuous; that is the reason why in the last chapter we were confronted with a discontinuity between the development of fief and of nation. The nation in a feudal society derived one side of its ideology from the fief, that of the personal relation of monarch and subject, but institutionally there was no necessary relation between fief and nation. That discontinuity might not have a deleterious effect upon the fief and upon feudalism in general; in Japan for a long time it did not. On the other hand, it offered an opportunity for the intrusion of other forces which might set the one institution against the other, more particularly nation against fief. Such a force did, in fact, enter by way of the other side of the nation's ideology, that derived from the empire—but even then it was incidental to the character of the nation; the nation was not intrinsically bound to destroy the fiefs it englobed.

Every nation is at once a reflection and a prefiguration of an empire. Every national monarch approximates imperial quality, but he may do so much or little, early or late. The more fully developed a nation, the more imperial it and its monarch become. In fact, a successful nation ends as a potential empire, and one nation in every society which has evolved as far has become an actual empire. Thus a nation is intrinsically an offensive institution (although a nation once feudal must remain also powerfully defensive), and in a society consisting of a number of nations there is of necessity war between the nations. There would be constant war if it were not for the intervention of other causal factors to restrain it; in Mesopotamia post-Hammurabi such other factors were few or weak, and there actually was something approaching constant war between the nations.

A fief differs from a nation. A fief may be extremely strong, but it is essentially a defensive institution; it is an in-group whose purpose is defence against out-groups. But a fief need not fight when its safety against other fiefs is assured. That assurance is attained for the fiefs englobed within it when the nation has become strongly established. Hence the coherence of those fiefs is likely to abate. The nation itself, however, having arisen in a feudal society, has the tough qualities of a fief which make it extraordinarily formidable when its characteristic offensive purpose is added to the purpose of defense. In its struggle with other nations, therefore, the feudal, or once feudal, nation will seek to strengthen itself by every possible means, and those means include the elimination of feudalism in favor of strong, centralized, bureaucratic, even in the last analysis totalitarian, government. Nor are the fiefs whose coherence as in-groups has been sapped by the dissolution of the danger from out-groups any longer able to resist as they did the first assaults of the monarch before the nation was well established. Hence feudal relations and institutions can now be eliminated by the monarch without serious resistance.

Thus we discover in theory the positive cause of the elimination of feudalism.

Before we proceed to the history of its operation, two matters require further theoretical elucidation. First, it was observed that monarchs approximate imperial quality much or little, early or late. Always they learn that quality from emperors, in feudal conditions from ghost emperors. Where monarchs begin their careers as vassals of ghost emperors, their vassalage may long inhibit the development of imperial quality; that is entirely to be expected, for their aims as feudal lords are inherently and essentially defensive. But in other cases, where they are national kings, actual or potential, from their origins, their imperialistic aims may become operative very early. Monarchs of the latter type tend to bring on international wars and consequent pressure upon feudal institutions at an earlier stage in the evolution of their societies and more precipitately than monarchs of the former type.

Second, we must note again that nations which were never feudal and their monarchs share imperial quality with those which have been feudal. But nations which have not been feudal do not share the tough in-group solidarity of those which have. On the contrary, non-feudal nations arise directly out of disintegrating empires,[1] inherit their sense of universality, and are thereby strongly inhibited from developing

[1] If consolidations of city-states should also be described as nations, possibly they have a different character, but it does not appear that those of the Diadochi in the history of Greece and Rome, which were so formed, had a different character.

in-group sense. Among non-feudal nations, therefore, international wars are apt to be rather mild; the people of one will submit rather easily to the imperial authority of another.[2] But among nations which have been feudal the wars become terrific struggles which must eventually be fought *à outrance*.[3] If by the time of those climactic wars any remains of feudalism survive, they are swept away. There is a grand historic irony in those struggles, for the strength and exclusiveness to which the nations owe their ability to fight them are descended from their feudal quality, and it is institutions of a feudal or post-feudal kind which are most surely and completely destroyed in the struggles.

Procedure cannot be simple in following out the history of the supersession and destruction of feudalism. The influence of economic change will be abstracted for review before the complex political processes are taken up. When political processes are considered, it will be found that a guide through them is furnished by the varying imperial quality of monarchs in the different societies.

Chou China, Europe, and Mesopotamia post Hammurabi must be considered as wholes, and China post-Han must be brought in because Japan is culturally an extension of it. It may have been noticed that nothing has been said in the theoretical discussion above about political thought in Mesopotamia. That is because there is no direct knowledge of it whatever. It will be treated as far as possible by inference and analogy in the concluding discussion at the end of the chapter. There also there will be suggestions, more solidly grounded, about political thought in Japan, for of that we are not very seriously ignorant. A probable explanation will be offered there for the curious facts that Japanese feudalism was dissolved as a result of international rivalries arising in Europe and was replaced by a new state formed largely in the light of European political thought.

The instrumentality of the rise of commerce and of the middle classes in the elimination of feudalism can be tested for Europe and for Japan. Unfortunately, there is scarcely any evidence to afford a test for other societies. As applied to Europe, the doctrine runs in part that monarchs

[2] Spengler observed this in the case of the wars which led to formation of the Roman Empire and made the error of thinking he had found in it a universal character of what he called "civilizations." See *The Decline of the West*, trans. C. F. Atkinson, one vol. edn. (New York, 1932), I, 36; II, 422.

[3] Cf. Spengler, II, 416-431; Toynbee, *A Study of History*, I, 53-124 and *passim*.

acquired from trade new sources of revenue which rendered them less dependent upon the services of their vassals, both military and administrative; hence they developed paid armies and government by functionaries which took away baronial power. This is true, but rather oversimple, for great barons were also able to have functionaries and paid armies, and thus might counter the methods of the crown against them with the same methods. It is sure that in France and England the greatest barons of the late Middle Ages were greatly involved in trade. They were often silent partners furnishing capital to merchants; they participated in merchants' profits in return for protection they could give merchants in their own territories and in relation to the government of the crown; and they could procure privileges, monopolies sometimes, for merchants from the government. It is indeed quite probable that in some times and places in Western Europe the great lords did better out of trade than the king did.

But it was otherwise with the small baron: he was not strong enough to sell his influence to the merchant, unless to the small merchant in mean ways, and he was damaged indirectly but seriously by the general rise in prices which the expansion of trade brought about since his small income was a fixed one derived from land. If his position became really precarious, the best thing he could do was to sell out and become a merchant himself, starting on the capital he obtained through sale of his landed rights. Many did this, and the usual purchasers of lands were the great barons, who often used for the purchases money made in trade. The great agglomerated fief was often partly formed in this way. Other small barons supplemented their incomes as mercenary soldiers or as personal retainers of a more conservative kind. In either case, they could hire themselves to the great barons or to the crown.

It was probably the large supply of mercenary soldiers and of liquid wealth to hire them which made the largest social change in late medieval and early modern Europe. But the political change which followed was far less. Armies ceased to consist of vassals doing their forty days service,[4] and came to consist of the mercenaries formed into bands of any size from a mere score to hundreds. They had regular leaders and they hired themselves out by contract. They were by no means "down-and-outers," but rather in the nature of speculators hazarding not only their fortunes but life and limb also. The key to their careers is ran-

[4] The serving vassal had too many rights to compete with the mercenary as a convenient fighting man, and the vassal as a rule was untrained and had out-of-date equipment.

soms: in any successful campaign they took prisoners, and every man in the band had his rights, the leader had his overriding rights, and a part of their contract with the crown or any other magnate who hired them secured their rights. One good campaign could make a man's fortune. On the other hand, a bad campaign might mean ruin, especially to a man who was taken prisoner.[5]

This was "bastard feudalism." It was the way the Hundred Years' War was fought, and was one reason why the war was fought for a hundred years, off and on. It was the way the Wars of the Roses in England and the struggles between the Princes of the Lilies in France were fought. The Spanish Peninsula, Italy, and much of Germany also became fields of battle and finance,[6] increasingly the latter rather than the former. Thus the last struggles in Western Europe between crown and baronage, fief and nation, were fought with mercenaries. The mercenary dominated warfare for a long time after that; the Thirty Years' War was fought almost entirely by mercenaries. A more truly national army appeared in France as early as the mid-fifteenth century, but in most countries it was much later.

There is an instructive resemblance between fourteenth- and fifteenth-century bands of mercenaries in Europe and the bands hired by great magnates before the time of feudalism in late Roman days. Full circle was, in fact, about to be reached, for the European monarchies began to seek the exclusive right to hire mercenary soldiers, and eventually they got it. When they got it, the army again belonged only to the state, as had last been the case in the days of the Roman Empire's strength.

The influence of the rise of commerce on the development of government by functionaries is quite another matter. The development of that kind of government was by no means wholly due to the influence

[5] There were many more interesting developments in connection with the practice. Merchants in London, Paris, Bordeaux, and elsewhere bought prisoners for cash as a speculation; the big merchants had their buyers with the armies and their private prisons at home where the prisoners were kept pending the raising of a down payment on their ransoms. Careful arrangements were made in view of men's social position, and there was a general feeling that men of importance ought not to be prisoners of nonentities so that nonentities sometimes sold prisoners to their betters. Military law courts developed to settle disputes about ransoms, and a large body of common law about them arose in Western Europe. One of the best examples of this sort of "business" is the story of the English knights Shakell and Haule and their prisoner, the Castilian Count of Denia; see G. M. Trevelyan, *England in the Age of Wycliffe*, 4th edn. (London, 1909), pp. 87-97.

[6] It is significant that the word finance entered European languages at this period with the meaning, ending of a ransom transaction.

of commerce. For a long time both crown and greater baronage could find officials to serve them, as experience improved administrative methods and demanded an increasing personnel, without resort to providing them with salaries. Small fiefs in demesne and advowsons to ecclesiastical benefices met the need even if the latter were in reality an abuse. Moreover, these two kinds of resource continued to be used throughout the Middle Ages and into modern times. On the other hand, salaries and large supplies of what we call consumers' goods which came into the hands of monarchs and other magnates through trade, were a great convenience in rewarding officials for their services, while the greater total revenue, irrespective of its form, to some extent[7] permitted larger total bodies of officials. It is clear that, in point of time, the rise of commerce was a secondary cause—if cause it may properly be called—of the growth of officialdom, and that it remained instrumentally secondary to deeper causes always.

Commercial men in some parts of Europe got free of both baronage and monarchs, but that did not greatly influence the development of feudalism except perhaps in Italy. There it restrained the rise of feudalism as much as it hastened its decline. In Germany also commercial cities largely got free both of the monarch and of the barons, and the overthrow of the power of the Holy Roman Emperor by the German princes was thus probably little affected by the expansion of commerce.

In Japan in the time of the Ashikaga Shogunate the effects of increasing commercial prosperity were in some ways, but not all, similar to those in later medieval Europe. An important difference is that commerce developed in Japan earlier in relation to political development than it did in Europe. Foreign commerce, with China that is to say, was largely organized by the Zen monasteries, and both the shogunate and the great barons became interested in it, but it would be hard to show that the one did better out of it than the other. Nor is there any indication that the leaders who effected the unification of Japan in the sixteenth century owed more to the profits of trade than their rivals whom they overcame. The profits of internal commerce may to some extent have been kept out of both baronial and shogunal hands, for merchants became independent, not on a basis of cities as in Germany, but on a basis of federated guilds.[8]

[7] To a limited extent only, for the rise in prices and the expansion of material needs consumed substantial parts of the increased revenue.

[8] Takekoshi, *The Economic Aspects of the History of the Civilization of Japan* I, 239-243.

It is very probable that commercial prosperity served to make life hard for the small baron as it did in Europe, but not to the same extent. No "bastard feudalism" arose in Japan, the Japanese feudal military system consequently remaining unchanged. Bureaucratic government developed in Japan, but probably not very much until the very late fifteenth century. It may have been facilitated indirectly through increasing wealth gained from trade by the barons, but that remains to be proved, and the evidence is that officials were provided for in the ordinary course of feudal government in which all persons got their livelihood in shares of rice revenue. The emergence of the *daimyo* in Ashikaga times occurred much as the emergence of the great provincial lords in France occurred; it was accompanied by decline in importance of other barons, who came usually to depend upon the *daimyo*. In Japan, the wealth arising from commerce during that process was probably relatively greater than it was at the corresponding time in France. It no doubt entered into the process, but it can hardly have affected its character much.

What happened under the Tokugawa is hard to interpret—though an interpretation will be offered later in this chapter. The facts are that the feudal structure of the polity was more or less fixed and that the government pursued a deliberate standstill policy, a vital feature of which was the narrowing down of foreign trade to a trickle through the Dutch. There is no doubt that by the eighteenth century the maintenance of the feudal regime was difficult under these circumstances, and that domestic trade increased in such a manner that the wealth of the country gravitated steadily into the hands of the merchants, especially of the large ones, and everybody else was impoverished. The picture of an enfeebled feudal nobility holding on to power in virtue of the conservatism of the shogunate is quite authentic.

Suppose, then, that the regime had transferred authority to the class which had the wealth, the merchants: would things have got better? Not, surely, unless it had also dropped the exclusion policy and, by permitting foreign trade, had opened a new source of wealth. That might have drawn the merchant classes away from pillaging their fellow countrymen, or might have enabled the *daimyo* and their dependents, as under the Ashikaga, to get additional wealth themselves with which to buy the town products the merchants sold them. Or, if the Tokugawa had dropped the exclusion policy, would there have been any compulsion upon them to drop their feudal policy also? It is hard to see that there would have been.[9] The *daimyo* would not then, presumably, have been impoverished, and ought to have been able to continue to be effective local rulers as they had been in the seventeenth century and earlier. That the day of the great feudal magnate was not necessarily over is suggested by the fact that some of the *tozama*, the greatest lords in Japan,[10] managed by intelligent policy to avoid the ill effects of the shogunate's exclusion rule and to maintain the prosperity of their fiefs.[11]

The rather strange history of Japan under the Tokugawa does not in fact, appear to furnish an argument for the incompatibility either o the power of great feudal lords or of feudal practices in governmen with a flourishing commerce. If it does furnish one for the incompatibility of a feudal polity with suppression of foreign commerce an growth of home commerce, that is quite a different thing.

Our knowledge of other societies sheds little light on this problem It looks as if commercial development in Chou China was quite late that it did not become appreciable until well after the great states ha been formed, but that impression arises from lack of evidence as muc as from evidence, and hence should not be relied on.

The upshot of the evidence for Europe and Japan is different, but onl largely so in the matter of the military change in Europe. Warfare between nations was another factor in the European situation, and th was absent from the Japanese situation. It may, therefore, have bee the warfare between nations rather than the rise of commerce whic promoted the transformation of European feudal armies into merc nary armies.

Apart from that question, the combined evidence of Europe an Japan suggests that the rise of commerce in a feudal country need n upset the regime. It seems to serve to reduce extreme devolution power down to the small, local baron, but the power so withdraw could be shared in any proportions by the monarch and the great barons. Undoubtedly, the larger territories which both monarch a great barons gained through mediatization of the small barons *cou* be ruled largely through functionaries when a large commercial re

[9] Unless perhaps through the influence of ideas from abroad, which might might not have prevailed.

[10] Those who submitted to the Tokugawa after the battle of Sekigahara in 16 Such were Shimadzu, Maeda, Chosu, and Date. They always maintained a deg of separation from the rest of the country.

[11] In at least one case, Satsuma, the intelligent policy included violation of isolation rule; see Takekoshi, III, 223-226.

enue facilitated such a development, but it is far from evident that they would necessarily be so ruled in those circumstances. The relation between increase in paid officialdom and decrease in feudal administration, is, in fact, one of considerable complexity and not at all a simple arithmetical relation. As between monarch and barons, the monarch's scale of operations and his traditional rights, such as that of taxation, enabled him to get more in the long run out of the profits of trade than the barons did. At any rate, unified nations arose both in Japan and Europe at the time when commerce became important, but the Japanese nation remained feudal, and some of the European ones had substantial feudal survivals.

We pass, then, to political questions. In order of importance they are: he pressure of international rivalry upon national governments, impelling them to reform; imperialist, or absolutist, character on the part of monarchs, the two characters not quite identical; and the rise of new political thought and its influence upon the structure of the state. The irst two are factors in the elimination of feudalism. The third, the ise of a theory of the state, is concomitant with later stages of elimination of feudalism, and it seems to have been subsequent to the earliest tage at least. In the cases of Chou China and Europe the new political hought was fundamentally conditioned by study of the feudal past. t was greatly complicated in Europe, as was the entire process of limination of feudalism there, by the remarkable European dichotomy f church and state.

The extent of imperialist character of the national monarchs proves) vary from society to society in a most interesting way, for it affords progressive series: in Chou China, Western Europe, Mesopotamia ost-Hammurabi, and China post-Han, taken in that order, there is a iminishing distinction between emperors and national monarchs, the vo types of magnate being entirely distinct from one another at one nd of the series, and completely merged at the other end. Moreover, it possible to distinguish Central Europe, the territories of the German Ioly Roman Emperor, as a separate society, or sub-society perhaps, ontained within the main society, as we have already noticed once efore.[12] When that is done, the series becomes a series of five cases, entral Europe coming first, preceding Chou China. The series is aversed between Chou China and Western Europe by a break conrning the origins of the national monarchs: in Central Europe and

[12] See pp. 237-238 above.

Chou China they began as vassals of the ghost emperor, and their nations were originally great fiefs; in the other three societies they arose independent of the emperor, their nations being determined territorially by historic and physiographic division.

The significance of the existence of the series will be considered again in the Conclusion of this study.[13] Meanwhile it serves as a very useful frame in which to treat the entire political process of the elimination of feudalism; indeed the economic factor already reviewed can be brought into the frame also. Accordingly, we proceed immediately to an analysis of the series.

In Central Europe the Holy Roman Emperor was always emperor and he always retained some power even though it was his power a a private feudal magnate rather than his power as emperor. The nationa monarchs, if they may be so called, were the German princes who be came virtually sovereign by the time of the Diet of Augsburg in 1555 They had for long been vassals of the emperor, and, although the feuda character of their relation with him really ceased in 1555, they re mained, most of them, his clients in international affairs. Never did th German princes approach imperial quality themselves. Brandenburg Prussia tried to achieve nationhood in the manner of great nations c Western Europe, and its very limited success emphasizes how little th other German states achieved in that direction.

In Chou China, the *wang* was always emperor—until indeed h ceased to exist—but he completely lost his power in the eighth centur as the Holy Roman Emperor never did. The nations were formed a or after the *wang* lost his power, and their rulers consequently had mo national, if not exactly imperial, quality than German princes. In th fourth century indeed the rulers of the Chinese states arrogated themselves the imperial title,[14] but that was of less importance in co trast with Central Europe than the *wang's* loss of power[15] for in Nap

[13] See p. 385 below.

[14] Between 370 and 315 B.C.; see Bodde, above, p. 69, and H. T. Lei, "T Rise of the Emperor System in Ancient China," *Chinese Social and Politi Science Review*, XX (1936), 253-254.

[15] The succession to the Holy Roman Empire became elective at an early ti through development then of a pre-feudal practice. As a result, the imperial cro could and did pass from one great family to another, as each was ruined in tu by the exigencies of the imperial position. By contrast, in Chou China the cro was practically inalienable. The doctrine of the "changing of the Decree Heaven" which provided for the passage of the imperial mandate to a new dyna had practical influence in the far future of Chinese history, but it is doubtful t it was known widely even as a theory before Mencius (373-288 B.C.). Hence, wh

leon's time a crop of kings, additional to the King of Prussia, who had existed then for a century, arose there, and the Holy Roman Emperor, like the *wang*, ceased to exist.

As we pass to Western Europe, the change in the character of na-tional monarchs, resulting from a change in the origins of the nations, takes place. At this juncture also it becomes necessary to study a little further the distinction between Western Europe and Central Europe which we discovered in considering the quality of the Holy Roman Emperor as a ghost emperor. "Central Europe" and "Western Europe" are not simple geographic terms as used here; rather, they denote two systems[16] of political development. Central Europe is primarily Germany, with northern Italy for a short time attached to it. It is the political system in which the German Holy Roman Emperors had dominion and were paramount lords. The popes had there a sort of uneasy co-ordinate authority with the emperors—as we have put it, pope and emperor were both ghost emperors—and because the Holy Roman Emperor was titular temporal head of Western Christendom, it was he more than any other monarch who led for the state in the great church-state conflicts with the pope. Hence the effect of those conflicts upon Central Europe was very great.

Western Europe is understood here to include Central Europe so that Central Europe is really a system within a system; Western Europe is, in fact, the whole European territory of the Latin Church. Both Holy Roman Emperor and pope had their places in Western Europe, but the places were not the same as those they had in Central Europe. Only Carolingian emperors had dominion in Western Europe; German Holy Roman Emperors never did. They were not even suzerains, but only senior monarchs, of greater dignity than other monarchs. The pope's position was similarly restricted in Western Europe, for he had no purely political rights, of coronation or anything else, in relation to any monarch other than the emperor.

There is, as we saw before, a perfectly clear historical bifurcation of Latin Europe into the two systems: the system of Western Europe originated with the first revival of empire, when Charlemagne became

---

e Chou Dynasty fled from Sian in 771 and thereby lost most of its possessions, e ruin of the *wang* proved definitive.

[16] Such a "system" is not, of course, a perfect system. Perfect systems exist only mathematics, and are of human invention. If systems in social evolution are ore imperfect than most systems, that differentiates them only in degree from e average system in nature. Cf. pp. 383-386 below.

ghost emperor, the system of Central Europe with the second revival of empire, when Otto I became ghost emperor; and on both occasions the pope, the co-ordinate ghost emperor, was the agent of the revival At no time after the second revival were Western Europe and Central Europe unconnected with one another. Their two heads were in each case the same person, though each functioned differently in the two systems. Besides that, Germany was a potential nation and eventually an actual nation of Western Europe even though it constituted many nations of Central Europe, the nations of Central Europe being fief in the system of Western Europe. Italy was curiously placed in relation to the two systems. South Italy and Sicily were wholly of Byzantine not Latin, Europe until the Norman conquest in the eleventh century and even after it they remained for a long time of mainly Byzantin culture. Northern and central Italy were for a couple of centuries a par of Central Europe, but after that they became rather a second sub society, this time of city-states, dependent more on Western than o Central Europe. But the pope's temporal state was an anomaly in it.

Western European nations, then, are unlike those of Central Europ and Chou China, but like those of Mesopotamia post-Hammurabi an China post-Han. Nations of this latter type exist *in posse* from the ver origins of their societies, preceding the rise of feudalism, even thoug they do not emerge *in esse* until feudal development has created suffi cient means for their political cohesion. Western European natior emerged in a territory girdling the territory of Central Europe in horseshoe formation. The earliest were the nations of the west side the horseshoe, France and England, but the Iberian nations were d layed somewhat by the intrusion of Islam. The chronological successic moved roughly northward to Scandinavia, and then eastward ar southward to the nations of the eastern fringe of Latin Europe. came last to Germany and Italy at a time when the system of Centr Europe had been broken down and the territories formerly involve in it were being fully absorbed into the system of Western Europe.

The monarchs of the Western European nations occupy the medi position in the series of types of monarchs. All of them were at fi feudal magnates even though they were also from their origins son thing more, as neither German nor Chinese princes were. Europe monarchs were, in fact, kings, a title which at its origin denoted barbarian war leader, hence a leading member of that aristocra which subsequently went feudal. If, then, Western European natior nonarchs were in origin actual members of the aristocracy and went eudal with it, they were always leaders in it, and so were strategically placed to acquire imperial quality as that quality became substantiable n effective power. The Holy Roman Emperor, viewed from Western Europe, was a great dignitary, greater in dignity than a king, but he was at the same time a dignitary *manqué* in that he never succeeded n converting himself into a national monarch or his dominions, vast hough they became in Habsburg times, into a nation. As the territories f Central Europe were absorbed into the political system of Western Europe, and after the Holy Roman Empire was suppressed, the title f emperor came to be used, ephemerally as it proved, by certain naional monarchs. But at all earlier times Western kings refrained from uch claims and the Habsburg emperors who ranked with them as great powers," ranked above them in honor and in the right to confer onor.[17]

Mesopotamia differs from Western Europe, Chou China, and Central Europe in that all national monarchs there used the imperial title "King f Kings" (or some equivalent)[18] at all times. It would seem, however, hat the Babylonian King of Kings was the legitimate claimant since e was the direct successor of Hammurabi and of other rulers of the ld empire, and there can be no doubt that the other monarchs copied neir style directly or indirectly from that of the Babylonian monarch. The Babylonian King of Kings was a national monarch as well as host emperor, and in that he actually was what the Holy Roman Emeror missed becoming. Thus Mesopotamia approached, but did not uite realize, a symmetry whereby every nation always professed to be n empire. The nations of Mesopotamia were, like those of Western urope, predetermined in territory and location historically and physigraphically, and did not originate as fiefs. The monarchs of some of nem originated as barbarian leaders, those of Hatti and of Persia, for xample, and those of Hatti, Urartu, Mitanni, and Assyria were all robably feudal kings, or something quite similar, for a time. We know nat Media and Persia were never truly feudal,[19] and it is not at all kely that Babylonia and Elam were. It seems thus justifiable to say nat Mesopotamian national monarchs, taken all together, were rather

[17] The European kings did not even use the imperial title "Majesty" until the oly Roman Emperor conferred it upon them; he began to do that in the sevententh century. See Zedler, *Universal Lexicon*, s.v. Majestät, quoted by Bryce, *oly Roman Empire*, p. 263, note j.

[18] See Ch. 4, n. 5.

[19] See pp. 327-328 below.

less feudal than European ones, for scarcely any European monarchs were not feudal to some extent in their earlier careers.[20]

Finally, in China post-Han every monarch called himself Son of Heaven and every state professed to be the empire. The difference from Mesopotamia is that there the Babylonian monarch was the "legitimate" emperor and the others were not, whereas no satisfactory criterion exists for choosing between the Chinese claimants. China after the Han split at once into nations, there being no question of any but physiographic and ethnographic—scarcely historic—divisions. The outermost nations arose later in territory to which Sinic culture was being gradually extended. Ghost empires, as we have observed in the instance of Japan came as a part of the culture into the new country, the ghosts, like the real empires, being multiple. It is to be noted that the ghost empires were one of the earliest cultural importations; they were the earliest considerable political importations so that in those countries there wa an "empire" long before there was anything solid enough to be callec a nation. In Japan, as we well know, feudalism reached classical development, and there was an important feudal development in Korea perhaps also in Tibet which was partly of Sinic culture. But in th main territory of China no feudal development occurred at all. Sinc China preponderates so largely in size and population in the whol society, then, that society saw the least feudal development of any c the five.

In one of our cases, Japan, the matter of chief interest is not th elimination of feudalism, but its long continuance. It appears strang that this, the classic case of feudalism, should occur in the society at th latter end of the series, the society in which every nation was at th same time an empire and there was, in the society as a whole, less feu dalism than in any other. Indeed in the Chinese post-Han society ex tremes meet: even the classic feudal nation was itself an empire. Bu that, in theory, is absurd, for feudalism and imperialism are in princip fundamentally antagonistic. Therefore, it is perfectly logical that i practice the antagonism should have been minimized by comple suspension of the emperor's power; emperors became the ghostliest

[20] In Scandinavia and the eastern fringe of Central Europe the feudal side institutions was nothing like so developed as in the other parts of Europe, but is not possible to find there states like Media and Persia which probably pass directly from a condition not unlike that of the "barbarian" states which succeed the Roman Empire to that of bureaucratically unified states. Mixed tribal-feuc institutions occurred in east central Europe, and they probably did also in Urar

ghosts. In the Chinese society emperors were far too important a feature of the culture either to be suppressed, or to suffer derogation. As to the latter, they could not become feudal lords themselves, and so the shogun came into existence. This, we may remind ourselves, is not an unusual thing to happen to a great dignitary. It happened to the Merovingian king, whose dignity was a reflection of that of the Roman emperor even though the king did not presume to use the imperial title. But the Mayor of the Palace eventually deposed and replaced the Merovingian king, remaining at the same time a feudal lord, as did all his successors. This could not happen in the Chinese society where the true quality of an emperor was well known and could at all times be seen actually in China itself. Thus the shogun could not aspire to that quality; he remained a vulgar, feudal ruler.

Hence the emperors continued to exist and shogunal government became completely feudal. When, therefore, Hideyoshi overthrew the *daimyo*, as European monarchs overthrew the great barons, and so unified the nation, he and his successors felt constrained to keep the nation in the form of a great, agglomerated fief. They dared not go very far with bureaucratic administrative reforms, for to do so could only have made the nation fit again for imperial rule, and the emperors, however ghostly, constantly and always remained a potential threat to the shogun's power. As at all earlier times in the nation's history, there was full knowledge of what an emperor's quality and function were. Japanese emperors had tried before to recapture the state, and there was the spectacle in China, and even in Korea, of an emperor in possession of power. Hence the state remained strictly feudal and Ieyasu and Iemitsu, first and third Tokugawa Shoguns, took special measures to ensure the isolation of the emperors from politics.

And, almost as if Clio had revealed to them the necessary condition for maintenance of feudalism, the Tokugawa Shoguns isolated Japan from contact with other nations. They were quite exceptionally fortunate in being able to do this, for it did not result from their own policy alone; it resulted also from the fact that the main country of the Chinese society, China proper, had been reunited more than a thousand years before the Tokugawa epoch in Japan, and had long been non-aggressive. Thus, the pressure of the international struggle, which in other cases enforced reform and the elimination of feudalism, was entirely absent from Japan for two centuries in Tokugawa times. Industrial and commercial prosperity put bureaucratic reform within easy reach of the Tokugawa government, but of that it did not wish to avail itself, and nothing compelled it to do so. This is the explanation of the maintenance of feudalism in Japan until the nineteenth century. It is not as mysterious as it is sometimes said to be.

Mesopotamia offers a sharp contrast with Japan. The international struggle there began very early, lasted very long, and often was exceptionally bitter; it was undoubtedly the severest of the great international struggles. There was more international warfare from the fifteenth to the eleventh centuries B.C. than in the corresponding period in the history of any other society; it probably increased in the tenth and ninth centuries, and it certainly reached a climax in the eighth and seventh centuries when the conquests of Assyria seemed always on the point of culminating in a final settlement and a new empire, and yet never actually did so. What happened finally was that extreme exhaustion on the part of all the nations except the new Persian nation set in, and in the late sixth century, Persia gathered the debris into a new empire The contrast, then, between Mesopotamia and Japan—more correctly between the Mesopotamian and the Chinese societies—in the matter of international strife is extreme.

The evidence for the development of national institutions in Mesopotamia, and so for the effect upon them of the terrific wars, is unfortunately slight. For what it is worth, however, it fits in with something already suggested for a limited region in an earlier time, the time when feudal institutions may have arisen. The suggestion is that disorder may then have been so great in the Assyrian region that even the elemental fief could not get established at all generally.[21] For the late period, any time from the twelfth or eleventh century, with warfare increasing, it would seem that the development of national institutions must have been even more inhibited, and that not only in Assyria, but in Babylonia and probably elsewhere also. And that is just what thos institutions look alike: soundly based, permanent reform, such as is necessary to the emergence of strong monarchies which are also stable, seem to have given place constantly to strength of a narrowly military kin hastily built up again and again to meet urgent threats of enemie Both Assyria and Babylonia from time to time suffered severe intern collapses which were probably the result of the strain of the almo incessant fighting. One of those collapses was the one we have studie in Assyria, lasting for about a century, when the country broke up int noblemen's estates, and was reunited by the conquests of Tiglath-Pilese III. It occurred in the ninth and eighth centuries, a very late date indee

[21] Above, p. 225. For further explanation of this matter, see below, pp. 323-32

for the nation to become fragmented into noblemen's estates, for Assyria was no backward frontier state requiring radical reform in order to catch up with older nations; it was the oldest considerable nation in the society after Babylon and Elam, and had been in the thick of the fight for hegemony for five hundred years before the collapse of the ninth century occurred.

What happened to other Mesopotamian nations is still more dramatic. Both Mitanni and Hatti ceased to exist in the twelfth century, as remarkably early a date for such eventualities as the ninth century is a late date for survival of noble political particularism in Assyria. It is true that the destruction of Hatti is commonly thought to have resulted in part from events outside Mesopotamia, even though Assyria also certainly took a part in it. Whether Assyria or some convulsion in the collapse of the Cretan society was mainly responsible, Hatti was wiped out within two hundred years or less of the emergence of its strong monarchy, a time at which it might be supposed to have been at the height of its vigor. Mitanni was certainly wiped out and annexed by Assyria, although in that Egypt may have had a certain part. Most calamitous and dramatic was the end of Assyria itself. Between 612 and 606, not twenty years after its conquests had reached their greatest extent, Assyria fell headlong before its enemies. Its leaders were killed, its cities destroyed, its people dispersed, its very identity rapidly lost.[22] What we encounter in Mesopotamia, then, is not the elimination of feudalism, probably not even reform of any constructive sort, but something more drastic, an exceptionally strong tendency toward elimination of the nations themselves, elimination being exceptionally early in the case of Mitanni and Hatti, and exceptionally complete and sudden in the case of Assyria.

The sharp contrast between the Chinese society post-Han and the Mesopotamian society post-Hammurabi in the severity of international warfare confronts us with a problem, though not an insoluble one. Standing next to each other in our series, both societies had nations of an imperialist character so that the explanation of the contrast lies in some factor other than that. It does not lie simply and plainly in large as against small feudalization, for, although the Chinese society was on the whole little feudalized, the Mesopotamian society was not as largely feudalized as the European society. Nevertheless, there was a great contrast between the institutional development of the two societies, and I believe that it is by that contrast that the great difference in

[22] Cf. an important passage in Toynbee, *A Study of History*, IV, 468-484.

their destinies is explained. Only a little subtlety is needed to see this Mesopotamia is a paradox. It was a society in which the struggles of the early stages of feudalism were never really concluded. The struggles went on and on, and neither feudal nor national institutions were, so we have supposed, adequately developed. These excessive struggles were, then, if our hypothesis is correct, of the same character as the struggles between feudal nations, and they were the greater, not the less, for the fact that feudal institutions could never be positively developed. The contrast with China post-Han is, therefore, essentially of the same kind as a contrast between much and little feudalization, but on the side of Mesopotamia, the political condition was one of abortiv feudalization.

In turn, this diagnosis explains the obstinacy of Babylonia's resistanc to absorption by Assyria. As a largely non-feudal nation, Babylonia migh be expected to have collapsed early before Assyria and to have bee readily absorbed. It often did collapse before Assyria in actual warfar but emerged with surprising regularity still a distinct political entit This, surely, was because Assyria never succeeded in developing th positive national character in which to absorb it.

Between the two extremes of China post-Han and Mesopotamia pos Hammurabi fall two means, Chou China and Europe; three if Centr Europe be considered distinct from Western Europe. Chou China di fers from Western Europe in that in the early national period dire action was taken to avoid international warfare. Thus, from the sevent century B.C. to the early fifth there was usually in existence politic machinery to that end, in the form of leagues of the nations for mai taining peace and a balance of power, often under the recognize hegemony of the nation which had preponderating power. This is, think, to be connected with the fact that the Chinese princes were sti in theory dependents of the *wang* and were not of imperial qualit The Chinese princes differed from German princes in that their en peror, unlike the Holy Roman Emperor, had become a cipher, so tha if they wished to preserve the peace, they had to provide new machine to do so, and could not rely on the imperial constitution, as the Germa princes did—to small effect.

The Chinese leagues are certainly to be connected also with the ve important political theories which began to appear in the sixth centur and have been considered in Chapter 6 to mark the rise of nationalit It is quite likely that those political theories were originally invent for the purpose of strengthening the state in its rivalry with other state that must have been one original purpose, and it is hard not to think that it was the predominating purpose, other purposes being ancillary. But the pressure of the international struggle was rendered less by the instrumentality of the leagues, and it may be that competition between the nations tended, under the powerful moral influence of Confucius, Mo Ti, and other such philosophers, to be sublimated into terms of competing social ideals. If this is really so to any extent, and there seems a good possibility that it is, the Chinese achievement in that age is one of the great, and somewhat rare, triumphs of human reason in a political problem of the first magnitude.

We do not know very well just how Chinese political theory affected the elimination of feudalism, but there is no doubt that it did so. It may quite possibly have slowed it up for a time, for Confucianism, by far the most influential theory, is strongly conservative. That very important doctrine, that political authority should be used under severe restraint, favors the idea of reciprocal obligations between lord and vassal found in feudalism; indeed that is very likely the inspiration of the doctrine. A transformation of institutions from feudal to another form could nevertheless take place under cover of the doctrine; and it seems probable that, by shifting emphasis from a particular institutional structure to the principle underlying it, the doctrine promoted the transformation. Yet how great and how rapid a transformation was it? When the tragic collapse of Chin occurred about three quarters of the way through the fifth century, it broke up into three states, Chao, Han, and Wei, each of which had been a great subordinate principality of the combined state before the collapse. Again, the great totalitarian-autarkic reforms of Shang Yang in Ch'in in the mid-fourth century eliminated at least an old nobility. The difficulty is that we cannot be certain either that Chao, Han, and Wei before the partition, or that the Ch'in nobility before their suppression, were still truly feudal. If, however, the probability is large that Chinese institutions were feudal between the ninth and seventh centuries, they were either feudal or post-feudal in the fifth and fourth. Mr. Bodde's important analysis of the disintegration of Chou feudalism puts most of it from the sixth century to the fourth.[23]

[23] Above, pp. 66-67. The importance of Mr. Bodde's demonstration will be understood when it is observed that in earlier sinological literature any kind of devolution of power to local magnates was customarily described as feudal, so that feudalism was not said to have been eliminated until the draconian reconstruction of China by Ch'in Shih Huang Ti after his establishment of the new empire, and

What we do know without any doubt about the elimination of old dependency relations in China during those centuries is that it was brought about by the exigencies of the international wars of the time. The worst of those wars, those between the *Chan Kuo* (fighting states), began in the latter period of the institutional changes,[24] and the rivalry of the nations had already been rising steadily all through the period. Ch'in at the end of the fourth century introduced cavalry and superseded the chariot fighting which had been the special practice of the feudal baronage. That was, however, probably of importance only in the technical history of warfare. It is scarcely possible that it can have affected the elimination of feudalism, for that was already nearly complete.[25]

Of much greater importance was the advent of Legalist political doctrine, the basis of the Ch'in reforms and possibly of other reforms at the time also. It was aimed, as we have already noticed, specifically at abolishing feudalism or feudal remains in the interest of strengthening the nations for their ordeal in the *Chan Kuo* wars.[26] And the fourth century was the century when the national monarchs took the title of *wang*, and the old Chou *wang* was at last suppressed. It would seem from this order of events that the exigencies of the struggle between the nations will affect the competency of monarchs to make administrative reforms: when the struggle reaches a critical phase, it will compel a change in the quality of the monarchs if they have not previously shown the needed aptitude to suppress feudal forms and set up new political forms which are potentially imperial and actually of maximum efficiency for waging war.

A similar deduction may be made from the events in the nineteenth century which finally brought about the overthrow of the shogunate in Japan and the radical reconstruction there of the empire. The exclusionist policy had economic effects which were in a high degree damaging, and might possibly have led in the end to the suppression of feudalism—or might indeed only have led to the dropping of economic isolationism. Actually, however, it was the menace of foreign nation

even then "feudalism" returned between the establishment of the Han in 206 B.C. and the Rebellion of the Seven Kings in 156 B.C.

[24] For an opinion about the transition which had occurred, see Maspero, *La Chine antique*, pp. 390-391.

[25] Was the Ch'in innovation even necessary because the old nobility had been suppressed there?

[26] The earliest, very simple law systems appeared in China in the sixth century but I know of no reason to think that the Legalist political theory arose before the late fifth century at the earliest.

and the example of their ideas and institutions which did bring about both the end of the exclusionist policy and the suppression of feudalism. To be sure, the menace of foreign nations to Japan was not very great at the crucial moment, but rivalry among the European nations was, as the intelligent Japanese observer could readily see, becoming strong, and their pressure upon the great Chinese Empire was something to impress the Japanese whose country in the mid-nineteenth century was still much weaker than China.

The complexity of the process of elimination of feudalism in Europe is remarkable. Yet the same factors as operated in other societies may be found operating in Europe also, though to some extent at different times and in different ways. In Western Europe the process began with war somewhat as it did in Mesopotamia, but only in a limited area and for a limited time. Imperialist aims were indeed quite general in late medieval Europe.[27]

The first great international struggle, the Hundred Years' War,[28] was, however, fought chiefly between the two leading monarchs of Western Europe, the kings of England and France. There is no mistaking the imperialist intentions of the houses of Plantagenet and Lancaster, which sought to conquer France and, in the case of Lancaster, momentarily succeeded.[29] The Iberian countries and some of western

[27] The wide extension of such aims is shown in the various claims to the imperial crown; many kings and even lesser magnates looked upon themselves as potential emperors. Alfonso of Castile and Richard of Cornwall, brother of Henry III of England, sought the Imperial crown at the time of the Interregnum. Charles of Valois sought it in the early fourteenth century, and Edward III of England was actually elected soon afterwards, but decided not to accept. George Podiebrad of Bohemia was elected in the fifteenth century, but failed to secure the crown. In 1519, when Maximilian I died, the kings of all three great nations of Western Europe, France, England, and Spain, competed for election, Francis I of France very urgently.

[28] It was the first "really national war," according to A. F. Pollard (*Factors in Modern History*, 3rd edn., London, 1932, p. 19).

[29] Imperialist aims were quite explicit in the case of Richard II of England. That was, of course, nearly half a century after the outbreak of the Hundred Years' War, and Richard's ambitions were directed toward exaltation of his authority within his realm, not to conquests outside it. But this only shows that both aspects of imperialist velleity were in men's minds in the period. Richard once referred to himself officially as "full emperor of his realm of England" (*Rot. Parl.*, III, 343). It seems fairly likely that Richard learned some of these ideas through his connection with the government of the Holy Roman Empire by his marriage to Anne of Bohemia, sister of Wenceslas and daughter of Charles IV. Charles was the successor of Ludwig IV, the patron of Occam and Marsiglio. For Richard's claim to absolutism and the extraordinary court ceremonies with

Germany got drawn into the war, and, had not the special European conflict of church and state intervened, it is not unlikely that a long series of international wars would have followed and engulfed the whole society.

We need no longer hesitate to think that it was the pressure of the war which led to the conversion of the feudal army into an army of mercenaries and at the same time brought in such technical military innovations as the longbowman and artillery. But neither the technical changes nor the entry of a cash nexus into the terms of military service necessarily led toward the elimination of feudal relations. Vassals could, as they did in Poland, render military service with new types of fighting men, and, especially in Central Europe, small barons who would hire themselves out as soldiers could sometimes thereby preserve the status of feudal gentry which would otherwise have been lost to them as a result of economic change. I doubt very much, in fact, that technical military change has ever upset an established feudal order. In the case of Chou China technical military change, as we have just seen, did not occur until about the moment when feudalism had been completely eliminated. It is, I believe, far more likely to be a result than a cause of the decline of feudalism.

The portent of the Hundred Years' War does not mean that the desire for peace was lacking in Europe by any means. It is only necessary to read Dante's *De Monarchia* to discover that, and in Central Europe there were direct attempts to establish peace; the parallel there is with Chou China in this matter as it is in other matters also. Thus there were serious, but abortive, efforts to rebuild the imperial constitution on its judicial side in the late fifteenth century so that it should serve to solve disputes, and various leagues, chiefly of cities, came into existence with the aim of protecting commerce, or more broadly of maintaining local peace and order. The earliest league, properly so called, in Western Europe, as distinct from those of Central Europe, was the League of Nations in 1919, but the so-called Concert of Europe came into existence in 1815, and there was a project for maintaining the peace by international cooperation in 1714. All of these schemes followed great wars between the nations, greater ones even than the Hundred Years' War.

Neither did Europe in the fourteenth and fifteenth centuries lack

---

which he sought to symbolize it, see T. F. Tout, *Chapters in the Administrative History of Mediaeval England*, IV (Manchester, 1928), 32-33.

the beginnings of new political theory concomitant with the beginnings of the change from a feudal to a new polity; it had them, as Chou China also had. Dante again, Marsiglio of Padua, William of Occam, Gerson, Nicolaus Cusanus, and, in a category of his own, Machiavelli, all made more or less important initial contributions to new ideas of the state. Especially in Marsiglio, Gerson, and Cusanus the right relations between ruler and ruled were prominent, taking a characteristic European form, for those thinkers saw or sought institutional restrictions on monarchical power through the parliamentary bodies which had begun to grow out of the councils of feudal kings in the later Middle Ages.

But those new theories were complicated from their very origin by the great conflict of church and state, for the conflict was fought as furiously in the realm of ideas as it was in the realm of politics. In the latter realm it brought to a sudden end the constructive movement toward order and peace in Central Europe, and it gave ironic meaning to the general desire for peace which Dante voiced. If there was any chance for realization of that desire in Western Europe after the Hundred Years' War, it was blasted anew by the conflict as it rose to its crisis. But it also cut right into the international struggle which the two great nations of Western Europe had begun. From the Hundred Years' War to the Thirty Years' War the military struggles of Europe were as often internal struggles within the nations as they were international, and they were almost all vitally concerned with religion or the interests of the Papacy. Conflict between crown and nobility of a post-feudal or a truly feudal character was a secondary issue in some of them. Indeed the process of transformation of the feudal polity into something new was interrupted, upset, and varied by the religious struggle; it was not stopped anywhere, but it became so much involved in many countries in the religious struggle that many strange, various, and unstable or unworkable political shifts resulted.

The great conflict of church and state was fought out in two stages, the earlier, lesser one the Conciliar Movement, the later, greater one the Reformation. The Papacy won in the first stage, the lay monarchies in the second. The beginnings of new political theory had been complicated from the outset by the conciliar issue in the church. With the failure of the Conciliar Movement important constructive theory was in effect set aside for a century and a half, and in its place there was a fevered and sterile development of theories of absolutism which culminated in the seventeenth century in the clumsy idea of the Divine Right of Kings. That idea was not really imperialist within the meaning of the term used here although Louis XIV was at various times an exponent of both ideas. Divine Right was an interim notion which expressed the victory of the king over both ecclesiastical and noble power, chiefly the former, but undoubtedly did lead back toward the imperialist trend as the dust of the conflict with the church cleared away.

Divine Right was a slogan, not an argument. The return to serious thought about the relations between ruler and ruled is marked by the rise of the extraordinary doctrine of Original Compact, or Contract. The doctrine was first propounded during the struggles of Huguenot and Catholic in France, and it contains quite remarkable distortions induced by the conflict with ecclesiastical power; but it had far more than those temporary aberrations. The distortions are not in the institutional, legalistic form of the doctrine, least of all in the idea of contract; a legalistic approach to politics had been characteristic of European thought and practice since at the latest the late eleventh century when the study of Roman law began to revive. The strangest distortion is in the conception of an original compact in some way preceding or conditioning the relations of ruler and ruled; it is hardly surprising that later thinkers could not decide whether the supposed compact had been actual, virtual, or merely metaphoric.

But contract in itself, being naturally compatible with European tradition, proved extremely fruitful. Nor can there be serious doubt that the idea was taken from feudal practice. Figgis regards it as forming a part of "the enduring legacy of feudalism to the modern world."[30] The *Vindiciae contra Tyrannos*, the most important of the early French documents propounding the doctrine of contract, was a direct resumption of the neglected ideas of Marsiglio, Gerson, and Cusanus on the relation of ruler to ruled. Thereafter the feudal past was earnestly studied for what could be deduced from it for application to the modern state. Yet it may well be that the prospects of establishment of a satisfactory relationship of ruler and ruled in that state had been irreparably damaged by the interruption and the furious passions aroused

[30] *Cambridge Modern History*, III, 762. The other part, he thinks, is the maxim "no taxation without representation." He is careful to say that it is the prevalence of the idea of contract rather than its origin in feudalism which is in question. It is a nice question whether contract should be traced to feudalism, to Roman law, or even to Greek thought. There is no doubt, of course, that agreement, even formal agreement, is of the essence of feudalism and is found wherever there is true feudalism. In Europe, however, the written contract with a part, not all, of its forms probably goes back to Roman models even if they were, strictly, without the law.

in the conflict of church and state. No clear and full understanding of feudalism was reached until that of Montesquieu in the mid-eighteenth century, and not long after that the makeshift political systems which had come out of the age of major conflict between church and state began to crack up in revolutionary upheavals.

Those political systems had contained feudal elements, or they had been of a post-feudal character closely influenced by the feudal past. But feudal or feudalistic survivals are to be expected since constructive thought about the feudal past had been interrupted so soon after it had begun. As a result, the changes from feudal relations had been almost completely uncontrolled and unplanned. It was ecclesiastical change which had been planned, and feudal institutions and practices had in some places been caught up in the ecclesiastical change, in others had been left little changed, in yet others had been allowed in a haphazard way to fall into desuetude. It was the nobility who constituted the most palpable and awkward survival from feudal times; they were not necessary to the new, unitary state, and only in a very few countries, such as England, were they effectively integrated into the state. There were, of course, countries which remained near enough to their feudal condition to need a landed aristocracy as a key part of their polities, and in those countries there survived conspicuously the diets or other assemblies, provincial and central, in which the aristocracy met the monarch as his vassals. In other countries the assemblies were mostly destroyed or allowed to fall out of use by the monarchs, while the nobles themselves survived as an incubus upon society. Those assemblies were in most cases the very ones which had in the late Middle Ages been growing into parliamentary bodies.

Central Europe had its own special change, consequent upon its being the focus and center of the conflict of church and state, the Reformation beginning there. The result was a remarkably rapid transformation, almost confined within the first half of the sixteenth century, of the great German barons, vassals of the Emperor, into independent princes. They had internal sovereignty by 1555 at the Diet of Augsburg which produced *cujus regio ejus religio*; external sovereignty, which is to say independent foreign policy, was denied them until the Treaties of Westphalia in 1648, but that was not much more than a formality. The transformation was in its suddenness like the one in China in the fourth century B.C. when the princes rapidly threw off the formal suzerainty of the Chou *wang*. In Central Europe it happened when the Emperor sought to protect the church against the attacks of Lutheran princes; in China it was a direct result of the bitter rivalry between the nations. In China the change was not more than formal, the object of it increase of prestige; in Europe, weak though the Emperor already was, the princes could still, on the crucial occasion in 1555, take from him the substance of his surviving rights over them. The similarity of the two transformations results directly from the slowness of states beginning as fiefs to emerge as nations.

The effect in Central Europe was to bring that society, or sub-society, into as nearly complete independent existence as it was to attain. While, in the Middle Ages, the Holy Roman Emperor had approximated—weakly, however—the character of a rising national monarch, and his dependents had been vassals, however turbulent, Germany had been as much a potential nation of Western Europe as it had been the main basis of the system of Central Europe. The sudden loosening of the system of Western Europe and strengthening of that of Central Europe did not prove enduring. It endured, in fact, for a century, and then in the latter part of the Thirty Years' War the great nations of Western Europe fell upon Central Europe and ruined it. The result was that its territories began to be re-absorbed into Western Europe, but the new transformation was not completed until 1871 or perhaps 1918. For Central Europe considered in isolation the Thirty Years' War was the culminating war of the nations which might, no doubt, have continued until one of them had conquered all the rest, had it not been for the supervention of greater events occurring within the predominating Western European system.

Among the nations of the Western European system feudalism survived the Reformation in Poland. Even the small nobility continued to exist there. The country cannot be called fully feudal, for so much that was pre-feudal survived and even developed along with the feudal. Thus the monarchy became completely elective, and progressively weaker. But the Polish army remained a thoroughly feudal force. The Hungarian nobility gained a position for themselves somewhat like the Polish, but did not make their monarchy elective. Elective monarchies, of pre-feudal origin, were, however, widespread in northern and east-central Europe where feudalism was late and imperfectly developed. Scandinavia had them, and it also had a remarkable oligarchic development of the nobility, or the greater nobility, wielded not only through the noble estates in the diets, but also through the royal councils (*Raad*, *Råd*); by capturing the councils the nobility usually acquired specific executive functions. In Denmark and Norway indeed the crown went virtually into commission to the *Raad* from the fifteenth to the latter end of the seventeenth century, the nobility retaining their feudal rights, but performing few of their feudal duties.

Brandenburg-Prussia, influenced from Central Europe, from Poland, and from Scandinavia, had a truly remarkable history of its own. Always approaching barbarian, even primitive, conditions very closely in certain ways, Brandenburg saw some increase in the Elector's power about the turn of the fifteenth and sixteenth centuries, but between Joachim II (1535-1571) and the "Great Elector" Frederick William (1640-1688) there was an astounding recrudescence of political-administrative feudalism. This was not unrelated to Scandinavian developments, but it also looks quite like what happened between the barons and the crown in England in the thirteenth century, when the king's Great Council was being transformed into a parliamentary body. In fact, the Diet of Brandenburg established an ascendancy over Joachim II remarkably similar to that which the embryonic English parliament established over Henry III. And, since there was no Prussian Edward I to succeed Joachim, the ascendancy continued until the reign of the Great Elector.[31] The Great Elector indeed did away with the powers of diets, and no constructive constitutional relation between monarchs and estates came out of late feudal developments in Prussia. Prussian Junkerdom seems scarcely to have equalled the English nobility in political sense. But, if a despotism prevailed heavily at the top of the Prussian polity from the Great Elector's time, a feudalistic substructure could still grow at its base: from the fifteenth century on the minor, local political functions of the Junkers had been increasing, and they went on doing so right into the eighteenth century.

A special development in Prussia, which must be called feudalistic, was that of the army. This also was started by the Great Elector. He set up a standing army for the first time, and an element in that army was the companies consisting of a Junker or a small group of Junkers and a following drawn from the serfs on their estates. This element came to predominate so largely by the time of King Frederick William I (1713-1740) that the Prussian army then looked in organization quite like the bastard feudal armies of late medieval England and France. The part played by the serfs in the Prussian army was much larger than that which archers, hobilers, and other simple people played in late medieval armies, but it was not fundamentally different. The standing

[31] Cf. S. B. Fay, *The Rise of Brandenburg-Prussia to 1786* (New York, 1937), pp. 22ff.

army in France immediately succeeded to the bastard feudal army; it was not the same thing, as it was in Prussia. These differences are minor, and it must be concluded that Brandenburg-Prussia, incompletely feudal in the Middle Ages, made up for that in the three succeeding centuries by the extension into that time of important particular feudalistic institutions.

In the old feudal countries of the west feudalism, even of the odd kind found in Prussia, did not last into the modern centuries. In England, as already remarked, even the nobility was fully absorbed into the growing national state. There indeed the transition was a smooth one, but for the Wars of the Roses, while the parliament was one of the few such bodies which successfully perpetuated restraints, of feudal origin, on monarchic power, and by far the most important of those few. Spain and Portugal are of minor interest, for there old institutions, including feudal survivals, were broken down by the sudden influx, and almost as sudden efflux, of wealth from the colonies. The Peninsula monarchies effectively did away with the power of the ruined nobility by the end of the sixteenth century, although in Spain especially the landed position of the nobility remained a permanent material burden upon the rest of the population.

It is France, of the western countries, which is of most interest, for there the feudal past left much behind it, much which was an unmitigated curse. In the fifteenth century the nobility had shown the same tendency to merge with the *roturiers* as their opposite numbers in England did, but in the sixteenth the government sought deliberately to stop this, and succeeded in doing so by legislation barring commerce and certain other lucrative activities to noblemen.[32] The trouble was that in France, as in most continental countries, the nobility had built up an immunity to taxation, and, if they went into trade, they carried their personal immunity with them, and the state lost some of its important new revenue. In England, where the nobility had no such immunity, passage from one class to another and from one function to another could be left completely free, so far as the state was concerned. But the Crown in France remained sufficiently afraid of the nobility not to dare to take away their immunity, which was the obvious way to meet the political and social changes coming about in the fifteenth and sixteenth centuries. Meanwhile, the Assemblies of Notables, in which the nobility were represented alone, and the Estates General, in which

[32] M. Szeftel, "La règle de vie exemplaire des nobles et l'évolution sociale de la France de l'ancien régime," *Revue de l'Institut de Sociologie*, XVI (1936), 603-606.

they formed one Estate, were deliberately allowed to fall into desuetude, as the Crown collected power into its hands. As a result, the nobility became a useless class without a sufficient function either political or economic.[33] Isolated from both people and government, they inevitably became an irresponsible public nuisance. With this sterilization of the nobility went a surprisingly unenterprising, timid preservation of the framework of the feudal polity. Such innovations as there were in this post-feudal polity culminated with Richelieu's intendants. These officers ruled the same areas as the old feudal magnates had ruled, but their administrative work grew steadily in volume from their establishment through the later seventeenth and eighteenth centuries, and it was done under the novel handicap of accountability for every considerable act and most inconsiderable ones to officials in Paris. The system was absurd and it led directly to 1789; only the great size and wealth of France prevented a collapse a century earlier.

It was the resumption of the struggle of the nations after the church-state issue had been settled[34] which enforced the elimination of feudal or feudalistic survivals. It was in the Central European society, or sub-society, that the struggle was first resumed, but it passed on with hardly a pause to the whole Western society as base. Thus, the Thirty Years' War, as we have already noticed, saw the culmination, so far as there ever was one, of the international struggle in Central Europe. But the struggle and the whole separate evolution of Central Europe were thereupon cut short by the intervention of the great nations of the Western European system, especially France and Sweden. As a result, the little nations of Central Europe were not permitted to eat each other up as nations ordinarily do in the struggle between them which leads

[33] Their functions remained in principle the same as those of the Prussian Junkers, and, had France been as simple a country as Brandenburg-Prussia, there might have been just sufficient for the nobility to remain a useful element in the state and the society. Especially in local political affairs, however, France had no need of a noble class; other classes had much at stake and were quite intelligent and energetic enough to deal with all such affairs. Hence the nobility let most of them go by default. Many noblemen treated the management of their estates in the same way, deputing it to stewards and bailiffs, for the serious agriculture of the country was not really in their hands. There remained to them only two useful occupations, military service and public office under the central government. They cared only for the high offices, however, and those were far too few, naturally, to afford any number of them an occupation. Military service gave a useful occupation to an appreciable number of noblemen, but a small minority even so, and they were not military organizers as the Prussian nobility were.

[34] The church-state issue was not finally settled until Napoleon's time, but it fell to a minor place in politics rather suddenly in the early seventeenth century.

to the establishment of empire. Instead, the great nations of Western Europe passed on almost at once to concentration upon their own internecine struggle, and it was because Sweden, then taking its place as a great nation of the Western society for the first time, played a major part in the Thirty Years' War that the first round of the Western struggle began in the north.

The northern wars and the wars associated with the ambitions of Louis XIV of France constitute the first round in those great internecine wars—"absolute wars" they were in Clausewitz's term. Then there was a pause of some eighty years in which the wars, though rather numerous and widespread, were only "limited wars." And then came twenty years more of absolute wars with France again in the position of aggressor. Louis XIV sought perhaps only hegemony over Western Europe, but Napoleon sought empire. Because Louis XIV's armies were largely contained by his adversaries and his aims frustrated, small states such as the Austrian Netherlands and the United Netherlands retained their old status, respectively of a Habsburg fief and an independent nation; nor was Spain closely united with France.

But the pressure of the movement toward empire was as great during the half-peace as it was during the great wars. The collapse and absorption of the weak nations began twenty years before the second round of great wars did, namely in 1772 with the first partition of Poland. Poland was the most feudalistic nation of the Western system, and it is significant of the weakness feudal and pre-feudal institutions imposed upon a nation that Poland succumbed completely and was destroyed in 1796. That gives the clue—if one is needed—to the disaster which befell Prussia a decade later. The Prussian army remained largely the feudalistic—bastard feudal—institution it had been in Frederick William I's time, and, if the Prussian army which retreated at Valmy was Frederick the Great's army grown thirty years older, the one the French overthrew at Jena and Auerstädt was the same grown nearly fifty years older. The Prussian state which was involved in the overthrow was neither feudal, nor, like the Polish state, a part feudal, part pre-feudal anomaly. It was a post-feudal despotism and a very efficient one when controlled by a genius like Frederick the Great or even by a highly competent martinet like Frederick William I. Without such control it was too superficial, too little penetrated, except for military matters, by the leading classes of its people, and that was because its architects could not contemplate a government shared with the nobility; nor were they wrong in all likelihood, for the narrow, factious, strongly localistic and feudalistic Junkers could scarcely have participated positively in the affairs of the nation.

The suppression of more than three hundred small German states by Napoleon is only tenuously an episode in the elimination of feudalism, for most of those states had ceased to be feudal. But it is their small size which made them an easy prey to Napoleon and their small size resulted from the fact that they had once been fiefs.

More directly relevant to feudal development is what happened to the Habsburg Dominions when eighteenth-century reforms were applied to them. Such reforms, the characteristic reforms of the enlightened despots, were the direct product of the increasing international rivalry, for the greatest claim to enlightenment the despots can make is that they understood the seriousness of the rivalry and knew that they must reform or perish. Joseph II (1780-1790), most enlightened of the Habsburgs, was one of those eighteenth-century statesmen in whose minds the logic of a political situation blotted out all other considerations. He plunged into a veritable orgy of reform. He proposed to complete the dissolution of ecclesiastical power, and he similarly proposed to absorb all noble power, which remained considerable, especially in Hungary, into the hands of the Crown. He planned judicial and penal reform, administrative rationalization, everything of the best known to eighteenth-century statecraft. And he planned it all at once, setting all parts of the machinery of reconstruction to work within months of his accession to power. What Joseph planned was no less than the conversion of the monstrous agglomerative fief of the Habsburgs into a nation, the transformation to be accomplished all in a generation.

It was impossible, of course, to accomplish such a vast number of changes so rapidly, and later events suggest that the main aim of consolidation into a single nation was by then impossible in any length of time; that, to have been successful, should have been begun in the sixteenth century or earlier. But another thing is also shown by Joseph's failure, namely that there was still a fair amount of vigor in the post-feudal institutions of the dominions. They were about as near to feudal institutions proper as it is possible for post-feudal institutions to be. The nobility were true local leaders, their diets not incapable of supplying some of the needs of the provinces. Above all, there was as a rule, except in Hungary, a balance of power between crown and nobility which promoted the interests of all parties, especially as it was reasonably harmonious. Joseph's reforms took their only lasting effect in upsetting the stability of the post-feudal regime permanently. Leopold II

(1790-1792) restored tranquility; in Napoleon's time Stadion tightened up administration a good deal, and the Habsburg Dominions got a new lease of life. But they were not able again to settle into any real stability, and it was only a matter of time before their various peoples each wanted liberal institutions and a separate nationality, not the single nationality Joseph would have liked and his successors could never hope for.

The fate of France under the pressure of the struggle of the nations is something really rather extraordinary, for it is hard to avoid the conclusion that the concatenation of events which led to the Revolution was a very narrow one consisting preponderantly of the shifting of the position of the nobility in society.[35] In the midst of and after the disasters which attended Louis XIV's wars, commercial and entrepreneurial occupation previously closed to noblemen was thrown open to them.[36] With unbelievable folly, Louis XIV and the regency for Louis XV maintained noble exemption from taxation in spite of the abandonment of noble exclusion from money-making occupations. This led directly to the ruin of the state and the revolution of 1789. The marvel is that breakdown did not occur long before that date and that so special a lesion as financial ruin of the state should seem to have been required to bring the crazy edifice down. The explanation certainly is the large population and great native wealth of the country. These fundamental advantages, indeed, had made France the greatest nation in Europe, actually or potentially, from the fifteenth century onward, and had afforded her the luxury of maintaining from that time, not only the noble class, but all manner of other anomalies derived from, or closely substituted for, feudal institutions. Once she had completely rid herself of these anomalies, France was a nation powerful enough to serve as the nucleus and basis of Napoleon's project of empire. That the great Revolution was aimed essentially at clearing away

[35] So clear a line of cause is unusual in history. It has in this instance been responsible for the attribution of the whole cause of the revolution to the position of the nobility, a fantastic error. The chaotic administrative structure was at least as large a source of weakness as the exemption of noblemen from taxation, while even the bankruptcy of the state was not wholly due to the exemption; the absurd incidence of the taxes even upon the taxables was another factor. And there were many other causes also.

[36] Maritime commerce was opened in 1669, wholesale commerce in 1701, banking at the time of the collapse of Law's commercial schemes, farming of the lands of the crown and princes of the blood in 1720, and participation in manufactures which were royal monopolies in 1722; Szeftel, *Revue de l'Institut de Sociologie*, xvi, 607-608 and notes.

the anomalies and survivals is witnessed by events which occurred in its early stages, especially in the resolutions of August 4th-5th, 1789, which abolished seigniorial and feudal rights, and the reconstruction of administration done between October 1789 and April 1790, whereby the departments replaced the old provinces.

Thus the elimination of feudalism in Europe was complete some time before the establishment of a new empire there—it was complete, that is to say, except for those insignificant vestiges which show only nature's abhorrence of absolutes. Yet, if feudalism has gone before a European empire has come into existence, and even if such an empire were never to come into existence, the history of Europe shows the connection between the elimination of feudalism and the advent of empire as clearly as do the history of China and the history of Mesopotamia. The increasing pressure of international rivalry is the main cause of the elimination of feudalism; the exaltation of the state, as carried out by national monarchs, is the next most important cause, one by no means independent of the main cause. Central Europe, like Chou China in so many ways, shows the same conversion of former feudal lords into national monarchs at a late date. Western Europe, by contrast, shows national monarchs who were never feudal dependents beginning the exaltation of the state at an early date and carrying it on at intervals over a very long period. Although the dichotomy of church and state in Europe is an altogether special development, lacking in other societies, it did not do more than interrupt and vary the process of elimination of feudalism; in essentials the process was the same in Europe as elsewhere.

The findings in the present chapter may be summed up in the form of a thesis. All civilized societies which have gone into decline and disintegration tend to revive and, after a period of national particularism, to be reunited politically. If the decline has been of comparatively minor extent, as in China post-Han and Egypt after the Sixth Dynasty, the monarchs of the nations consider themselves as emperors and one or another of them will succeed after a few centuries in reuniting the society, so setting up a new empire which will not be very greatly different from the old empire. We know from earlier parts of this essay that the new empire usually covers more territory than the old, but that it does not take in all peoples to whom the civilization has spread. If the decline has been profound and disintegration far reaching, a feudal period is likely to intervene in large areas of the society before particular national formations become effective and powerful. In such cases, although reunification of the society will come about in the end, there can be considerable variation in the course of development followed. A leading variable factor is the relative status of emperor and national monarchs. In some societies, such as Chou China and Central Europe, the monarchs remain essentially feudal magnates, sharply distinguished from the emperor, until, as it appears, circumstances force them into competing imperial roles. In other societies, national monarchs are more or less imperialistic from an early time, in extreme cases, such as Mesopotamia post-Hammurabi, almost as much so as in societies which do not go feudal to any extent. In all societies which have an important extent and period of feudalism the international wars, through which political reunification is eventually brought about, tend to be very severe. Special factors in particular societies may mitigate the severity of the wars or interrupt them. It looks too as if there is a general correlation between the severity of the wars and two particular factors, the strength of the imperialist urge in the monarchs and their nations, and, far back in the society's history, the magnitude of barbarian incursions.

This is, as stated, a thesis. It is not intended to be completely general, as witness the special cases, not covered by the thesis, to be treated in the next two chapters. Further, it is highly experimental even for the extent of its application.

There remains an important incidental matter which has arisen in this chapter and must be discussed shortly, the circumstances of the rise of new political theory.

In the Chinese society post-Han no fundamentally new political theory was invented; the dominant theory remained Confucianism, with a certain modification by Legalism inherited from the earlier cycle of Chinese history and quite a minor, perhaps finally nugatory, reshaping by Buddhism in the new cycle. I think it was the prestige of Confucianism in late feudal Japan which prevented the rise of an effective new political theory there. It would seem that even a very constructive feudal age in a single country—or a few minor countries, if such ages occurred also in other Sinic countries—will not affect the dominant political principles of an old, developed society which goes into a decline of small depth and degree at the end of a cycle of its history. On the whole, I do not think it probable that the absence of new political theory was a cause of the Tokugawa conservative feudal policy. As we have seen in two other cases, new theory follows the breakdown of feudalism; it does not precede it. The explanation offered above in terms of the shogun's fear of the revival of the emperor's power is more probable. The accessibility of Japan to European political theory in the nineteenth century, then, requires special explanation. That would seem to be in the main the great prestige of Europe at the time. Japan was not the only country so affected: Russia, though not truly feudal, was also moved by the pressure of European nations to get rid of a polity of as loose a kind as a feudal polity, and to attempt to substitute for it one of the European character. It cannot be said in the Japanese case whether a Confucianist state rather than one of European type would have been adopted if China had not been in decline at the time, but the possibility is worth bearing in mind.

That Central Europe, a society much like Chou China, never produced a political doctrine comparable with Confucianism, or indeed any political doctrine of its own, is explained, of course, by its relation to Western Europe: its parts were at all times parts of Western Europe also, and European doctrine belonged to Western Europe. The events and institutions which first exhibited it were the medieval parliamentary bodies of England, France, to a lesser extent the Iberian states, and perhaps one or two Italian states. The first theories include the work of Europeans of several nationalities, an Englishman, a German, a Frenchman, and the very great Italian, Marsiglio, but the ideas they propounded were the property of the great universities of Europe, French, English, and Italian. The resumption and full development of those theories in the late sixteenth century and thereafter were in France and England almost to the exclusion of other countries. The early experimentation in application of the fully developed theories occurred in seventeenth-century England, eighteenth-century England beyond the seas, and eighteenth-century France; it produced revolutions in each country. Central Europe was as much dominated by the great Western European theory as Japan was by the great Chinese theory; for that matter, the nations of the northern and eastern regions of the Western European system were similarly dominated by theory produced by the western nations.

What, then, about Mesopotamia post-Hammurabi, in whose history so far we have not discovered any very significant political theory? It would be idiotic to think that there never was any tendency for such a theory to arise there. Yet there seems a certain probability that no important one was developed. The history of Iran, which will be studied in the next chapter, supports the probability, for Iranian culture was

—more or less—Mesopotamian, and Persia, the latest of the Mesopotamian nations to arise, showed substantially negative political quality: its polity was a combination of certain pre-feudal and para-feudal relations with a rather crude royalism, or imperialism, similar to that of Assyria. It would seem that, if Mesopotamia had succeeded in developing an important political doctrine as it emerged from its feudal era, the doctrine would have been actively received in Media and Persia which were coming into existence at that time. Media and Persia were capable of producing a very striking new theory of another kind on their entry into the Mesopotamian society: Zoroastrianism. A failure to produce political theory seems consistent too with the failure to produce effective and stable national institutions which we have supposed to have been a feature of Mesopotamian history. In fact, in seeking to explain Assyria's repeated failure to absorb Babylonia after conquest, we begged the question of political theory, so far as Assyria's contribution to it goes, by supposing that Assyria had no effective national character.[37]

The presumptive political failure of Mesopotamia, both in ideas and in institutions, does not in the least prevent the conclusion that feudalism often leads on, as it comes to an end, to constructive political achievements; it merely means that it does not do so invariably and always. Mr. Strayer's discernment that in Europe it was the countries in which there was a major feudal development which afterwards made the greatest contributions to the society's characteristic political institutions receives in this chapter the support of an analogy in at least one other society. In spite of uncertainties due to gaps in evidence, we are entitled to say that feudal evolution tends to lead in later history, when feudalism itself no longer exists, to forms of government in which there is restraint of governing power and a sense on the part of the governed of political solidarity and the duty of cooperation. It may lead on to wide popular participation in government, but does not necessarily do so. Not every feudal era is the source of a new political doctrine of this valuable kind, but, where there is need for such doctrine in post-feudal times, there seems to be some possibility that it will be forthcoming, provided that there is no crushing inhibitory condition to obstruct it.

[37] Above, pp. 304-306.

8. THE CASE OF IRAN

IF there is in history an evolution from empire to empire midway between the feudal and the non-feudal course, it is the evolution of Iran from the breakdown of the Achaemenian Empire to the establishment of the Sassanian Empire. This evolution took some seven centuries from the decline of the old empire which was first evident in the reign of Xerxes (486-465 B.C.) until the beginning in A.D. 226 of the conquests by which Ardashir established the new one. Even if the total reckoning be reduced, the time is more than twice as long as the longest evolutions of a strictly non-feudal character. Yet, so far as we can judge, it is shorter than the evolutions which have feudal stages, perhaps about half as long if we strike an average.[1] Like the feudal societies, Iran had a ghost empire, the Parthian Empire. Like them again, it had in Mithradates II (124-87 B.C.) a great ruler of the caliber of Charlemagne or Yoritomo who conquered a large, ephemeral dominion; that dominion indeed looks in some ways proto-feudal. But we do not know that there was ever truly feudal tenure in Iran, and we have some reason to think there was not. One reason for thinking there was not is that there was always an important amount of commerce across Iran, the Mesopotamian cities, which were usually subject to the Parthian Empire, serving as prosperous entrepôt towns.

Both countries which went feudal and countries which did not were subject to barbarian invasion as their old empires broke down, and the so-called Parthians were just such invaders. In that political authority fell into their hands, they resemble the invaders of country which went feudal rather than invaders of country which did not. They have, in fact, a place in the history of Iran not unlike that of the Franks in the history of Western Europe. During the decline of the empire they established themselves in the province of Parthava, whence the name by which we know them, and then they spread west between the Caspian and the Iranian desert into Media and beyond it some distance into Mesopotamia. This took about a century, ending in the time of Mithra-

[1] Judgment is difficult because Western Europe has not yet achieved a new empire even though fifteen centuries have passed since the fall of the old one. The doubt about Shang China is a difficulty too, but there were about eleven or twelve centuries between the time when the old empire, if any, began to break down and the establishment of the new empire. It is impossible to make any calculation based on the history of Japan. In the case of Mesopotamia, whether feudal or not, the period is about fourteen centuries.

dates I (pre-160-138 B.C.). Subsequently, this territory manifested some degree of cohesion, and it may not unfairly be compared both with the Frankish dominions in Europe and with the Holy Roman Empire. Although this main Parthian territory had been more important in the Achaemenian Empire than Gaul had been in the Roman Empire, the high culture of Mesopotamia by its antiquity and achievements overshadowed the culture of Iran about as much as the high culture of Rome overshadowed the culture of Gaul. Politically, Parthia and Francia were alike in being the leading states among a number of states arising in a dark age of abasement of the culture after the fall of an empire.

The Parthians themselves were originally barbarians, as the Franks were, and, as such, they had been affected in some degree by the high culture of the civilized area before they invaded. That the Parthians had been steppe nomads, whereas the Franks had been settled agricultural villagers, before their respective migrations made little or no difference to events after the migrations, for nomad war organizations closely resemble war bands formed by previously settled barbarians when they migrate into the territory of an empire.[2] Thus the Parthians after they were settled in Iran were socially much similar to the Franks. The Parthians were fighting aristocrats who lived in the saddle and preferred, when there was no fighting to be done, to occupy themselves with hunting. Their famous method of cavalry warfare almost certainly came with them from the steppe. It was very likely that which enabled them to make their conquests, and it probably put all warfare in the Middle Eastern region on a new basis from then on.[3] Personal loyalty was of paramount importance to them and was sealed in blood brotherhood.[4] This is a social ethic familiar to us now, not only in the case of the Franks and other European barbarians, but also in every other case investigated so far. We are unable in the case of the Parthians, however to search forms of tenure for vassalage descended from these barbarian traits, for the evidence is not available. All we are able to substantiate is that some form or forms of dependent tenure did develop within the ranks of the Parthian aristocracy, and that the aristocracy must have owed some sort of war service to the King of Kings.[5]

[2] See Ch. 5, n. 11 above.

[3] See pp. 209-210 above for discussion of a different opinion held by Tarn.

[4] *Cambridge Ancient History*, IX, 589.

[5] Tarn remarks that what Parthian suzerainty meant is "unknown" (*Cambridge Ancient History*, IX, 590). It is not completely unknown in the cases of some

There is a suggestion that Parthian "feudalism" derived directly from Achaemenian institutions and not from anything introduced by the Parthians, and this must now be considered. Christensen makes the most reasonable statement to this effect: "Voilà [in the Achaemenian Empire] les origines du féodalisme en Perse. Toutefois, le féodalisme ne s'était pas encore développé sous les Achéménides."[6] Rostovtzeff thinks similarly but more positively.[7] It is evident from Mr. Brundage's investigation of this[8] that it is an error to regard the Achaemenian regime as feudal in any sense, but the error has its interest, for it draws attention to a non-feudal way in which formerly barbarian personal relations may become involved in a civilized polity.

The Persian Empire was to a rather large extent a continuation of the Assyrian Empire via the feeble Chaldaean Empire which carried on during the period of less than a century after the sudden fall of the Assyrian Empire. The transition was not unlike that between the Dynasty of Akkad and the Third Dynasty of Ur at an earlier time in the history of Mesopotamia. What has been described as feudalism under the Achaemenids was the personal immunities of the *vithpaitis* nobility and probably the self-containedness of the satrapies which some of them ruled—the latter being perhaps an inheritance from the Assyrians. Ehtécham, to whom Brundage refers, gives a twofold origin for the power and dignity of the *vithpaitis*, their landed property and their considerable number of personal dependents during their period of establishment in Iran before they took over the empire. This is most interesting; it was not a tribal arrangement, but something which grew up while the Medes and Persians were limitrophic barbarians to the empire. Thus, on the side of the personal dependencies it fits quite well into Chadwick's picture of such barbarians. As to the landed property, that may or may not have been characteristic of limitrophic barbarians; we scarcely know, but I am inclined to suggest that, in the Persian

Mesopotamian cities, but otherwise it is: neither in the cases of tenants in the main Parthian territory, nor in the cases of dependent monarchs outside it, do we know what service or tribute, if any, was owed the King of Kings.

[6] A. Christensen, *L'Iran sous les Sassanides*, 2nd edn. (Copenhagen, 1944), p. 16.

[7] *Cambridge Ancient History*, XI, 117. Rostovtzeff speaks of feudal structure as being characteristic of Iranian monarchies and in contrast with centralization as found in Egypt and Assyria and passed by them to the Hellenistic monarchies and so to the Roman Empire. This will not do; the vital continuity of the Assyrian and Achaemenid monarchies is now well known, while the profound difference between Egypt and Assyria has recently been probed by Frankfort (*Kingship and the Gods*, Chicago, 1948, pp. 6, 215).

[8] Above, pp. 108-110.

instance, it resulted from imitation of land practices in the empire and that its adoption was possibly a factor in the success the Persians later had in taking over and reviving the empire. The Medes and Persians, Brundage says, underwent three centuries of acculturation and "absorbed large doses of Valley ideas and techniques" before their conquest began. They did not, in fact, conquer Mesopotamia as barbarians at all, but as a nation—more correctly perhaps, two closely related nations—belonging to the society. They remained culturally somewhat different from the rest of the society, as Ch'in remained from the rest of Chou China, but in all aesthetic matters and some intellectual matters they were fully Mesopotamian; their language was their own, and their religion was special and remains rather a mystery. This substantial assimilation did not reduce the power or break up the personal relations of the *vithpaitis*, which thus found their way into the imperial structure as an incident of the Persian conquest.

It is clear that they might have become much more than an incident, however, since Cyrus gave his satraps both military and civil powers over the local territories they were to rule. Hence, as his vassals—if that term is allowable—they were well placed to become feudal lords if the empire had subsequently gone to pieces. Nor were there wanting some moves by satraps to make themselves independent local lords.

But the empire did not go to pieces; it did the very opposite, and to that fact *prima facie* is due the non-development of feudalism. Thus, under Darius the satrap became civil ruler only, a general and a secretary standing beside him and coming independently under the direct authority of the King of Kings, while all three came under the supervision of travelling inspectors, the "eyes and ears of the king." What was potentially feudal in this system was far less than what Cyrus had left, but the government of the satrapy did remain entirely self-contained except for inspection and rendition of taxes to the central authority; there was no centralization in the sense of ministers at the center controlling a local bureaucracy directly. Besides this, the satrap remained personally an immunist with great privileges, a magnate of even greater dignity than of actual power. Clearly, the system is properly described as federal, not feudal in the sense in which the word is used here.

Now comes the question whether the existence of this system contributed anything to the rise of dependency relations under the Parthian regime. In the course of the four centuries or so which divided the two periods, the Achaemenian regime had gone into decline and had been succeeded by the regime of the Seleucids which was likewise in decline and finally extinguished as the Parthian regime arose. It is hard to believe that, under the Parthians, the independent power of the local magnate owed much to the past. The dynamics of that situation were obviously those of the time itself, the disintegration of the empire and the conquest and attempted restoration by a new flood of barbarians, the Parthians. It is true that some honorific paraphernalia of the Achaemenian regime appeared again under the Arsacids, for example, the "Seven Families" who disposed of various court privileges and claimed many more solid rights. But this seems in principle to be of the same character as the Arsacid revival of the Achaemenid title of "King of Kings," in short, to be a part of the evocation of the ghost of the old empire. The powers of those families were really great under the Arsacids, but that was with a new substance imparted to old forms. It would seem, in fact, that the error of Rostovtzeff is to mistake form for substance, Christensen sharing in the error to a lesser extent: the private political power of Arsacid times arose out of the facts of those times; what it owed to Achaemenid precedent was names and forms.

If we turn from the power and dignity of the political magnate to the territorial system, we get similar results. Conceivably, the self-containedness of the Achaemenian satrapy served to preserve the old geography of Iran-Mesopotamia. But it is notable that it preserved; it did not create. Media had been Media before it became the Tenth Satrapy under Darius; Uvaja had been Elam before it became Uvaja, the Eighth Satrapy, and it was to become Elymais under the Parthians. It is not conceivable that the federal form of the Achaemenian Empire was an actual incentive, a dynamic beginning, of disintegration, still less of feudalization, in Parthian times. If it had been, surely disintegration would have proceeded under the Achaemenids themselves. Confirmation of this is found in the actual disintegration which occurred under the Parthians. Media remained Media under the Seleucids, but it broke into five dependencies under the Parthians, even though it became the real center of Parthian power. It is true that Uvaja became Elymais with a local king over it and under the Parthian King of Kings, but a diverse fragmentation developed below the local king, and the same happened in Persis and other old territorial units of Iran proper. It is clear, in fact, that the disintegration of Parthian times is something quite different from the federal system of Achaemenian and Seleucid times even if it occurred to a fairly large extent within the territorial forms left by the Seleucids and Achaemenids, and indeed by much earlier regimes than theirs. To regard the Achaemenian Empire as a half-feudal polity, or as an "undeveloped" feudal polity waiting, in some kind of suspension to be fully developed when the Parthians came along, is a misinterpre tation of the facts.

The Achaemenian Empire was not the only great empire in the his toric background of Parthian Iran: the Seleucid Empire was there also and that is a very special feature of Iranian history. The conquest by Alexander the Great and the subsequent establishment of the Seleucid were not mere superficial, political episodes; indeed their effect wa least in politics. The more powerful movement of Hellenization bor upon other aspects of the culture. Mesopotamia and Bactria were quit deeply, although not permanently, Hellenized, but it is interesting tha western Iran, seat of the Medes and Persians and of the main strengt of the Parthians and of the Sassanids as well, was less Hellenized. Th most remarkable phenomenon was the Hellenization of the cities o Mesopotamia proper. The old Mesopotamian culture died right ou even the religion ceased,[9] and there was, not exactly a cultural vacuum for it was refilled before that could happen, but a most remarkabl cultural transformation: where the region was not Hellenized, it wa Judaized, and in Parthian times and later more of the culture of Mes opotamia survived on the Iranian Plateau than in Mesopotamia prope —and not a great deal of it survived on the Iranian Plateau.[10]

Hellenized subjects were certainly an important element in the Par thian Empire, and the Arsacid rulers recognized that fact by assumin the title "Philhellene." But the Parthian Empire was in all its particula a ghost of the Persian Empire, and the Arsacids saw themselves a successors of the Achaemenids. If Hellenization was less effective i politics than in the rest of the culture, it was least effective politicall upon the imperial tradition. The Seleucids had to rule much in th

[9] Both H. S. Nyberg (*Die Religionen des Alten Iran*, trans. from Swedish, H. H. Schaeder, Leipzig, 1938, p. 406-407) and J. M. Unvala (*Observations on the Religi of the Parthians*, Bombay, 1925, p. 5) speak of Hellenistic influence on religion Mesopotamia. This is rather misleading. Greek religion, except for a few rath special things like Orphism and the cult of Tyche (Fortuna) was at a very lo ebb, and, though some forms were set up, they had no life in them. Sometim they yielded to Mazdaism, sometimes to Judaism, and later they were swamped b various Gnosticisms, Christianity and Manicheeism.

[10] P. Sykes in his short work on Persia (*Persia*, Oxford, 1922, p. 30) speaks the Parthians as a people who remained nomads and governed from a camp. Th is an exaggeration. I should think it actually an impossibility for nomads to ru for five hundred years over even a much degenerated civilized people witho amalgamating with them, but the general level of the culture fell very low.

manner of the Achaemenids, although the Seleucid army and a few administrative practices were Macedonian. The effect of the intrusion upon the main course of the main, cyclic, political evolution was not great. At most, it prolonged the political decline between one and two centuries; it hardly even reversed it, for, Jouguet remarks, the Seleucids were compelled "by the very nature of things" to be content with a looser authority over Iran even than the later Achaemenids had wielded.[11]

It was a very different matter with commerce. The important trade which passed across the Parthian and then the Sassanian Empire was thoroughly Hellenized; it became essentially a Greek trade, a trade between the Greco-Roman world and China and India. Certainly it was not a Parthian or even an Iranian trade; non-Greeks in it were Syrians, Jews, or Armenians and they were usually more or less Hellenized. The Mesopotamian cities had, of course, been great trading cities long before Greeks had been heard of, but it may well be asked whether their trade would have continued in Parthian times if the Greeks had not taken it over. In short, without Hellenization would not trade, cities, and high culture in every manifestation have ceased in Mesopotamia, or fallen as low as to become of little consequence in the subsequent development of Iran-Mesopotamia? This is a very important question for the character of Parthian and Sassanian institutions and we shall return to it below.

Some of the leading events of political history must now be reviewed for their bearing on the development of institutions. The reign of Mithradates II (124-87 B.C.) was a key period in development of the Parthian state. He was a great conqueror. Besides obtaining all Parthia in the north of Iran, he became superior lord of Elymais and of Persis, the latter the original home of the Achaemenids and probably the strongest Iranian state after Parthia itself. Outside Iran proper he acquired for a time Babylonia, which was more or less the territory in the Tigris-Euphrates Valleys known by that name from later Kassite times. He enlarged the northern valley territory, to which at this time the name Mesopotamia is usually confined, beyond that part which was usually under the Arsacid King of Kings. He conquered also a large piece of steppe territory in the north and ruled right up to the Oxus.

[11] P. Jouguet, *Macedonian Imperialism and the Hellenization of the East*, trans. M. R. Dobie (London, 1928), p. 365. Jouguet cites G. Radet in *Journal des savants*, 1913, p. 301, in support.

In this conquest it is likely that he provoked the invasions of the Saca, the Yüeh Chih and other nomads which became one of the main series of events of his reign. He successfully defended western Iran against this menace, but, like the Norse invasions of Europe, the Saca invasions took large effect in some areas, brought a second incursion of barbarians akin to those of the first invasion, and may have promoted militarization of government. The area of Iran most affected was the east, where the Hellenistic state of Bactria was established. That state disappeared and was succeeded by Sacastene (Seistan) which eventually became a province of the Sassanian Empire. Iran was saved from some of the Saca fury when the Sacas passed beyond Bactria and penetrated into India where they brought about still greater political changes.

Mithradates' empire was ephemeral, and it is clear that Mithradate and his successors did not dispose either of the wealth, the skilled administrative personnel, or even on a reliable, enduring basis of the mili tary strength to hold the empire together. We are reminded irresistibl of Charlemagne's empire, and, when Debevoise says that Mithradate had to devolve much power upon subordinates in order to rule th immense territory,[12] we may ask whether the devolution was made on a basis of feudal relations. But, of course, there is no clear answer.[1] Gotarzes, Mithradates' *marzban* of *marzbans*,[14] was given charge o Babylonia, and he probably made himself independent (though nc permanent) monarch there before Mithradates' death; was he a feuda vassal who became contumacious, or was he just an unreliable, traitor ous official? Christensen has noticed that the relations between th King of Kings and his immediate great vassals were less firm than thos between the great vassals and the lesser gentry.[15] Such is very usua

[12] N. C. Debevoise, *A Political History of Parthia* (Chicago, 1938), p. 44.

[13] Herzfeld describes a sculpture (bas-relief?) among those at Behistun c Mithradates II and four other persons, one of whom is Gotarzes. Herzfeld say that the picture is of the investiture by Mithradates of four feudal houses wit their fiefs and adds, "Mithradates, the actual founder of the empire, must hav created its feudal organization" (*Archaeological History of Iran*, Schweich Le tures of the British Academy, 1934, London, 1935, pp. 54-55). For "feudal" rea "proto-feudal," and it is then useful to have Herzfeld's opinion, but a picture figures in certain attitudes to each other is not strong evidence of feudal relation.

[14] *Marzban* is the usual Parthian word for an official ostensibly discharging th function of satrap in the old empire. The *marzban* of *marzbans* was the hea *marzban*, just as the King of Kings was the head king. Surely the *marzban* *marzbans* should have been occupied, in a properly run kingdom, entirely wit general administration; that he became ruler of a province suggests irregularit

[15] *L'Iran sous les Sassanides*, pp. 18-19.

in a proto-feudal state or a feudal state in its earlier days, and it is noticed by Strayer for Europe in the later Carolingian period.[16]

We are painfully ignorant of the main three centuries of Parthian history which followed the reign of Mithradates II. Almost all our information is from Josephus and Roman authorities, who were reporting at second hand. The one exception, the local *Chronicle of Arbela* of Msiha Zkha, is so very local that it is risky to generalize from it. From this basis, such as it is, the period might tentatively, rather doubtfully, be interpreted as an age of formative feudalism like that of the Ashikaga Shogunate in Japan or of ninth- to eleventh-century France. There certainly must have been a great deal of internecine warfare. The misfortunes of Ardawan III, a particularly able king, suggest the onset of a period of baronial ascendancy and disorder in the latter part of his reign, the late 'twenties and the 'thirties of the first century A.D.; for some of that time the king went into hiding until he could rally his followers. On the other hand, Roman authorities often report solid resistance to Roman invasion by king and barons together; such solidarity was perhaps provoked by alien attack. I think it is likely that institutions were being consolidated in this period and certain that personal dependency of some sort was important in them. But it is also likely that the monarchs continued to operate government chiefly through paid, removable functionaries. Vologases II in the latter part of the first century A.D. was able to reduce the kingdom of Adiabene to the status of a province under a *marzban* after a rebellion; a *marzban* was presumably an appointive official, and the former King of Adiabene had certainly been a dependent in some form of the King of Kings.

This brings us to the remarkable conquests of Ardashir and Shahpuhr I, which were given at the opening of this chapter as the conquests whereby the whole society was reunited, but in Chapter 6 were compared with the revolutionary emergence of strong nations in Europe, Japan, and Chou China. There need be no hesitation about the real character of Ardashir's and Shahpuhr's achievement: it was reunification of the whole Iranian-Mesopotamian society.[17] But it is interesting that it does resemble so much the emergence of the strong nation in a feudal society, coming, as it does, just at the moment in the evolution of Iran when strong monarchies might be expected. Indeed, Arda-

[16] Above, p. 21.

[17] The fact that the Romans made serious inroads and sometimes held part or, rarely, all of Mesopotamia did not really affect the evolution of Iran-Mesopotamia, being a very superficial and, as it always proved, impermanent intrusion of an alien society.

shir and his father, Pabhagh, did set up a strong monarchy in Persis, their own nation, immediately before Ardashir set out upon the greater conquests; the latter thus were extensions of the emergence of a strong nation.

We may get an idea of the magnitude of the Sassanid achievement if we make an imaginary transposition of it to medieval Europe. Upon that basis we might suppose that Robert I of Normandy, William the Conqueror's father, instead of helping Henry I to the throne of France, had rebelled against him, driven him out, and made himself king—for Pabhagh began his career as a mere local magnate in Persis, who rebelled against and displaced his king. William himself would then have suppressed his own great vassals throughout France, introducing perhaps an administration of officials to run the whole country—something scarcely possible actually in France before the fourteenth century if then. After that would have followed William's chief undertaking the overthrow of the house of Franconia in the person, presumably, of Henry IV, and the acquisition of the imperial crown. To William Rufus perhaps would have fallen the task of conquering England and the lesser territories of Scandinavia and the east.

This flight of fancy serves to suggest rather forcefully that Iran in Parthian-Sassanian times was rather different from medieval Europe. In area it was some three-fifths the size of Western Europe so that the conquests of Ardashir and Shahpuhr are to be discounted to that extent for purposes of comparison. Even with the discount the proposed conquests of Robert I, William I, and William Rufus are unthinkable. The Norman rulers did not, in the first place, dispose of sufficient armies, whereas Ardashir built up and kept on a permanent war footing a very large army. In the second place, no service of officials like the Sassanian *dibherân* could have been set up in eleventh-century Europe, and, if the comparison be shifted to fourteenth- or fifteenth-century Europe when perhaps such a service was possible, the Hundred Years' War was then fought by the monarchs of one nation seeking to conquer another nation. This raises a third consideration which will prove to be the vital one: Ardashir and Shahpuhr met resistance from the several other nations of Iran they conquered, but it was not, in my judgment, the resistance which the tough nations formed in a feudal society would have put up. If this is correct, Iran was not and had not been feudal when it was reunited at the establishment of the Sassanian Empire. The hypothesis that it was not must now be tested.

Nations, worthy of the name, arose as the Seleucid Empire broke up, but not in all parts of Iran. Persis in the south was one of these. It is an example of historic determination, for it was the original Persian territory of the Achaemenids, and was now ruled by the Basrangi; it had the gulf on its southwest and the desert plateau north of it, but no clear frontiers northwestward or eastward. Bactria in the northeast was very Greek. It was also in the main a mountain kingdom, embracing the Hindu Kush and the Pamirs. Hyrcania in the Elburz around the southeast corner of the Caspian was another mountain kingdom, though a small one. In the extreme northwest was yet another mountain kingdom, Armenia, which was also ethnically quite distinct from both Iran and Mesopotamia; it was not Graecized and had its own language and institutions. Media Atropatene, southeast of Armenia, became a nation early and proved a stable political unit. It was Iranian, and it occupied the less high mountains next to Armenia lying between the line of the Zagros on the southwest and the southwest coast of the Caspian on the northeast. It had no physical frontier southeastward. Parthia itself, southeast of the Caspian between Hyrcania and Bactria, must also be considered an early nation, one consisting of the historic province of Parthava and having the steppe nomad immigrants who have been called Parthians as a special ethnic element.

These nations, except Bactria, would presumably have appeared just as early, perhaps earlier, if the Seleucid Empire had not supervened for a couple of centuries upon the decline of the Achaemenian Empire. Armenia and Media Atropatene already had appeared earlier than the rest. The early rise of nations suggests a non-feudal evolution in the main part of the society, but it should be noticed that nations did not develop in Mesopotamia either north or south, or in a large region eastward of the great valleys, consisting chiefly of Greater Media, and perhaps also including Elymais, the ancient Elam. This last indeed is problematical; we just do not know whether Elymais acquired an effective national individuality as the Seleucid Empire broke down or not. What happened in this other region at first was that the Parthian King of Kings conquered a good half of it, the northern half including most of Media and a little northern Mesopotamian country. This with Parthia proper became his chief territory, which thus resembled geographically the German Holy Roman Empire in Europe, although it had come into existence in another way. The Parthian King of Kings was, however, clearly a somewhat more effective ghost emperor than the Holy Roman Emperor. There are good reasons for thinking that, wobbly as he was in his position in his main territory, he usually had more power there than the Holy Roman Emperor had in Germany. Besides that, he became for most of the time acknowledged suzerain over the nations, as the Holy Roman Emperor did not over those in Europe, even though the Iranian nations were developed at a far earlier date than the European ones, and presumably were stronger when the King of Kings—Mithradates II in most cases—gained his suzerainty over them. We scarcely know enough to say whether the lands ruled directly by the King of Kings produced nations at the sort of date that might be expected if the lands were feudal.

The Mesopotamian territories are really no help with our problem. To be sure, we know more about the form of relation of the states there with the King of Kings than we do about those of other states with him, and we know more about the city-states of that region than we know about any other states of the society in the Parthian period. The Greek cities, as they had become, always had the typical Greek political structure in some form with *boule*, magistrates, and *demos*. Some of those cities, too, did depend in a quasi-feudal manner on the monarch as is true of some medieval European cities, but that does not constitute a real feudalism. There were other cities in which a condominium existed between the city officials and assemblies and a resident representing the monarch—a system which can be found also in some cities of Germany in the sixteenth century, as the power of the territorial princes increased. Besides the cities, there were a number of other kind of principality, the territorial principality of Adiabene in the far north whose rulers adopted for a time Judaism, Jewish and Arab tribal states among the latter the rather famous "kingdom" of Hira, and others. They came into existence at all sorts of times.

Mesopotamia-Babylonia filled a place in Iran much like that of Ital in medieval Europe, even to the point of being in touch culturally, an sometimes politically, with the neighboring society, Byzantium in th case of Europe, the Greek world under successive different authorit in the case of Iran. Mesopotamia is thus not the place to look for im portant feudal developments, while the rest of the society's territor seems rather decisively not to have developed nations at the time or i the manner we expect in a society at all largely feudal.

There is less evidence about the development of fiefs than there i about that of nations. We do not hear of fiefs which tended to becom nations as in Central Europe or Chou China. The nations of Iran wer clearly of the kind which arose from physiographic and historic deter minants, and yet, contradictorily, the admitted suzerainty of the King of Kings put them in a dependent position which causes them to approximate to the status of fiefs in a very general sense. But, as we have just seen, there were other kinds of dependency than that of the nations. The cities of Mesopotamia and tribal principalities in Mesopotamia and other places were dependent upon the national monarchs, or upon the King of Kings, by some special tenure. Also dependent upon the King of Kings were the members of the Seven Families we have found to have been a part of the apparatus of empire copied from that of the Achaemenids; their tenures can scarcely have been like those of national kings. A remarkable thing we know about the Suren, one of the Seven Families, is that its lands were so large that in military service they yielded an entire army. It was that army which fought and won the great battle of Carrhae against Crassus while the King of Kings himself was operating against Crassus' communications. Plutarch's description of that army does not suggest quite a feudal army, for the large vassal does not appear; the army consisted rather of small vassals and partly of armed personal servants, probably both of the Suren family itself and of its vassals, all of them mounted.[18]

Carrhae was fought in 53 B.C., thirty-four years after the death of Mithradates II, actually in the first stage of true feudalism by the European and Japanese analogies. The Suren estate would seem to have been extremely large for a feudal estate at so early a moment in feudalization. This with the lack of the chief feudal element in the army suggests that it was not truly a feudal estate. It seems instead like one of those great *latifundia* of later Roman times which in Byzantium developed into estates of the *dynatoi*. Those had a feudalistic feature in the form of vassalage of some of the chief retainers, and it looks as if the Suren estates had a similar feature. But that feature in the Byzantine case was not truly feudal; it was pre-feudal in type, but never became feudal because the old structure of the state never finally col-

[18] ". . . *εἶχε δὲ τοὺς σύμπαντας ἱππεῖς ὁμοῦ πελάτας τε καὶ δούλους μυρίων οὐκ ἀποδέοντας*" (*Crass.* xxi.6). A *πελάτης* is nearly always a landed dependent, a *cliens*, usually a person of no great importance socially. Δοῦλος is the difficult term to interpret. It is hardly likely to mean slave since slaves would hardly be reliable fighting men; I have taken the view that they must have been personal servants since a *δοῦλος* usually was a personal slave. Cf. the translations of Perrin (*Plutarch's Lives*, Loeb edn., London and New York, 1916, III, 37) and Dryden-Clough (*Plutarch's Lives: The Translation Called Dryden's*, New York, n.d., III, 22), neither of which, however, is particularly suggestive. The army may well have been of a pre-feudal type, and such armies need never have given place to truly feudal armies.

lapsed so that the society was never exposed to the violent struggle for survival out of which the elemental strong fief arises. It looks as if the same was true in Iran-Mesopotamia (many Suren possessions were in Mesopotamia); large estates governed mainly by a service of officials, even if defended by a force of troops partly maintained on a feudalistic basis, could survive in circumstances of that sort.[19]

There is confirmation of this in a number of small data, but most effectively in the survival under the Arsacid rulers of a service of offi cials. The *marzban* were great local officials who remained, at least in most cases, removable by the crown under the Arsacids; the degrada tion of the Kingdom of Adiabene to the status of a province under a *marzban* by Vologases II has already been cited, and that occurred in the latter part of the first century A.D., a late date in Parthian times. A thing like that could not happen in a truly feudal society. In the class system of Sassanian times, for which we have official record, the *Vu zurgan*, the third class, consisted of the high functionaries and adminis trative heads of the empire, while in the fourth class, the *Azadhan*, th "free," were a host of lesser functionaries, mostly provincial. These, th *Vuzurgan* and the *marzban* (the *marzban* belonging to the topmos class, the *Shahrdaran*) were all *dibheran*, officials. In the centralizatio which was the consequence of Ardashir's and Shahpuhr I's conquest o the society, the *dibheran* in the service of the empire were rapidly in creased in numbers. But they can scarcely have been created by th conquerors out of unskilled personnel; they came, obviously, from th service of the great nobility and the princes whose lands were bein conquered.

It is, in fact, reasonably clear that the Parthian polity was a rathe loose federal polity consisting of two main kinds of unit, the kingdor or principality and the noble estate, possessions respectively of the tw topmost classes, the *Shahrdaran* and the *Vaspuhran*. Both types of un were ruled mainly by a service of officials, but within both the lord ha some dependents owing him military service on a feudalistic basis. Th basis of tenure may have existed as between the *Shahrdaran* and *Va puhran* and their own overlord, the Arsacid King of Kings, but, if did, it was obscured by involvement in a complex of the reciproc

[19] There may be something in the idea that such estates readily arose all ov the Near East, and so that they are something which Iran-Mesopotamia and th eastern end of the Roman Empire had in common. If Jacques Pirenne is to trusted, the nomarchs in Sixth Dynasty Egypt came to have dependents on feudalistic basis also (*Revue de l'Institut de Sociologie*, Brussels, XVI, 1936, 29 but, as has been shown above (pp. 257-261), Egypt at that time did not go feuda

duties and rights and traditional honorific conditions.[20] Nevertheless, these great "vassals" were expected to follow the King of Kings in war and often did so. Among the rights the King of Kings had was the right to replace his dependents, probably of both classes, certainly of the *Shahrdaran*, when they were contumacious, either with substitutes in the same relation to him, or with mere officials, the former substitution being consistent with feudal ideas, the latter not being. This right resulted in a number of principalities finding their way into the hands of Arsacid cadets; among those usually in such hands was Armenia. Whether the King of Kings could similarly remove the *vaspuhr* is not clear, but he could certainly, when strong enough, seize some or all of the *vaspuhr's* land and annex it to the imperial domain.

Typical of the character of this polity is the parallel between functionary and landed magnate. The king found his equal in the great *marzban*, and, if the *vaspuhr* took precedence of the *vuzurg*, no gulf divided them, for they were neighbors in dignity, while the ordinary free *azad* might be a small gentleman or he might be a village headman.[21] The *vaspuhr* very likely still was in some of his functions an official under the crown, while yet his position as landed magnate was his salient political trait; the *vuzurg*, who had remained always primarily a great official, yet had to have land in order to live. Christensen introduces here telling evidence for Armenia: the administration there got muddled sometimes between the words *nakhararut'iun*, which meant a local government, and *nahapetut'iun*, which meant a fief.[22] The source is a chronicle of the fifth century A.D., and it surely indicates a polity not fully feudal even at that late date. If in the rest of Iran-Mesopotamia verbal confusion between the two things did not arise, then feudalization had occurred there less than it had in Armenia.

The reason a feudal polity did not eventuate in Iran-Mesopotamia is not the diversion of events in a totally different direction by supervention of overwhelming alien influence as in "Libyan" Egypt or in India post-Gupta. This is not an evolution cut short. It is perhaps one held back and eventually foreshortened. Such a diagnosis is not proven,

[20] This is the substance, I think, of the closer liens Christensen finds between he great "vassals" and their dependents than between the former and the imperial crown (pp. 18-19). Such a contrast is usual in truly feudal societies in the early tage of their development.

[21] The headman, *dekhan*, might himself be a small gentleman, or he might be a mere senior peasant, depending upon the size of the village. The incomplete differentiation of classes is itself suggestive.

[22] p. 22. Christensen's fifth-century source is Moses of Chorene's *History of Armenia.*

but there is reasonable probability in it. The continuing vigor of commerce across Iranian-Mesopotamian territory quite probably served to postpone the final collapse of the old regime so long that it never actually took place. Our enquiry into the effects of the rise of commerce in feudal countries does not show a necessary incompatibility between the two, but clearly shows that a rising commerce facilitates the growth of the size of political units. Large political units are, in many cases, precisely what we encounter in Iran—much larger units than we should expect in early feudal times. It seems eminently probable that the lords of those political units were enabled by wealth gained from commerce to maintain the administration and the military forces required to keep large political units together. It would presumably be easier to keep together relatively large territories already in being than it would be to build up large territories anew with wealth newly acquired, and, if there is not an incompatibility between feudalism and well-developed commerce, there is an affinity between well-developed commerce and bureaucracy.

The polity of Iran in Parthian times, then, is comparable with that in late feudal times in Europe and Japan, but it is not closely comparable: it was in all likelihood much less feudal and much more bureaucratic. In the same way, the conquest of Iran by the Sassanids is comparable with the establishment of strong nations in Europe and Japan, but it was a much greater change than those changes. Usually in Europe, when the struggle of monarchy and baronage came to an end a good deal of the feudal structure in government fell away; in Iran most of the feudalistic development fell away with Ardashir's, Shahpuhr I's, and their two successors' construction of the new unified government. Christensen thinks that the majority of the knights then became castellans dependent on the imperial crown, and not upon the *vaspuhrs*, as they had been under the Arsacids. The *vaspuhrs* indeed continued under the Sassanids to go to war at the head of the levies of their subjects; it was no doubt difficult and not worth while to abrogate completely so venerable a custom; but their levies were now "paysans . . . mal organisées et . . . de mauvais soldats," for the *vaspuhrs* had lost their only fencible dependents.[23] Such elements in an army might be called feudalistic, but it is hardly possible that peasants could hold in true feudal tenure of their lords. The real army came to be one of mercenaries, as also happened at the corresponding stage in Europe.

[23] *L'Iran sous les Sassanides*, p. 259.

The Sassanid conquest, being a conquest not merely of one nation but of many, presented the new imperial government with a problem of nationalities. There cannot be much doubt that the government dealt with it successfully, for there is very little in the record of subsequent troubles from that source; troubles there certainly were, but they had not much to do with national particularism. The Sassanids developed and transformed the Arsacid policy of placing their relatives on the thrones of the nations. Whereas this often led to hereditary cadet lines under the Arsacids, the Sassanids aimed at a true appanage system, the heir to the imperial throne in particular being given the throne of one of the important nations. Probably other thrones were given to other Sassanids than the heir,[24] but not all the nations were brought into the system; probably there were too many for it to be possible. The Sassanids, however, seem to have managed to control the personnel of the other royal houses fairly well also. No doubt, this policy, together with the administrative centralization, served to inhibit, perhaps even to reverse, the growth of nationality. We do not know much about centralization in detail, but it was certainly a fact, a policy maintained permanently. But centralization and control of royal personnel together do not explain the absence of all signs of nationality in Iran. It has been postulated above that the Sassanid conquest would never have been possible if nationality had been developed in Iran as strongly as it was developed in feudal societies. By the same token, the centralization of the Sassanian Empire and the management of its subordinate monarchies would never have been possible if the nations had been developed into strong, coherent in-groups like the nations which arose in feudal societies.

The troubles of the Sassanian Empire did not arise from any conflict of nations; the international struggle of feudal societies was almost wholly lacking, and in that regard Iran is to be classed with non-feudal societies. What the empire did have was a turbulent nobility and, with it, dynastic strife within the house of Sassan itself. The nobility no longer aimed at local independence; they had been brought to court, and their aims centered upon influencing imperial policy. Local particularism gave way completely to faction at the center in the politics

[24] In the first century B.C. and a part of the first century A.D. there had been a system of rotation of thrones with each new succession to the paramount throne in the Saca-Pahlava confederacy of southeastern Iran and the Indus Valley (Debevoise, pp. 63-69). Whether that idea came from the steppe with the Sacas, or whether it was Iranian, we do not know, but it was certainly much the same system as the Sassanids adopted for their empire.

of Iran as a result of the Sassanid conquest. The completeness of this change is one of the two remarkable things about the new regime; the other is the constancy and violence of the new factiousness. The house of Sassan was indeed secure in its tenure of the imperial crown, but no individual member of the house was. Few indeed of them died in their beds, and maiming and assassination were more common than death in battle. For centuries—for almost the entire four centuries of the empire's duration—the nobility were *frondeurs*, more than *frondeurs*, for there were times when they actually governed. In this respect Sassanian Iran was somewhat like a nation in a post-feudal society, burdened with a formerly feudal nobility which had become the leading estate of the realm. Yet no post-feudal nation suffered from noble and dynastic faction as Iran did. Neither can Sassanian Iran be compared in this respect with other societies whose empires were restored without resort to feudalism, for those societies, as we have seen in the cases of T'ang China, Byzantium, and Twelfth Dynasty Egypt, suffered from the threat of local particularism, the danger which, surprisingly enough, the Sassanid conquest of Iran brought to an end. The Sassanian Empire was *sui generis*.

But it is not, finally, very strange that the evolution of Iran-Mesopotamia should lead to a state which cannot be classified with other states, for the evolution itself was quite unusual. We need not expect to find a class of societies of which Iran-Mesopotamia was one. There is no such class, half way between those which went feudal and those which did not. One other society, Russia, which underwent an influence similar to that special influence which affected Iran-Mesopotamia, evolved quite differently.

It was said above that the peculiar evolution of Iran-Mesopotamia did not result from supervention of an overwhelming alien influence. It surely did result, however, from an alien influence which was less than overwhelming. When the Achaemenian Empire went into disintegration and the culture of Mesopotamia almost faded away entirely, the commerce of which Mesopotamia had been the center would, in normal circumstances, have dwindled to nothing also. In all likelihood indeed it did dwindle to something much less than it had been. But, as Mesopotamia declined, Greece grew. The Seleucid Empire, a political product of Greek growth, proved indeed of merely temporary effect upon the political evolution of Mesopotamia and Iran. The Greek aesthetic and intellectual culture, however, possessed Mesopotamia; its cities, most of them, became Greek cities, and formed an advanced base for Greek long distance commerce. That commerce prospered throughout Parthian and Sassanian times, and gave Iran a source of wealth which had profound effect upon the course of its history.

It is instructive to find that the course of evolution of one society can be so greatly influenced by penetration of the commerce of another society. We shall find in the next chapter that Russia, another society with an anomalous history, was also profoundly influenced, and very early influenced, by penetration of commerce from outside it.

9. RUSSIA AND BYZANTIUM

IN Chapters 4 and 5 above the restoration of empire in Byzantium after the disintegration of the old, unitary Roman Empire has been examined, and it has been shown that feudal institutions did not occur in the course of that transition. It was one of those transitions in which disintegration did not go far enough to need the feudal remedy. Russia's relation to Byzantium has also been noticed, but not more than that. The development of Russian and of late Byzantine institutions, the connection of Russian and Byzantine development, and the approach to feudal conditions in both Russia and later Byzantium remain to be investigated. It is because these are all matters which are at least unusual that they have been left for special treatment in this chapter, and for the same reason their treatment must begin with a clear characterization of the position of Russia and Byzantium—Byzantium-Russia—in history.

Byzantium had been one of the two nuclear regions of the Roman Empire. It was the older one, the earliest and always one of the greatest cultural centers of the Graeco-Roman society. Southern Russia had been an outside, limitrophic region of the empire, with steppe land penetrating into it, while the rest of Russia was simply further external territory, penetrable perhaps by the Graeco-Roman high culture. Its inhabitants were probably few and much subject to influences from the steppe and from Asia beyond, as well as from Byzantium. When the general decline of the Graeco-Roman culture and the break-up of the Roman Empire came about, southern Russia and Byzantium were, respectively, in the same historic positions as Germany and Italy, the one barbarian country with a prospect of being drawn fully within the civilized area as and when the civilization should recover, and the other, as a nuclear civilized region, having the prospect of leading the recovery if the recovery should begin soon. Two other circumstances vitally affected the positions of Russia and Byzantium. One was the odd fact that the Graeco-Roman society was in two parts, Greek and Roman, not simple and single, and the other was that at least two distinct civilized societies had flourished eastward of the Graeco-Roman world and had tended to be drawn within it.

From these various antecedent circumstances the destiny of Byzantium and Russia took shape. Byzantium, as we know, realized the prospect of leading a rapid recovery of the high culture, as Italy, at the other end of the old society, did not. But Russia failed rather miserably where Germany succeeded: Russia was not brought fully into the civilized area; in fact, it was hardly brought in at all. As we shall see below, except in commerce, its civilization remained very simple, while the civilization of Byzantium, which was never simple, grew rapidly; from this contrast, it would seem, there arose a cultural barrier between the two countries.[1] The difference between Greece and Rome became a more and more obtrusive fact as the culture and empire declined; it was as if the old high culture shrank back ultimately upon its oldest and strongest center, Greece, threatening to die out everywhere else. As a result, east and west diverged and constantly tended to break apart and go separate ways. In a large degree they actually did so, even though the connection between them could not be completely severed, and their two cultures always retained important common elements. They became separate enough to constitute substantially different entities so that Byzantium-Russia had a close and formidable neighbor to the west. And it had a neighbor to the east also. For some centuries this was Sassanian Iran, but from the seventh century on it was Islam which swallowed up Iran, Egypt and all else which lay eastward of the true Byzantine world. Byzantium's rapid recovery gave her a chronological advantage over both her western and her eastern neighbors, while Russia's distance from both western and eastern political centers saved her for a time from their power. But Russia was really wide open to threats from both directions, when they should materialize, and Byzantium itself proved unable to fend them off forever.

The movement of peoples in Russia during the disintegration of the Roman Empire was greater than it was in Germany, perhaps because the steppe stretched into Russia and mobility was of the essence of all steppe culture. Russia was the immediate source of the multitudes of barbarians who flooded the Byzantine region, and indeed of some who in the end went much further afield, notably of the Goths who landed eventually in Italy and Spain. Yet the Goths had only been temporary sojourners in Russia, as they subsequently were in the Balkans. The Varangians, again, credited with setting up the earliest forms in the

[1] The barrier was due more to the simplicity of the culture of Russia than to the complexity and rapid development of that of Byzantium. This follows from the fact that no such effective barrier developed between China and Japan; it would be hard to show that T'ang China was more highly developed than Byzantium, whereas it is plain that Japan developed more effectively than Russia.

main Russian political evolution, came from Scandinavia, as the Goths had done; and the Varangians also played a part, though a small one, in Byzantine affairs. The Bulgars, yet again, came to Russia from elsewhere, this time from the steppe. In Russia they divided, one part establishing themselves on the upper Volga where they were forerunners of the Tartars, who had an important part in Russian history much later; the other part passing into the Balkans where they made a contribution to politics but became ethnically and linguistically Slavonized. The Slavs, the main ethnic basis probably of historic Russia, are first found in what is now Poland and extreme southwestern Russia north of the steppe. From there between the fifth century and the eighth they spread over most of Russia and the Balkan Peninsula, as well as certain other European territories, profoundly modifying the ethnic character of all the lands they occupied.

The common barbarian elements in Russia and the Balkans, especially the Slavs, show the close relationship of the two regions from the earliest times with which we are here concerned. Had the Byzantine state disintegrated as the Roman state of the West did, it is conceivable that a feudal order would have developed first in the Balkans and then in Russia. It is not hard to imagine, on the Western model, the growth of feudal relations out of Slav and Bulgar war-bands within the empire's territory and their subsequent spread north and east beyond it. Under such circumstances no barrier would have arisen between Russia and Byzantium. The cultural frontier would have remained what Toynbee calls a *limen*, a threshold, and it would, presumably, have been a moving one, receding outward as the high culture spread. But, as we have seen, the eastern center of the old empire never went into dissolution as the western center did. On the contrary, it made a decisive recovery in the sixth and seventh centuries, and the Byzantine Empire thus took shape. As a result, the disparity between the level of its culture and the level of Russian culture, which had always remained great, became greater; there was scarcely a *limen*, but instead a *limes*, a limit which the high culture could pass only with great difficulty. In Byzantine-Balkan territory the revived state—two states actually, the Byzantine and the Bulgar—rapidly repressed feudal tendencies, which therefore could not spread to Russia, while those tendencies in Russia itself, where they also arose independently of developments in the Balkans, became subject to quite a different influence exerted from Byzantium—one which was essentially economic.

The revival of Byzantium was, as just remarked, the emergence of the Byzantine Empire, as distinct from the old empire, for the first time.

The themes were formed at this time, and they, we have said, virtually constituted the Byzantine Empire, forming a strong military structure under the domination of the empire's bureaucracy which solved in a non-feudal manner the problems which feudalism elsewhere arose to solve. Yet this oversimplifies the picture. Alongside this new structure the *dynatoi*, the great landlords, continued to exist, it may be said in a kind of symbiosis with the new structure. If they were for a time somewhat effaced, they were nevertheless always there. It cannot even be said that the empire in its many crises could have dispensed easily with the local leadership the *dynatoi* gave. They lingered on, therefore, a constant threat to the theme system since they constantly tried to bring its soldiery under their own command. The Byzantine Empire may thus be described as dual. It was, on the one hand, a new political growth and, on the other, it was still the old empire, arrested in its disintegration, but liable to return to it. And this description is more than merely figurative; it may well be that it approximates to the real character of the Byzantine Empire.

And, if the Byzantine Empire came to have a dual character, so also did Russia. There was still the Russia which had acquired the character of a disturbed outer territory of the Roman Empire as it disintegrated: the barbarians there found their mode of existence threatened by reason of the breakdown of the economic system of the empire on which they had become dependent, but, as they sought to find a new mode of existence, they began to acquire the rudiments of the high culture of the old imperial territory. Soon, however, there arose also a new Russia, the Russia beyond the Byzantine *limes*, debarred from further acquisition of the high culture, but, in compensation, becoming firmly attached to the new economic system which the rising Byzantine Empire rapidly built up. The Russia of this latter character was superimposed upon the Russia of the former character, and predominated over it, but it would be a mistake to think that the Russia of the former character ceased to exist.

Thus it was the former character which gave the new Russia some, not all, of the earmarks of a country destined to go feudal. Most evidently Russia had the barbarian war-band, the *druzhina*, as it is called there. Every word of Chadwick's which is true of the Teutonic comitatus is true also of the *druzhina* in its early days; for centuries the *druzhina* remained, in fact, virtually the same institution as the comitatus. It was, no doubt, of Scandinavian origin on the primitive side which is, to all intents and purposes, the same as German origin. But, in its latter character, as an economic appanage of the rising Byzantine Empire, Russia underwent a change which cut across and inhibited the rise of the *druzhina* into a position of political primacy. There seems to be no doubt that the important new trade with Byzantium was one of the fundamental reasons for the non-feudalization of Russia at this period. The effect of the trade was both direct by influence upon relations within the *druzhina*, and indirect by promotion of the growth of powerful cities. Hence there was an important causal chain between the rise of Byzantium and the anomalous character of Russian history.

Qualifications must now be added to this last statement, but none which detract from its plain truth. The Russian river system is universally recognized as having provided an ideal network of communications for traders. It served as a series of highways for traders to and from the steppes and the lands beyond the steppes and somewhat later for traders to and from northwestern Europe via Novgorod, as well as for traders to Byzantium who bought Russian furs and honey. Steppe peoples, such as the Chazars and Cumans, both of whom had no doubt their respective kinds of formative influence on Russia, were habitual traders in a way that primitive agriculturalists were not. But it was certainly Byzantine economic needs that were of greatest effect upon the economic, social, and political system of Slavic, Kievan Russia as it came into existence in the eighth and ninth centuries.[2]

That trade served as an obstacle to feudalization accords with an old doctrine, but the doctrine must be accepted with caution. It was remarked in the Introductory Essay[3] that the commercial centers of Byzantium radiated an influence over Russia, Iran, and Asia Minor, and that the results of that influence, though different in the three cases, were alike in obstructing the feudal tendencies which existed in all of them. As to Iran, it has subsequently been shown that that commerce did not by any means prevent feudalistic developments there.[4] It may not be taken for granted, then, that a vigorous commerce always has the same degree of anti-feudal effect. For Russia, however, the effect of commerce was both direct and indirect, as has been suggested, and hence probably very great. Directly, Russians drew profits from the trade, and large ones. Among the Russians who did this were the princes who led the *druzhinas*. They were able, therefore, to pay salaries to their faithful followers, or to cut them in on the commercial profits.

[2] Cf. G. Vernadsky, *Kievan Russia* (New Haven, 1948), pp. 118-121, and Szeftel, above, p. 168.

[3] Above, p. 8.

[4] Above, pp. 339-340, 342-343.

Hence they did not need to provide for them with land fiefs, and, when they, the princes, happened to be much concerned with land, which was not always, their practice was to employ the boyars and *muzhi*, chief men in their *druzhinas*, as *salaried officials* to administer it. If those officials themselves had estates, which they often had not, the estates ordinarily had nothing at all to do with their lords—although at this early date probably the principle, which later became very strong, that land and personal dependency were to be kept strictly apart, was not yet clearly formulated.

The indirect effect of trade in restraining feudalization, its promotion of the rise of cities, is its usual, well-known effect. This process in Russia was certainly the same as had long before given rise to the Greek cities. Russian princes had their seats in the cities, and their importance in city government varied from city to city, probably also from time to time. It is scarcely sure how great the power of the princes was in Kievan times, but Vernadsky thinks that the "city-state was the basic pattern politically."[5] Princes certainly did not fall as low as Greek kings did, but neither did Russia inherit in its earliest days (or ever) a large share in the central commerce of the world, as Greece did.[6] Even so, the northernmost of the important early cities of Russia, Novgorod, was substantially a commercial, oligarchical republic, in which the prince for a long time might not hold land and to which he was bound under contract; sometimes he was an outsider, prince in another city.[7]

Among themselves the princes developed a system of succession to power, sometimes called the "rota system," whereby ideally, all members of the house of Riurik held the cities of Russia in accordance with their seniority, Kiev being the leading seat, other cities following. Thus, as each prince died, there should be a general shift around among the survivors. For long the princes all felt themselves to be "grandsons of a common grandfather," and their relationship was certainly a factor in holding Kievan Russia together. It can hardly be supposed that the rota system worked exactly as it was intended to work, however, and it did not by any means prevent internecine wars, but, by and large, it contributed to maintaining the cohesion of Kiev until some time in

[5] *Kievan Russia*, p. 212.

[6] It may well be asked whether the rise of cities to political importance in the early stages of the history of a civilized society must always be ascribed to the need of commerce. Cf. pp. 234-235 above and pp. 378-383 below.

[7] Cf. the arrangement of the Netherlands estates with the house of Orange-Nassau.

the twelfth century and did not even then entirely cease to influence politics.[8]

The Kievan regime was a historical anomaly. Mirsky says that it arose virtually out of nothing, "with no roots in pre-Russian Slavdom, but with no roots in Norse tradition either. It may be regarded as a beginning."[9] It branched off from the route toward feudalism at an early juncture. It did so, in fact, before the tribes had completely broken down, for they remained in existence in the west, where the Slavs were indigenous or had long been established, while the cities were first growing up. The development of the rota system is, I think, to be regarded as something arising out of tribalism, something non-feudal, invented to supply a form of unity since other forms were insufficient owing to the barrier against Byzantine influence. The *druzhinas*, of course, signify a heroic age with great disorders in some regions, presumably eastward, but the rise of strong cities precluded the movement toward feudalism, for it superseded the *druzhinas* as a means of establishing order. There was certainly personal vassalage within the *druzhinas*, but there was never any need for it to be brought to the support of a tottering government, for there was no tottering government. Vassalage therefore remained a military relation which did not broaden out politically. Hence there was no proto-feudal regime; the movement toward feudalism ceased before that stage was reached.

Kievan Russia thus always retained its anomalous, dual character. In the main it was territory beyond the Byzantine *limes*, attached to Byzantium by a commerical nexus—commerce always being the most superficial of relations. Yet the other kind of relation persisted in a minor way, as witness the fact that, in the middle course of its history, Kievan Russia began to be converted to Christianity. It was indeed a remarkably late date for conversion to begin. And, when the church was established in Russia, the infiltration of Christian feeling was extremely slow. It is hard to think that it ever got a grip on the masses, or even on the majority of political leaders, in the days of the Kievan state. It remained largely formal and nominal, and indeed alien, for the upper clergy continued to be Greeks.[10] It was mainly an inapt and feeble instrument of Byzantine political influence. And yet the slow penetration of the outward, ritualistic forms of Christianity in Kievan times must not be ignored.

[8] Cf. Vernadsky, *Kievan Russia*, pp. 179-181.

[9] *Russia: A Social History* (London, 1931), p. 34.

[10] Cf. P. Miliukov, *Outlines of Russian Culture*, I (Philadelphia, 1942), pp. 7-11.

The curious history of Russia and of Byzantium was turned in a radically new direction by a tremendous "pincers movement" exerted upon the two countries by Western Europe and Islam, their neighbors to the west and the east. Yet that movement was not pressed home, hardly began indeed, until degenerative processes had begun both in Byzantium and in Russia. Was the pincers movement a consequence of the degenerative processes? It is not unlikely, but the imponderables are too many to permit a firm statement.

Contrasted with that probability, but not exclusive of it, is the growing strength and expansiveness of the two neighbors. From the west the crusaders attacked Byzantium; the Lithuanians, Poles, and later the Germans, some of them professedly crusaders also, attacked Russia. From the east, Russia was overrun by Tartars, and Byzantium was constantly assailed by Turks. The earliest of these movements began in the twelfth century, and their dramatic result was completely manifest in the fifteenth. They began at the moment when the Byzantine-Russian relationship was at its weakest—when perhaps in other circumstances it might have snapped altogether and the two peoples have gone in entirely different directions. That was not to be: both Russia and Byzantium were almost suppressed, and Byzantium did eventually fall into a kind of half-life under the rule of the Ottoman Turks, but the Russia which survived, Muscovy, learned and bore forward the Byzantine tradition as the old Russia had never known it; we have already encountered "Moscow, the Third Rome." In their near-suppression both Russia and Byzantium developed institutions which have been called feudal.

But both had entered on internal degeneration before they met the pressure from east and west. For Byzantium the source of this is mysterious. Certainly, the dual character of the Byzantine polity was concerned in it. The overthrow of Bulgaria, accomplished early in the eleventh century by Basil II (976-1025),[11] seems also to have been concerned in it. That event, however, ought to be seen a little more largely, for the struggle between the empire and the Bulgarian Khanate was complicated in the tenth century by attempts of the Russians to conquer both Byzantium and Bulgaria, and Basil's overthrow of Bulgaria involved also the defeat of the last Russian attempt upon Constantinople.

[11] This is the event that Toynbee regards as fatal to the empire. His view of the matter is different from the one propounded here, however, and is advanced as an example of a regular historical occurrence, which the view in the text is not. (Cf. *A Study of History*, IV, 371-404.)

The greatest Russian attack had been that of Sviatoslav I, which had been foiled by Basil's predecessor, John Tzimisces (969-976). The emperors John Tzimisces and Basil II may be said, in fact, to have solved the barbarian problem, both of Russians and of Bulgarians.[12] As a consequence, the empire in the mid-eleventh century appeared to be a greater power than it had ever been before. That is probably one reason why a great change in its internal system began. The *dynatoi* had been more than usually disloyal during the Bulgarian troubles and Basil had assailed them as violently as Justinian had done. But in the new era, after Basil, they were tolerated and even encouraged by the basileus, while over some two centuries the theme structure underwent great changes and its farmer-soldier system crumbled away. It seems, then, that the Byzantine Empire, resurgent in the sixth and seventh centuries, could from then until the eleventh face adversity and overcome it, but could not meet the challenge of success.[13] Events a little later tend to support the truth of this diagnosis. And yet, if it is true, it can scarcely be the whole truth, so that an element of mystery remains.

There is no similar mystery about the beginning of the decline of Kievan Russia. It began perhaps with the pressure of the Pechenegs from the east, but that was a small matter compared with the ruin of the trade with Byzantium. The reason for this was a secular change in both commercial and political relations in the Mediterranean, consequent upon the crusades: those relations ran henceforward from east to west. The process was fully accomplished in the thirteenth century at about the moment when Russia had to meet the great attacks from east and west. Byzantium had encountered the Seljuks from the east in the later twelfth century, and, in the fourth crusade at the beginning of the thirteenth century, the West dealt it a body blow.

It is not too much to say that the history of Russia began anew at this juncture. There was, in fact, a new beginning now just as truly as there had been when the Kievan polity arose. Indeed, that Russian history had several new starts—some of them false starts perhaps—is an enlightening comment upon it. The great blows of the Tartar invasions, which mark dramatically the ending and the new beginning on this occasion, were combined with an absorptive movement by the Lithuanians and Poles, more subtle but also more effective and lasting. The old Kievan polity utterly ceased to be, the greater part of its territory

[12] The Russians attacked Constantinople once more, in the time of Zoë (c. 1043), but that attack was an aftermath.

[13] Cf. Toynbee's doctrine of the "stimulus of pressures" (II, 112-207).

and people being drawn into Europe where they became an irredenta for the later Muscovite state.

Kiev left little behind it, no prosperous agricultural system, for example, such as many societies inherited from the past when they had to make a new start. The princes were Kiev's most evident legacy, and they were now very numerous, had inevitably lost the recollection, in any useful political form, of the common ancestor, and had long been engaged in destructive internecine struggles. Loss of the trade to Byzantium had impoverished them, for they had all been interested in it. They were thrown back upon their landed rights or claims. Each of them, therefore, came to have a patrimony of his own, his *udêl,* which was divided at his death between his heirs, with the result that, as the generations passed, the princes became more numerous, more poverty-stricken, and consequently more bellicose.

The struggles of the princes and the great invasions from east and west were certainly, all of them, circumstances which could very well have led in a feudal direction, provided that no other positive political development should arise to forestall such a movement. Nor did one arise for some two centuries, for Russia as yet remained outside the great empire, the source of political ideas. Yet no true feudalism grew up in Russia during those centuries. The reason, clearly, was what Kliuchevsky called the "peculiar conjunction of circumstances which caused the history of Russia to become the history of a country for ever undergoing colonization . . . the boundless and inhospitable plain . . ."[14] of Russia, so great as always to be drawing the settler onward, so infertile in large parts as to be constantly driving out the primitive farmer who did not know how to fertilize it.

We need not dwell upon this situation, for Mr. Szeftel has already treated it.[15] It was one of endemic instability, land being at a discount and the ultimate lord of the land, the prince, thus always at a disadvantage as against the peasant who could make the land produce and the boyar who could organize and protect it for him. Hence the boyar did not become truly a vassal: his service to his prince remained as it had

[14] V. O. Kliuchevsky, *A History of Russia*, trans. Hogarth (London and New York, 1911), I, 2. The passage quoted is not one which requires acceptance of Kliuchevsky's theory of migration of the Russian population in its extreme form. Following Mr. Szeftel (above, p. 169), I accept the view that some migration did occur. I think indeed that the Russian population has always remained somewhat migratory. Thus I find it impossible to go all the way with Vernadsky's criticism (pp. 99-102) of Kliuchevsky although I have no doubt that Vernadsky is right in what he says about agriculture in early times in Russia.

[15] Above, pp. 169-173.

been, neither hereditary nor even of long duration, his agreement to serve easily breakable,[16] his land often becoming an allod.[17] Similarly, the peasant did not become a serf, bound to the soil, Russia in this stage of some two centuries remained anomalous, and, by contrast with its prosperity in the Kievan stage, was in miserable distress. Of princely territories in the fourteenth century Kliuchevsky says "not a single one of them stood upon a secure footing or possessed a source of income which could be looked upon as trustworthy."[18] The position of the boyar in such a territory he contrasts with the position of a Western baron:

"In the West a freeman secured his freedom by confining himself strictly within a ring of permanent, inherited relations—relations which permitted of his making himself the centre of the lower social forces in his locality, and thus creating around himself a little world of which he was both the director and the supporter. On the other hand, the free servitor of the Russian appanage[19] could find, in the ever-shifting local community, none of the elements necessary for a durable environment of that kind, and therefore sought to secure his freedom by conclusion of a personal, temporary agreement with his prince, with the right of at any time tearing it up and departing into service in some appanage to which he was not bound by any ties consolidated through lapse of time."[20]

This period, the thirteenth to fifteenth centuries, was, then, one of the periods in which feudalism might be expected to have developed in Russia had the necessary circumstances existed. The break-up of the Kievan regime and the invasions were such circumstances, but other circumstances were lacking. In particular, land was of little value in Russia. Hence, conspicuously missing in Russia is the tough baron of the Western type, compelled on pain of losing his land to defend it and at the same time to learn its economic and social needs and to foster them. If feudal Europe was a school of politics, Russia in the age of the *udêl* was not.[21]

[16] A. Eck, "La vassalité et les immunités dans la Russie du moyen âge," *Revue de l'Institut de Sociologie*, XVI (1936), 106. Mirsky (*Russia*, pp. 105-106) describes the situation as the outcome of the "essentially individualistic character" of Russian society.

[17] See Mr. Szeftel, above, p. 171.

[18] *History of Russia*, I, 267.

[19] This is Hogarth's translation of *udêl*. See Mr. Szeftel's n. 24 for objections to its use.

[20] *History of Russia*, I, 264-265. Cf. a similar passage from a later work of Kliuchevsky quoted by Mr. Szeftel, above, p. 181.

[21] Cf. Mr. Strayer, pp. 22-25 above, for European feudalism as a school of politics.

On the other hand, although much was in dissolution in Russia, there was also positive development. It was the opening up of new country on the upper Volga and the Oka and, beyond that region, far northward, ultimately up to the Arctic Ocean. On a tributary of the Oka arose Moscow. The pressure from east and west actually drove some of the Russian people of the southwestern regions in a migration into the vast central and northern spaces where pressure was no longer felt.[22] But those spaces were a refuge not only for the Kievan-Russian population. As the pressure on Byzantium became critical, Greeks and Bulgar-Slavs fled northward and found refuge in the "Mesopotamian" region of central Russia where Moscow eventually became paramount. The numbers of Greeks and Bulgars did not compare with those of the Kievan Russians who moved, but almost all the Greeks and Bulgars had been leading persons in Byzantium and Bulgaria, and what they brought with them was the civilization. This proved before long more important than the mere movement of population. If, then, there was a new beginning of Russian history when the great pressure from east and west began, the first great positive development after the new beginning came about with the concentration in central Russia of the makings of a civilized society, the high culture from Byzantium and an increment of population from southern Russia.

Meanwhile, under pressure Byzantine society became more and more the society of the *dynatoi*. The free peasantry who had supplied the men for the imperial armies fell more and more into serfdom under the magnates, who in turn were taking over more and more of the powers of the state. With the accession of the Comneni (1081), the *dynatoi* became the state. Here, it would seem, was a pre-feudal society like that of seven or eight centuries earlier when the whole Roman Empire had for the time been in dissolution. And yet it is unwise to be too sure of the character of late Byzantine society. We have noticed the internal weakening which followed the disposal of the Slav-Bulgar barbarian problem by John Tzimisces and Basil II. The chief palpable factor in that, the slow dissolution of the theme system, continued, but the rest of the Byzantine system reacted vigorously against the new dangers from east and west as those materialized. This would seem to confirm the proposition that the empire could meet adversity more effectively than it could meet success. It could, that is to say, meet adversity of the magnitude of Bulgar or Kievan barbarian attacks, but

[22] See note 14 above.

the crushing process Byzantium had to meet from east and west from the thirteenth century in the end proved more than it could sustain. Nevertheless, it went down fighting. There was not really a withering away of the state; there was no true loosening of grip, no weakening, but instead a desperate distribution of power and wealth to the *dynatoi* to strengthen them in the local warfare they had often to maintain against enemies in part possession of the territories of the empire.

On their part, the *dynatoi* became greater magnates than ever. They acquired vassals and they led armies of cataphracts scarcely distinguished from the armored knights of the West. And yet there was a regularity about their power that makes it look unlike power destined to be shifted on to a feudal basis. True, they fought one another and the emperor too when it suited them to do so; as individual houses they rose and fell. But the system they embodied was too much a system; it was potentially stable in itself, provided that an effective central government could be restored to confirm the potential stability. It lacked the inherently changing character of a feudal society. Too much has been made of the linguistic development whereby the Greek *pronoia* came to be used as a translation of the Latin *feudum* when Latins settled in the Peloponnese and elsewhere. *Pronoiai* were indeed dependent holdings for which military service was rendered, but for a long time they were not hereditary, and they then resembled Russian military benefices under Moscow more than Western fiefs. When they did come to resemble Western fiefs the political relations on those fiefs were late feudal relations in which government was done in part by other than feudal means. It was so on a Byzantine estate also; the lord had his army of retainers who had usually both small lands and wages and upkeep, but the government of the estate was not really feudal; it was a little Byzantine administration, and the estate was a little principality rather than a fief.

That this was the character of the late Byzantine polity is confirmed after the empire's fall, for the Ottoman Turks for a time supplied a strong government which imparted stability to the system, and the system thereupon stayed as it was, looking like rather a heterogeneous federation, certainly not like a feudal state. Commerce and industry, damaged in the two bad centuries before the conquest, and suffering at first through Italian competition, recovered, and all the general social qualities derivable from it were in fact derived and made the society a wealthy society again, the government able to govern by an officialdom. Yet the Ottoman Turks were the very people who could have led the society in a feudal direction if it had had inherent tendencies in that direction. They were not the most barbarous of barbarians, but they were barbarians, and, not long before, had tended in southeastern Russia to develop a feudal-like society when they passed partially out of nomad into settled life. The regime they set up in former Byzantine territory never was truly bureaucratic even though it certainly could have been made so if its rulers had understood how to make it so and had wished to make it so. The Ottoman Empire was always a federal regime ruled by great pashas who tended to make themselves hereditary. Under the surface of the regime many and various political growths arose, but few, if any, of them were feudal. The large estate, or half-state, or indeed full state, was usual. Even prosperous pig-farming could become the basis for a series of estates and for a sort of a state set up over them. The church could become a bureaucratic state within the non bureaucratic state, and in fact there was more than one such church-state, the one headed by the Patriarch of Constantinople being the strongest. When the empire in a few centuries began to break up it was states and estates of these kinds which emerged from it, not a feudal system.

There are few might-have-beens in history which are calculable. That the future which the Byzantine Empire did not have should be one of them is due, of course, to the fact that the society and the lower structures of the polity lived on under the Turkish regime. If there had been no Turkish regime—nor any other alien conqueror—it would seem likely that Byzantium would have recovered itself without experiencing a feudal stage, and that, like Twelfth Dynasty Egypt, T'ang China, and like itself in the sixth and seventh centuries, it would have emerged with some new characteristics, but in the main the character of the old society.

Russia in the Muscovite period continues to show a dual character. It is no longer the same dual character as the old, for the *limes* of Byzantium had been broken by the Byzantine refugees fleeing to Moscow. Moscow, therefore, became on the one hand a ghost empire reflecting the Byzantine Empire, as we have seen in Chapter 4. On the other hand, Moscow had behind it its history as barbarian country which might, in different circumstances, have become feudal. As successor to that barbarian Russia, Moscow showed some of the traits of a strong monarchy. Of its two characters the former predominated. Moscow qualifies poorly as a strong monarchy because it was not really strong enough.

It was, however, a far stronger state than the petty *udêli* among which it arose, and the policy of the Princes of Moscow toward the rights and claims of the princes of those estates is strongly reminiscent of that of national monarchs in Western Europe toward the rights and claims of barons.

Perhaps the most remarkable feature of Muscovite Russia is that it so soon became, and then remained, a unified state. In so great an area as Russia, strong monarchy might be expected to have emerged multiple and national: we should expect several distinct states, not one. Of course, Novgorod and Pskov did exist at first as separate principalities. They were city states, Novgorod having acquired a fairly broad territory. Although, then, no feudal order existed in fourteenth- and fifteenth-century Russia, some development of the city-state regime did so. But Novgorod was absorbed by Moscow in 1478 and Pskov in 1510; they must be regarded as special developments left over from the Kievan period. We have learned to seek national boundaries in physiography, rather rarely in ethnography, and otherwise in historic differences. All of these fail in Russia, which, like North China, is, in the main, a featureless plain and had in the period in question scarcely any significant ethnographic differences except around its edges. Yet North China in Chou times had produced a series of nations which descended from certain of its great agglomerative fiefs. Since, however, Russia on the eve of the rise of Moscow was not feudal, there could be no great fiefs to be transformed into nations. Both great fiefs and physiographic-historic frontiers failing, therefore, a single state arose, not properly to be called a nation, but rather an empire. And it was a ghost empire, for the material resources did not permit of anything more palpable. Nor was there in the country, except temporarily in Novgorod and Pskov, any other state strong enough to oppose the ghost.

Moscow arose gradually out of the welter of thousands of petty *udêli* which, as we have seen, composed the Russia of the time. To unify this fluid mass did not require the achievement of a great conqueror like Ardashir in Iran, or like Ch'in Shih Huang Ti in the more usual case of China. A series of predisposing circumstances, and not a dramatic succession of wars, were all that was needed to bring unification about: the taxing of all Russia by the Tartar conquerors for which function in 1328 the Prince of Moscow became their agent; the urgent desire of many *udêlni* princes for protection—at one period hundreds of them voluntarily submitted to Moscow and became subjects; above all, the influence of the church which made Moscow its capital in 1326.

This mode of unification was quite anomalous by comparison with the other two modes we know, those which followed a comparatively minor decline of the high culture of the society, and those which followed a profound decline, a feudal period and a national period.

Yet we must not look upon the church's part in this as in itself wholly anomalous; the anomaly is in the combination of circumstances and the absence of need for heroic military exploits. The church's part was, in fact, quite analogous to the part the Western church had played in bringing the Holy Roman Empire into existence, to the part which religion probably played in upholding the position of the *wang* in early Chou China, and somewhat analogous to the part the Theban priesthood played in the restoration of unity to Egypt by the Eleventh and Twelfth Dynasties.[23] The church's part in the unification belongs, in fact, in the main to Moscow's character as a ghost empire, something we should expect to precede or accompany feudalization, and not to its character as a strong monarchy, which we should expect to arise in late feudal times. But it was not wholly and exclusively of the former character, for the church had been established in Russia since the late tenth century, and, from then until the fourteenth, it had, very slowly and superficially, made for itself a place in the society. That place served in the fourteenth and fifteenth centuries, while calamity was overwhelming Byzantium and Bulgaria, as a refuge and rallying ground for ecclesiastical-political power of a very different order from that which Russia had formerly had. Russia now became the leading Orthodox Christian country instead of a distant and not very important mission field of the church.

I do not think it should be said that this process was anomalous except perhaps for the existence of the early Russian church and its function as a conductor for ecclesiastical refugees; that, the immediate result of Russia's dual character, cannot be paralleled in the history of Western Europe, or in that of Chou China; nor is there for any other society evidence to show a parallel development. Nevertheless, in Chapter 4 Muscovy was described as a refugee ghost, and it may be that the existence of the early Russian church was a necessary link in the chain of events which gave the ghost its refuge. Since, then, there are other

[23] It is usually said that the Amon-Re priesthood gained large influence in politics after the Hyksos intrusion in Egypt (e.g. Drioton and Vandier, *Les peuples de l'Orient Méditerranéen*, I: *L'Egypte*, pp. 326-327, 339-340, 436, 451; Wilson, *The Burden of Egypt*, pp. 169-170, 216-217). Mr. Edgerton puts this back further; see above, p. 130, and his note 23. I would put it back yet further.

refugee ghosts, it is conceivable that there are analogies also to the early Russian church. But there is nothing at all unusual, of course, in Moscow's character as a ghost empire; in that Moscow resembles other ghost empires even if there is something unusual in the circumstances of its origin, and something else unusual in the fact that, as a ghost empire, it was nevertheless not superseded and pushed aside later by nations.

But that is to anticipate. Before the rise of nations we should expect a feudal period. Was there anything of that kind in the history of Muscovy? There was; not indeed a true feudal period, but something bearing a resemblance to it—and this, from the standpoint of the present study, is the most remarkable anomaly of all in Russian history. In the late fifteenth century Moscow began to develop its army and at the same time to attempt to devise means to hold together the large territory it had. From this came the *pomêst'e*, something quite new in Russia, for it was a land tenure conditional on service, usually military service: those who served in the army or the administration obtained a *pomêst'e* because there was no other way of providing for them. But some feudal relations were lacking, most evidently vassalage. There was no truly personal relation of loyalty to the Prince of Moscow (now beginning to call himself Czar), no homage or fealty; the relation was one of serving persons to the government. Nor was the tenure at first hereditary, though it became so after about a century. Not long after that the tenure began to lose its military character: the landed class gradually got out of the obligation of service—and that perhaps seems to make nonsense of the whole idea that it was like feudal tenure.

The dropping of military service was scarcely like anything we know of in other societies even though a long struggle was waged between monarchy and nobility in Russia; and the escape from service obligation, which occurred mainly in the seventeenth century, was a part of the struggle. Whereas strong, post-feudal national monarchies dispensed with the feudal services of their nobility in order to demilitarize and disarm them and made their armies into soldiers of the central government, the Russian government reluctantly let its nobility off a service which it still needed: whereas post-feudal monarchies did away with feudal service when they were strong enough to do so, the Russian government let it go because it was too weak to insist on maintaining it. The government remained dependent upon the *pomêshchiki* for police work, for justice in all small cases, and for tax-collection. In this last capacity the *pomêshchiki* enriched themselves, legally and illegally, and came to hold the government itself at their mercy. The peasantry, partly through the exercise over them by the *pomêshchiki* of these various political functions, and partly by actual legal changes in their status, had become not merely serfs (as they are usually described in European books) but something nearer to slaves. This, again, was not the usual agrarian concomitant of a feudal order, but a depression far more extreme.

The status of the peasantry became inevitably a factor in the struggle between monarchy and nobility, and the final victory of the monarchy is signalized by the emancipation of the peasants; that did not occur until the nineteenth century, with the edict of 1861. It is important to note that most of the work of building a modern state in Russia remained to be done after that edict. Russia before that was not like a post-feudal European state with a nobility which had no logical place in the polity and was maintained, as pre-eminently in France, by something like artificial legal means. On the contrary, the Russian nobility were quite essential and it often looked as if they might swallow up the czardom and consign it to the fate of other ghost empires. Yet it is hard to imagine nations emerging in Russia if the nobility had succeeded. The struggles between autocracy and aristocracy were, in fact, prodigious, as much exaggerated by the usual standards of feudalism as the depression of the peasants was. Hence the ferocious rule of such monarchs as Peter the Great (1689-1725) and Ivan the Terrible (1533-1584), the frightful anarchy after Ivan during the Time of Troubles (1604-1613), the appalling destruction of Pugachev's Rebellion in the reign of Catherine the Great (1762-1796) from which both autocracy and aristocracy, assailed by the peasants, emerged prostrated, and the autocracy made its last great concessions to the aristocracy. Even when honors were even the results were strange, as when Ivan divided the land for administration between autocracy and aristocracy into the *Oprichnina* and *Zemshchina*.

This interpretation of Russian history, then, requires, first, five or six centuries, the seventh to the thirteenth, when it was vitally related to Byzantine history, and both Byzantium and Russia showed a dual character. Byzantium was at once a prolongation of the Roman Empire in a limited region and a new, peculiar polity and society, Christianized, militarized, and centralized. Russia, correspondingly, was first barbarian territory at and beyond the Roman frontier which looked as if it might become more and more merged with the failing civilized society, and showed certain important signs of going feudal. But there was always a barrier between Russia and Byzantium, a barrier consisting of the great difference between their respective levels of culture, and it became the greater as the rapid rise of Byzantium occurred. Hence Russia, while retaining certain of the qualities of a territory being drawn within the aura of civilization, came at the same time to have again those of a territory beyond the civilized region and attached to it as a sort of economic appanage.

Then followed two or three centuries, the thirteenth to fifteenth, of violent change, when both Russia and Byzantium were ground between expansive movements of alien societies from east and west. At the end of those convulsions the Byzantine Empire had ceased to exist and so had Kievan Russia. Instead, there was a new polity, descended from both of them, arising in a new place, central Russia: this was Muscovy. Muscovy, like its two predecessors, shows a dual character; one character was derived from each. The one character was superimposed upon the other, that of a ghost empire reflecting the Byzantine Empire upon that of a strong monarchy—yet hardly a nation—following the feeble and anomalous states of the *udêl* period in which Kievan Russia ended. In its dual character Muscovy produced no nations; that political form failed altogether. Muscovy neither was as whole a nation when it arose in succession to the remains of Kievan Russia; nor did it ever split up at a late time in its career as a ghost empire into a series of nations, as Chou China and Central Europe did. It is not even possible to imagine some of its great provinces of the seventeenth or the eighteenth century as potential nations, for they never had that inner coherence or that distinction from one another and from the whole society which nations have. Physiographic, ethnographic, and historic frontiers to divide nations from one another were substantially lacking in Russia, and so was the essential feudal development—that ethical-political process which first makes an in-group of the fief, and later makes an in-group of the nation, expanding and deepening the loyalties of lord and vassal into those of king and subject.

But Muscovy did produce a polity which might be called para-feudal.[24] It produced the *pomêshchik*, a dependent of the monarch, or perhaps rather of the central government, without a feudal contract and without the relation of personal vassalage, at first not hereditary, at first owing military service for his land, but later dispensed of that

[24] Cf. Mr. Szeftel, who considers that term but prefers to call the institutions in question "abortive feudalism"; p. 181 above.

important duty. Is Muscovite Russia, then, after all the missing link between a feudal and a non-feudal polity—a true semi-feudal polity, standing mid-way between the two types? Certainly, Muscovite Russia had some feudal features and lacked others. But, if to reach that condition such extraordinary circumstances as those of Russia's early history and of its early and its late relations to Byzantium are necessary, then a reason has been found for the apparent tendency of other societies to fall clearly within the category of societies which had feudal periods or to fall clearly without it. Russia indeed does offer suggestive evidence of the strength of the tendency towards feudalization and so of the reason why feudalism is a repetitive phenomenon in history. Russia was at all times with which we are concerned a barbarian or near-primitive country. Being such, it three times witnessed the rise of feudal tendencies—if the *udêl* period be considered such a period—and on the third occasion there was what I have called a para-feudal development.

We have seen that Parthian-Sassanian Iran offers another exception to the strict division of the society with feudal forms from the society without them. In that case also there were special conditions which explain the non-occurrence of true feudalism, namely the sharp difference between Iran proper and Mesopotamia which had become attached to it, and the existence of a vigorous commerce based in part in the Mesopotamian cities. It is unquestionably significant that commerce played a part in the unusual developments both in Iran and in Russia. The Iranian case is less extraordinary than the Russian. It is the Russian case rather than the Iranian, therefore, which looks like an exception, not indeed to prove any rule of social evolution, but instead to establish the probability we have found for growing civilized societies to have either a well-marked feudal stage of development, or else virtually no such stage at all.

10. CONCLUSION

FEUDALISM is a political phenomenon, but politics is not separate from other human affairs in a system of its own. On the contrary, politic is but an aspect of the movement of culture. Feudalism is not full understood, then, until it has been placed in its largest context, th movement of the whole culture. Nor will it be sufficiently understoo until some attempt has been made to deal with that very large problem which was stated but left unsolved in Chapter 4, the problem whethe feudalism is primarily a phenomenon of the original rise of civiliza tion rather than one of revival of civilization after collapse. Only th almost complete lack of evidence has justified postponing treatmen of so very important a problem until now.

This concluding chapter, therefore, extends the relation of feudalism from politics to the intellectual and the aesthetic culture. There follow a thesis, since it cannot be more than that, concerning possible feuda or feudalistic phases in the rise of the first civilized societies of the Ol World. Finally, feudalism and certain other phenomena we have en countered are considered for their significance as uniformities in histor since it is the largest purpose of this book to offer an example of wh can be done in present knowledge to distinguish the uniform, the re petitive, from the unique in the history of human societies.

Feudalism has been found here to be a mode of revival of a societ whose polity has gone into extreme disintegration. The disintegratin polity was in every known case a great empire, but feudal institutio may occur either in territory which belonged to the old empire or i territory which was outside its limits. Feudalism is by no means necessary stage in political recovery. It occurs, in fact, only in regio in which recovery has been slow and weak. The nuclear, usually t larger, part of the old empire recovers its political vigor without reso to feudal methods. Feudalism is thus a phenomenon of the margin a civilized society which has fallen into decline, not a necessary d velopment even there however. But the margin of such a society m be quite extensive: it may be as extensive as the larger part of Wester Europe, or as Japan, Korea, Tibet, and parts of Manchuria, perha also of Mongolia.

The decline and revival of civilized societies constitute one of t major processes of history. The process is a cyclic one—if the term cyc is accurate enough to describe it.[1] It is still rather a mysterious matter although a certain convergence of opinion is discernible about it today, at least on the part of a few prominent scholars. It is clear, on any of the various analyses which have been made, that the whole high culture in these processes of transition moves to some extent together. But the extent and the manner of relatedness of the several expressions of the culture remain obscure; the relations appear, so to speak, elastic, and they are probably somewhat variable from case to case. Many attempts have been made to find a single, simple causal factor of decline, far fewer attempts to find one of revival. None of these has been successful, in my judgment. No fundamental "social force" has been found, and the most successful treatments of the problem have been those employing rather synthetic concepts, such as the anthropologists' concept of culture. I think it highly probable, however, that the formation of religion is an important part of the transition from decline to revival; such an opinion has had serious advocates at least since Giambattista Vico at the turn of the seventeenth and eighteenth centuries. It is to be added that the formation of religion is in no wise simple; it is complex and multiple, consisting in substantial ways of the formation of relations with other parts of the culture. Most of those who have thought religion important in the transitions we are considering have professed to find in it, or through it, the ultimate force controlling man and society. I regard it, by contrast, as a creation of man, a special form he imparts to culture, when he faces the decline of culture and society. Thereafter religion becomes an agency of the revival in the manner best expressed by Bergson.[2]

It can be argued that there is no direct relation between feudalism and religion. Yet feudalism is invariably a phenomenon occurring in

[1] I admit that it may seem rather inaccurate, but it is the only convenient word which will carry the meaning I want, and I hate to invent jargon. It is only necessary to say that my use of it does not require repetitions that are at all close; that it excludes the special idea of endless repetitions which, in my opinion, is absurd; and that it does not imply the possibility of simple mathematical abstractions from the movements of culture. Toynbee rejects the word on the tacit assumption that it must mean only endless repetition, quarreling with the various authorities, Plato and Aristotle particularly, who have so used it (*A Study of History*, IV, 23-39). Endless repetitions, absurd in our present mode of thought, were not absurd in Greek or in Arabic thought. Why not, then, rescue so useful a word as cycle from use restricted to an absurdity?

[2] *Les deux sources de la morale et de la religion* (Swiss edn., Geneva, 1945), pp. 201-254. Cf. my "Concept of the Conglomerate Myth," *Proceedings of the Tenth International Congress of Philosophy*, I, 74ff.

an age of faith, and the part of religion in such an age has to be examined before it becomes possible to place feudalism in its relation to the whole culture. This is for the general reasons that the rise of religion is a far greater phenomenon than the rise of feudalism and that religion is in operation long before the rise of feudalism, but also for the special reason that both religion and feudalism are agencies of the society's revival. Indeed the building up of a new religion is apparently a sufficient, completely successful, agency of revival in those regions of a society in which revival is accomplished relatively rapidly and the extent of decline is not great. But in those marginal regions (however extensive) in which resort is made to feudalism, the construction of religion is apparently not sufficient to save society. The feudal remedy is then applied to the crucial, material-political fabric whose disintegration would entail the society's final destruction; nor, as we have found is this very special remedy applied until the last moment, the moment in which final destruction actually threatens.

To say, then, that there is no direct relation between feudalism and religion is to say that they are independent remedies applied to the same purpose. But they seem to be very different remedies. Feudalism is special, applied only in some cases and in limited regions at one face of the culture, the political facet. Religion, on the contrary, is genera applied in all cases and in all regions of the society and affecting much perhaps all, of the culture. There will be more to say on this matte below.

When a civilization is in decline, religion is the one element in which runs counter to the general direction of change: it is in growth This contradiction has baffled many scholars and has led to doub whether such a thing as decline really occurs, whether in reality the change is simply a transformation, a movement from one system of forms to another. I believe that it is such a movement, but also that the old forms do in truth decline and, further, that much old substance of culture, as well as forms, is eventually lost. It is surely a fact too that our concepts of decline and revival are not wholly adequate for grasping the ultimate character of these great historic transitions; som semantic analysis might profitably be applied to them. But I do no by any means propose a wholesale jettisoning of old concepts, and, i any case, this is not the place for large experiments in such matters.

New religions and fundamental reconstructions of old religions begi to appear as soon as decline affects a society; their appearance is a suffi cient indication of the approach of a general decline, as distinct from mere transformation of a particular and limited function of the culture. All functions of the culture are affected, but not all to the same extent or at the same time. Nor, it would seem, are all related to the same extent to the rise of religion. Some even appear not to be so related at all. Moreover, the extent of relationship to religious change is undoubtedly different in different societies. This indeed is one of the most difficult problems, and its difficulty suggests strongly that our understanding of religion, probably also of all the relations of the parts and functions of culture, contains false assumptions. In these circumstances we simply have to do the best we can.

The functions of the culture are considered here to fall into three main categories, the intellectual, the aesthetic, and the political. Certainly, these give no ultimate analysis of culture. Rather they are categories of end-products whose composition overlaps, which are inseparably—and obscurely—related to one another in practice, but of which we have some working knowledge. We shall use their respective relations to the growth of religion as a frame in which to trace decline and revival.[8]

Decline can first be observed in the movement of the intellectual culture. It begins when intellectual innovation comes to an end, or perhaps it is truer to say that its onset is first shown as intellectual innovation becomes more and more attenuated, concerned with smaller and smaller items of knowledge. Just how early in this attenuation the student will clearly discern decline is a conceptual problem, but he must surely do so when he finds in addition that old knowledge is being lost. He may well feel that he discerns it in such an episode as the rejection by the learned of the Graeco-Roman world of Aristarchos's discovery that the earth revolves around the sun, an event of the third century B.C. Aristarchos's new idea was too large to be received: it upset too many intellectual vested interests, frightening their proprietors into a search for a defense, a means of fixing known truth. Intellectually, the onset of decline is, in fact, shown when the search for truth becomes the search for an orthodoxy. As the transition proceeds, ignorance spreads, critical standards fall, philosophy gives place to theology, knowledge to myth, theology and myth being of one substance and serving to direct thought to the purposes of religion.

[8] What follows in the next few pages is greatly compressed from manuscript material of my own on comparative cultural history which I hope to publish at some future time. It has been drawn from secondary sources too numerous to list here, but a special debt must be acknowledged to Mr. Kroeber's *Configurations of Culture Growth* (Berkeley, 1944).

The movement of the intellectual culture is, in fact, in very close relation with the growth of religion. It is not true that the two are identical, for religion affects far more than the intellectual culture, and it may even be that some knowledge escapes the domination of religion. But the movement of the two is very intimately related. Thus, as religion grows, the movement of the intellectual culture sustains a subtle change. Reduced to myth, or constrained within theological forms, knowledge nevertheless after a time ceases to be lost and begins to accumulate once more. Even the beginnings of a new criticism emerge, a criticism which is never completely and quite safely confined within the limits of the new orthodoxy. The revival has begun. But we must note at once that it begins in the central territories of the society long before it does in the marginal territories, and long before the time when feudalism may arise in the marginal territories.

The aesthetic culture follows a related course, but not the same course. Literature may move much as thought does, for some of its many forms carry a large intellectual freight. Epics and similar songs of barbarian origin, however, are not dominated by religion, though they may be affected by it. But it is the practical arts which move the more freely and the more variously. They are more resistant to decline than thought is—architecture is especially enduring—and they usually escape religious domination far longer; not that resistance to decline and to religion necessarily, or even very often, go together. Religion always has its own captive arts, or schools of art, and these may emerge early and contribute forthwith vigorously to the supervention of revival upon decline. Yet other arts, remaining apparently quite independent of religion, may nevertheless early show new inspiration, essay new subjects, put forth new techniques, and contribute also to the revival. The distinction between the arts which serve religion and those which do not, or which do so only incidentally, is a conspicuous one, but it is not very clear what it means. It may mean that the decline in question is the less severe, the less its arts fall under religious domination, but there is scarcely enough evidence to make that sure. At any rate, there is variation from case to case in that matter.

So, most religions have their own architecture, but the architecture of the Sinic world at the Han-T'ang transition was used by Buddhists, not formed by them. In Parthian-Sassanian Iran there were two architectures, the magnificent palace architecture entirely secular, the lesser architecture of the fire-temples entirely religious. Most religions have their own sculpture and painting, but Islam in most regions rejected and actually suppressed both. In China from Han to T'ang the exquisite grave figurines were of the ancient ancestor worship which Confucianism sanctioned, there was a Buddhist sculpture in large figures of indifferent quality, the great poetry of Li Po and Tu Fu was of loose Taoist affiliation, and historiography, which was not of high quality during the transition, was secular.

Both in thought and in the arts there is a vast difference between the transition in the main, central territories and in the marginal territories of a civilized society. In the central territories, knowledge and thought always show marked decline, but are by no means altogether lost; the arts are sure to undergo changes of school, but may remain fairly active throughout the transition, while the practical arts at least may achieve excellence again quite soon. In the marginal territories, decline continues long, though sometimes with a noticeable pause in the protofeudal stage, and in the end a veritable dark age descends. Knowledge there has indeed shrunk calamitously by that time, and even theology is small in volume and very simple in theory; the literary arts can fall into illiteracy and almost into silence. Architecture, in spite of its endurance, is slower to revive and quantitatively less in its product in the marginal countries, and, more important probably, such excellence as it attains there is appreciated only by a very restricted aristocracy.

Nor is it at all sure that these differences are explained by a lesser antecedent participation of the marginal regions in the greatest achievements of the high culture. I doubt very much that such a difference, even if a fact, explains the later difference in the course and the depth of the decline in the two regions. Ideas are very mobile, and it may be very hard to say where, if indeed anywhere geographically, a certain school of thought really belongs. As to the arts, local schools have a way of turning up in marginal regions during the early stages of decline at the center, for there is usually a time-lag in the margin.

The difference in the relative strength of religion between the margin and the center is of special importance for present purposes. In any one society in the same transition religion develops a more powerful hold over the intellectual and aesthetic culture in the marginal territories than it does in the central territories, but that is not at all to say that it is feeble in the central territories. Thus, it was more powerful in Western Europe than in Byzantium; in Japan, Korea, and Tibet than in T'ang China; probably in Further India and the East Indian Islands than in Gupta India. Nevertheless, it was powerful in Byzantium, China, and India. It is by no means a fact that religion is more powerful in the marginal territories of one society in transition than it is in the central territories of another society in transition. The generalization in this matter is limited to the relative power of religion as between the central and marginal territories in each particular transition.

We may now turn to the relation of politics and political institutions to religion, and there we shall encounter feudalism again. The decline of political institutions may continue for centuries quite aloof from the rise of new religion. When political revival comes about, however, there is in no case any doubt of the active engagement in it of religion. The revival takes the form of restoration of the empire or establishment of a new empire, and in this religious leaders are always prominent. There are cases, such as Islam, in which the head of the new state is primarily a religious leader; others, such as Byzantium, in which he is primarily head of the state but secondarily is admitted to overriding power over religious institutions; yet others, including both T'ang China and Gupta India, in which the head of the state stands outside religion but is powerfully influenced by priests. In all cases religion requires the rejuvenation—usually also the purification—of the state, and priests take an active part in promoting it.

It is this which fails in some marginal territories. The ghost empire in those territories witnesses to it directly, and we already know well that the authorities of religion are actively concerned in the attempted political revivals whose failure leaves the ghosts. Feudalism is a logical (but not necessary) concomitant of the state which has degenerated into a ghost. It arises free of the old state, very clearly so since the proto-feudal relation between them is invariably a failure. It may arise, then, free also of religion since religion always seeks to promote the recovery of the old state—unless indeed religion can also promote the feudal mode of political recovery. At least in Western Europe and Japan this was not so: religion in those societies was not concerned in feudal practices so that feudal politics stood outside the sphere of religion much as some of the arts have done.

Religion is not necessarily, then, a form neatly and logically superimposed over the whole of a declining culture to bring about its recovery. Politics, arts, presumably thought too, may in part move independently of religion; system has its limits in the development of human societies. The meaning of this is a little clearer in the case of politics, feudal politics at least, than it is in the case of the arts. The inner substance of politics is ethics, and, except where it builds a great institutional church, religion promotes political revival by ethica means alone; ethics is, in fact, as effectively covered by a rising religion as thought is. Feudalism, we know, is based upon the ethic of the barbarian war-band. It is, in fact, so simple, so elemental, that it adds nothing to the ethic in creating its political structure, except a simple idea about rights to the use of land.

Feudalism and religion thus meet in the sphere of ethics even though a caesura may continue to divide them there. Is feudalism, then, a kind of religion? Or, are feudalism and religion variants of some general quality a human society needs and may dangerously lack? The question may seem fantastic, but it must not be unthinkingly dismissed. In one feudal society, Chou China, church and state were one, and there religion was profoundly concerned in feudal practices. Indeed in Chou China ethics was and remained a matter of the quality of personal character and of the relations between persons, just as it is in the barbarian war-band. The clergy-nobility of Chou China knew no ethic but this, and they sought to revive the failing empire by promoting and strengthening that ethic. We cannot be surprised, therefore, that this empire, like the empires of marginal territories in other societies, became a ghost. Nor can we be surprised that China, in which that ethic has never been fundamentally changed, has never developed a state of great material power or complex political articulation, even though a bureaucracy eventually replaced the feudal hierarchy.

Nor is Chou China the only civilized society in which the ethic of the barbarian war-band, or something very like it, was the ethic fostered by religion. It is Toynbee who points out that the religion of the Greeks was a religion directly reflecting the conditions of a barbarian society:[4] Zeus was a barbarian war-leader and the other Olympians were his followers. If in this case their personal relations could become somewhat sophisticated, and their ethical conduct not altogether reliable, we know that the same happened in feudal societies too. And we may notice that the Greeks, like the Chinese, did not develop a great political edifice of complex articulation; they had great difficulty in transcending the city-state.

It appears, then, that in two civilized societies which were, in their several ways, simply formed politically, the divergence between the barbarian ethic and that prescribed by religion did not occur. There the development of society was rather systematic; religion did neatly and

[4] *A Study of History*, I, 96; III, 113. My student, Isaac R. Barfield, first noticed the relevance of Greek religion, as Toynbee sees it, to the relation of feudalism with religion, and drew my attention to it. I am glad to acknowledge my debt to him.

logically cover at least the political culture, perhaps the rest of the culture too, and promoted the society's growth, or its recovery. The deduction is clear that some religions lose touch with the barbarian mind and fail to offer it an ethic it can understand and follow—it is indeed always in regions in which the barbarians hold political power that feudalism arises. But that is not because religion is less powerful in every way in the marginal regions where the barbarians may preponderate than it is in the central regions; we have found that religion is, case by case, more powerful in the marginal regions. It is, I think, because the religions in question, Christianity, Buddhism, Mazdaism, possibly Hinduism, contain the relics of great philosophies which fit and demand large imperial political edifices incomprehensible to the barbarian mind. The failure of these religions is thus quite local and special even within the political culture. But their failure is very important, as witness the deepseated antinomy, already mentioned earlier in this book,[5] which Bryce found between feudalism and imperialism. It is important enough to block the reversal of the trend from decline to revival in politics.

And it would appear that the intellectual and aesthetic culture becomes to a large extent involved in the blockage, that a general cultural revival cannot occur until revival has been decisively started in the crucial material-political sphere. This is confirmed rather strikingly by what happens in the aesthetic and intellectual culture once the feudal remedy has been effectively applied to the polity and sufficient order has been imparted to society. The aesthetic culture surges forward dramatically, and the intellectual culture, always less free than the aesthetic, follows.

Thus, the eleventh to the twelfth centuries saw the culmination of feudalism in the old, leading countries of Western Europe, the establishment of an effective order in society. And those were also the centuries when medieval European thought began in earnest, when architecture first showed its great promise, and when the study of Roman law was taken up. The next two centuries, in which the intellectual and aesthetic achievements reached their height, saw the feudality beginning to fall in behind the new leadership of the national monarchs. Iran, a society of poor achievement, nevertheless fits well with Western Europe in the development of its architecture. The great age was the third century A.D., the first Sassanian century, in which whatever had been feudal in Iran was brought effectively under the authority of tha

[5] Above, pp. 270-271.

remarkable imperial monarchy. In Japan it is painting which shows the chronological relation most clearly, for a new departure began in the late fifteenth century after the feudal order had become well established. It must be noticed, however, that Japanese architecture reached its highest point very early in the feudal period, namely in the late fourteenth century. This exceptional achievement can be traced to special influences of Chinese origin, as can other disturbances of the usual chronological succession in the case of Japan. In China itself, in the Chou feudal age of the ninth to seventh centuries B.C., there occurs one of the clearest records of the rise of an art in a society being brought to order by feudal means; it is the record of the working of bronzes, which has been traced through the decline of the late Shang and earliest Chou periods, then through changes of school to a strong revival at the height of the feudal age.[6]

This significant chronology, repeated in society after society, makes the place of feudalism in the growth of civilization appear a large one. Nor can there be any doubt that feudalism has played a crucial part in the history of several great civilized societies. But we must guard against exaggerating its importance. Feudalism is not a kind of religion. In Chou China it was an ordinary product of the application of religion to politics. In other societies it marks the omission of something from religion. The arts which surge forward in feudal societies very rarely have intrinsic relation to feudal ideas—which is hardly surprising since feudalism has few and extremely simple ideas. On the other hand, they frequently relate intimately to the religion of the time; they may, as in the case of Gothic architecture, be one of its greatest expressions. Nor is the political failure of religion complete: feudalism does not supply an ethic in the complete absence of an ethic from religious sources; where the feudal ethic is not itself backed by religion, feudalism strengthens the general ethical structure, probably only at the crucial point, that of the barbarian mind, which religion has failed to capture. That religion contributes much else to politics in a feudal society is so obvious that it scarcely needs mention. In the case of Western Europe it is abundantly evident in the political structure of the church, which was better developed for many centuries than that of the state, whose clerks indeed were the first skilled administrators the society had, so

[6] See Bernhard Karlgren, "New Studies in Chinese Bronzes," *Bulletin of the Museum of Far Eastern Antiquities* (*Ostasiatiska Samlingarna*, Stockholm), IX (1937), 1-118, especially 81-88, 95-96.

superior to the state's officials that the state borrowed their services, often to the church's detriment.

That feudalism is a process which brings barbarians, or primitives, into civilization is a consideration of large consequence. It suggests the proposition that feudalism belongs more logically at the original rise of civilized societies, when all peoples were at first primitives, than it does at the revivals of civilized societies after decline—that it was a phenomenon of construction before it was a phenomenon of reconstruction. If this is sound, then most, perhaps all, of the cases of feudalism which have been treated in this book are really cases of incidental, marginal repetition of events which occurred on a greater scale and with far greater consequences at the genesis of civilization.

Thus, feudalism in Japan is classic for the cases of feudalism at the revival of civilization because it played a part in introducing primitives for the first time to civilization. Feudalism in Western Europe is less than classic for those cases because the people most strongly affected, those of northern France, had been to some extent civilized before, while the peoples of central and northern Europe, who had not been civilized before, were not completely feudalized.[7] What was classic feudalism for the revivals of civilization, that is to say, was most like the feudalism of the actual genesis of civilization. Our non-typical cases, Iran and Russia, which were feudalistic but not truly feudal, fit admirably into this structure of theory, for in them the incidental repetition was far less than in the classic case of revival, Japan, and very substantially less than in the next case, Western Europe. The repetition was inhibited in the non-typical cases through the instrumentality of commerce and the survival or the rise of city polities, which is something we shall shortly find significant. Moves in what seems to us a feudal direction which stopped much short of feudalism in Byzantium and in China post-Han fit equally well,[8] for in them the undoing of

[7] The theoretical argument can be varied to bring the cases of Japan and Western Europe closer together if we say that both the people of central Japan and the people of northern France had been civilized before feudal times, those of central Japan under the early Japanese Empire, those of northern France under the Roman Empire and the early Frankish kingdom, and that the peoples of northern Japan and of central and northern Europe were civilized for the first time with the aid of feudalization.

[8] So, no doubt, does the case of Egypt between the Fifth Dynasty and the Twelfth, but I doubt that in that case, the shortest chronologically of all the transitions from decline to revival which we have considered, there was anything which can even be called a move in a feudal direction.

civilization did not go even far enough to call into operation anything which may correctly be called a feudalizing process.

Here, then, is an issue out of all our perplexities, a bold interpretation of the place of feudalism in history which satisfactorily explains all that we know and provides a frame for future discoveries, serving especially well as a directive in the search for data on the origins of civilized societies. Unfortunately, however, we have at present very few data on origins which support the proposition; those we do have can also be otherwise interpreted, and there are other data which at least appear to be incompatible with it. The proposition therefore remains no more than an experimental hypothesis. It is a sufficiently attractive and plausible one, nevertheless, to make mandatory a very careful review of the few data.

The first important data are those which show that barbarians invaded and settled in the four valley countries of the Old World in which we know that civilized societies originated, Egypt, Mesopotamia, Northwestern India, and North China.[9] Archaeology actually establishes those settlements beyond a doubt in the first two countries, virtually does so in the other two. Perhaps it could even be said that the fact of settlement is established *a priori* for all four cases. But there is a doubt whether the settlers ought properly to be called barbarians within the meaning used in this essay, where it has a special relation to the rise of feudalism. Yet I do not think the doubt is very important. I think that the first settlers migrated into the valleys across desert country, or country becoming desert or steppe, only a short time before the civilizations began to rise; if so, the migrations are analogous to those of barbarians who entered declining civilized societies in later history. But, even if their migrations occurred long before the civilizations began to arise, and there were undoubted primitive societies in the valleys at the dawn of civilization, those societies must have broken up and something like barbarian war-bands have arisen as the civilized societies began to be formed; if that was so, the primitives were somewhat analogous to the primitives in Japan and elsewhere who began to be transformed *in situ*.

And besides, we know very well that the settlement in the valleys was not the consequence of a single migration, or even of a single series of migrations. The early remains from all the valleys—all four valley countries—show that migration and settlement occurred originally in

[9] We do not know that they did not settle and originate civilized societies in other places in the Old World, valley countries or countries of other physiography.

waves, later waves being superimposed upon earlier ones. In the case of Mesopotamia, Kramer has proposed that a wave of Sumerian barbarians overran an already established Irano-Semitic civilized society some time in the third millennium B.C., and that a heroic age followed.[10] This proposed episode is of a type familiar to us, and it prompted Mr. Brundage to suggest that a feudal age could in turn have followed the heroic age.[11] Thorkild Jacobsen's valuable study of Mesopotamian origins also requires, and, I think, shows beyond reasonable doubt, a heroic age and an invasion.[12] At least two such ages must have been involved in the episodes Jacobsen and Kramer propose, which suggests waves of conquerors, or at least of immigrants, entering Mesopotamia on several early occasions.[13] If that happened in Mesopotamia, something similar presumably happened in the other valley societies also. And, if a feudal age followed each invasion, then it is worth considering whether the repeated feudal experience, with its known effect of toughening the political fiber, was a vital factor in the origin of the four known primary civilized societies of the Old World. The rise of civilized societies, I am fully persuaded, is not something which resulted from a Darwinian accumulation of minuscule modifications of primitive societies. It requires for its explanation a series of large changes proceeding from a chain of causes, chiefly large causes. Repeated intensification of the in-group out-group struggle in a feudal or similar manner could be a series of links in the chain.[14]

We have no evidence for Mesopotamia, unfortunately, of tough political units which might have been fiefs at the origin of civilization there. Nor have we for any of the four primary civilized societies evidence of such units at a very early date. For Egypt, however, we have found that the nome, the main unit of local government, was an exceptionally tough political entity in the period between the Fifth and the Twelfth Dynasties;[15] its exceptional character arises from compari-

[10] "New Light on the Early History of the Ancient Near East," *American Journal of Archaeology*, LII (1948), 155-164.

[11] Above, pp. 94-95.

[12] "Primitive Democracy in Ancient Mesopotamia," *Journal of Near Eastern Studies*, II (1943), 159-172.

[13] Thus Kramer finds his central evidence for the Sumerian invasion in the sharp break between the archaeological types found in the Mesopotamian strata known conventionally as "Uruk VIII" and "Uruk VII." Other similar breaks occurred earlier (and later) in Mesopotamia, and there are several in each of the other four valleys.

[14] For other, larger factors, see my "Concept of the Conglomerate Myth," 74-81.

[15] Above, pp. 260-261.

son with local units in other societies at similar times in their history. So tough was the nome then that it is reminiscent of those very durable Japanese and French provinces which had at one time been fiefs, and we have been led to suspect that the nome also had been a fief. If it had been a fief, then that was in the days of origin of the Egyptian society in the fourth or fifth millennium B.C.[16]

Jacobsen's theory requires that his heroic age occurred at the time when the Mesopotamian religion was first being formulated.[17] We must not and need not stop to investigate that fully here; it is adequately treated by Jacobsen himself, forming one of the two main premises of his argument. Obviously, however, it is of great importance also to the argument being developed here, for it brings our proposed feudalism at the genesis of civilization into the same kind of relation with the rise of religion which we have found to occur between feudalism and religion in later history; the relation is especially close to that we have found to have occurred in Chou China.

There is, further, at least a suggestion that the physiography and climate of the great valleys in which civilized societies arose required something like feudal organization. Human survival in the valleys

[16] The antiquity of the nome has been a matter of difference of opinion, but I do not think it can now be seriously disputed. True, Elise Baumgärtel has recently revived a demurrer of Steindorff to the opinion that the nome is very ancient, but she does not prevail against Newberry and others. To show that the nomes of Lower Egypt have been reorganized at relatively late dates does not prove that there were no nomes there in prehistoric times, while many of those of Upper Egypt have been traced back to such early historic dates that it is certain they were already there in prehistoric times. The main literature is as follows: Eduard Meyer, *Geschichte des Altertums*, II-I (2nd edn., Berlin, 1928), 176-178; G. Steindorff, "Die ägyptischen Gaue und ihre politische Entwicklung," *Abhandlungen der sächsischen Akademie der Wissenschaften*, XXVII, no. 25 (Leipzig, 1909), 878ff.; W. M. Flinders Petrie, "The Nomes of Egypt," British School of Archaeology in Egypt, *Studies*, II (London, 1911), 22; P. E. Newberry, "Some Cults of Prehistoric Egypt," *Annals of Archaeology and Anthropology*, V (1912-13), 132ff.; *idem*, "Notes on Some Egyptian Nome Ensigns and their Historical Significance," *Ancient Egypt*, 1914, pp. 5ff.; A. Moret, "Une liste des nomes de la Haute-Egypte," *Comptes rendus de l'Académie des Inscriptions et Belles-Lettres*, 1914, p. 565; G. Bénédite, *Journal of Egyptian Archaeology*, V (1919), 225ff. Moret sets up a persuasive argument to the effect that the earliest nomes, but not, of course, every individual nome known from a late date, arose as the people settled and gave up a clan organization for a fully territorial organization (*From Tribe to Empire*, pp. 129-130; *The Nile and Egyptian Civilization*, pp. 40-53). Drioton and Vandier give an excellently clear account of nome administration under the unified regime of the central government, and they sum up the argument about the age of the various nomes. (*Les peuples de l'Orient Méditerranéen*, II: *L'Egypte*, pp. 43-47.)

[17] "Primitive Democracy in Ancient Mesopotamia," pp. 167-172.

depended preeminently upon a system of canals and embankments, both to prevent the settlements from being swamped and drowned out by the annual floods of the great rivers and, most vital, to save and distribute the water of the floods for agriculture in a climate which afforded little or no rain. It may be, then, that the firm discipline maintained within a fief offers an effective means of ensuring the care necessary to keep a system of canals in serviceable operation. Thus König remarks: "It should be expressly noted that a good canal development, which rendered the soil effectively fertile, was only possible under a feudal regime. An intensive canal system and feudalism are bound together inseparably in the ancient Orient."[18] To this may be added the conviction of Lattimore that water-works were an essential feature of the economy of feudal Chou China.[19]

It is, of course, obvious that König's statement is too strong. If it were completely correct, there would never be, or have been, any but a feudal regime in the great valleys. We know, however, of other regimes effective enough to keep the canals, embankments, and other water-works serviceable. Even so, we also know that weak regimes in some of the valleys, Mesopotamia in particular, could lead to disaster through failure of water-control, and it is not impossible, not indeed unlikely, that a feudal regime could be an effective early political method, leading later to other, stronger methods, of enforcing water-control. If this is true, it may mean that more attention should be paid than has been paid in this book to the protection and development of the material subsistence of a feudal society. The special provision of water-control as a part of subsistence in the primary civilized societies may, too, imply a special quality in the proposed feudalism of those societies. I do not suggest, however, that these considerations could require any modification of the concept of the nuclear ethic of a feudal society which has been propounded here.

We come now to the data which appear to be incompatible with the occurrence of feudalism in the original formative stages of civilized societies. The data are confined to the single case of Mesopotamia, but in the general dearth of evidence they must be given relatively great weight. They point to the rise of city polities directly out of the domina-

[18] F. W. König, *Älteste Geschichte der Meder und Perser: Der Alte Orient*, XXXIII, Parts 3/4 (Leipzig, 1934), 13-14: "Es sei ausdrücklich bemerkt, dass eine gute Kanalisation, die tiefgreifend und befruchtend auf den Boden wirkt, nur unter feudalen Machtverhältnissen möglich war. Intensive Kanalwirtschaft und Feudalismus sind im alten Orient unzertrennlich miteinander verbunden."

[19] *Inner Asian Frontiers in China*, pp. 40-41, 317, 370-376.

tion of barbarian war-bands in heroic ages. Both Kramer and Jacobsen, neither of them concerned to combat the idea of feudal developments in the period, find that cities arose in and after the "Enmerkar-Lugalbanda-Gilgamesh era," which was the supposed heroic age after Kramer's Sumerian conquest.[20] Gilgamesh, a barbarian leader, is indeed traditionally represented as lord of the city of Uruk, and Jacobsen, using some of the epic material, argues that Gilgamesh shared his power with two city assemblies, one of elders and the other of ordinary citizens.[21] If this is correct, it sounds, not like feudalism, but rather like an alternative and related development to feudalism. Thus, the smaller assembly at Uruk (and elsewhere in Mesopotamia) could well be descended from the war-band, the comitatus of advisers and assistants to the leader, which in a feudal system would become a council, or court, of vassals. The great assembly was the successor to the entire body of barbarian freemen, as is very plain from the fact that this assembly remained at the same time the body of fighting men.[22] In a feudal system this mass of warriors has often, not always, lost its relation to the original leader, but retained its rights in the main by becoming a body of rear vassals, vassals of the leader's vassals, and vassals of one another.

The Frankish *Campus Martius* was a general body of free, barbarian fighting men which later became feudalized in that manner. The Homeric *agora* was another such body, which, however, led on, so far as we know, directly to such city general assemblies as the Athenian *Ecclesia* and the Spartan *Apella*— and both of these bodies remained in the early city, as the corresponding assembly of Uruk did, a body of fighting men. The similarity of Greek to Mesopotamian city institutions seems, in fact, to have been quite close. It has been thought that certain features of later Greek society resulted more or less directly from the fact that Greece had not been feudalized. Thus Zimmern argues that class differences were less in Greece than in Europe because there had been no feudal past in Greece.[23] It is, of course, still debatable whether they really were less, and, even if they were, it is a completely open question whether Mesopotamia was like Greece in that respect.

[20] "New Light on the Early History of the Ancient Near East," p. 163.

[21] "Primitive Democracy," pp. 165-166.

[22] "Primitive Democracy," p. 166, n. 4.

[23] A. E. Zimmern, *The Greek Commonwealth* (3rd edn.; Oxford, 1922), pp. 89-92. Zimmern goes on to describe "mediaeval Greece," relying chiefly upon Hesiod (pp. 93-96). I doubt, however, that the village life he depicts is very different from that in, say, Merovingian Gaul.

Greece was heir—the younger of two co-heirs, Phoenicia being the elder—to one of the greatest systems of trade the world had then seen, the "thalassocracy of Minos." This, together with certain characteristics of the Greek terrain, is usually taken to have determined, not from Greek origins but from an early time in Greek history, the powerful growth of Greek cities with their preponderance over other political forms. Conceivably, something similar happened at an early time in the history of Mesopotamia. The great importance of commerce in later, historic periods in Mesopotamia is well established, and it is not at all unlikely that the country so greatly needed foreign products that commerce became important at a very early time. That may well mean that the city polity was urged forward in development and that it supervened upon, perhaps overwhelmed, feudalistic forms. River valleys are a notoriously special kind of environment: they usually lack some vegetal products and most or all minerals, while their alluvial soil and constant water supply serve to provide certain foods and other products in great abundance. If, then, Mesopotamia had from an early time to trade its surpluses to make up for its lacks, that is no more than might be expected. And, if this seems a good argument for Mesopotamia, is it not likely to be a good one also for the other great valleys where civilized societies arose out of primitive ones? The city form may thus have been urged forward at the expense of the feudal form in all the valleys.

But the cases of China and Egypt do not support this idea. Maspero's picture of the unit in the Chou feudal polity shows it as at first a nobleman's castle, the peasants' dwellings clustered near it so that the peasants could take refuge when an enemy approached; such a unit was only a village. Later, the population increased and diversified and a city, at least a town, emerged, but it remained under domination of its lord; and it was still a very small town even after these apparently feudal conditions had been transformed during the development of nations.[24] In Egypt also village populations took refuge inside some sort of stockade, for in the time of the early settlements there the bedouin of the desert constantly raided the valley farms. But we have no indication whether the stockades were maintained by feudal lords. There were chieftains, elders, the "Saru," in the more important villages, and those villages became before long political centers for surrounding areas containing less important villages. Territorial administration on the basis of these areas developed and replaced the blood relations of the clan: these were

[24] *La Chine antique* (Paris, 1927), pp. 24-25.

the areas which became nomes. This picture of early Egypt is Moret's and Eduard Meyer's.[25] Both of these pictures, that of Chou China and that of Egypt, are very largely speculative, of course, but they are not very different from one another. The main difference, if there was one, was in the occurrence or non-occurrence of the feudal lord. But we do not know of that difference as a fact: the feudal lord was there in China, and we do not know that he was not there in Egypt. And we do have another reason to think that the nome originated as a fief.

We are confronted, then, with contrary indications: one, consisting of general considerations for early Egypt and China, of the supposed frequency of invasions in the early valley societies, and of the exigencies of civilized societies arising on a material foundation which required water-control, supports the likelihood of feudal or feudalistic developments; the other, consisting of certain of Jacobsen's findings for Mesopotamia, of inferences from the better known Greek analogy, and of considerations of the commercial needs of societies situated in river valleys, supports the likelihood that cities were the earliest effective civilized polities. Are we to conclude that the primary civilized societies in the valleys actually developed differently in different cases? Only, I think, to the extent of differences in degree. One thing we know is that cities did arise fairly early in all four societies, but that does not exclude the possibility of a feudal principle of political relations also. In the Chinese case we think we see the city and feudal principles in combination. We may think, then, that the two were combined in the other valley societies also, but that each society produced its own particular combination, the two principles varying in relative importance from case to case. So, in China the feudal principle was predominant over the city principle, while in Mesopotamia, if Jacobsen is correct, the city principle was soon predominant over the feudal principle.[26]

In later history, when the primary cycles of civilization were over and the civilized societies had passed through phases of decline, there appears a certain antinomy between the feudal and the city political principles. The rise of the city in those later times accompanies the displacement of feudal relations by other relations although it does not directly cause the displacement. In the anomalous case of Kievan Russia the

[25] See note 16 above.

[26] Jacques Pirenne, who thinks that feudalism existed at Egyptian origins as well as under the Fifth and Sixth Dynasties, argues that it was confined to Upper Egypt, the valley, while in the delta, Lower Egypt, city-states predominated. (*Histoire des institutions et du droit privé de l'ancienne Egypte*, I, Brussels, 1932, 51-104.)

rise of the city-state probably signifies the actual forestallment of the formation of feudal relations through the instrumentality of an unusually early and rapid growth of commerce. Commerce between the Graeco-Roman world and the Chinese and Indian worlds passed across Iran-Mesopotamia in Parthian times, and very possibly provided the means to prevent the development then in Iran of a fully feudal regime. Commerce both in Kievan Russia and in Parthian Iran was thus to a large extent something alien, which possibly sharpened the difference of political principle between city and feudality. But, as a matter of fact, some alien quality always attached to commerce in a feudal polity in historic times: the trade which was more than local, small-scale trade carried on under a feudal regime was always in those times a survival or revival of trade which had existed before feudal times in the old empire and around its frontiers. Even in feudal Western Europe all trade of any consequence led back to Italy and Italy's economic relation with non-feudal Byzantium and the Levant.

Trade in the primary civilized societies cannot have had that alien quality since it arose to supply the material needs of the river valley which was the society's seat, and its center of organization and control was in the valley society itself. The difference of principle between city polity and feudal polity may thus have been more potential than actual in those societies, or it may have become actual only with the passage of time. Our supposed city-feudality in Chou China fits very well into this thesis if China was then still in its primary cycle of civilization, as present expert opinion holds. For, if that was so, trade in Chou China cannot to any important extent have been a survival or revival from the past; it cannot have had an alien quality because there was no civilized society surviving from the past in any region at all near the Yellow River Valley from which it could have derived that quality.[27] And the indications are that trade was not very important in Chou China so that the predominance of the feudality over the city there is just what we should expect, and there need not have been any appreciable conflict between the two principles.

One more consideration arises, an entirely theoretical one for the primary societies. It is that the feudal principle is anterior to and more fundamental than the city principle. In historic times the city follows the feudality wherever the feudality becomes firmly established. The feudal principle, where it arises, is elemental to the reviving civilized society: it is concerned with its actual survival, the prevention of the

[27] Further away there were such regions, namely, in India, Mesopotamia, and further west. Hence there is a weakness in this argument.

annihilation of the society, the preservation of the lives of its members upon something approaching a subsistence level. But the city arises later, when subsistence has already long been secure and there are wants to be supplied above and beyond mere subsistence. The rise of the city marks a stage above subsistence, therefore. This must be true of the primary civilized societies also. They required to survive before they required to trade. If, then, they secured survival by feudal means, they had feudal polities before they had city polities.

But there is, I must admit with regret, no answer in this argument to the question whether feudalism actually had a part in the genesis of civilization. The argument shows only what part feudalism is likely to have had if it had a part at all. To show whether it did have a part we need more evidence. The place of feudalism in history, therefore, so far as we can discover it, is that of a very important political device for the revival of a declining civilization, and for the extension of civilization to new peoples not formerly civilized. Its place may indeed be a far greater one than this, namely as a part of the process of the genesis of civilization, but that we have not shown to be fact.

The word uniformity is used in this study in a broad and somewhat variable way. In general, it denotes the type to which any class of things, entities, or events conforms in a significant respect. The uniformities we are concerned with are found among the major processes in the historical development of civilized societies. The causes which control those processes are obviously very complex, and conformity to types among them cannot often be very close. It is possibly closer among the elemental things in social development, that is to say, among social relations of the simplest kinds; we shall have to take notice of those relations. For major uniformities I propound as a guide to our inquiry only a very broad criterion: a uniformity is a repetitive type emerging strongly enough to be unmistakable to common sense informed by the special experience of the historian; the repetitive sequences of events which exhibit such uniformities are, or at least appear to be, more alike than unalike.

The final operation in this book is, then, an attempt to give substance to the concept of uniformities in history, using feudalism as the leading example; it will appear that it is a peculiarly useful example. We shall be able in performing this operation to throw a little light upon the obscure problem of causes in the evolution of societies, and at the same time to show a few particular reasons for which the major uniformities in history cannot be very strong types. These demonstrations will lead to certain suggestions about proper method in history and social science as compared with proper method in biological science and in physical science.

Feudalism is obviously one of the major uniformities in history by the criterion propounded. Another major uniformity is the cyclic movement of civilization. Viewed as a whole, the recovery of a civilized society after a decline is uniform to a fairly high degree in the cases we have considered here: we have noted the decline of the high culture, beginning with the attenuation of creation of knowledge; the disintegration of the political fabric (and of the economic system) occurs at later stages; at an advanced stage the society will usually divide into two parts, a central part, including the old geographic nucleus of the civilization, which is making a fairly rapid recovery without utter ruin of the high culture, and an outer, marginal part in which political disintegration eventually becomes nearly complete and the general culture sinks very low. But at once it is to be noted that this uniformity does not actually extend to all the cases studied: Chou China, for example, did not divide into two parts. It may be that this is because in China the decline began differently; that is something we do not know; but we do know that there was a decline before the recovery in Chou times. The whole society in this early Chinese case followed a course of development so much like those of the outer regions of other civilized societies, those regions which go feudal, that we find a new rather broad uniformity covering all these cases. It is a uniformity parallel, similar in some ways, dissimilar in others, to the uniformity of development in the other parts of civilized societies, those which make a rapid recovery without ruin of the high culture.

Thus, uniformities in history overlap upon each other a little irregularly: civilized societies, considered as wholes, show an extensive uniformity in their cyclic declines and revivals, but the uniformity does not include every case; if such societies be then divided into regions of lesser and of greater decline, two new uniformities are found, and one of them includes the society which is recalcitrant to classification in the uniformity of societies considered as wholes. This sort of argument can be extended. At least one of the two divisions of civilized societies can be divided again to produce new uniformities: these are the feudal regions in former barbarian country and the feudal regions in former marginal country of the old empire; but the Chinese society post-Han does not show any feudal region in former marginal country—another irregularity. It may be that the other division of civilized societies, the non-feudal one, can be subdivided also, say into territories ruled rather directly by the government of the new empire, and territories ruled indirectly; but that has not been investigated here. The course of development of the aesthetic and intellectual culture, which has been noticed shortly in this chapter, can, however, be studied for uniformities and a considerable number of new ones found.

The uniformities discoverable in aesthetic and intellectual development do not coincide with those in political development or with one another, but they tend to do so. That is to say, if the developing structure of like societies be analyzed on one basis, the uniformities found will not quite coincide with those found when analysis is made upon another basis. And again, a vertical view of like societies will show uniformities among like component institutions, movements, etc. which do not fit neatly within the uniformities among the greater institutions, etc., which the lesser ones compose. There is, as has been said, an irregularity in the structure of uniformities into which the major processes of history fall. It is as though the history of civilized societies were built up out of a number of forms, each form being a developmental process, not all of them used for every society: here and there among the various societies one form, or more than one, is missing altogether; here and there some rather anomalous shape has been put in instead of one of the stereotyped forms; for some historic processes more than one form is available, and thus for different societies major differences of development occur even though broad correspondences can be recognized between the differences. And, to carry on the figure, the stereotyping of the forms is itself a pretty rough business: it is, as we said, unmistakable, but the forms are of different sizes in time and space (duration and geographical area); their proper shape—of order and succession of events—varies somewhat from case to case even though remaining unmistakable.

Sometimes a series of differing forms or of differing modes of fitting the forms together permits the serial comparison of societies. Such occurred when we were able to establish a series of societies roughly progressive in terms of the imperialistic propensities of national monarchs. It is no fluke that such a series can be found; there are certainly others. That it should be quite rough and traversed by the difference between feudal and non-feudal origin of the territorial extent of the nation fits in perfectly consistently with the general roughness of the uniformities.

Such, it seems to me, is the kind of morphology the history of civilized society has. It is quite foolish to pretend that this amounts to close repetition in history, but still more foolish to pretend that there is no repetition at all, that history entirely lacks uniformities. The element of irregularity may be taken, I think, to support the thesis that society and culture are not products of a single force unified at the social or cultural level. The element of regularity, *per contra*, may be taken to show that the various causes operating in the evolution of culture and society tend towards unification. Those causes tend towards unification, then, but are not completely unified. That they tend towards unification explains why monistic views of social or cultural evolution have arisen and have received some support; that the unification remains incomplete is a reason why such views must be rejected.

There is in progress at the moment, chiefly among anthropologists, a discussion of causes in culture. It began with Durkheim's demonstration against Comte and Spencer that events occurring in society are largely caused in society,[28] and since that time has tended to veer between the

[28] *The Rules of Sociological Method*, 8th edn., trans. S. A. Solovay and J. H. Mueller, ed. G. E. G. Catlin (Chicago, 1938), pp. 101-102, 107-108. The largest contributor, by far, to this subject is Mr. Kroeber, and most of his material, which began to appear in 1917, has just been collected in Part I of his *The Nature of Culture* (Chicago, 1952); items 11 and 12 there, which concern causes, are newly published. In addition, his *Configurations of Culture Growth* is directly or indirectly concerned with the matter throughout. Other literature is as follows: David Bidney, "On the Concept of Culture and Some Cultural Fallacies," *American Anthropologist*, XLVI (1944), 30-44; Leslie A. White, "The Expansion of the Scope of Science," *Journal of the Washington Academy of Sciences*, XXXVII (1947), 181-210; *idem*, *The Science of Culture* (New York, 1949); Edward W. Strong, "A Question of Interpretation," *American Anthropologist*, L (1948), 216-224; A. L. Kroeber, "White's View of Culture," *American Anthropologist*, L (1948), 405-415; J. H. Steward, "Cultural Causality and Law," *American Anthropologist*, LI (1949), 1-27; A. L. Kroeber, "Configurations, Causes and St. Augustine," *American Anthropologist*, LIII (1951), 279-284; Rushton Coulborn, "Causes in Culture," *American Anthropologist*, LIV (1952), 112-116; Philip H. Bagby, "Culture and the Causes of Culture," *American Anthropologist*, LV (1953), 535-554. Marginal, but important material is: Frederick J. Teggart, *Theory and Processes of History* (Berkeley, 1941), pp. 77ff.; Sidney Hook, *The Hero in History* (New York, 1943); *Causality, Lectures Delivered before the Philosophical Union, University of California*, ed. G. P. Adams, J. Loewenberg, and S. C. Pepper (Berkeley, 1932).

The attempt in some of this literature to discredit the concept of cause has not convinced me. I think it all boils down to the plain fact, which we all admit, that cause is an exceedingly difficult thing to unravel. I agree for that reason that it may often be a good thing to evade consideration of cause and work with probability, regularity, and other more viable concepts. But for that reason also the larger concept of cause must not be forgotten, and it must be used, however difficult, where it is the only concept which will work, as is the case here where we are dealing with events as wholes. The only constructive criticism of the concept of cause which I know is that it is so closely bound up with that of existence that it can (perhaps) not be dissociated from it; cf. Loewenberg in *Causality*, pp. 3-37. It is, in my opinion, a sound dictum that doctrine is in the last analysis answerable to common sense: we still must use cause in our common-sense reasoning.

monistic extreme of cause solely on the social or cultural level and the "reductionist" extreme of cause operating exclusively upward from the biological and physical levels. To make our contribution here to that fruitful discussion, certain comparisons between uniformities in the history of society and culture and uniformities in the biological and physical worlds must be brought in.

The social, cultural, or socio-cultural world is far younger than the biological or the physical world; it is therefore unlikely that cyclic processes in the social world have had time to become as closely repetitive as those in the biological and physical worlds.[29] It would appear that both the physical and the biological worlds have produced characteristic repetitive processes of major magnitude. Those in the physical world are the cyclic processes of movement of satellite bodies about primary bodies together with a number of derived oscillations. Those in the biological world are the reproductive processes whereby the species are continued by birth, development, and death successively of individual organisms. It needs no demonstration that the repetitions in the physical world are far closer than those in the biological world. The cyclic process of rise and fall of civilized societies[30] began perhaps seven thousand years ago. It has therefore endured for a mere moment in comparison with the duration of biological processes, scarcely even a moment in comparison with physical processes. It is hardly possible to imagine the emergence of repetitions in that moment comparable in closeness with the repetitions of the biological and physical worlds.

The simple argument in relative ages is, however, not enough alone to explain the divergences from type in the repetitions of the social world. Possibly relative ages are not even very important. There is also the matter of relative complexity of process, the most evident, possibly the largest, source of which lies in the structural connections between the three worlds. Our ignorance of the limits of the physical world is something which must make the argument following a tentative one, but it appears to me sure that the argument has some validity and possible that it has great importance. In the organic world the palpable, observable cause of change in evolution is environment,[31] fundamentally

[29] For "worlds" as used here the term "levels" is used in some of the literature listed in the previous note, and the three worlds are often there referred to as inorganic, organic, and superorganic. I do not happen to have used those terms here, but no criticism of the usages is intended; they are perfectly good terms, in my opinion.

[30] Cf. n. 1 above.

[31] There is no need here to enter into the vexed question of the full cause of biological mutations. It may indeed be quite relevant to our subject, but it is too obscure to be introduced profitably into an already complicated argument.

physical environment, and physical environment also conditions the development of the individual organism. When we search the inorganic, physical world for an analogous underlying basis, our ignorance halts the inquiry. We may guess perhaps that we ought to divide the molar from the nuclear physical world and regard the latter as "environment" to the former. But this is only a guess, and, even if it is correct, the next question which suggests itself is whether the nuclear physical world itself has an environment, and to that we have no answer whatever.

However many worlds, levels of existence, underlie the physical world, it is undeniable that the physical world underlies the biological world, and—what is important to our present concerns—that both the biological and the physical worlds underlie the social world: the social world has a conditioning environment which is at least twofold. If, then, environmental cause is important at all, it is likely to be more important in the social than in the biological world.

Before proceeding to the obvious deductions from this proposition we may examine what I think is corroborative evidence to be found in the elemental things of the three worlds. Let us assume, as long used to be thought, that atoms are the elemental things in the physical world—the neglect of nuclear things being covered by the tentative character of the argument. Cells are, without dispute, the elemental things in the biological world. In the social world world they are, I think also without dispute, social relations of the simplest kind, such as those between employer and employee, between the state and its officials, between persons engaged in any institution operating by division of labor, or indeed operating in any way at all. I shall say that cells in their various classes conform less closely to type than atoms in their classes do, and that social relations in their various classes conform less closely to type than cells do. The former perhaps cannot quite be proved, but at least nobody —I presume—ever thought that like cells are identical, whereas from the seventeenth century to the nineteenth physicists, consciously or unconsciously, proceeded as if like atoms were identical (and they still do so for many useful purposes).

It is obvious perhaps that like social relations vary quite considerably, but there are ascertainable reasons for it, one in particular. In a military formation the relations between a sergeant and the privates under him should ideally be the same in each case since it is more immediately and practically important that military relations conform to type than that any other social relations do so—we consciously try to make these relations approach the typological standard we call mechanical, which means, of course, physical. But we know perfectly well that, even with the same sergeant, the relation varies for every individual private. This is because individual men differ very largely; their relations with other men, therefore, being functions of their varying personalities, must vary also.

But we should notice here, as we have not needed yet to do, that civilized societies are not the only human societies known; there are also primitive societies. There is a real difference between elemental social relations in primitive and in civilized societies, and those in primitive societies almost certainly approach type in many of their classes more closely than those in civilized societies do. This is, I think, mainly because of the *gemeinschaftlich* quality of those in primitive societies: they are largely carried in the culture and learned unconsciously at an early age by the persons involved in them.[32] That primitive societies are far simpler, smaller structures than civilized societies is another, probably an independent, reason for close approach to type among relations in primitive societies. Another important factor in the matter is the far greater age of primitive than of civilized societies. Primitive societies of some sort are possibly as old as the species itself, or not a great deal younger, which suggests that a process very closely parallel to that of biological evolution was (and no doubt still is) in operation to form the type of relations in the various classes of primitive *Gemeinschaft*.[33]

Yet, however strong the type of relations in primitive societies, they cannot escape the influence of the variety of human personality. I contend that the variations from type so brought about must be greater than variations from type among the cells of the biological world, and that variations among cells are greater than variations among atoms.

Return, then, to the matter of causality in social evolution. Because the social world has at least a twofold environment, events occurring

[32] Cf. Redfield in *American Journal of Sociology*, LII, 300.

[33] For the parallel between biological and social evolution in the early ages of human society, see the brilliant speculative passage at the end of Kroeber's "Superorganic" (*The Nature of Culture*, pp. 49-51).

I suspect that it was chiefly the close approach to type reached among relations in primitive societies which made possible the theories of such scholars as Bachofen and L. H. Morgan propounding a single course of social evolution among all societies—and, moreover, permitted those scholars to advance knowledge in spite of their large error.

Insect societies are vastly older than any human societies, and they contain far closer repetitions of type than human societies do. This, of course, is not due only to their greater age, but also and probably far more to their greater simplicity. It may, no doubt, be assumed that personality varies much less in some insects than in human beings, but that is a nice point on which it would be inadvisable to dogmatize!

in it are subject to causal influences of origin in each of the underlying worlds and sometimes in both; it follows that variety in the social world is likely to be greater than in the biological world, greater again than in the physical world. This is confirmed at the elemental level in the social world, for human personality, which lessens conformity to type of the elements in that world, is itself, in an important part, determined biologically, and, in a part whose importance it is hard to assess, determined physically.[34] If the very elements in the social world are thus variable, how much more variable are major events likely to be.

Elsewhere I have argued that in ordinary, small, continuous events in the history of human societies, the influence of cultural prevails powerfully over other causes, but that in large, extraordinary, "historic" events the preponderance of cultural determination is not a fact.[35] The major uniformities of history, as studied here, illustrate very well the combination of the ordinary and the extraordinary of which the broadest history[36] consists. It is the influence of culture which tends to unify the causes of the development of human societies, and the repetitive character of long sequences of large events which I call uniformities exhibits the action and reaction between the influence of the culture and the influence of causes arising from the biological and physical worlds. It is to be noticed that the boundary between the biological and social worlds passes across the stream of human actions: some human actions, especially in primitive societies, are culturally produced, but others, the

[34] Kluckhohn and Mowrer, "Culture and Personality," *American Anthropologist*, XLVI (1944), 1-27, esp. 7, 9-14; Mowrer and Kluckhohn, "Dynamic Theory of Personality," *passim*, in *Personality and the Behavior Disorders*, ed. J. McV. Hunt (New York, 1944), pp. 69-135; Otto Klineberg, *Race Differences* (New York, 1935). It is not easy to assess even the biological determinant, and there is rather a dearth of useful literature on the subject. I am afraid the dearth happens because it is very hard to approach quantitative assessment of these matters. In my judgment, social scientists lose half the battle, gravely endangering their sense of proportion in their science, when they run away from problems which can be carried only to a stage where a few facts and factors, important but incommensurable, can be discerned. Where would history be if the historians avoided the periods for which the data are scanty? I flatly disagree with Ralph Linton in his approval of analysis of personality in abstraction from biological influences; *The Cultural Background of Personality* (New York, 1945), pp. 84-85. This is an example of the bad influence the prestige of physical science and its methods has upon social science.

[35] *American Anthropologist*, LIV (1952), 114.

[36] See reference in previous note. The word "history," like the word "historic," as just used in the text, is often used with the restricted meaning of large, extraordinary events. I ordinarily use it, however, to cover all events in any sequence, and in this study I always do so unless otherwise noted. Thus here "broadest history" is simply history, as I ordinarily use the term.

actions of men as individuals, actions within the sphere of each man's "free will," must be said to be biologically produced; there are, no doubt, plenty of actions jointly produced.

It is still mysterious that the struggle between social causation and biological and physical causation follows a cyclic course, a course of repetition of what we think of as long sequences of events. The mystery is to some extent dispelled, however, when we realize that any repetition is in reality a repetition of a sequence of events; even what we customarily think of as a single event can be subdivided for observation into, is in fact composed of, a sequence of smaller events; the durationless instant is a figment of the mathematician's imagination. It is, then, chiefly and immediately (not only) the length of sequence relative to the history of society as a whole which needs explanation. I think the explanation of this is simple, namely the recent origin of society; when human society is even a million years old, the rise and fall of civilized societies and the uniformities subordinate to those main movements will not appear so long. Of course, the core of the mystery remains: why does nature do things in repetitive cycles at all? The solution is presumably the same for all cycles, the rise and fall of societies, the lives of organisms, the many periodicities of the physical world. About this we know nothing, and, if it is any comfort, we might as well conclude that nature does it because nature knows no better!

We know nothing about the addiction of nature to cyclic repetitions even though we are able in some instances, in all perhaps, to unravel some of the outer mechanism of the cycle. The biologist can show that ontogeny repeats phylogeny and so claim that he has demonstrated the systematic storing up of the forces which make the organism follow out its life career—all he has actually demonstrated is the fact that nature stores up the forces, not much about how or anything about why nature does so. Similarly, the social scientist can describe what happens as a civilized society declines and revives. He can, as we have done in this essay, show that the formation of religion and of feudalism has to do with the storing up of forces which make the society follow out another cycle of its history.[37]

[37] Bergson offers the same formula to explain the storing up of forces, both of those which direct the life of the organism and of those which direct the history of society, the formula of the *élan vital; L'évolution créatice* (Swiss edn.; Geneva, 1945), pp. 101-110 and *passim* for the *élan* in the organism; *Les deux sources de la morale et de la religion* (Swiss edn.; Geneva, 1945), pp. 108ff. for the *élan* in society. The formula is, of course, no explanation; it is a mere trick—with which, in my opinion, Bergson deceived both himself and others. Nevertheless, Bergson was a thinker of great perspicacity, and his equating of the two occasions is suggestive.

We may venture a step further now in that demonstration and suggest that the formation both of religion and of feudalism shows culture being put through social convolutions in its development by man as a biological agent. The formation of religion is a conscious, purposeful reconstitution of most of the high culture in its political-ethical, intellectual, and aesthetic manifestations in such a way as to render it an inspiration, an impetus, to man to return to the social tasks. Feudalism, when it arises independently of religion, is something far narrower, but its formation is a process whereby the culture of a jaded civilized society is reinforced in its elemental nucleus, the relation of man to man, by an ethic drawn from a primitive source. In neither of these processes is cultural determination preponderant. On the contrary, the men who form, or re-form, religions and the men who form war-bands and fiefs do so as individuals, acting within the sphere of their free-will, to restore to the culture the quality it needs in order to determine its own development and, consequently, the ordinary, small, continuous events of social evolution. I regard this as biological determination, man using his mind, his leading biological asset, to create something of a social order. Let the anthropologists see if they can fit this into their theories of culture, or else let them discredit my doctrine.[38]

From this exposition of process in the social world follows an entire rationale governing the appropriate modes of acquiring knowledge of that world.[39] There are, in fact, two modes of acquiring knowledge of that world, as also of the biological and physical worlds, the historical

[38] For the sake of brevity I omit reference to other causal influences at such crises as the decline and revival of civilization. These are the whole biological and physical environment acting obstructively to the operation of the old culture, permissively to the operation of the new. When the obstruction offered by a particular thing in the environment becomes very conspicuous, the historian may be misled into thinking he has unearthed the "cause" of the decline. Hence, for example, Liebig, Sigwart, and others who attributed the decline of the Roman Empire to exhaustion of the soil. It is often possible by careful inquiry to give a fair definition of the extent of such physical difficulties—Rostovtzeff has done it in this instance (*The Social and Economic History of the Roman Empire*, Oxford, 1926, pp. 329-330)—and they usually turn out to be individually quite minor, such as would attract little notice by the historian but for accompanying or ensuing decline. The economic determinists are only a little more sophisticated than others who make the error of particularizing cause in that they see the recalcitrance of environment as multiple instead of single.

[39] I have once previously ventured to discuss those modes, and on that occasion I relied rather upon the relatively small numbers of things in the social world. I think the reliance is sound in general, though I do not use it here, but my previous venture was certainly faulty in some ways; see "Note on Method in Anthropology," *Southwestern Journal of Anthropology*, 1 (1945), 311-317.

and the theoretical. As Hugh Miller showed fifteen years ago, the historical method is primary and the theoretical secondary.[40] Nature has created things, all things, historically, and when the human mind seeks to trace the historical steps by which things are related to each other it is following nature as closely as possible. Such procedure tells, however, only what nature has done in a single instance, and there is scarcely any indication that nature will ever do the same thing again: that is to say, history is of almost no use as a basis for prediction. If, however, the scholar finds that nature has followed the same, or a much similar, course on several occasions, some probability exists that nature will do it yet again; the more often nature has done it in the past, the more probable, other things being equal, that nature will do it again in the future. This is the purpose of theoretical knowledge. Theory is what is abstracted as common to a series of similar courses of events and used to predict the character of future courses of events. It is far more useful than history, but, for plain numerical reasons and for other reasons, it is often much harder to get. And, when theory is hard to get, the scientist must resort to the discovery of all the relevant history he can find, for that may eventually yield him the material for the establishment of theory.

This resort, so insistently forced upon the social scientist by the character of his material, is far from unknown to the biological and the physical scientist. A few decades ago the physical scientist revelled in theoretical knowledge, proclaimed that all "real" knowledge is quantitative and affected to despise all other modes of knowledge and those who worked with them. The biological scientist hoped much from theory, but failed rather often to establish it securely. Then Darwin brought salvation to biology, and since that time the history of living organisms has been fundamental to the science. And it is becoming clear at the present time to the physical scientist that the historical side of astronomy is fundamental to his science as a whole. It ought always to have been clear to him that the historical side of geology is fundamental to the terrestrial part of his science, but he hardly noticed it until recently. The reason the physical scientist is now coming to realize the historicity of things in his world of knowledge is that the great difficulties of nuclear physics have forced upon him the tracing of particular histories that he may get to irreducible data.[41] History is

[40] *History and Science: A Study of the Relation of Historical and Theoretical Knowledge* (Berkeley, 1939), pp. 5-8 and *passim*.

[41] Irreducible in present knowledge. New histories, found in the future, may reduce data now irreducible.

the fundamental knowledge in every world of existence, and the physical scientist is at last being forced to recognize this.[42]

The social scientist never had it easy, and for that reason he is potentially the most sophisticated of scientists. His types are so rough and imperfectly formed, even at the elemental level of his science, that any abstractions he dares to make are sure to violate the particulars—twist the facts—to some extent. Hence the meaning the abstractions carry is narrowly limited, the actual knowledge they afford relatively small, the danger of error they involve relatively great. Thus the vast field and great utility of statistical and mathematical operations in and near the elements of the physical world is not repeated in the social world; it is not repeated even in the biological world. Sir James Jeans thought that God is a mathematician. But that is the god of the physical world. If the god of the social world is a mathematician, he is a thoroughly bad one!

This does not mean that statistical knowledge and mathematical use of the statistics are not feasible at all in social science. It means that their use is very much restricted. Statistical-mathematical operations are useful only with the simplest basic social relations, and even there their usefulness is drastically restricted by the roughness of the approach of the individuals to type. From the rough quality of this approach arises the usefulness of averaging in the statistical side of social science. Whatever is based upon averages, and clearly so understood, thereby protects the scholar from error, while, of course, it also drastically curtails the meaning of the statistics; the latter is the inevitable price paid for the safety and soundness of the meaning which survives. But it must be remembered, and it is highly significant, that averaging is not peculiar to social science. There is a fair probability that many, perhaps all, of the close repetitions of physical science are themselves the outcome of vast averaging processes; the container of gas whose pressure is in a constant relation to its temperature is the classic example. The difference in this matter between physical and social science is that nature does the averaging in physical science, but the scientist has laboriously to do it himself in social science.

It is with the major uniformities in social science that this study has been concerned. They may be considered outside the realm of "quan-

[42] An important landmark in recognition of this truth by physical scientists is the appearance of C. F. von Weizsäcker's *The History of Nature* (trans. F. Wieck; Chicago, 1949). The material first entered knowledge as a course of lectures at Göttingen in 1946. For the importance of the book and for a serious weakness in it, see my review in *Ethics*, LXI (1951), 236-238.

titative" knowledge altogether, but this does not mean that they are unimportant. On the contrary, the variability of the cases within uniformities makes those uniformities which can be discerned and are unmistakable, not the less, but the more valuable. If they concern current events, they may even have a very special predictive value; that value is there, however much mischief may be done under its sanction by Marxists, Spenglerians, and other cranks. The cranks can, in fact, only be discredited, the danger they constitute forestalled and suppressed, by serious pursuit of comparative historical social studies. Where theory fails in those studies, history is the proper resort. The nearness of approach to type in any uniformity in history is therefore to be carefully assessed and thereafter the failure of type, the differences. So, in the method proper to the larger issues of social science, theory occupies a central position: first, the history of each case which falls into a uniformity must be studied; second, the uniformity itself is to be educed; and third, the history of the differences is to be reconsidered as it is set off by the uniformity.

The excellence of feudalism as an example of this kind of study lies first in the unusually distinctive character of feudal institutions and of the order of events in their development; the uniformity running through the various cases of feudalism is, therefore, itself clear and distinctive, more so than most uniformities in history. Second, the various histories of cases aberrant from the uniformity and of the divergences of the cases which fall within it are significant: they nearly all point to reasons for their divergence or aberration and beyond those reasons to the reasons for the uniformity of feudalism itself. Both these excellences arise from the elemental, crucial, and so very clear, place of feudalism in the history of civilized societies.

BIBLIOGRAPHIES

II · FEUDALISM IN WESTERN EUROPE

BY JOSEPH R. STRAYER

(compiled by William Bowsky)

WESTERN FEUDALISM IN GENERAL

Bloch, Marc. "Feudalism. European," *Encyclopaedia of Social Sciences*, vol. 6 (London, 1932), pp. 203-210, bibliography on p. 219.

Bloch, Marc. "Les formes de la rupture de l'hommage dans l'ancien droit féodal," *Nouvelle revue historique de droit français et étranger*, vol. 36 (1912), pp. 141-177.

Bloch, Marc. *La société féodale*. I. *La formation des liens de dépendance*. II. *Les classes et le gouvernement des hommes*. 2 vols., Paris, 1939-1940.

Calmette, J. *La société féodale*, 4th edn., Paris, 1938.

Ganshof, F. L. *Feudalism*, tr. P. Grierson, foreword by F. M. Stenton, London-New York-Toronto, 1952.

Halphen, L. "La place de la royauté dans le système féodal," *Anuario de historia del derecho español*, vol. 9 (1933), pp. 313-321.

Hintze, O. "Wesen und Verbreitung des Feudalismus," *Sitzungsberichte der Preussischen Akademie der Wissenschaften, Phil.-Hist. Klasse* (Berlin, 1929), pp. 321-347.

Keeney, B. C. *Judgment by Peers*, Cambridge (Mass.), 1949.

Kienast, W. "Unteraneid und Treuvorbehalt," *Zeitschrift der Savigny-Stiftung für Rechtsgeschichte, Germ. Abt.*, vol. 66 (1948), pp. 111-147.

Krawinkel, H. *Feodum*, Weimar, 1938.

Lot, F. *L'art militaire et les armées au moyen âge*, vol. I, Paris, 1946.

Lot, F. *La fin du monde antique et le début du moyen âge*, 2nd edn., Paris, 1951. (English translation of 1927 edn. by P. Leon and M. Leon: *The End of the Ancient World and the Beginnings of the Middle Ages*, New York, 1931.)

Mitteis, H. "Zur Geschichte der Lehnsvormundschaft," *Festschrift Alfred Schultze* (Weimar, 1934), pp. 129-174.

Mitteis, H. *Lehnrecht und Staatsgewalt*, Weimar, 1933.

Mitteis, H. *Der Staat des hohen Mittelalters*, 4th edn., Weimar, 1953.

Société Jean Bodin. Recueils. I. *Les liens de vassalité et les immunités* (*Revue de l'Institut de Sociologie*, vol. 16 [Brussels, 1936], pp. 7-118). III. *La Tenure*, Brussels, 1938. IV. *Le Domaine*, Wetteren, 1949. (Each volume contains articles by several authors dealing with various aspects of the central problem in different countries.)

Stephenson, C. *Mediaeval Feudalism*, Ithaca, 1942.

IXe *Congrès International des Sciences Historiques*, Paris, 1950. I. *Rapports.* (Section on medieval institutions by R. Boutruche, C. Cahen, P. Dollinger, and Y. Dollinger-Leonard, pp. 417-471, esp. pp. 440-447 on feudalism.)

THE ORIGINS AND THE FRANKISH PERIOD

Bosl, K. "Vorstufen der deutschen Königsdienstmannschaft," *Vierteljahrschrift für Sozial- und Wirtschaftsgeschichte*, vol. 39 (1952), pp. 193-214, 289-315. (Merovingian period through tenth century.)

Cronne, H. A. "Historical Revisions, xci. The Origins of Feudalism," *History*, vol. 24 (1940), pp. 251-259.

Dopsch, A. "Beneficialwesen und Feudalität," *Mitteilungen des Oesterreichischen Instituts für Geschichtsforschung*, vol. 46 (1932), pp. 1-36.

Ganshof, F. L. "Benefice and Vassalage in the Age of Charlemagne," *Cambridge Historical Journal*, vol. 6 (1939), pp. 149-175.

Ganshof, F. L. "La juridiction du seigneur sur son vassal à l'époque carolingienne," *Revue de l'Université de Bruxelles*, vol. 27 (1922), pp. 566-575.

Krawinkel, H. *Untersuchungen zum fränkischen Benefizialrecht*, Weimar, 1937.

Leicht, P. S. "Gasindi e Vassali," *Rendiconti della Reale Accademia Nazionale dei Lincei. Classe di Scienze morali, storiche, e filologiche*, 6 ser., vol. 3 (1927), pp. 291-307.

Lot, F. "Origine et nature du bénéfice," *Anuario de historia del derecho español*, vol. 10 (1933), pp. 174-185.

Odegaard, C. E. *Vassi and Fideles in the Carolingian Empire*, Cambridge (Mass.), 1945.

Sánchez-Albornoz, C. *El 'stipendium' hispano-godo y los orígenes del beneficio prefeudal*, Buenos Aires, 1947.

Sánchez-Albornoz, C. *En torno a los orígenes del feudalismo*, 3 vols., Mendoza (Argentina), 1942.

Schlesinger, W. *Die Entstehung der Landesherrschaft. Untersuchungen vorwiegand nach mitteldeutschen Quellen*, vol. I, Dresden, 1941.

Schur, J. *Königtum und Kirche im ostfränkischen Reiche vom Tode Ludwigs des Deutschen bis Konrad* I, Paderborn, 1931.

Stephenson, C. "The Origin and Significance of Feudalism," *American Historical Review*, vol. 46 (1941), pp. 788-812.

FEUDALISM IN DIFFERENT COUNTRIES

FRANCE

Bloch, M. "Un problème d'histoire comparée: la ministérialité en France et en Allemagne," *Revue historique de droit français et étranger*, ser. 4, vol. 7 (1928), pp. 46-91.

Bongert, Y. *Recherches sur les cours laïques du Xe au XIIIe siècle*, Paris, 1949.

Carabie, R. *La propriété foncière dans le très ancien droit normand.* I. *La propriété domaniale*, Caen, 1943.

Chénon, E. "Le rôle juridique de l'osculum dans l'ancien droit français," *Mémoires de la Société nationale des Antiquaires de France*, 8 ser., vol. 6 (1924), pp. 124-155.

Declareuil, J. *Histoire générale du droit français des origines à 1789*, Paris, 1925.

Dhondt, J. *Études sur la naissance des principautés territoriales en France*, Bruges, 1948.

Dillay, M. "Le 'service' annuel en deniers des fiefs de la région angevine," *Mélanges Paul Fournier* (Paris, 1929), pp. 143-151.

Dumas, A. "Encore le question 'Fidèles ou Vassaux?'" *Nouvelle revue historique de droit français et étranger*, vol. 44 (1920), pp. 159-229.

Ganshof, F. L. "Depuis quand a-t-on pu en France être vassal de plusieurs seigneurs?" *Mélanges Paul Fournier* (Paris, 1929), pp. 261-270.

Guilhiermoz, P. *Essai sur les origines de la noblesse en France au moyen âge*, Paris, 1902.

Haskins, C. H. *Norman Institutions*, Cambridge (Mass.), 1918.

Kienast, W. *Unteraneid und Treuvorbehalt in Frankreich und England*, Weimar, 1952.

Lot, F. *Fidèles ou vassaux?* Paris, 1904.

Luchaire, A. *Manuel des institutions françaises: Période des capétiens directs*, Paris, 1892.

Petot, P. "L'hommage servile: essai sur la nature juridique de l'hommage," *Revue historique de droit français et étranger*, ser. 4, vol. 6 (1927), pp. 68-107.

Richardot, H. "Francs-fiefs. Essai sur l'exemption totale ou partielle des services de fief," *Revue historique de droit français et étranger*, 4 ser., vol. 27 (1949), pp. 28-63, 229-273.

Sczaniecki, M. *Essai sur fiefs-rentes*, Paris, 1946. (See review by F. L. Ganshof in *Revue Belge de Philologie et d'Histoire*, vol. 27 (1949), pp. 237-243.

Schramm, P. E. *Der König von Frankreich*, 2 vols., Weimar, 1939.

ENGLAND

Cam, H. M. "The Decline and Fall of English Feudalism," *History*, vol. 25 (1940), pp. 216-233.

Chew, H. M. *English Ecclesiastical Tenants-in-Chief and Knight Service, Especially in the Thirteenth and Fourteenth Centuries*, Oxford, 1932.

Douglas, D. C. *Feudal Documents from the Abbey of Bury St. Edmunds*, London, 1931. (Important introduction.)

Douglas, D. C. "The Norman Conquest and English Feudalism," *Economic History Review*, vol. 9 (1939), pp. 128-143.

Gibbs, M. *Feudal Order*, New York, 1953.

Keeney, B. C. "Military Service and the Development of Nationalism in England," *Speculum*, vol. 22 (1947), pp. 534-549.

Kienast, W. *Unteraneid und Treuvorbehalt in Frankreich und England*, Weimar, 1952.

Kimball, E. G. *Serjeanty Tenure in Medieval England*, New Haven, 1936.

Lyon, B. D. "The Money Fief under the English Kings, 1066-1485," *English Historical Review*, vol. 66 (1951), pp. 161-193.

McFarlane, K. B. "Bastard Feudalism," *Bulletin of the Institute of Historical Research*, vol. 20 (1943-1945), pp. 161-180.

Painter, S. "Studies in the History of the English Feudal Barony," *Johns Hopkins University Studies in Historical and Political Science*, series LXI, no. 3, Baltimore, 1943.

Painter, S. *The Reign of King John*, Baltimore, 1949.

Painter, S. *William Marshall*, Baltimore, 1933.

Plucknett, T. F. T. *A Concise History of the Common Law*, 4th edn., London, 1948.

Pollock, F. and Maitland, F. W. *The History of English Law before the Time of Edward I*, 2 vols., 2nd edn., Cambridge, 1899.

Poole, A. L. *From Domesday Book to Magna Carta, 1087-1216*, Oxford, 1951.

Round, J. H. *Feudal England*, London, 1895. (Reprinted 1909.)

Stenton, F. M. *Anglo-Saxon England*, 2nd edn., Oxford, 1947.

Stenton, F. M. "The Changing Feudalism of the Middle Ages," *History*, vol. 19 (1935), pp. 289-301. (English feudalism, *ca.* 1066-1500.)

Stenton, F. M. *The First Century of English Feudalism*, Oxford, 1932.

Stephenson, C. "Feudalism and Its Antecedents in England," *American Historical Review*, vol. 48 (1943), pp. 245-265.

GERMANY

Barraclough, G. *Medieval Germany, 911-1250*, 2 vols., Oxford, 1938. (Articles by German historians. See esp. vol. 2, ch. VII, by Heinrich Mitteis: "Feudalism and the German Constitution.")

Below, G. von. *Der deutschen Staat des Mittelalters*, vol. I, 2nd edn., Leipzig, 1925.

Brunner, H. *Deutsche Rechtsgeschichte*, vol. 2, 2nd edn., revised by C. Freiherr von Schwerin, Munich-Leipzig, 1928.

Bosl, K. *Die Reichsministerialität der Salier und Staufer*, 2 vols., Stuttgart, 1950-1951. (Vol. 10 of *Schriften der Monumenta Germaniae Historica*.)

Hirsch, H. *Die hohe Gerichtsbarkeit im deutschen Mittelalter*, Prague, 1922.

Mayer, Th. *Adel und Bauern im deutschen Staat des Mittelalters*, Leipzig, 1943. (Articles by German historians.)

Mayer, Th. *Fürsten und Staat. Studien zur Verfassungsgeschichte des deutschen Mittelalters*, Weimar, 1950.

Scheidung-Wulkopf, I. *Lehnsherrliche Beziehungen der fränkisch-deutschen Könige zu anderen Staaten vom 9. bis zum Ende des 12. Jahrhunderts*, Marburg, 1948. (*Marburger Studien zur älteren deutschen Geschichte*, Reihe 2, 9.)

Schroeder, R. K. H. *Lehrbuch der deutschen Rechtsgeschichte*, 7th edn., revised by E. Freiherr von Künssberg, Berlin-Leipzig, 1932.

Stengel, E. E. "Land- und Lehnrechtliche Grundlagen des Reichsfürstenstandes," *Zeitschrift der Savigny-Stiftung für Rechtsgeschichte, Germ. Abt.*, vol. 66 (1948), pp. 294-342.

Tellenbach, G. *Königtum und Stamme in der Werdezeit des Deutschen Reiches*, Weimar, 1939.

Thompson, J. W. *Feudal Germany*, Chicago, 1928.

LOW COUNTRIES

Blécourt, A. S. de. *Kort begrip van het oud-vaderlandsch burgerlijk recht*, 5th edn., Groningen, 1939.

Didier, N. *Le droit des fiefs dans le coutume de Hainaut au moyen âge*, Lille-Paris, 1945. (See review by R. Latouche in *Revue du moyen âge latin*, vol. 1 (1945), pp. 423-428.

Genicot, L. *L'économie rurale namuroise au bas moyen âge (1190-1429)*, vol. I. *La seigneurie foncière*, Namur, 1943.

SCANDINAVIA

Bobé, Graae and West. *Danske Len*, Copenhagen, 1916.

Bolin, S. "Medieval Agrarian Society in Its Prime: Scandinavia," *Cambridge Economic History of Europe*, vol. I (Cambridge, 1941; ed. J. H. Clapham and E. Power), pp. 467-492.

Erslev, Kr. "Europaeisk Feudalisme og dansk Lenvaesen," *Historisk Tidsskrift* (Copenhagen), 7 ser., vol. 2 (1899), pp. 247-304.

Löfquist, K.-E. *Om riddarväsen och frälse i nordisk medeltid*, Lund, 1935.

Lönnroth, E. *Statsmakt och statsfinans i det medeltida Sverige*, Stockholm, 1940.

Rosén, J. I. *Kronoavsöndringar under äldre medeltid*, Lund, 1949.

Styffe, C. G. *Skandinavien under unionstiden*, 3rd edn., Stockholm, 1911.

Swedlung, R. *Grev- och friherreskapen i Sverige och Finland. Donationerna och reduktionerna före 1680*, Uppsala, 1936.

ITALY

Cahen, C. *Le régime féodal de l'Italie normande*, Paris, 1940.

Ficker, J. *Forschungen zur Reichs- und Rechtsgeschichte Italiens*, 4 vols., Innsbruck, 1868-1874.

Haskins, C. H. "England and Sicily in the Twelfth Century," *English Historical Review*, vol. 26 (1911), pp. 433-447, 641-665.

Leicht, P. S. "L'introduzione del feudo nell'Italia franca e normanna," *Rivista di storia del diritto italiano*, vol. 12 (1939), pp. 421-437.

Leicht, P. S. "L'organisation des grands domains dans l'Italie au Nord pendant les Xe-XIIe siècles," *Société Jean Bodin*, Recueil IV. *Le Domaine* (1949), pp. 165-176.

Leicht, P. S. *Storia del diritto pubblico italiano. Lezioni*, Milan, 1938.

Monti, G. M. *Lo stato normanno svevo*, Naples, 1934.

Mor, C. G. *L'età feudale*, 2 vols., Milan, 1952. (In the series *Storia Politica d'Italia.*)

Padovan, C. *Delle origini economiche e finanziarie del feudalismo*, Padua, 1935.

Sestan, E. "L'Italia nell'età feudale," in E. Rota, ed., *Questioni di storia medioevale* (Como-Milan, 1946), pp. 77-127.

SPAIN

Mayer, E. *Historia de las instituciones sociales y políticas de España y Portugal . . . siglos V a XIV*, 2 vols., Madrid, 1925-1926.

Ríus, J. M. Font. *Instituciones medievales españolas*, Madrid, 1949.

Sánchez-Albornoz, C. "La potestad real y los señoríos en Asturias, León, y Castilla en los siglos VIII a XIII," *Rivista de Archivos, Bibliotecas, y Museos*, 3 ser., vol. 31 (1914), pp. 263-290.

Valdeavellano, L. D. de. *Historia de España. De los orígines a la baja Edad Media*, Madrid, 1952.

HUNGARY AND POLAND

Grodecki, R. *Początki immunitetu w Polsce*, Lvov, 1930. (Beginnings of immunity in Poland.)

Hötsch, O. "Adel und Lehnswesen in Russland und Polen," *Historische Zeitschrift*, vol. 108 (1912), pp. 541-592.

Hóman, B. *Geschichte des ungarischen Mittelalters*, 2 vols., Berlin, 1940-1943 (Without scholarly apparatus. Translated into German by H. von Roosz and M. Pfotenhauer, ed. J. von Farkas.)

Jansák, S. *Slovensko v dobe uhorského feudalizmu. Hospodárské pomery od. r. 1514 do 1848*, Bratislava, 1932. (Slovakia during the time of Hungarian feudalism. Economic relationships from 1514 to 1848. This book contains an introduction on the character of feudalism by A. Štefánek and, pp. 197-228, an abstract in German.)

Rutkowski, J. "Medieval Agrarian Society in Its Prime: Poland, Lithuania and Hungary," *Cambridge Economic History of Europe*, vol. I (1941) pp. 398-417.

Szekfü, G. *Serviensek és familiarisok*, Budapest, 1913. (*Servientes and familares.*)

Uhlirz, M. *Handbuch der Geschichte Osterreiches und seiner Nachbarländer Böhmen und Ungarn*, vols. I-II, 1, Graz, 1927-1930.

Váczy, P. *A királyi serviensek és a patrimoniális királyság*, Budapest, 1928. (The royal *servientes* and patrimonial kingship.)

Váczy, P. *A szimbolikus államszemlélet kora Magyarországon*, Budapest, 1932. (The age of the symbolic conception of the state.)

Wojciechowski, Z. "La condition des nobles et le problème de la féodalité en Pologne au moyen âge," *Revue historique de droit français et étranger*, 4 ser., vol. 15 (1936), pp. 651-700, and vol. 16 (1937), pp. 20-76.

Wojciechowski, Z. *L'Etat polonais au moyen âge. Histoire des institutions*, Paris, 1949.

THE PAPACY

Jordan, K. "Das Eindringen des Lehnswesens in das Rechtsleben der römanischen Kurie," *Archiv für Urkundenforschung*, 1931, pp. 13-110.

CRUSADER STATES

La Monte, J. L. *Feudal Monarchy in the Latin Kingdom of Jerusalem 1100 to 1291*, Cambridge (Mass.), 1932.

III · JAPANESE FEUDALISM

BY EDWIN O. REISCHAUER

THE history of Japanese feudalism is excellently documented, perhaps better than that of any region of similar size in the Western world and certainly far better than that of any other non-Occidental land. Thus, Japanese feudalism and the feudalism of Western Europe may in time be coupled as the two best known and, in that sense, classic examples of feudalism in world history. Unfortunately, a detailed study of the ample records of Japanese feudalism is still largely to be made. Japanese scholars during the past five or six decades have made an excellent beginning, revealing the general outlines, but there is still much work to be done on the integration and interpretation of the vast body of available data.

Relatively little of the recent scholarly work on Japanese feudalism is available in Occidental languages, but, fortunately, a few of the most valuable contributions are in English. K. Asakawa's *The Documents of Iriki* (New Haven, 1929) is a pioneer work which is fundamental to an understanding of Japanese feudalism; and his article on "The Life of a Monastic Shō in Medieval Japan" (*Annual Report of the American Historical Association for 1916*, I, 311-346) describes an important facet of the problem. "Some Aspects of Japanese Feudal Institutions," *Transactions of the Asiatic Society of Japan*, XLVI, Part I (1918), 76-102, is another stimulating article by the same author.

John Carey Hall has contributed translations of the primary legal codes of feudal Japan. These translations, which are published under the general title of "Japanese Feudal Law" and the specific titles of "The Institutes of Judicature, Being a Translation of the 'Go Seibai Shikimoku,' The Magisterial Code of the Hojo Power-Holders (A.D. 1232)," "The Ashikaga Code, Translation of Kemmu Shikimoku A.D. 1336," and "The Tokugawa Legislation," appeared in the *Transactions of the Asiatic Society of Japan*, XXXIV (1906), 1-44; XXXVI, No. 2 (1908), 3-25; XXXVIII, No. 4 (1911), 269-331; XLI, No. 5 (1913), 683-804.

Sir George Sansom in his *Japan: A Short Cultural History* (New York, 1938 and 1943) provides a good overall account of Japanese feudalism. James Murdoch's *A History of Japan* (Kobe, 1903, 1910, and 1926) and Yosoburo Takekoshi's *The Economic Aspects of the History of the Civilization of Japan* (New York, 1930) are huge three-volume compendia containing a wealth of valuable but often disorganized details about the subject.

Eijiro Honjo's *The Social and Economic History of Japan* (Kyoto, 1935) covers some of the same material as Takekoshi in much briefer but more systematic form. André Gonthier in "Le régime féodal au Japon." *Revue de l'institut de sociologie*, Instituts Solvay, XVI, No. 1 (Brussels, 1936), 71-84, presents a short general statement on Japanese feudalism written in the same spirit as the present paper.

For further details on the Occidental bibliography of Japanese feudalism, see Hugh Borton, Serge Elisséef, William W. Lockwood, and John Pelzel, *A Selected List of Books and Articles on Japan in English, French, and German* (Cambridge, Mass., 1954).

IV · FEUDALISM IN CHINA

BY DERK BODDE

SPACE permits the listing of only major primary sources and, among secondary accounts, only those written in Western languages, thus excluding from the latter the large literature in Chinese and Japanese. References to several Chinese articles and monographs, however, will be found in notes 3, 11, 22, 25, 42, 48, and 54 in the text.

The Shang is the earliest dynasty whose historicity has been confirmed by archaeological remains. These include numerous divination texts inscribed on bone or tortoise shell, which, however, are restricted in content and often obscure, and only a handful of which are available in Western translation. Probably none of the literary sources traditionally said to be of Shang or earlier date actually antedate the beginning of the Chou Dynasty.

For the first half of the Chou (prior to ca. 600 B.C.), the primary archaeological texts are inscriptions on bronze ritual vessels (very few of them available in Western translation). More important, both in size and content, are the following literary works: the original corpus of the *Yi Ching* [Book of Changes], a work of divination; the *Shih Ching* [Book of Odes], a collection of folk and court poetry; portions of the *Shu Ching* [Book of History], a collection of historical documents; and the *Tso Chuan*, a detailed historical chronicle covering the period 722-481 B.C., which, however, did not assume its present form earlier than the fourth or third century B.C. Many gross misconceptions about early Chinese history have been created through indiscriminate use of such idealized accounts as the *Li Chi* [Book of Rites] and *Chou Li* [Rites of Chou], which, though purporting to describe the institutions of the early Chou, were actually compiled only during the last two or three centuries B.C. They and the other major classics listed above have all been translated into Western languages by James Legge, Edouard Biot, Séraphin Couvreur, Arthur Waley, Bernhard Karlgren, and others. Invaluable though they are, they often leave unanswered those questions on which we should most like to be informed.

For the second half of the Chou (ca. 600 B.C. onward), the literature becomes too extensive to be listed here, owing to the rise of many political and philosophical thinkers, among whom Confucius (552/551-479) was the earliest. They contribute much information, not only on their own but on the earlier age. Most of them have been translated into Western languages.

The Han Dynasty saw the appearance of the extremely valuable *Shih Chi* [Historical Records], by Ssu-ma Ch'ien (ca. 145-ca. 86 B.C.), a work traditionally regarded as the first of China's many "dynastic histories," but actually a universal history of China from earliest times to about 100 B.C. Roughly half of it has been translated by Edouard Chavannes as *Les mémoires historiques de Se-ma Ts'ien*, 5 vols. (Paris, 1895-1905). Its successor, the *Ch'ien Han Shu* [History of the Former Han Dynasty], by Pan Ku (A.D. 32-92), contains an important section on Chinese economic history from earliest times until the birth of Christ, which has been translated by Nancy Lee Swann as *Food and Money in Ancient China* (Princeton, 1950).

For the Period of Disunity, the situation is the reverse of that of the Chou: the original sources, while far more bulky, have been far less studied from the point of view of our subject. Of prime importance are the dynastic histories, of which there are no less than eleven for this period—a fact which helps indicate the magnitude of the task involved.

Among secondary materials, there are, first of all, several general historical surveys, of varying value but all covering both the Chou and the Period of Disunity. Among them are Otto Franke, *Geschichte des chinesischen Reiches*, 5 vols. (Berlin, 1930-52); K. S. Latourette, *The Chinese, Their History and Culture*, 3rd rev. edn., 2 vols. in 1 (New York, 1946); Wolfram Eberhard, *A History of China* (Berkeley, 1950), which is particularly detailed on the Period of Disunity; C. P. Fitzgerald, *China: A Short Cultural History*, 2nd rev. edn. (London, 1950); and L. Carrington Goodrich, *A Short History of the Chinese People*, 2nd rev. edn. (New York, 1951).

For the dynamics of Chinese society, important analyses include K. A. Wittfogel, "The Foundations and Stages of Chinese Economic History," *Zeitschrift für Sozialforschung*, IV (Paris, 1935), 26-60 (one of several writings); Owen Lattimore, *Inner Asian Frontiers of China*, 2nd edn. (New York, 1951); and Wolfram Eberhard, *Conquerors and Rulers: Social Forces in Medieval China* (Leiden, 1952). The two latter works have been discussed in detail on pp. 71-82 above.

General surveys, covering pre-Han China only, include Henri Maspero, *La Chine antique* (Paris, 1927), still excellent in part, though a good deal of it antiquated by reason of later archaeological discoveries; and H. G. Creel, *The Birth of China* (London, 1936, and New York, 1937), which makes full use of archaeology and is by all odds the most reliable account down to ca. 600 B.C.

The numerous works of Marcel Granet, including his *Chinese Civilization* (London and New York, 1930), though widely known, contain some theories of dubious validity and hence should be used with considerable caution. Granet's *La féodalité chinoise* (Oslo, 1952), uncompleted at the time of his death and now published posthumously, unfortunately reached this writer too late to be utilized in the present study. Like all of Granet's writings, its main emphasis is sociological rather than historical. It devotes much space to such matters as the social groupings, the mores, and the mythological, cosmological, and magico-religious conceptions of the early Chou Chinese (especially the aristocracy). On the other hand, it pays but scant attention to the dynamic aspects of Chou feudalism, i.e., those pertaining to its historical growth and decay. Unlike Maspero (in the articles listed below), Granet makes no use of archaeological data (notably the bronze inscriptions), but relies entirely on literary materials, including some that are late and probably considerably idealized, and others that he dates a good deal earlier than most scholars would allow. The result, as far as this writer is concerned, is a book more theoretical, less concretely linked to time and space, and hence less satisfactory, than are the studies of Maspero.

Many of Granet's findings, nonetheless, agree essentially with those presented (necessarily more briefly) in the present study. In particular, Granet rightly insists (pp. 24ff.) on the appropriateness of the word "feudal" to describe the society of the Chou Dynasty, and points to significant institutional parallels between it and medieval Europe. Basic to both societies, in his opinion, is the bifurcation between an elite warrior class on the one hand, living according to an elaborate code of honor and having as its main function the performance of military service on behalf of the suzerains by whom it is invested with landed estates, and, on the other hand, a mass of despised peasants who lack this code of honor, play only a subordinate role in warfare as conscripted footsoldiers, and possess no rights to the land which they cultivate.

Studies particularly pertinent to feudalism, especially for the Chou period, include Otto Franke, "Zur Beurteilung des chinesischen Lehenswesens," *Sitzungsberichte der Preussischen Akademie der Wissenschaften*, XXXI, Pt. I (1927), 359-377, and his summarizing article, "Feudalism, Chinese," in the *Encyclopaedia of the Social Sciences* (New York, 1937), VI, 213-214—both somewhat conventional surveys; Ch'i Ssu-ho, "A Comparison between Chinese and European Feudal Institutions," *Yenching Journal of Social Studies*, IV (Peiping, 1948), 1-13, which is based on earlier articles in Chinese by the same writer; and Yang Lien-sheng, "Notes on Dr. Swann's *Food and Money in Ancient China*," *Harvard Journal of Asiatic Studies*, XIII (1950), 524-557, which contains a useful summary of theories by several contemporary Chinese scholars on Chou systems of land tenure. On the God of the Soil and his connection with the Chou ritual of feudal investiture, see E. Chavannes, *Le T'ai Chan: Essai de monographie d'un culte chinois* (Paris, 1910), Appendix, "Le Dieu du Sol dans la Chine antique." Above all, however, should be cited the three striking articles by Henri Maspero in Volume III of his *Mélanges posthumes sur les religions et l'histoire de la Chine* (Paris, 1950): "Le régime féodal et la propriété foncière dans la Chine antique" (pp. 109-146); "Les régimes fonciers en Chine, des origines aux temps modernes" (pp. 147-192); "Les termes désignant la propriété foncière en Chine" (pp. 193-208).

For the Ch'in Dynasty, the standard work is D. Bodde, *China's First Unifier* (Leiden, 1938). For the Han system of government, see Chapter I of C. Martin Wilbur, *Slavery in China during the Former Han Dynasty* (Chicago, 1943), and Wang Yü-ch'üan, "An Outline of the Central Government of the Han Dynasty," *Harvard Journal of Asiatic Studies*, XII (1949), 134-187, both excellent studies.

For the Period of Disunity, the few available pertinent studies include Yang Lien-sheng, "Notes on the Economic History of the Chin Dynasty," *Harvard Journal of Asiatic Studies*, IX (1946), 107-185 (covering particularly the period 265-419); Wang Yi-t'ung, "Slaves and Other Comparable Social Groups during the Northern Dynasties (386-618)," *ibid.*, XVI (1953), 293-364; Etienne Balazs, "Le traité économique du 'Souei-Chou,'" *T'oung Pao*, XLII (Leiden, 1953), 113-329 (covering primarily the Sui Dynasty, 590-617, but also presenting rich and abundant data on the preceding Period of Disunity); and Wolfram Eberhard, *Das Toba-Reich Nordchinas* (Leiden, 1949) (dealing with the Northern Wei Dynasty, 386-535). See also Eberhard's *History of China* and *Conquerors and Rulers*, both cited above.

V · FEUDALISM IN ANCIENT MESOPOTAMIA AND IRAN

BY BURR C. BRUNDAGE

The list of works below has been selected in general for easy introduction into the history and archaeology of ancient Mesopotamia and Iran. Some few are standard, and others have been selected for their bibliographies. Except in the initial instance, monographic material does not appear. The pertinent volumes of the *Cambridge Ancient History* should in all cases be consulted.

Albright, W. F. "A Third Revision of the Early Chronology of Western Asia," *Bulletin of the American Schools of Oriental Research*, No. 88 (December 1942), pp. 28-36. To orient the reader into the latest advances in Near Eastern chronology.

Albright, W. F. *The Archaeology of Palestine*, Harmondsworth, England, 1949. Chapter V is probably the best recent summary of the Hyksos period from archaeological evidence. The second printing contains a selected bibliography.

Christensen, A. *L'Iran sous les Sassanides*, 2nd edn., Copenhagen, 1944. One of the best accounts of this period. It unfortunately contains no bibliography, but ample footnotes give the reader access to all the important primary and secondary sources.

Debevoise, N.C. *A Political History of Parthia*, Chicago, 1938. A difficult period due to scanty sources. Excellent classical references.

Delaporte, Louis. *Les Hittites*, Paris, 1936. A convenient summary. Part II and the bibliography "Lois Hittites" (pp. 354-355) should be particularly consulted on the subject of feudalism.

Ehtécham, M. *L'Iran sous les Achéménides*, Fribourg, Switzerland, 1946. Primarily a study of the political institutions of the first Persian Empire. Excellent references. The picture can be supplemented and filled out with references to A. T. Olmstead, *History of the Persian Empire*, Chicago, 1948.

Hrozny, Bedrich. *Histoire de l'Asie antérieure, de l'Inde, et de la Crète*, Paris, 1947. Useful bibliography. Though he is a notable worker in the field, Hrozny's interpretations in this text must be accepted with much caution.

Meyer, Eduard. *Geschichte des Altertums*, new edn., 5 vols., Stuttgart-Berlin, 1909-1939. A standard overall account of ancient history to the end of the Hellenic period.

O'Callaghan, Roger T., S. J. *Aram Naharaim: A Contribution to the History of Upper Mesopotamia in the Second Millennium B.C.*, Rome, 1948.

The author's conclusions are sometimes hasty, but his survey of the Mitannian problem is useful. He covers northern Syria as well as upper Mesopotamia.

Olmstead, A. T. *History of Assyria*, New York, 1923. Crammed with material and often colorful, but difficult to read at times.

VI · THE QUESTION OF FEUDAL INSTITUTIONS IN ANCIENT EGYPT

BY WILLIAM F. EDGERTON

THE best histories of Egypt are:

Etienne Drioton and Jacques Vandier, *Les peuples de l'orient méditerranéen,* II: *L'Egypte* (Paris, 1938). The second edition (Paris, 1946) is an unchanged reprint with an added Appendix (pp. 633-663) in which Vandier has brought the most important matters up to date. There are excellent bibliographies.

Hermann Junker, *Die Ägypter, Die Völker des antiken Orients* (Freiburg-im-Breisgau, 1933).

The Egyptian sections of Eduard Meyer, *Geschichte des Altertums* (I, Part II, 5th edn., Berlin, 1926, an unchanged reprint of the 1913 edn.; II, Part I, 2nd edn., Berlin, 1928), though old, are still of great value and can be used by outsiders with more confidence than many more recent works.

George Steindorff and Keith C. Seele, *When Egypt Ruled the East* (Chicago, 1943) deals chiefly with Dynasties Eighteen to Twenty. Earlier and later periods are briefly summarized.

The best systematic description of Egyptian civilization is Hermann Kees, *Ägypten* (Tübingen, 1928).

The best introduction to Egyptian law is Erwin Seidl, *Einführung in die ägyptische Rechtsgeschichte bis zum Ende des Neuen Reiches,* I: *Juristischer Teil* in *Ägyptologische Forschungen*, ed. Alexander Scharff, No. 10 (Glückstadt-Hamburg-New York, 1939).

An important and recent general interpretation of Egyptian cultural development is J. A. Wilson, *The Burden of Egypt* (Chicago, 1951).

The following are monographs bearing especially on the subject of this paper:

Hermann Kees, "Beiträge zur altägyptischen Provinzialverwaltung und der Geschichte des Feudalismus," *Nachrichten von der Gesellschaft der Wissenschaften zu Göttingen*, 1932, pp. 85-119; 1933, pp. 579-598. This deals with the organization and administration of Egypt from the Fifth Dynasty through the First Intermediate Period.

Alexander Scharff, "Der Historische Abschnitt der Lehre für König

Merikarê," *Sitzungsberichte der Bayerischen Akademie, phil.-hist. Abt.*, 1936, No. 8. An important contribution to the history of the First Intermediate Period.

Eduard Meyer, "Gottesstaat, Militärherrschaft, und Ständwesen in Ägypten: Zur Geschichte der 21. und 22. Dynastie," *Sitzungsberichte der Preussischen Akademie der Wissenschaften, phil.-hist. Kl.*, 1928, No. 28.

William C. Hayes, "Royal Decrees from the Temple of Min at Coptus," *Journal of Egyptian Archaeology*, XXXII (1946), 3-23. This includes a full bibliography of the decrees from Coptos, which are among the most important sources for the breakdown of the Old Kingdom, with some discussion of their significance. Among the earlier works which Hayes cites, the non-Egyptological reader should consult especially Gardiner, *Proceedings of Society of Biblical Archaeology*, XXXIV (1912), 257-265, and Sethe, *Göttingische gelehrte Anzeigen*, CLXXIV (1912), 705-726.

The writings of Jacques Pirenne contain many original ideas, and therefore deserve and receive attention from specialists. Unfortunately Pirenne himself is totally incapable of any sound scholarly criticism in Egyptological matters, and his works should therefore be avoided by scholars who are not trained in Egyptology. Especially relevant to this paper are: *Histoire des institutions et du droit privé de l'ancienne Egypte*, 3 vols. to date (Brussels, 1932-52); and "La féodalité en Egypte," *Revue de l'institut de sociologie,* XVI (Brussels, 1936), 15-36. The same criticisms, both favorable and unfavorable, apply to G. Dykmans, *Histoire économique et sociale de l'ancienne Egypte*, 3 vols. (Paris, 1936-37).

VII · FEUDALISM IN INDIA

BY DANIEL THORNER

THERE is no single work that can be cited as a suitable comprehensive guide to the history of India. For the period from the beginning of the first millennium B.C. down to A.D. 1000, a standard political handbook is that of Vincent Smith, *Early History of India* (4th edn., Oxford, 1923).

For the period from A.D. 1000 down to the nineteenth century a heavily detailed account of political development is given in the *Cambridge History of India*, III, IV, V (Cambridge, Eng., 1928-29). These volumes, as well as the first volume (which covers the ancient period), provide extensive bibliographies of original sources and secondary materials. The second volume, dealing with medieval India, has long been promised but has not yet been published. The flavor of ancient Indian politics in its most realistic aspect is provided by a treatise probably put together in the early centuries of our era: Kauṭilya, *Arthasastra*, translated by R. Shamasastry (2nd edn., Mysore,

1923). A secondary work that bears upon the same general subject is Beni Prasad, *The State in Ancient India* (Bombay, 1928).

The outstanding original source for the Mughal period in northern India is Abul Fazl, *Ain-i-Akbari*, edited and translated by H. Blochman and H. S. Jarrett, 3 vols. (Calcutta, 1871-94). Four secondary works on the Muslim regimes of northern India are: I. H. Qureshi, *The Administration of the Sultanate of Delhi* (Lahore, 1942); W. H. Moreland, *Agrarian System in Moslem India* (Cambridge, Eng., 1929); Moreland, *India at the Death of Akbar* (London, 1920); and Moreland, *From Akbar to Aurangzeb* (London, 1923).

A specialized work on the Marathas of the Deccan is: S. N. Sen, *Administrative System of the Marathas* (rev. edn., Calcutta, 1925). The classic work on the Rajput states is: James Tod, *Annals and Antiquities of Rajasthan*, edited by William Crooke, 3 vols. (London, 1920). A critical discussion of Tod's treatment of Rajputana is available in A. C. Lyall, *Asiatic Studies* I (2nd edn., London, 1907).

Sir Henry Maine treated India as "pre-feudal" in a number of chapters in three of his works: *Village Communities in East and West* (3rd edn., London, 1876), *Early History of Institutions* (London, 1875), and *Early Law and Custom* (London, 1883). A brief restatement on Sir Henry Maine's views on India is available in Thorner, "Sir Henry Maine," *Some Modern Historians of Britain: Essays in Honor of R. L. Schuyler*, edited Herman Ausubel et al. (New York, 1951). Maxim M. Kovalevski, although a friend and disciple of Maine, described the evolution of "feudalism" in India in *Obshchinnoye Zyemlevladyenie, Prichini, Khod i Posled'stviya evo Razlozheniya* [Communal Landholding: Causes, Course, and Results of Its Disintegration] (Moscow, 1879). B. H. Baden-Powell, also in opposition to Maine, repeatedly draws on feudal analogies in his work, *The Indian Village Community* (London, 1896).

The German sociologist, Max Weber, devoted virtually an entire volume to India in his studies of the sociology of religion: *Gesammelte Aufsätze zur Religionssoziologie*, II: *Hinduismus und Buddhismus* (Tübingen, 1923). (Hans Gerth of the University of Minnesota has translated, but not yet published, this work by Weber.) Weber's account, which draws heavily on Baden-Powell, presupposes a good deal of background on India. It should be used with caution by those unfamiliar with this field.

Two convenient reference works for students of India's history are: C. C. Davies, *Historical Atlas of the Indian Peninsula* (London, 1949); and C. H. Philips, ed., *Handbook of Oriental History* (London, 1950). This last work is particularly useful for its glossary, list of dynasties, place names, and related matters.

VIII · FEUDALISM IN THE BYZANTINE EMPIRE

BY ERNST H. KANTOROWICZ

(Compiled by William Bowsky)

Brehier, L. *Les institutions de l'empire byzantin*. Paris, 1949. (This is vol. II of Brehier's Le monde byzantine, 3 vols., Paris, 1947-1950.)

Charanis, P. "Economic Factors in the Decline of the Byzantine Empire," *Journal of Economic History*, vol. 13 (1953), pp. 412-424.

Charanis, P. "The Monastic Properties of the State in the Byzantine Empire," *Dumbarton Oaks Papers*, no. 4 (1948), pp. 51-118.

Charanis, P. "On the Social Structure and Economic Organization of the Byzantine Empire in the Thirteenth Century and Later," *Byzantinoslavica*, vol. 12 (1951), pp. 94-153.

Charanis, P. "On the Social Structure of the Later Roman Empire," *Byzantion*, vol. 17 (1944-45), pp. 39-57.

Ostrogorsky, G. "Agrarian Conditions in the Byzantine Empire in the Middle Ages," *Cambridge Economic History of Europe*, vol. I (1941), pp. 194-223.

Ostrogorsky, G. "Le grand domaine dans l'empire byzantine," *Société Jean Bodin*. Recueil IV. *Le Domaine* (1949), pp. 35-50.

Ostrogorsky, G. *Pronoia, A Contribution to the History of Feudalism in Byzantium and in the South-Slavic Lands*. Belgrade: Serbian Academy of Science, Special Editions, CLXXVI, Byzantine Institute, vol. I, 1951 (in Serbian). See the English summary by Ihor Ševčenko, "An Important Contribution to the Social History of Late Byzantium," in *The Annals of the Ukrainian Academy of Arts and Sciences in the United States*, vol. II (1952), pp. 448-459.

Ostrogorsky, G. "Die Wirtschaftlichen und sozialen Entwicklungsgrundlagen des byzantinischen Reiches," in *Vierteljahrschrift für Sozial- und Wirtschaftsgeschichte*, vol. 22 (1929), pp. 129-143.

Vasiliev, A. A. *History of the Byzantine Empire*, 2nd edn., Madison (Wisc.), 1952, esp. pp. 536-579.

Vasiliev, A. A. "On the Question of Byzantine Feudalism," in *Byzantion*, vol. 8 (1933), pp. 584-604.

IX · ASPECTS OF FEUDALISM IN RUSSIAN HISTORY

BY MARC SZEFTEL

THE most important primary sources for the study of political aspects of feudalism in Central Russian principalities (including the principality of Moscow) are treaties between the princes which contain numerous clauses on commendation, vassalage (we use this term tentatively), and immunity. They cover a period from 1341 to 1531, and have been published in *Sobranie Gosudarstvennykh Gramot i Dogovorov* [Collection of State Charters and Treaties], I (Moscow, 1813).[1]

Next in importance are the very numerous charters of immunity granted to monasteries, bishoprics, and churches by the princes of Central Russia from 1303 to 1598.[2] Many of them have been published in collections of charters and scholarly monographs; many unpublished ones are described in published repertories of archives. This rich source of documentation has not been at all fully published, but the available printed materials provide an ample opportunity for study and conclusions.

Finally, charters dealing with immunities granted to lay landlords are less numerous and more recent. There are 109 of them, from 1394 to 1594.[3] All but two have been published in different collections of charters, and upon them as basis it is possible to analyze the institution of immunity in lay allods around the middle of the fifteenth century and earlier.

For the study of the military and manorial aspects of feudalism three categories of sources are available for the sixteenth and seventeenth centuries: (1) transactions of central administrative agencies (*prikaz*'s), (2) private archives, and (3) monuments of legislation.

Among the *prikaz*'s, the *Razriadnyĭ Prikaz* [Board of Classes of Service] dealt with the military organization of Muscovy from 1535 to 1711, and its papers comprise an enormous number of registers, files, and rolls. Much of

[1] Together with the princes' treaties, the princes' wills (published in the same volume) are important for the study of this period. Both have been republished most recently by the Academy of Arts and Sciences of the U.S.S.R. in *Dukhovnye i dogovornye gramoty velikikh i udel'nykh kniazeĭ, xiv-xvi cc.* [Wills and Treaties of the Grand and Patrimonial Princes, 14th-16th centuries] (Moscow-Leningrad, 1950)—hereafter cited as *Dukh. i dog. gram.*

[2] The earliest recorded is the charter given by Mstislav of Smolensk to the St. George monastery in Novgorod (1130), published in *Dopolneniia k Aktam Istoricheskim* [Supplements to Historical Records] (St. Petersburg, 1846), I, No. II.

[3] They have been enumerated in S. B. Veselovsky, *K voprosu o proiskhozhdenii votchinnogo rezhima* [On the Origin of the Manorial System] (Moscow, 1926), pp. 113-118.

it has been published, but the major part still awaits publication. The *Pomêstnyĭ Prikaz* [Board of Military Tenures] dealt with landed possessions under every kind of title, military tenure, or hereditary property, and with changes which occurred in tenure from the second half of the sixteenth century to 1713. There, too, only a portion of the transactions has been published, mostly terriers. An immense quantity of registers and rolls remains practically untapped.

Among the private archives, the best preserved are those of monasteries, such as St. Trinity-St. Sergius, the Volokolamsk monastery (both in the region of Moscow), or the Solovki monastery (on the White Sea). Substantial parts of these archives have been published. Less well preserved are the archives of lay landlords. But the archives of Boris Morozov, Tsar Alexis' uncle, and those of Andrew Bezobrazov, dapifer of the same Tsar, contain particularly important materials for the study of the manorial system in Muscovy in the seventeenth century. Morozov's archives have been published *in extenso*, those of Bezobrazov in excerpts.

The legislative sources include (1) the Code (*Sudebnik*) of 1497; (2) the Tsar's *Sudebnik* of 1550; (3) the Book of Ordinances (*Ukaznaĭa Kniga*) of the *Pomêstnyĭ Prikaz* (1587-1649); and (4) the Code (*Ulozhenie*) of 1649, all published and carefully studied with commentaries.[4]

All military aspects of feudalism disappear with Peter the Great's reform at the beginning of the eighteenth century. Its social aspects, however, not only survive in the Russian Empire, but the dependence of the population of landed estates on the landlord grows immensely in the eighteenth century. Whether this is still feudalism is questionable in view of the extreme centralization of power in the Russian Empire, but historically the situation of the landlord's "subjects," as bonded peasants are called in the language of the law, is a direct outcome of the principle of military tenure as established in the sixteenth century. The problem of Russian feudalism thus leads to the problem of serfdom in the eighteenth and nineteenth centuries, for the study of which very rich sources, both of official and private origin, are available. They are too numerous and manifold to be detailed in this short study. A long list is given in the bibliographic index of Peter Lyashchenko's *History of the National Economy of Russia Prior to the 1917 Revolution*, translated by L. M. Herman (New York, 1949), pages 801-807, and in G. T. Robinson's *Rural Russia under the Old Regime* (New York, 1932), pages 312-326.

The problem of feudalism in Russia was raised toward the end of the nineteenth century by Nicholas Pavlov-Sil'vansky, who devoted to it a series

[4] Detailed information on sources of Russian history is to be found in *Istochnikovedenie istorii SSSR* [Studies of the Sources of the History of the U.S.S.R.], 2 vols. (Moscow, 1940). Vol. I, by M. N. Tikhomirov, extends from most ancient times to the end of the eighteenth century; Vol. II, by S. A. Nikitin, covers the nineteenth century to the beginning of the 1890's.

of studies written with great force and talent, but overstressing the analogy of institutions.[5] Pavlov-Sil'vansky's views did not get the applause of Russian historians, and at the time of the Revolution of 1917 not very many of them accepted the idea that there was a genuine analogy, amounting to more than mere external similarity, between Russian and Western institutions in the Middle Ages.[6] Pavlov-Sil'vansky's views were, however, provocative, and in spite of the insufficiencies of his inquiry, he drew the attention of scholars to phenomena hardly noticed before. Then, after 1917, the Marxian school in its Russian variety made it almost heretical not to recognize feudalism in Russian history. The Marxian school defined it, however, in a technically misleading manner, not as a system of institutions, but as a social and economic "formation" based on the appropriation by the landlord of a portion of the cultivator's work. The landlord effects this by means of three successive forms of "feudal land rent": labor, commodities, and money. This appropriation is made possible by "extra-economic constraint," i.e., the personal legal dependence of the cultivator on the landlord. In the historical development of human society the "feudal formation" normally precedes "capitalism" and follows upon the "patriarchal and community regime" either directly or indirectly via the "slave-owning formation." In the case of Russia a prefeudal, "barbarian" period provides the transition.

This conception of feudalism not only stresses its manorial aspect, but practically reduces its study to that of social dependency in a rural society. As such dependency had existed *in some form* in Russia at all times from the ninth to the beginning of the twentieth century, most of pre-Revolutionary history becomes either "prefeudal" or "feudal." This chronological overextension has greatly reduced the methodological value of the concept of feudalism, whatever its interpretation,[7] and the study of it has become identi-

[5] "Zakladnichestvo-patronat" [Commendation and Patronage], *Zapiski Imperatorskago Arkheologicheskago Obshchestva* [Memoirs of the Imperial Archaeological Society], IX (St. Petersburg, 1897), Parts I-II, was the first of them. It was followed by other essays in which Pavlov-Sil'vansky dealt with different aspects of old Russian law. His doctrine was finally stated in two books: *Feodalizm v drevneĭ Rusi* [Feudalism in Old Russia] (St. Petersburg, 1907), and *Feodalizm v udêlnoĭ Rusi* [Feudalism in the Russia of the *udêl's*] (St. Petersburg, 1910), a posthumous, unfinished work.

[6] A bibliography of books, articles, and reviews touching on the problem of feudalism in Russia in connection with Pavlov-Sil'vansky's ideas is attached to *Feodalizm v udêlnoĭ Rusi*, pp. 505ff.

[7] The not too bulky literature considered to be authoritative texts on feudalism in the U.S.S.R. has been given in the bibliography, "Classical Writers of Marxism-Leninism," *Istoriia SSSR* [History of the U.S.S.R.], Academy of Arts and Sciences, I (2nd edn., Moscow, 1948), 703-704. In spite of the very rigid formulation of the concept of feudalism by the writers of those texts, difficulties of application exist and lead to periodic revival of discussions dealing with the principle itself, as, for example, in the second half of the 1930's in connection with the anti-Pok-

fied in the U.S.S.R. mostly with the study of the peasant problem in the historical past. At the cost of a terminological adjustment, Russian historians specializing in rural history have not been too much disturbed by the Soviet concept of feudalism, and outstanding studies have been produced in this field, besides the publication of important source material.[8] B. D. Grekov's *Krest'iane na Rusi s drevneishikh vremen do XVII v.* [Peasants in Old Russia from Most Ancient Times to the Seventeenth Century] (Moscow-Leningrad, 1946) is to be specially mentioned in this connection.[9]

---

rovsky reinterpretation, or, as recently, with its use to divide Russian history into periods the boundaries of which would satisfy all facets of Marxian-Leninist ideology and also the "general line."

The monthly *Voprosy Istorii* [Problems of History] inaugurated this discussion in its issue of November 1949, and it continued until March 1951, when the editorial board devoted to its results a concluding article (pp. 53-60). The discussion seemed to have shown that forthwith: (1) Karl Marx's doctrine on precapitalistic rent cannot be the main criterion of the division of the feudal era into periods—this would be "economic materialism" and oversimplification of the historical process; (2) changes in the political superstructure, i.e., forms of government, cannot be the criterion either—this would revive the institutional approach of the Russian "bourgeois" historiography; (3) the struggle of classes is the chief feature of the feudal regime (as it is that of the capitalist regime), its landmarks being the main halting points of the historical process within every "class-formation." Still, even that is not an absolute criterion in all cases: sometimes political forms are more revealing of the "development of productive forces and relationships of production"; sometimes even the reflection of social and economic processes in the consciousness of the people; but since domestic development and external political events are interrelated, history cannot be rigidly divided into periods, and this applies to feudalism as well as to capitalism.

In spite of this qualified approach, division into periods continues as a major pursuit, with references to Stalin's "indications": pre-Kievan Russian history is "prefeudal," the Kievan period is "early feudal" from the 9th to the 11th century, and then "feudal fragmentation" sets in; after that, as it seems, the old *terminus ad quem* has not been changed, i.e., the middle of the 15th century, and only the importance of the Mongolian invasion as "substantial inside limit" is stressed more than in the former "periodization." As to the rest of the "feudal age," the editorial board does not offer any pertinent new suggestion, and we may conclude *ex silentio* that the former division into periods continues, at least for a time: "feudal monarchy" (middle of the 15th century to 1613) and "feudal-absolutistic monarchy" (17th, 18th, and 19th centuries to 1861). New discussions on "periodization" are imminent, and the article already suggests that in the future consideration should be given for this purpose not to the history of Russia in isolation, but to the history of all peoples of the U.S.S.R. as an organic unit. This "broadening" of perspective is not too hopeful a sign for the future study of Russian feudal institutions in the U.S.S.R.

[8] Cf. S. N. Valk, *Sovetskaia arkheografiia* [Soviet Archeography] (Moscow-Leningrad, 1948).

[9] This work is the first volume of a comprehensive history of the Russian peasantry (until after 1917) in several volumes, to be published by the Historical Institute of the Academy of Arts and Sciences of the U.S.S.R.

Nevertheless, some Russian historians have continued to study feudalism primarily as a system of institutions. S. B. Veselovsky, for example, has devoted his lifelong scholarly activity to the study of the political and manorial aspects of feudalism in northeastern Russia from the fourteenth to the sixteenth century. In his method he follows not so much Pavlov-Sil'vansky as Seebohm, Maitland, and Fustel de Coulanges, and he has built his conclusions on years of research in Russian archives, putting aside all comparative considerations. In 1947, Veselovsky began the publication of *Feodal'noe zemlevladenie v Severo-Vostochnoĭ Rusi* [Feudal Landownership in Northeastern Russia], his major work. It was planned in four parts: (1) private landownership; (2) the landownership of the metropolitan's economy; (3) the landownership of monasteries; and (4) the landownership of peasants. The first two parts had already been published as Volume I when the publication was interrupted and Veselovsky's "bourgeois" methods virulently assailed in public meetings and in the scholarly and non-scholarly press. Still, even in this unfinished form, Veselovsky's works represent the most competent existing study of immunities, allodial property, and the *pomêst'e*'s as far as the Time of Troubles.[10]

Political, manorial, and (to some extent) military aspects of feudalism in Russia have been studied by Alexandre Eck in his *Le moyen âge russe* (Brussels-Paris, 1933) on the basis of printed materials available in Western Europe. An exhaustive analysis of sources extensively quoted in a most scholarly French translation done by the author himself makes this work particularly valuable for non-Russian historians. The book has been followed by a series of essays dealing with particular problems of the Russian Middle Ages, which for Eck cover the period from the thirteenth century to 1613: "La vassalité et les immunités dans la Russie du moyen âge," *Revue de L'Institut de sociologie*, XVI (Brussels, 1936), 103-118; "L'asservissement du paysan russe" in *Le servage* (Société Jean Bodin: Brussels, 1937), pages 243-264; "Les modes de la possession agraire dans la Russie du moyen âge," in *La tenure*, Receuils de la Société Jean Bodin, III (Brussels, 1938), 245-285; and "Le grand domaine dans la Russie du moyen âge," *Revue historique du sud-est européen* (Bucharest, 1944), pages 82-136.[11] Since translation of terms involves interpretation, Eck's feudal terminology suggests analogies, but the author carefully refrains from all comparisons *expressis verbis*. He presents in a foreign language a complete and convincing picture of the "Russian Middle Ages"; the latter is a term of his own which enables him to some extent to avoid use

[10] There should also be mentioned Veselovsky's study quoted in note 3, above, and his *Selo i derevnia v Severo-Vostochnoi Rusi* [Village and Hamlet in Northeastern Russia] *XIV-XVIcc.* (Moscow-Leningrad, 1936).

[11] These problems were treated by Eck at four meetings of the *Société Jean Bodin pour l'étude de l'histoire comparative des institutions*, successivly devoted to each of them. The meetings took place in Brussels and Paris, 1935-1938.

of the concept of feudalism and so to avoid committing himself to analogies.

On the basis of largely the same source material as is used by Eck, another Russian scholar-in-exile, V. B. El'ïashevich, has studied the legal history of landed ownership in Russia, *Istoriïa prava pozemel'noï sobstvennosti v Russii*, 2 vols. (Paris, 1948-1951).[12] Writing in Russian makes it possible for the author to avoid all foreign terminology, and he does it on purpose in order not to violate national historical reality. Moreover, even legal concepts generally accepted by Russian historians, such as "*votchinnyi* (usually translated as manorial, but actually allodial) regime," are rejected by El'ïashevich in order to remove any screen of dogmatism which might obscure genuine historical evolution. All forms and legal aspects of landownership are studied, however, including the privileges of jurisdiction, and this inquiry leads him to insist on the lack of resemblance between Russian legal institutions before Ivan IV and those of feudal Europe. Only in the landownership of previously independent patrimonial (sing. *udêl'nyï*) and serving (sing. *sluzhilyï*) princes does he see an analogy with Western European feudalism.[13]

There is no book in Russian historical literature dealing comprehensively with the military and social aspects of feudalism as expressed in the system of *pomêst'e*'s.[14] This subject has been treated *in toto* only as a part of the his-

[12] Vol. 1 (the only one which we have been able to consult) deals with the legal regime of landed relationships between the 13th and the second half of the 16th century.

[13] This situation arises when a ruling prince enters "with his patrimony" the service of another ruling prince (*sluzhba iz votchiny*, service from patrimony, i.e., service while keeping his patrimonial principality). A variation of it is the *priêzd* (arrival) of a prince who already served a suzerain but now chooses another suzerain and at the same time relinquishes his patrimony; in this case, the new suzerain would give him new landed possessions as princely patrimony. The patrimonial princes who lost their independence to Moscow without losing their patrimonies were following the same regime as serving princes. El'ïashevich analyzes these relationships in the chapter on "The Lands of Serving Princes" (pp. 215-230) on the basis of numerous quoted texts from treaties, chronicles, judgments, and decrees. Referring further to this regime in some additional concluding remarks, he points out its analogy with Western feudalism in the following terms: "Precisely here appeared with a particular clarity the system of multiple rights existing on top of each other in the same land: that of the ruling prince as a sovereign; that of the serving prince still keeping his former rights; and, finally, that of the peasant" (p. 386).

[14] Military aspects only: Ivan D. Belïaev, *O storozhevoï stanichnoï i polevoï sluzhbê na pol'skoï ukrainê Moskovkago gosudarstva* [On Guard, Post, and Field Service in the Polish Frontier Area of Muscovy] (Moscow, 1846). The legal aspects of the system have been studied by such eminent historians of law as K. Nevolin, A. Lakier and V. Sergêevich, but they hardly paid attention to other aspects or to the unpublished materials in the archives. A comprehensive study, based largely on archive material, exists for the 16th century: S. V. Rozhdestvensky, *Sluzhiloe zemlevladênie v Moskovskom gosudarstvê XVI vêka* [Landownership Carrying Public Service in 16th Century Muscovy] (St. Petersburg, 1897).

tory of the Russian gentry, and one may refer particularly to Pavlov-Sil'vansky's *Gosudarevy sluzhilye lı͡udi* [The Sovereign's Serving People] (St. Petersburg, 1898) as the best available study. In this book, Pavlov-Sil'vansky is not preoccupied with comparative considerations, and this history of the Russian gentry from Kievan times to 1762, nourished by a thorough knowledge of source material, is an excellent historical treatise.[15]

Attention should be drawn to Otto Hötzsch's "Adel und Lehnswesen in Russland und Polen und ihr Verhältniss zur deutschen Entwicklung," *Historische Zeitschrift,* CVIII (1912), 541-592, in which general acceptance of analogies between the institutions of the Russian and the German[16] Middle Ages as emphasized by Pavlov-Sil'vansky is accompanied by reservations pointing out differences. The simultaneous brief treatment of three different developments cannot be considered as successful, but there are pertinent remarks in this essay both on parallels and, still more, on differences.

Professor George Vernadsky, of Yale University, has written a paper "Feudalism in Russia" (*Speculum*, July 1939, pp. 300-323), where the problem is treated very extensively with attention paid to different ethnic and cultural components of the present U.S.S.R. from the very beginning of Russian history to 1861. In the notes a detailed bibliography has been given which greatly enhances the value of this study, rich in documentation and suggestive by reason of the author's consolidation of different lines of study.

[15] To follow up the history of the Russian gentry in imperial times, see A. Romanovich-Slavatinsky, *Dvorı͡anstvo v Rossii s XVIII stolêtı͡a do otmêny ḳrêpostnogo prava* [The Gentry in Russia from the 18th Century to the Abolition of Serfdom], 2nd edn. (St. Petersburg, 1912).

[16] Hötzsch says "especially Eastern German development" (p. 589). This distinction between regions of Germany is important, and Heinrich Mitteis in his *Lehnrecht und Staatsgewalt* (Weimar, 1933) shows much discrimination of different regional patterns within Germany (less in *Der Staat des Hohenmittelalters*, 3rd edn., Weimar, 1948, offered as a comparative constitutional history of the feudal age). Also, among criticisms of Pavlov-Sil'vansky's theses, the most pertinent one concerns his disregard for differences within European feudalism: so N. Karêev, *V ḳaḳom smyslê mozhno govorit' o sushchestvovanii feodalizma v Rossii?* [In What Sense Is It Possible to Talk of the Existence of Feudalism in Russia?] (St. Petersburg, 1910), and T. Taranovsky, *Feodalizm v Rossii* [Feudalism in Russia] (Warsaw, 1902), among those who are generally favorable to Pavlov-Sil'vansky. The latter critic points out that Pavlov-Sil'vansky entirely left out of consideration English feudalism, taking his data exclusively from Western Germany and France and, moreover, from one epoch only, that of the origin and the earliest stages of feudalism.

INDEX

(The Bibliographies to Part Two are not included in the Index. They will be found on pages 397-419.)